Tourism, Mobility and Second Homes

ASPECTS OF TOURISM
Series Editors: Professor Chris Cooper, *University of Queensland, Australia*
Dr C. Michael Hall, *University of Otago, Dunedin, New Zealand*
Dr Dallen Timothy, *Arizona State University, Tempe, USA*

Aspects of Tourism is an innovative, multifaceted series which will comprise authoritative reference handbooks on global tourism regions, research volumes, texts and monographs. It is designed to provide readers with the latest thinking on tourism world-wide and in so doing will push back the frontiers of tourism knowledge. The series will also introduce a new generation of international tourism authors, writing on leading edge topics. The volumes will be readable and user- friendly, providing accessible sources for further research. The list will be underpinned by an annual authoritative tourism research volume. Books in the series will be commissioned that probe the relationship between tourism and cognate subject areas such as strategy, development, retailing, sport and environmental studies. The publisher and series editors welcome proposals from writers with projects on these topics.

Other Books in the Series
Natural Area Tourism: Ecology, Impacts and Management
  D. Newsome, S.A. Moore and R. Dowling
Tourism and Development: Concepts and Issues
  Richard Sharpley and David Telfer (eds)
Tourism Employment: Analysis and Planning
  Michael Riley, Adele Ladkin and Edith Szivas
Marine Ecotourism: Issues and Experiences
  Brian Garrod and Julie C. Wilson (eds)
Classic Reviews in Tourism
  Chris Cooper (ed.)
Progressing Tourism Research
  Bill Faulkner, edited by Liz Fredline, Leo Jago and Chris Cooper
Managing Educational Tourism
  Brent W. Ritchie
Recreational Tourism: Demand and Impacts
  Chris Ryan
Coastal Mass Tourism: Diversification and Sustainable Development in Southern Europe
  Bill Bramwell (ed.)
Sport Tourism Development
  Thomas Hinch and James Higham
Sport Tourism: Interrelationships, Impact and Issues
  Brent Ritchie and Daryl Adair (eds)
Tourism, Mobility and Second Homes
  C. Michael Hall and Dieter Müller
Strategic Management for Tourism Communities: Bridging the Gaps
  Peter E. Murphy and Ann E. Murphy
Oceania: A Tourism Handbook
  Chris Cooper and C. Michael Hall (eds)
Tourism Marketing: A Collaborative Approach
  Alan Fyall and Brian Garrod
Music and Tourism: On the Road Again
  Chris Gibson and John Connell
Tourism Development: Issues for a Vulnerable Industry
  Julio Aramberri and Richard Butler (eds)

For more details of these or any other of our publications, please contact:
Channel View Publications, Frankfurt Lodge, Clevedon Hall,
Victoria Road, Clevedon, BS21 7HH, England
http://www.channelviewpublications.com

ASPECTS OF TOURISM 15
Series Editors: Chris Cooper (*University of Queensland, Australia*),
C. Michael Hall (*University of Otago, New Zealand*)
and Dallen Timothy (*Arizona State University, USA*)

Tourism, Mobility and Second Homes
Between Elite Landscape and Common Ground

Edited by
C. Michael Hall and Dieter K. Müller

CHANNEL VIEW PUBLICATIONS
Clevedon • Buffalo • Toronto

Library of Congress Cataloging in Publication Data
Tourism, Mobility, and Second Homes: Between Elite Landscape and Common
Ground/Edited by C. Michael Hall and Dieter K. Müller.
Aspects of Tourism: 15
Includes bibliographical references.
1. Second homes. 2. Vacation homes. 3. Tourism. 4. Residential mobility.
I. Hall, Colin Michael. II. Müller, Dieter K. III. Series.
HD7289.2.T68 2004
333.33'8–dc22   2004002643

British Library Cataloguing in Publication Data
A catalogue entry for this book is available from the British Library.

ISBN 1-873150-81-4 (hbk)
ISBN 1-873150-80-6 (pbk)

Channel View Publications
An imprint of Multilingual Matters Ltd

UK: Frankfurt Lodge, Clevedon Hall, Victoria Road, Clevedon BS21 7HH.
USA: 2250 Military Road, Tonawanda, NY 14150, USA.
Canada: 5201 Dufferin Street, North York, Ontario, Canada M3H 5T8.

Typeset by Wordworks Ltd.
Printed and bound in Great Britain by the Cromwell Press.

Contents

Part 3: Patterns and Issues

Part 4: Future Issues

Acknowledgements

I, Dieter, do not own a cottage. I should not – at my age you are usually engaged in other things in life. However, a lot of other people opened their homes to me, and hence there are a lot of people to whom I owe thanks. First of all, I would like to thank Michael who invited me to join him in writing and editing this book and who introduced me to the international research community. For several weeks Jody and Michael hosted me in their home in Dunedin, where the first steps towards this book were taken. Great cooking, fishing trips, antiques stores, and some Swedish pop music provided the perfect mix for some late-night work sessions. Thanks also to Donna Keen, Stephen Boyd, David Duval, Mel Elliot, Tom Hinch and all other people at the Department of Tourism at the University of Otago who gave me a great time on the opposite side of the world. Friends in Umeå and my colleagues at the Department of Social and Economic Geography at Umeå University welcomed me more than 10 years ago and made Umeå my new home. After more than 9 years of second home research, they are now used to my interest in that topic, but continue to provide a supportive environment for scientific investigations. I particularly want to thank Bruno Jansson for his never-ending support and cooperation. I also want to thank Backa Fredrik Brandt, Lotta Brännlund, Erik Bäckström, Einar Holm, Urban Lindgren, Anders Lundgren, Linda Lundmark, Roger Marjavaara, Albina Pashkevich, Robert Pettersson, Linda Rislund, Olle Stjernström, Margit Söderberg, Kerstin Westin, Ulf Wiberg, and all other colleagues who in one way or another have provided essential practical and academic support. However, this book is for Åsa.

By the way, if you are thinking of coming to northern Sweden – I think you should.

Dieter K. Müller
Umeå, August 2003

We had hoped that, by the time this book was finished, we would own a second home. Unfortunately, owing to the international demand for second homes on Banks Peninsula and the lack of rural subdivisions by the Banks Peninsula Council, this has not been the case. However, despite the absence of a second home, this book still represents a personal as well as a professional interest. There is nothing so reflexive as having to examine where you want to live and the people you want to encounter on a regular basis.

Working with Dieter has meant more than acquiring a collection of Swedish music and a taste for polarbröd; it has meant working with someone who has a dress sense not unlike to my own and who also shares a professional passion for seeking to understand patterns of mobility and their contribution to regional development while at the same time recognising that serious research should also be fun. I should also note that visits to Umeå mean that that city has begun to acquire some of the characteristics of home in terms of a comfortable sense of place when I am there. This is due not only to the familiarity of Dieter's spare room and the kitchen chair (which still hasn't been repaired) but also to the hospitality of his Department, which is always a stimulating environment to work in. I would also like to acknowledge a number of other people who have stimulated my thoughts on second homes, particularly Dick Butler, Rebecca Arnold, Nick Cave, Elvis Costello, David Duval, Thor Flognfeldt, Derek Hall, Tom Hinch, Bruno Jansson, Donna Keen, Alan Lew, Stephen Page, Jarkko Saarinen, Annadorra Saetorsdottir, David Sylvian, Dallen Timothy, Gustav Visser, Geoff Wall, Lucinda Williams and Allan Williams. Terry Coppock must also be acknowledged as, although I have never met him, his work provides a benchmark for the study of second homes which we cannot hope to meet and which was also a major stimulus for my interest in rural geography as an undergraduate student. The support of the ICCS Transculturalism project is also acknowledged. Mel Elliott and Frances Cadogan deserve great thanks for doing the administrative work that I get the credit for as Head of Department; they also usually manage to keep me sane. Undertaking this book has not only meant that Jody has had to put up with me being away working on second homes, but she still doesn't have one herself. For her continued understanding I am always grateful, particularly as the time taken to do this book is as much hers as it is mine. After living in Dunedin for six years I also think that we should go to Sweden, especially as I think that Dieter is more than old enough for a second home!

C. Michael Hall
Dunedin, August 2003

Contributors

Lars Aronsson: Baltic Business School, University of Kalmar, SE-391 82 Kalmar, Sweden. E-mail: lars.aronsson@hik.se.

María Angeles Casado-Díaz: Faculty of the Built Environment, Centre for Environment and Planning, University of West England, Coldharbour Lane, Bristol, BS16 1QY. E-mail: maria.casado-diaz@uwe.ac.uk.

David T. Duval: Department of Tourism, University of Otago, PO Box 56, Dunedin, New Zealand. E-mail: dduval@business.otago.ac.nz.

Thor Flognfeldt jr: Faculty of Tourism and Applied Social Sciences, Lillehammer College, N-2626 Lillehammer, Norway.
E-mail: thor.flognfeldt@hil.no.

Warwick Frost: Department of Management, Monash University, Caulfield Campus, 900 Dondenong Road, East Caulfield, Victoria 3145, Australia. E-mail: warwick.frost@buseco.monash.edu.au.

C. Michael Hall: Department of Tourism, University of Otago, PO Box 56, Dunedin, New Zealand. E-mail: cmhall@business.otago.ac.nz

Greg Halseth: Geography Program, University of Northern British Columbia, Prince George, BC, V2N 4Z9, Canada. E-mail: halseth@unbc.ca.

Bruno Jansson: Department of Social and Economic Geography, Umeå University, SE-901 87 Umeå, Sweden. E-mail: bruno.jansson@geography. umu.se.

Donna Keen: Department of Tourism, University of Otago, PO Box 56, Dunedin, New Zealand. E-mail: dkeen@business.otago.ac.nz.

Russel King: Department of Geography, University of Sussex, Falmer, Brighton, BN1 9RH UK. E-mail: r.king@sussex.ac.uk.

Dieter K. Müller: Department of Social and Economic Geography, Umeå University, SE-901 87 Umeå, Sweden. E-mail: dieter.muller@geography. umu.se.

Bernadette Quinn: School of Hospitality Management and Tourism, Dublin Institute of Technology, Cathal Brugha St, Dublin 1, Republic of Ireland. E-mail: bernadette.quinn@dit.ie.

John Selwood: Department of Geography, University of Winnipeg, 515 Portage Avenue, Winnipeg, Manitoba, R3B 2E9, Canada. E-mail: j.selwood@uwinnipeg.ca.

Stephen Svenson: Faculty of Environmental Studies, York University, Toronto, Ontario, Canada. E-mail: stephensvenson@sympatico.ca.

Dallen J. Timothy: College of Public Programs, Department of Recreation, Management and Tourism, Arizona State University, PO Box 874905, Tempe, AZ 85287-4905, USA. E-mail: dtimothy@asu.edu.

Matthew Tonts: Department of Geography, University of Western Australia, Nedlands, Western Australia 6907, Australia. E-mail: mtonts@geog.uwa.edu.se.

Gustav Visser: Department of Geography, University of the Free State, South Africa. E-mail: VisserGE.SCI@mail.uovs.ac.za.

Tony Warnes: Sheffield Institute for Studies on Ageing, University of Sheffield, Community Sciences Centre, Northern General Hospital, Herries Road, Sheffield S5 7AU. E-mail: a.warnes@sheffield.ac.uk.

Allan M. Williams: Department of Geography, University of Exeter, Amory Building, Rennes Drive, Exeter UK EX4 4RJ. E-mail: a.m.Williams@exeter.ac.uk.

Part 1

Context

Chapter 1

Introduction: Second Homes, Curse or Blessing? Revisited

C. MICHAEL HALL AND DIETER K. MÜLLER

Second homes are an integral part of contemporary tourism and mobility. In many areas of the world, second homes are the destination of a substantial proportion of domestic and international travellers, while the number of available bed nights in a second homes often rivals or even exceeds that available in the formal accommodation sector. For many destinations, particularly in more peripheral areas, second homes are a major contributor to regional economies, while they may also represent a significant heritage resource because of their use of vernacular architecture and the ongoing use of buildings that may otherwise have fallen into disrepair. At the level of the individual, second homes may also be important for concepts of identity and sense of place, particularly as they may represent a connection to family and/or childhood place affiliations. All this is not to say that second homes are universally welcomed. In some areas, second homes are seen as putting further pressure on existing housing stock and forcing up prices, thus making it harder for permanent residents to obtain housing. Similarly, where there are substantial seasonal variations in second home use, these may be perceived as exacerbating seasonal patterns in employment and economic demand, rather than assisting with regional development strategies. Finally, in some circumstances second home households may be seen as outsiders and even as invaders, which at times has created substantial resentment, even leading to destruction of the second home property. The various dimensions of second home development point to both the complexity and significance of the subject. This book therefore aims to explore such complexities with the aim of providing an informed contribution to the debate as to the value and significance of second homes.

The present chapter provides an introduction to the concept of second homes and discusses its historical and spatial characteristics as well as some of the motivations of second home ownership. One notable point in examining second homes is that, in comparison with some other areas of tourism and leisure mobility, they have a relatively long history of scholarship, often within particular national traditions. In the case of Scandinavia Ljungdahl (1938) was reporting on second homes in the Stockholm archi-

3

pelago before the Second World War. This study was followed up in the 1960s and early 1970s by such researchers as Aldskogius (1968, 1969), Finnveden (1960) and Bielckus (1977). In North America second home research was pioneered by the work of Wolfe (1951, 1952, 1962, 1965, 1977) in Canada (see also Lundgren, 1974), with substantial early research also being undertaken in the United States (Ragatz, 1970a, 1970b; Ragatz & Gelb, 1970; Burby *et al.*, 1972; Clout, 1972; Geisler & Martinson, 1976; Tombaugh, 1970). Continental Europe also witnessed a significant amount of early research (Barbier, 1965; Cribier, 1966, 1973; David, 1966; David & Geoffroy, 1966; Clout, 1969, 1971, 1977; Grault, 1970). Nevertheless, it was the publication of Coppock's (1977a) book *Second Homes: Curse or Blessing* that was to provide a benchmark for second home research, reflecting as it did contemporary debates over the value of second homes, especially bearing in mind the substantial opposition to second homes in some parts of the United Kingdom, Wales in particular (Coppock, 1977b; Rogers, 1977). Yet despite the significance of Coppock's (1977a) publication, somewhat ironically, relatively little was published on second homes in the late 1970s and early 1980s, leading Whyte (1978) to enquire, 'Have second homes gone into hibernation?' Indeed, it was not until the later part of the 1980s and the 1990s that a substantial number of publications on second homes once more began to emerge. There may have been several reasons for this re-emergence:

(1)   the growth in inter-regional and international second home related retirement migration;
(2)   increased recognition of the economic, environmental and social implications of tourism by government;
(3)   the deliberate use of second homes as an economic development tool; the re-emergence of conflict between second home development and permanent populations in some localities, making second homes a significant policy issue.

The present book takes stock of much of this second wave of second home research, but the contributors to this volume are mindful of much of the pioneering work of Coppock (1977a) and contributors, and the substantial insights that they demonstrated on tourism, which we now have the opportunity to revisit.

Defining Second Homes

There is a great variety of terms that refer to second homes: recreational homes, vacation homes, summer homes, cottages, and weekend homes. In the context of this book, the term 'second home' is used as an umbrella for these different terms, which all refer to a certain idea of usage. It should be

Table 1.1 Second home characteristics

Type	Structure	Buildings/Vehicles
Non-mobile	Houses and apartments	Solitary cottages and houses
		Second home villages
		Apartment buildings
Semi-mobile	Camping	Trailers/mobile homes
		Recreational vehicles
		Tents
		Caravans
Mobile	Boats	Sailing boats

Source: Newig (2000)

noted that the term 'cottage' which is also used in this book (Halseth, Chapter 3; Svenson, Chapter 4) does not primarily address the physical form but the function of the second home, usually referring to small houses that are mainly for recreational use. Similarly, second homes can also be apartments.

In contrast to other forms of tourism mobility, such as day tripping, second home tourism is covered relatively well in census data and national statistics. Nevertheless, there is a lack of comparable data, for example because of different national definitions as to what constitutes a second home. For example, in some jurisdictions caravans and boats may be regarded as second homes (Coppock, 1977c; Newig, 2000), while in others (Keen & Hall, this volume) unoccupied houses in rural areas are not officially classified as second homes and have to be occupied on census night in order to be officially recognised. Three groups of second homes may be recognised: stationary, semi-mobile; and mobile (Table 1.1). However, most researchers employ a pragmatic approach where data access determines the definition of second homes. Therefore, the primary focus is on non-mobile second homes. Furthermore, although time shares demonstrate some similarities with second homes, they are not usually included in second home data (although see Timothy, this volume). In addition, although urban second homes exist, they have not generated significant attention because they are relatively few in number. Instead, focus has long been placed on second homes in rural and peri-urban areas, and this book, too, focuses on privately-owned rural second homes.

Definitional approaches to second homes are also made more complicated because interest in second homes is not limited to tourism research, and has attracted attention from urban and regional planning (Langdalen, 1980; Gallent, 1997; Gallent & Tewdwr-Jones, 2000), rural geography (Pacione, 1984; Buller & Hoggart, 1994a) and population geography

(Warnes, 1994; King *et al.*, 2000). This is also mirrored in the terminology used to characterise second home tourism. For example, Casado-Diaz (1999) uses the term 'residential tourism'; Flognfeldt (2002) prefers 'semi-migration', Finnveden (1960) 'summer migration', and Pacione (1984) writes about 'seasonal suburbanisation'.

The Nature of Home

To complicate definitional matters further, both the term and the concept of second homes have been increasingly brought into question (Kaltenborn, 1997a, 1997b, 1998; Müller, 2002c) by the growing number of households in the developed world with the ability to allocate their time independently of a single workplace, and so are able to adopt more mobile lifestyles, and may have several homes (Williams & Hall, 2002). Kaltenborn (1998) argues that second homes are seldom sold, but are sometimes passed on through generations. Hence, they may form a first home because of the strong emotional place attachment of their owners, and Kaltenborn (1998) uses the term 'alternate home' to indicate the emotional meaning that is otherwise hidden by the term second home. The extent of this phenomenon, however, is often concealed owing to administrative practices that require house-holds to register a primary residence (Müller, 2002c).

Müller (2002c) criticises the administrative practices that fail to recog-nise the complexity of current mobility patterns and forms. Departing from Williams and Hall's argument (2000a, 2002) Müller argues that neither space–time use nor the motivations for mobility are sufficient indicators to distinguish tourism from migration. Hence, whether a house is a primary residence or a second home is entirely the owners' decision. This decision can depend on a variety of factors, such as local taxation rates and the order in which homes are purchased. However, evidence also suggests that the most owners are hardly aware of the consequences of this decision (Williams & Kaltenborn, 1999; Müller, 2002c).

In reality, it can be predicted that a considerable number of people have more than one place that can be called a home. However, practical matters concerning, for example, taxation, statistics, voting and other citizenship rights force individuals and households to state exactly where they are at home. This administrative practice clearly fails to acknowledge the complexity of life and mobility by defining people as static and immobile in their day-to-day everyday life (Müller & Hall, 2003). Administrative proce-dures simply do not accept that people are at home in two places at once, in the same way that travel arrival cards usually do not allow more than one reason for a visit. Setting the notion that individuals are mobile against this bureaucratic background is not a trivial concern. In fact, in many ways the term second home has arisen as a result of these administrative practices. In many jurisdictions, the power of such practices may be so significant as to exclude second *home owners* from some of the local community institutions and practices. In this respect, the term second home may provide an additional meaning as it may identify second *home owners* and households as only partial members of the local community when it comes to the ability to participate in certain rights and duties.

The consequences of this practice can be significant not only for the single individual, but also for the local communities. Having only a second home rather than a primary residence in some communities may mean that the second *home owners* are excluded from certain citizenship rights by virtue of their capacity to vote, and from access to some public amenities and institutions. Accordingly, they may not be able to influence the local society to the same extent as 'permanent' residents. Such regulatory barriers may also serve to reinforce the perception in some circumstances, for example, that they are outsiders who can be accused of displacing 'real' locals from the housing market (Gallent & Tewdwr-Jones, 2000). Moreover, they may be perceived as temporary residents, even though they might live there more than six months a year and thus spend more time in the host community than 'permanent' residents (Müller, 1999; Flognfeldt, 2002). Indeed, in some countries the local community tax income and other public transfers depend on the number of 'permanent' residents, which does not necessarily correspond to the actual number of residents (see Chapter 2). In other jurisdictions, second *home owners* may pay local community taxes but not be allowed the right to vote. The number of residents, ideally expressed as the result of an equation that represents the actual time spent in the community by 'permanent' residents and second *home owners*, is usually unknown (Müller & Hall, 2003). Nevertheless, the lack of appropriate measurements and statistics can be mirrored, for example, in a deficit of local service provision (see Frost, this volume) or in disagreement over what the actual level of service provision should be (Keen & Hall, this volume).

The Historical Geography of Second Home Tourism

The origin of second homes can be traced back to ancient societies where the house in the countryside was an exclusive asset for the nobility (Coppock, 1977c). During the 18th century, second homes could be found in spa towns and later in coastal towns (Löfgren, 1999) and were often used on a seasonal basis to escape city life. New means of transportation had a substantial influence on the geography of second homes. In the Stockholm archipelago, for example, second homes were built along the steamboat lines (Ljungdahl, 1938), and Flognfeldt (this volume) has noted a similar pattern of development along the Oslo Fjord. During the first part of the

Table 1.2 Second home relative space–time characteristics

Second home function	Frequency of visits	Length of visit	Form of mobility	Location relative to primary residence
Weekend home	high	short	circulation	dependent
Vacation home	low	long	seasonal migration	independent
Future permanent home	decreasing	increasing	migration	independent

Source: Müller (2002a)

20th century, second home ownership spread to other groups outside the upper classes together with changed ideas regarding contact with nature and wilderness. In North America, second homes were constructed in wilderness areas, partly as a cultural reminder of frontier development (Coppock, 1977c; Wolfe, 1977; Löfgren, 1999). In New Zealand and Australia many of the first coastal second homes were little more than fishing huts on public land (Selwood & Tonts, this volume; Keen & Hall, this volume) that provided households with cheap holidays by the beach and an escape from the warmer inland areas. In the Nordic countries, second home construction was supported as a mean of social tourism and entailed the construction of a large number of second homes in metropolitan hinterlands, particularly between 1950 and 1980 (Nordin, 1993b).

However, the main increase in second home ownership since 1960 can be explained by the increased personal mobility offered by growing car ownership and access. The idea of owning a weekend refuge for relaxation contributed to the development of second homes within easy access of urban areas (Wolfe, 1951; Lundgren, 1974; Jansson & Müller, 2003). Accordingly, most second *home owners* live close to their property. Even in an international context, long-distance second home ownership is still the exception (Hoggart & Buller, 1995). Space–time distance forms an obstacle for second home ownership that favours second home ownership within the weekend zone of the owners' primary residences and, thus, most second homes may be labelled 'weekend homes. These weekend homes can be visited frequently and also for short periods (Table 1.2). In contrast, second homes outside the weekend zone, 'vacation homes', are visited only occasionally but often for longer periods (Müller, 2002c).

These patterns mirror geographical assumption regarding interactions, gravity and mobility (Bell, 1977; Hall, 2004a, 2004b). Müller (2002b) established empirically that the second home demand decreases in a logistic curve with increasing distance from the primary residence, implying that second home ownership loses its attractiveness as soon as the weekend leisure zone is passed. The weekend leisure zone of Müller (2002b) is analogous to Hall's (2004a) 'zone of overnight' stay within the recreational hinterland of an urban centre. The zone of overnight stay refers to an area in which the tendency for travellers to stay overnight increases and the likelihood of same-day return trips decreases because of

(1) availability of time to travel (time budget) and engage in tourist-related activities;
(2) limitations related to the need for rest while travelling (i.e. tourists cannot continue to drive continuously without sleep);
(3) time/distance trade-offs between returning home to sleep and the travel time involved in that versus stopping overnight.

The time sensitivity of leisure travel means that overnight stays from a tourist-generating region tends to cluster at a location related to time and distance from a point of origin. This means that second home ownership outside the weekend leisure zone is relatively independent of the location of the primary residence; the second home is visited once or twice annually. However, second home location is not dependent solely on travel times. It is also influenced by the geography of amenity-rich landscapes that

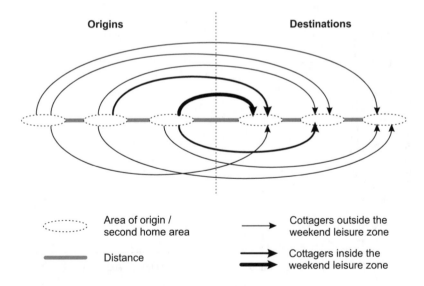

Figure 1.1 Origin–destination relationships

Source: Muller (2002a)

concentrate at least purpose-built second homes within coastal and mountain areas (Tombaugh, 1970), as well as making existing housing stock in such areas attractive for conversion to second homes (Hall, 2004b). Therefore, primary economic determinants in the selection of second home locations are space–time accessibility, amenity values and real estate costs. Nevertheless, second homes, often converted former permanent rural housing, can be found in all locations, simply because they also represent links with places of childhood and family origin.

In the Swedish case, Jansson and Müller (2003) have demonstrated that 25% of all second home owners have their property within 14km of their primary residence, 50% are within 37km of their property, and 75% within 98km. However, amenity-rich areas disturb the otherwise very regularly declining pattern of second homes. Figure 1.2 shows the second home ownership patterns of the citizens of Umeå, a town in northern Sweden. Here the distance-decay effect is very clear. The peak in ownership patterns between 300km and 400km represents the mountain area that attracts a greater number of second *home owners* than predicted. Hence, space–time functions, land-use patterns and the geography of amenity-rich areas greatly influence the geography of second homes.

Additional factors in the distribution of locational choices for second

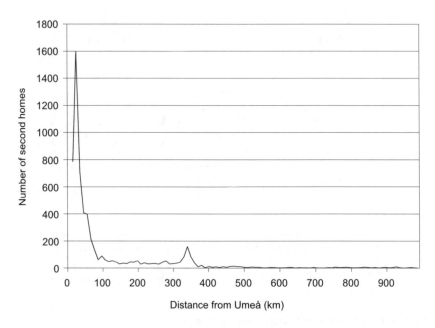

Figure 1.2 Distance decay for second home owners from Umeå, Sweden 1996

homes are the role of real-estate agents, and the availability of land through government land use policies. The role of real-estate agents for the distribution of second homes may be regarded as significant, at least in terms of international second home ownership. Research in France (Hoggart & Buller, 1994) and Sweden (Müller, 1999) suggests that second *home owners* are channelled to certain destinations by the promotional activities of real-estate agents, although this mainly applies to the more inexperienced segment of the demand market. The agents not only act as gatekeepers to the second home area, but may also play an important role in offering post-purchase services and social activities (Müller, 1999). Land availability is also a significant factor in the selection of sites for second homes, as land use planning regulations may limit the minimum size of land sections that can be sold, thereby contributing to the scarcity value of desired second home locations (Keen & Hall, this volume). Such government land use controls therefore play a significant role in influencing land and housing stock values and, depending on the local rating or tax system, may even be manipulated to maximise rates returns from housing developments. Although such regulatory measures will often be justified by local government on the basis of landscape or environmental protection (Jansson & Müller, this volume; Keen & Hall, this volume), they nevertheless will have enormous impacts on the availability of land for second home development.

One further aspect of second home location, and an issue that provides one of the points of departure for the present book, is the extent to which second home location as well as the decision to purchase a second home may be regarded as status symbols. Depending on the national context, second home ownership can arguably be seen as an expression of elitism (Wolfe, 1977; Jaakson, 1986; Halseth & Rosenberg, 1995; Halseth, 1998). With reference to Canada, Halseth (1998, this volume) argues that second home landscapes are turning more and more into playgrounds of the elite. In contrast, second home ownership or access is part of everyday life in Scandinavian countries. However, even there second home ownership in certain amenity-rich locations can be perceived as conferring status to owners (Müller, this volume). Nevertheless, there is an increasing perception of second homes as the domain of the rich in parts of the United Kingdom, mainland Europe and New Zealand and, undoubtedly, such scarcity values may initiate their own purchasing dynamic with respect to the status that second home ownership may confer in certain locations.

Motives for Second Home Ownership

There is a wide range of reasons for purchasing or owning a second home and these have to be seen in the context of second home ownership for the individual owners. Most households purchase second homes in order to achieve some dimension of lifestyle that is not available at their primary residence. These lifestyle decisions appear to have an increasing importance in travel decision-making, including leisure tourism and second homes, and imply, in some cases, greater mobility at the international level (Fountain & Hall, 2002; Timothy, 2002).

It has long been recognised that removal or inversion from everyday urban life appears to be a main attraction of second homes (Wolfe, 1951, 1952; Jaakson, 1986). For example, in the Canadian context, Wolfe (1952) described cottaging as a 'divorce' from the urban environment. This inversion is related not only to the focus on leisure rather than work, but also to a general relaxation and informality that exists in the second home (Kaltenborn, 1997a; Williams & Kaltenborn, 1999; Jansson & Müller, 2003). Chaplin's (1999) two-year study of British second *home owners* in France characterised such behaviour as an 'escape' aimed at providing a balance in life. Chaplin (1999) found that issues of second home ownership were closely linked to a desire to 'get away from it all'. On closer investigation, these issues were closely connected to ideas of production and consumption, namely that the second home provided people with the ability to experience something that was no longer regarded as present in their normal 'lives'. As Kaltenborn (1997a) observed, second homes are often responses to two phenomena: where the second home is seen as more 'authentic' and where it is seen as a representation of 'real' life. This quest for the authentic and the real is an often-cited motivation behind many forms of tourism (e.g. Selwyn, 1996). Furthermore, according to Jaakson (1986), such second home use is both full of ritual (the return to the same place and the same activities over and again) and control (the search for the authentic and real).

Second home ownership can also be interpreted as a step 'back to nature' (Jaakson, 1986; Williams & Kaltenborn, 1999), with some people adapting the surrounding of the second home to the nature of their imagination, while others move towards an idealised simple rustic lifestyle in which ideas of rurality become extremely important (Jaakson, 1986; Geipel, 1989; Löfgren, 1999; Müller, 2002d; Hall & Page, 2002). Accordingly, the activities second *home owners* mainly occur locally and usually include creative work on the property or outdoor activities such as hiking and berry or fruit picking. Indeed, maintaining and changing the interior and exterior of the second home itself forms an important motive for second home ownership (Jaakson, 1986; Müller, 1999). Chaplin (1999) even sees such creative work not only as property maintenance but also as a means by which owners can express their identity.

Second home ownership may be strongly related to personal identity (Jaakson, 1986). This is particularly true in cases where second homes represent emotional connections with places of childhood, family or ancestry

(Kaltenborn, 1997a, 1997b; Löfgren, 1999). Such familial connections may also positively influence the extent to which second *home owners* may be integrated into the local community (Pacione, 1979). Jaakson (1986) even argued that a major reason for second home ownership is as a perceived means of keeping a family together. Many second *home owners* inherit their properties, which thus represent a significant place of family heritage. In fact, some second *home owners* state that they invest in a second home so that they can pass it on to the next generation (Jansson & Müller, 2003). However, Jansson and Müller (this volume) argue that rapid social and economic changes in developed countries, including greater personal mobility, may serve to make long-term ownership of second homes increasingly difficult and hence imply a shift to a more touristic validation of second home purchase.

The transnational nature of some second homes also leads some commentators, such as Kaltenborn (1998), to argue that second home ownership constitutes a turn towards the local as a response to globalisation. For example, Buller and Hoggart (1994a) argue that British second *home owners* are actually trying to find a lost British countryside in rural France. However, local responses to globalisation may be quite varied. In his study of German second *home owners* in Sweden, Müller (1999, 2002a, 2002d) draws, however, a slightly different conclusion from Buller and Hoggart and suggests that second home ownership mirrors a form of internationalisation itself. Müller (1999) argued that for some respondents owning a property abroad was viewed as a self-evident right within the new Europe and ownership itself becomes an expression for a changing geographical identity.

Recent developments in Europe, Australasia and North America indicate that second home ownership can also usefully be approached from a life-cycle perspective, particularly in the context of retirement second home ownership, which attracts retirees to amenity-rich and often sunny places (Buller & Hoggart, 1994a; Warnes, 1994; McHugh *et al.*, 1995; King *et al.*, 2000). In general it can be noted that the majority of households owning a second home are older than 35 years (Jansson & Müller, 2003). After becoming established on the housing and the labour market and often having teenage children, households identify second homes as objects for investment and creative focus. Evidence also suggests that a substantial proportion of second *home owners* actually purchase a property for later retirement, even if it is never used as such (Robertson, 1977; Buller & Hoggart, 1994a; Müller, 1999). Hence, second home ownership may sometimes represent a precursor to permanent domestic or international migration. However, in many cases permanent migration is not registered, because households choose to keep a link with their formerly permanent home (Müller, 1999; King *et al.*, 2000; Williams *et al.*, this volume). Therefore, it is almost impossible to pinpoint the households that retire into their second homes. Nevertheless, second home retirement is clearly emerging as a significant planning issue from both domestic and international perspectives (Williams *et al.*, this volume), particularly given the aging of the demographic profile in many developed countries and the demands that such aging places on infrastructure and services (Müller & Hall, this volume).

Summary

This chapter has reviewed both the definition of second homes and some of the motivations for their purchase and continued ownership. In so doing it has indicated some of the complex structures of consumption that surround second homes. Significantly, the chapter has noted that second homes are important not just in terms of their contribution to leisure and tourism but, at a deeper level, of there role in influencing identity; senses of belonging, family and place; and ideas of heritage. These motivations are expressed in second home locational decision-making processes which may then serve to affect the communities and places in which individuals locate. Many of the issues arising from such second home location and household activities are taken up in the following chapters.

Second homes are undoubtedly significant in the consumption of production of leisure travel. They are also important in assisting us to better understand the nature of contemporary circulation and mobility (Müller, 1999; Hall, 2004a). However, they also represent some of the broader tensions which exist in present-day understanding of tourism and travel access issues and social equality. To some second homes represent access to low-cost holidays and a more authentic experience, to others they are increasingly expressions of elitism and exclusion. Clearly, depending on circumstances both of these positions will have elements of truth about them, yet such extremes also connect discussions of second home tourism to broader issues of access, circulation, mobility and regulation, and the insights that such discussions may bring to our understanding of contem-porary society. It is hoped that this book will be one such contribution to such debates not only within tourism and migration studies but also the wider social sciences.

Chapter 2

Second Home Tourism Impact, Planning and Management

DIETER K. MÜLLER, C. MICHAEL HALL AND DONNA KEEN

As the previous chapter noted, research interest in second homes has undergone a significant rejuvenation since the late 1990s (e.g. Müller, 1999; Gallent & Tewdwr-Jones, 2000; Hall & Williams, 2002). New and more flexible forms of labour and new spatial patterns of production provided an increasing number of households with the opportunity to spend more leisure in the second home. At the same time, rural economic restructuring and depopulation have made rural properties available for potential second home owners and hence have entailed new patterns of consumption thanks to the conversion of rural areas into arenas for recreation, leisure and tourism (Müller, 2002d). This development is sometimes associated with a transformation of the countryside into what is described as a more post-productive state or into a consumption landscape (Ilbery & Bowler, 1998). In this context the countryside is no longer mainly considered to be an arena for agricultural or forestry production. Instead it is consumed for its amenities, its housing environments, and an imagined rural lifestyle. The new consumers appear as tourists, second home owners, and lifestyle migrants, all embodying a particular often-idealised image of the countryside (Bunce, 1994; Halfacree, 1995). Sometimes this is accompanied by conflicts over rural resource use between the traditional local population and the newcomers (Butler, 1998; Hall & Johnson, 1998; Fountain & Hall, 2002). However, it can also entail both conservation and revival of the rural environments as shown, for instance, in the case of German second home owners in Sweden (Müller, 1999).

Second home owners are tourists and so the impacts of second home tourism are often similar to the impacts of other forms of tourism (e.g. see Mathieson & Wall, 1982; Hall & Page, 2002; Hall, 2004b). However, the characteristics of second home tourism, such as the long duration of visits in the destination area, imply that certain impacts on change are more prominent. Similarly, second home tourism is different from other forms of tourism in that it has also required the second home household to purchase property in the destination, therefore implying the development of different sets of social and economic relationships than would apply to leisure or business travel. This chapter addresses issues related to this shift in countryside use by reviewing and discussing the literature on the impacts of second home tourism on the rural economy, culture, and environment. It also addresses the attempts to manage and plan second home developments and their associated impacts.

Second Home Landscapes

Undoubtedly, the geographical patterns of second home ownership influence the geography of change induced by second homes. A major factor influencing the impact on rural change that has not been sufficiently discussed in previous studies of second homes is the composition of the second home stock. Ongoing conversion of permanent homes to second homes in rural regions usually arises as a result of population decline and, related, economic decline. In contrast, the construction of purpose-built second homes in addition to the existing housing stock usually means a temporary increase in population, an intensified consumption of the environment, and an increasing inflow of economic resources into the area. Differences may also exist between areas with weekend homes and those with vacation homes (see Chapter 1). This depends on the location of the second homes areas in relation to the most important regions of origin. Accordingly, it can be argued that different types of second home settings occur in specific landscapes (Table 2.1). Sole converted homes in extensively-used peripheral areas have different impacts than highly concentrated purpose-built second homes in amenity-rich urban hinterlands, often located along a coast. Different rural settings have different capacities to respond to the impact caused by second homes. As the remainder of the chapter suggests, this is true not only for rural societies, but also for rural environments.

Table 2.1 Second home types and their areas of occurrence

	Weekend homes ◄————————————►	*Vacation homes*
Converted homes	Ordinary rural landscape in urban hinterlands	Extensively-used peripheral landscapes
↕		
Purpose-built homes	Amenity-rich hinterlands, coast and mountain landscapes	Major vacation areas, coast and mountain landscapes

Economic Impacts

All tourism, including second home tourism, contributes to change both in the destination area, and in the tourist-generating area (Fridgen, 1984; Hall, 2004b). According to Clawson and Knetsch (1966) tourism causes economic impacts along the route between origin and destination. As this review will demonstrate with few exceptions the focus of academic attention has been on the impacts of second home tourism in the destination area. However, it should be noted that second home tourism also induces various impacts even in the primary home districts. In particular, the rather frequent and long use of second homes implies a considerable outflow of consumption from the primary home area although the implications of this are rarely taken into account when second home flows are considered (Müller & Hall, 2003), even when national tourism accounts are developed. In addition, the purchasing patterns of second home owners along travel routes between the primary and second homes may also contribute to economic change (Flognfeldt, 2002).

A positive economic impact of second homes is central to the decision making of the rural planners and politicians who decide on land use and tourism development (Green *et al.*, 1996). Generally, second home development is considered an option in rural environments, usually after a period of economic decline and changes to the traditional agricultural or service base, because of the potential benefits such a development may bring to the regional economy (Clout, 1972; Deller *et al.*, 1997). For example, Deller *et al.* (1997) argue that municipalities are mainly interested in second home tourism because they anticipate a growth of tax incomes and increased spending in local businesses. However, to be an effective strategy this requires that second homes would be hitherto-unoccupied housing. If second homes displace permanent homes, then the economic effect is likely to be negative because of a reduction in the overall population with potential impacts not only on expenditure patterns but also on municipal taxes. However, it is difficult to estimate the economic impact of second home tourism, simply because there is a lack of reliable statistics (Müller & Hall, 2003).

In this context it has to be pointed out that the distance between second home and primary residence also influences the expenditure patterns of the households of second home owners (Bohlin, 1982a; Nordin, 1993a; Müller, 2002c). The greater the distance between second home and primary residence, the smaller the amount of goods that can be taken from the primary residence (Bohlin, 1982b). Hence, peripheral second home areas and vacation areas can expect relatively high incomes, although rather short visitation, from second home tourism.

Shucksmith (1983) identified a number of economic impacts related to second home acquisition, improvements and other consumption of goods and services. Besides the input of economic capital, second home tourism entails employment in banking, real-estate sale, craft and retail. However, it cannot necessarily be assumed that second home tourism will contribute to the generation of new employment, especially outside amenity-rich areas. In many cases, expenditure is too low to permit the economy to specialise only in the needs of the second home market. Nevertheless, second home tourism may contribute to the maintenance of a local service supply by generating a marginal income that enables local entrepreneurs to continue to run their businesses (Marcouiller *et al.*, 1998; Müller, 1999; Jansson & Müller, 2003).

The economic impacts of second homes are, however, not always positive. Second home tourism also leads to increased costs in providing, for example, additional infrastructure and services (Frost, this volume). Increases in property values in particular are considered a threat to a sustainable rural development (Shucksmith, 1983). However, this situation primarily occurs in areas with high amenity values and therefore considerable pressure on the second and primary home market rather than in all second home destinations. Boschken (1975) similarly deemed second home development as an unfortunate deal for rural communities; while in a study in Vermont, USA, Fritz (1982) argued that second home development increased the tax burden for the local population. In contrast, Gartner (1987) argued that, following second home development, costs will be shared between more households, thereby reducing economic pressure on the permanent population. Unfortunately, infrastructure and service investments and other economic impacts of second home development are usually not assessed comprehensively, and hence systematic accounts of the economic effects of second homes are not developed. Nevertheless, Deller *et al.* (1997) estimated that for the United States second homes generate revenues that just cover their increased cost to public services.

In other parts of the world, second home tourism is considered an important cornerstone for many rural economies. Second home owners tend to favour small rural shops and therefore contribute to the maintenance of service levels in the countryside (Nordin, 1993a; Müller, 1999; Velvin, 2002). For example, The Finnish Islands Committee (*Skärgårdsdelegationen*) identified the importance of second home tourism for the rural economy by comparing figures between the permanent population and second home populations (Leppänen, 2003). Between 1980 and 2000, the population living permanently in the countryside had declined by 31% to about 900,000. At the same time, the number of persons using second homes had increased by 79% to more than 1.8 million people using a second home between 80 and 109 days per year. Müller (1999) established that four German second home owners in Sweden spent as much a permanent

Swedish household. Another study in the Nordic countries showed that the consumption of between 3 and 32 second home households equalled the consumption of a permanent household. The differences depend primarily on the quality of the housing stock and the owners' intention to actually use the second home (Jansson & Müller, 2003). Similarly, in a study of recreational homes in Wisconsin and Minnesota in the United States, Marcouiller *et al.* (1998) demonstrated that second home owners played an important role in generating local business activity mainly because they use their properties throughout the year (albeit with greater use in summer). 'On average, recreational home owners spent about [US]$6,000 per year on items directly used or attributed to their recreational homes. Purchases made locally ranged from 20-70% of this amount, including remodelling and meals' (Marcouiller *et al* 1998: i). Interestingly, Marcouiller *et al.* (1998) also found that at the county level the expenditure patterns of the residents and the recreational home owners were generally similar with respect to how much money they spent outside the county.

For the public economy it is also of interest how second homes are dealt with on a national level (Jansson & Müller, 2003). In cases where a local property tax has to be paid, the local community receives a certain income and has an impetus to develop second home tourism. When property taxes are primarily raised on a national or state/provincial level, second home tourism will often provide only indirect revenues for the local municipality. In the US case, the taxation regime means that second home tourism can lead to additional public spending with respect to infrastructure and public services (Fritz, 1982; Deller *et al.*, 1997). Similarly, the rating base of local councils in Australia, New Zealand and the United Kingdom also means that second home owners will make direct taxation payments to municipalities. However, in the Nordic context public expenditure due to second home tourism is extremely limited (Jansson & Müller, 2003).

Social Impacts

During the 1960s and 1970s the social impacts associated with second home ownership caused great concern among rural populations and planners (Coppock, 1977a, 1977b; Rogers, 1977; Jordan, 1980). Even in the 1990s these concerns were alive despite the fact that the fears of an invasion of the countryside expressed in the 1970s never occurred (Gallent & Tewdwr-Jones, 2000). Indeed, in Britain in 2001 *The Times* (Bruxelles, 2001) ran a front-page story noting that Exmoor National Park in the south-west of England may ban outsiders from buying second homes because of a dramatic increase in property prices. However, as a more detailed article in the newspaper noted (Naish, 2001: 6), 'Exmoor's proposal reflects the genuine concern that local people are being squeezed out of their homes by encroaching city-dwellers, but this strategy fails to address the ultimate problem: there is not enough decent low-cost housing in the area.'

Concerns regarding the replacement or displacement of the traditional permanent population by second homes are often expressed in terms of increased property prices (Coppock, 1977d; Gallent & Tewdwr-Jones, 2000). In these situations it is usually claimed that young families are unable to purchase a property. As a consequence of such processes, villages that were once permanently occupied may be transformed into seasonal resorts implying, for example, increased crime rates (Coppock, 1977d; Jordan, 1980). However, such a perspective is overly simplistic. An alternative interpretation lies with the notion of rural change due to economic restructuring as a result of globalisation, new trade regimes and technological innovation, which leads to rural unemployment and out-migration (Jenkins *et al.*, 1998). Hence, it is the growth of a service-based economy favouring urban living that causes the changes in the countryside by also pushing the limits of recreational hinterlands further away from the urban core (Lundgren, 1974). Accordingly people leave the countryside not only for employment, but also for education and an urban lifestyle (Garvill *et al.*, 2000). Therefore, implicitly it can be argued that second home owners only fill the gaps caused by rural out-migrants (Müller, 1999, 2001). However, these openings are usually filled only on a seasonal basis.

Both interpretations imply that recent developments call into question the sustainability of rural areas, and also challenge their very survival as the living rural environments they have been portrayed as for much of the last century. It could even be argued that second home tourism may actually destroy its own amenities, i.e. the living countryside. It is also argued that amenity landscapes are transformed into elite landscapes with access limited to only affluent members of society (Halseth, this volume), thereby transferring urban segregation to the countryside and converting formerly common ground into elite playgrounds.

The mechanisms causing the displacement of rural population are usually seen in the rural property market and particularly in the way property values are assessed for taxation purposes. Recent sales influence the values of all properties in the geographical neighbourhood and hence competition for the attractive environment also affects the costs of living for primary residents. In this context, primary residences and second homes are treated equally, which means that amenity landscapes in particular are areas of increasing costs – although such demand tends to be highly seasonal. This situation is most likely to occur in amenity-rich metropolitan hinterlands, where the combined demand exceeds the existing property supply (see Müller, this volume). A similar demand also occurs in leisure destinations of national and international interest. Clearly, the high-profile Welsh experience was perceived in that way (Coppock, 1977d; Gallent &

Tewdwr-Jones, 2000). However, most rural areas do not experience such a displacement of the local population. Indeed, Müller (1999) argues that second home tourism instead fills the vacancies caused by out-migration.

It is also argued that second home owners interfere in the daily life of rural villagers (Jordan, 1980). In the Welsh case, the situation was made worse because the second home owners were English and so the acquisitions were perceived as depriving the local population of what belonged to them (Coppock, 1977d; Rogers, 1977; Shucksmith, 1983; Gallent & Tewdwr-Jones, 2000). In addition, second home owners benefited from government grants aiming at modernising rural housing, and were thus perceived by the rural population as competitors for such funding (Gallent, 1997). Similarly, German second home owners in Sweden were sometimes met with resentment. In Scandinavia it was feared that traditional rights of strand access would be contested owing to an increasing occupation of shorelines by second home developments (Jansson & Müller, 2003).

Another reason for dislike of second home development seems to be the potentially different social and economic backgrounds between second home owners and locals (Halseth & Rosenberg, 1995; Halseth, 1998). At least outside the Nordic countries second home owners often tend to be wealthier, entailing a potentially considerable economic and social distance between them and the inhabitants of the host community (Jaakson, 1986; Girard & Gartner, 1993; Halseth, 1993). Second home development can also be perceived as a form of rural gentrification, which implies the clash of traditional rural lifestyles with urban images of rural life (Müller, 1999). Halseth (this volume) argues that second home development in Canada is often isolated from the rural landscape and thereby contributes to the transformation of the countryside into an elite landscape. In Sweden Aronsson (1993) reported that encounters between second home owners and other residents are rare and limited to certain places. Flognfeldt (2002) draws a different picture for an area of second homes in Norway. There, second home owners are partly perceived as local patriots and hence are increasingly seen as a resource that can be utilised to attract additional businesses.

The social integration of second home owners into the local community is, however, not self-evident as it is partly dependent on the social ambitions and strategies of the second home owners themselves (Albarre, 1977; Buller & Hoggart, 1994b). Second home owners in traditional resorts, where residents are outnumbered by tourists, probably have a primary interest in the local amenities and not in social contact with locals. In contrast households with relatives in the second home destination may already have social contacts in the area. Limited social distance enhances the opportunities for becoming fully integrated (Pacione, 1979). International second home ownership causes problems regarding language and traditions (Buller & Hoggart, 1994b; Müller, 1999). Moreover, an inaccurate image of the modern countryside forces second home owners to look for social contacts among those who inhabit the rural area in the daytime. This often means contacts with other second home owners (often of the same nationality) as a substitute for the desired countryside life among the locals (Müller, 1999, 2002d).

Environmental Impacts

Second home ownership does not always imply new environmental impacts. According to the Finnish Islands Committee (Leppänen, 2003), transportation between primary and second homes forms the most prominent environmental impact. Mathieson and Wall (1982) list three major issues related to second home tourism: wildlife disruption due to the clearance of vegetation, disposal of human waste, and aesthetics. However, these impacts will apply to any building development. In cases of former rural permanent homes, no new infrastructure is needed. In cases of purpose-built second homes the situation is obviously different. Unplanned and unregulated housing developments raise pollution concerns, particularly for lakes and rivers that are attractive to second home development (Ragatz, 1977; Gartner, 1987). Langdalen (1980) and Clout (1971) suggested planning restrictions to limit the impact of second home development on the landscape. However, it is readily apparent that, at least in the European context, second home standards have widely improved since the 1970s (Gallent, 1997; Jansson & Müller 2003; Flognfeldt this volume). In Finland the shares of carbon dioxide, phosphorus, and nitrogen emissions related to second home tourism are estimated to be less than 1% of the total national figure (Leppänen, 2003). Even energy consumption by second homes is below 1%. Particle emissions caused by heating with wood are also estimated to be limited. Hence, compared to some forms of rural development, second home tourism may be regarded as being relatively environmentally friendly (Leppänen, 2003).

Although second home owners tend to appreciate the same aspects of the local community as the local population, they clearly differ in their view of future development in the second home community. Second home owners are usually more conservative and less positive towards change (Aronsson, 1993; Boschken, 1975; Girard & Gartner, 1993; Green et al., 1996; Fountain & Hall, 2002), particularly if it involves industrial development. Instead they care about the physical qualities of their second home environment and therefore tend to favour land use control and preservation (Burby et al., 1972). Moreover, they are usually interested in hindering further large-scale tourism development. Indeed, Leppänen (2003) suggests that there is a role for second home life in fostering an understanding of ecology and a respect for the environment.

Conflicts have also been noted with respect to second home development and some agricultural practices. For example, in the Nelson area in the north of the South Island of New Zealand, the price of suitable land for wine growing is inflated by high demand from 'lifestylers' migrating from urban centres (Gillion, 1998). Similar problems have also been recorded for the Martinborough area on the North Island. In addition, viticultural practices may not be welcome by second home owners, who are attracted in their purchasing behaviour by tranquil images of vineyards in pleasant rural areas. For example, in order to deter birds, which may cause substantial damage by pecking at grapes on the vine, many vineyards will employ birdscarers such as loud air guns. Similarly, helicopters are sometimes employed to improve circulation between warm and cold air layers, and thus prevent frosts from damaging tender grape buds. However, the noise from such activities has been opposed by a number of people in some grape-growing areas to the point where limitations have been imposed on helicopter use (Hall & Johnson, 1998).

These differences of environmental perception contributed to what the Wine Institute of New Zealand (WINZ) Chairman called the 'intrusion of urban values and expectations into rural working environments' (WINZ, 1997: 10). Unless the 'right to farm' is preserved and vineyards remain a part of rural life, the key resource of viticulture as well as winery tourism is undermined, to the clear detriment of the landscape features that attracted people to the area in the first place (WINZ, 1997). Therefore, any sustainable development of second home tourism in agricultural landscapes will have to balance these competing demands on resources. Similarly, concerns may sometimes be expressed over the biocide spray programmes employed on some vineyards. However, rural holidays will impact on the everyday lifestyle of urban tourists when they return home, and this includes changes to their mind-set regarding rural concerns (Swarbrooke, 1996). As a Michigan tourist council director described it, agricultural tourism (including second home tourism) is an opportunity for agriculture to create urban stakeholders in rural issues (Waldsmith, 1997). Second home tourism may in certain circumstances therefore even become an ally in retaining the 'right to farm'.

Managing Seasonality in Second Home Tourism

A common problem linked to the renewed interest in second homes is the seasonality in population patterns induced by second home tourism (Ragatz, 1970a; Casado-Diaz, 1999; Frost, this volume). As shown recently in the case of Sweden, second home tourism accounts for considerable *de facto* population changes usually neglected in official population statistics. Some peripheral municipalities are estimated to have 20% more inhabitants than actually recorded in the statistical tables (Müller & Hall, 2003).

In many parts of Europe second home owners are usually not registered as citizens in their host municipality. Instead, they are citizens only in their municipality of stated primary residence. Resorts with a significant second home population may therefore suffer from this situation in relation to access to government funding. Casado-Diaz (1999) reports that in the Spanish municipality of Torrevieja a population of only about 35,000 inhabitants is officially recorded, which means that the approximately 70,000 second home owners who have residences there are not considered to be citizens of the municipality, but instead are regarded as tourists. Hence, the municipal authorities can only estimate the numbers of the second home owners by observing their consumption of water and their demand for social services, which is significantly higher for second home owners who are usually retired and thus older than the average inhabitant of Torrevieja (Casado-Diaz, 1999). Comparable issues with respect to estimates of population levels in the United States and the implications for regional development were also recognised by Ragatz (1970). Nevertheless, official population estimates usually fail to consider the population mobility of second home owners, a situation made even more problematic in some second home areas as second home ownership in turn creates additional mobility with respect to VFR-tourism (Visiting Friends and Relatives) and retirement migration (Williams & Hall 2002).

Throughout the world, current administrative practices fail to recognise the complexity of current mobility patterns and forms (Müller & Hall 2003). Neither space–time use nor the motivations for mobility are sufficient indicators to distinguish tourism from some forms of migration (Müller 2002c; see also Duval, this volume). Hence, whether a house is a primary residence or a second home is entirely the owners' decision. This decision can depend on a variety of factors, for example, local taxation rates, the purchase order of homes, and diverse social and economic issues. Nevertheless, it is highly likely that most owners are hardly aware of the consequences of their decision with respect to nomination of permanent residence and consequent issues of governance and monetary transfers between levels of government (Williams & Kaltenborn, 1999; Müller 2002c).

In some jurisdictions, the nomination of one primary residence restricts the second home owners' right to participate in municipal elections to the municipality where the primary residence is located. Hence, in some circumstances, second home owners have to pay tax in their host municipality, but are excluded from democratic means to influence the situation there. Such limitations may reinforce the marginal positions of second home owners in the host municipality where they may also be regarded as second-class citizens. However, in contrast, in some countries (such as Finland and Canada) second home owners may be invited to establish local community associations in order to convey opinions regarding local issues to decision-makers (Halseth, 1998, Leppänen, 2003).

In many countries, second home owners' registration of residence may also be used as an index to redistribute national tax money from the central level of government back to the regional or municipal levels or to raise tax from the local population. Such indices may also be drawn on to assess economic transfers within national regional policy schemes. Therefore, many administrative systems assert the value of high municipal population numbers. In some situations, maximising the economic impact of second home tourism therefore equates to increasing the registered population, in other words, convincing the second home tourists to convert themselves into primary residents by promising better services or providing lower tax rates. However, such successful place-marketing solves the mobility problem only at a local level as the second home owners' former primary municipality then becomes the loser in the competition for citizens. In countries that do not raise local property taxes, the introduction of administrative systems that acknowledge individual mobility and recognise people as having several homes would therefore be most beneficial in equalising some of the unintended taxation consequences of mobility (Müller & Hall, 2003).

Planning and Management Issues

The responsibility for housing and land use planning, and therefore second home planning, generally lies within the realm of local government, whose involvement in second home development has been almost continually called for by researchers (e.g. Shucksmith, 1983; Gallent, 1997). Shucksmith (1983) observes that the perception exists that second homes are a problem to be dealt with by local, not central, government. This perception is arguably correct, given the uniqueness of second homes in each location. Yet, little has been specifically achieved on behalf of local government in terms of policy, planning and regulation for second homes. One of the difficulties that emerges in planning for second home development is the extent to which the impacts of second homes may be differently interpreted. For example, as noted above, the fears of the 1970s represented a perception of the rural communities as passive victims of the impacts of urban change. From this perspective planning is compelled to conserve the state of the countryside. In contrast, recent research argues that second home tourism itself is an expression as well as an agent of rural change (Müller, 1999). Hence, planning should aim to maximise the positive impacts of second home tourism and allow services to adapt to the changes caused by it instead of trying to prevent development. This is particularly so because the opposite scenario (conservation of the countryside) does not necessarily imply conservation in its current state, but instead implies rural depopulation and poverty. Behind every property that is sold to a second homeowner there is usually a household that decided not to live in the countryside.

Coppock (1997c: 12) recognised that, 'Effective solutions depend on understanding what is happening, on seeing second homes in the wider context of leisure time and the total pattern of living, and on devising effective policies which do not solve one problem and create another'. Therefore, the understanding of the issues, which this chapter has already discussed, is vital for appropriate strategic planning with respect to second homes. Nevertheless, little research has been conducted on the understanding that local government has of second home development issues. For example, while Gallent and Tewdwr-Jones (2000) provided a review of the planning controls available to government in various European jurisdictions there was no comprehensive overview of how these various controls may be applied and why.

In March 2001 a national survey of second homes and local government was sent to all regional and territorial authorities in New Zealand (Hall & Keen, 2001). A total of 58 of the country's 86 councils responded. The survey examined five specific areas of interest; the maintenance of records, perceived impacts of second homes, second homes and tourism development, regional development and planning (Hall & Keen, 2001). The results are detailed below as they provide one of the few accounts of how local government perceives second home issues.

Maintenance of statistics

As noted in Chapter 1, lack of effective statistics is a worldwide issue for second home research. There is a dearth of information at both the national and local levels on the numbers and characteristics of second homes in New Zealand (see Keen & Hall, this volume). As Table 2.2 shows, none of the councils kept any record, and only one council noted actual locations of second homes within its jurisdiction. The main reason identified for not maintaining a record of second homes was that there was no inherent benefit in doing so (44.6%), and that second homes were not the council's responsibility (18%). A number of councils noted that there are not enough second homes in their jurisdiction for them to be regarded as important (10.6%). In relation to this it should be noted that only 10 of the responding 58 councils have indicated that second homes are not an issue; hence the issues relating to second home should theoretically be of importance to the remaining councils. For many councils, second homes are identified as an issue; however, lack of resources (8.5%) and a difficulty in identifying or recording second homes (7.4%) were given as reasons for having no records. The difficulty in identifying second homes highlights the need for

Table 2.2 Reasons why New Zealand councils do not keep records of second home numbers or locations (*n* = 58)

Reasons for not maintaining a record of second homes	Frequency*	Percentage
Not enough second homes in jurisdiction	10	10.6
Lack of resources	8	8.5
No inherent benefit in doing so	42	44.6
Too difficult	7	7.4
Second homes are not the council's responsibility	17	18.0
Other	10	10.6
Total	*94*	

*Multiple response

clear definitions and consistent statistical records at both the local and national level.

Qualitative responses to the survey also provide an insight into the views of local government regarding second homes. One of the most frequently mentioned comments was the difficulty in identifying second homes. One council stated: 'Second homes are often no different from retirement homes and therefor[e] difficult to distinguish'. Another council simply stated: 'How can you possibly identify second homes?' The problem of identification is probably one of the most fundamental issues in relation to second homes. A failure to identify second homes results in a lack of understanding on behalf of councils regarding their role and impact. Related to this is the decision at a council level to identify second homes as no different from first homes. As one respondent commented: 'All homes are treated equal. For council purpose they are all the same – same provisions apply if it is the first, second or third home'. As another council noted: 'This is not an issue under the district plan – residential activities are not noted as either permanent or seasonal as can change without notification' (Hall & Keen, 2001).

Given present regulatory conditions in New Zealand, councils may be justified in treating all components of the housing stock in the same way. However, in terms of tourism and wider community and economic impacts, substantial differences clearly exist between first and second homes that impact on local government functions and responsibilities other than housing and resource consent issues. Table 2.3 shows how councils responded to the request to judge the significance of second homes within their jurisdiction. It is interesting to note that some of the councils that directly stated that second homes were not an issue were well known to the researchers from fieldwork they have conducted. Two of these areas have some of the largest concentrations and range of second homes in New Zealand and in some cases second homes are vital to community survival.

Table 2.3 Importance of second homes within New Zealand councils ($n = 51$)

Level of importance	Frequency	Percentage
1 Very important	2	3.9
2	4	7.8
3 Somewhat important	10	19.6
4	9	17.6
5 Not important	26	50.9

Impacts

Economic contribution was seen as being the most beneficial effect of second home development (62.5%); however the social effects of second homes were also seen as being highly beneficial (30%). The importance that local government attaches to the economic advantages of second home development is not unexpected, given the economic restructuring of many rural regions (e.g. Jenkins *et al.*, 1998; Marcouiller *et al.*, 1998).

In relation to social effects it appears that many of the adverse effects felt in some countries, are not an issue that local governments in New Zealand must deal with. In the case of Britain, local antagonism towards second homes has been fuelled by issues of status and insufficient housing (e.g. Dower, 1977; Gallent, 1997). In this survey these same issues were important only for a small minority of cases. The only notable negative effect is a concern over properties being empty out of season. The major positive effect was the enhancement of community lifestyle; this is particularly important in terms of regional and community development of tourism resources. In addition, local government in New Zealand recognised the negative physical impacts of second homes as a significant issue, although second homes are also seen by some councils as having a positive effect.

Green *et al.* (1996) argued that second homes had adverse effects on local government in terms of rate (local tax) returns versus expenditure on infrastructure and services. Table 2.4 shows that a number of the local governments felt that second homes increased the cost of infrastructure and service provision to local government. It is also interesting to note that other issues such as increasing land costs, costs beyond locals means and increasing rates cost are seen as having a degree of importance.

Ways in which second homes can contribute to tourism and regional development

Table 2.5 shows that second homes are perceived as contributing to tourism in a variety of ways. Most notably, the attraction of friends and relatives and the provision of economic benefits are seen as being of particular value.

Table 2.4 Impacts associated with second home tourism by New Zealand councils (*n* = 35–37)

Impacts	1 Very important	2	3 Somewhat important	4	5 Not important	Mean
SOCIAL EFFECTS	%	%	%	%	%	%
Positive						
Enhanced community lifestyle	-	16.2	48.6	18.9	16.2	**3.5**
Input of new ideas into community	2.4	7.5	26	34.1	29.3	**3.8**
Creation of facilities	-	7.5	30	35	27.5	**3.83**
Increase in local pride in the area	2.5	15	37.5	17.5	27.5	**3.53**
Preserves a traditional way of life	2.5	7.5	35	25	30	**3.73**
Use of redundant housing stock	2.6	18.4	10.5	21.1	47.4	**3.92**
Negative						
Second home/local antagonism	5.3	2.6	15.8	18.4	57.9	**4.21**
Increase in crime	-	5.3	18.4	23.7	52.6	**4.24**
Loss of cultural identity	2.6	5.3	5.3	28.9	57.9	**4.34**
Properties empty out of season	5.1	15.4	25.6	17.9	35.9	**3.64**
Insufficient housing stock	5.3	2.6	7.9	23.1	60.5	**4.32**
Disruption of rural life	2.6	-	15.4	23.1	59	**4.36**
Change in social structure	2.5	5	15	37.5	40	**4.08**
Limits access to recreational areas	2.5	7.5	20	30	40	**3.98**
Over crowding	-	5.4	10.8	18.9	64.9	**4.43**
PHYSICAL/ENVIRONMENTAL						
Positive						
Beautification of area	-	7.5	35	22.5	35	**3.85**
Protection of natural areas	4.9	17.1	17.1	22	39	**3.73**
Protection of heritage buildings	7.5	10	12.5	25	45	**3.9**
Wildlife protection	7.5	5	17.5	17.5	52.5	**4.03**
Facilities/services	7.5	17.5	20	27.5	27.5	**3.5**
Negative						
Loss of visual amenity	4.9	26.8	24.4	22	22.4	**3.29**
Inadequate waste disposal	23.3	25.6	23.3	11.6	16.3	**2.72**
Environmental degradation	14.6	19.5	22	24.4	19.5	**3.15**
Stress on road systems	10	10	25	25	30	**3.55**

Table 2.4 *(continued)*

Wildlife deprivation	10	15	17.5	25	32.5	**3.55**
Exploitation of natural areas	11.9	21.4	16.7	21.4	28.6	3.33
Poor design construction of houses	5	17.5	20	22.5	35	3.65
Land being taken from conservation areas	7.5	2.5	10	40	40	4.03
Inadequate water supplies	12.5	23.3	14	32.6	18.6	3.23
ECONOMIC						
Positive						
Restoration of land values	7.5	17.5	25	32.5	17.5	3.35
Increase in employment opportunities	10.3	15.4	23.1	28.2	23.1	3.38
Creation of new economic base	7.3	22	24.4	24.4	22	3.32
Revitalisation of construction industry	10.3	2.6	20.5	35.9	30.8	3.74
Creation of service industries	10.5	5.3	26.3	31.6	26.3	3.58
Increase in rates	4.8	23.8	28.6	28.6	10.3	3.24
Help to maintain existing services	7.7	23.1	30.8	23.1	15.4	3.145
Negative						
Land values beyond means of locals	7.1	11.9	28.6	31	21.4	3.48
Increase in rates	5	12.5	30	25	27.5	3.58
Increase in property prices	2.4	11.9	35.3	31	19	3.52
Increase in cost of local goods and services	2.6	7.7	23.1	30.8	35.9	39
Increasing cost to local governments	12.2	17.1	24.4	24.4	22	3.27

Regional development is one of the ways in which second homes can be most beneficial to communities. The use of tourism as a regional development strategy is well recognised (e.g. Jenkins *et al.*, 1998; Marcouiller *et al.*, 1998; Hall, 2000; Town of Hamden, 2000). Tourism was the second most important strategy for regional development identified by New Zealand local and regional councils – the most important being the increase of horticultural and agricultural possibilities. Nevertheless, such significance does not readily correspond to the overall understanding of second homes by councils. Some 64% of councils noted that second homes do make a contribution to regional development. The most notable factor was the increase in spending into local economies as a result of second homes: 94.5% of respondents indicated this was significant. Other important issues were the attraction of retirees (45.9%), the contribution to an increase in permanent

Table 2.5 The importance of second home tourism to tourism development

Importance	1 Very important	2	3 Somewhat important	4	5 Not important	Mean
Provides a supply of tourists	13.5	21.6	24.3	18.9	21.6	3.14
Creates facilities for other tourist types	7.9	13.2	28.9	23.7	26.3	3.47
Facilitates domestic tourism	5.1	28.2	38.5	15.4	12.8	3.02
Provides economic benefits	13.5	27	27	24.3	8.1	2.86
Highlights benefits tourists can bring to the area	-	15.2	24.2	36.4	24.2	3.48
Instigates regional development	2.8	13.9	27.8	30.6	25	3.61
Attracts friends and relatives to area	7.7	38.5	20.5	23.1	10.3	2.84

residents (48.6%), and contribution towards business growth (40.5%). Both the positive and negative effects of these trends upon local government are considerable: 15 councils (35.7%) said that they have already seen evidence of second homes becoming retirement properties. The impact of this will probably be an increase in the demands on infrastructure and services, changes to the local rating (tax) base and changes to visitor flows. Eleven councils (26.1%) councils noted that there has been a trend in their jurisdiction for people to use the second home as the primary residence prior to permanent retirement. Such population shifts may well have significant implications for the structure of communities as well as for the development of business opportunities and increasing demands on infrastructure and services.

The results of the New Zealand survey suggest that second homes are perceived by New Zealand's local governments as both a curse and a blessing. Such a situation is not confined to New Zealand. As this chapter has argued, and as many of the subsequent chapters in this book demonstrate, second homes have different effects. However, they are now an integral component of rural areas and not an aberration, and should therefore be incorporated into the strategic planning processes that local and regional councils should be undertaking if they are to ensure sustainable regional development. In order to provide effective planning, local government must therefore recognise the inherent unique qualities of second homes as a housing, tourism and development factor.

Summary

The potential impacts of second home development necessitate effective planning. Planning from the municipal and regional government perspective should not deal solely with housing regulations or planning controls, nor with the negative issues associated with second homes, but should also be created to effectively gain the most benefit from second homes now and in the future. The current importance of regional development strategies to rural areas, and the overall economic significance of second home tourism to rural and peripheral areas that are otherwise suffering the loss of intellectual capital, population, services and income cannot be ignored, and increase the importance of second homes in many jurisdictions. However, the lack of understanding of, and research on, second homes makes effective planning and policy setting extremely difficult. As Marcouiller *et al.* (1998: 1) recognised, the implications of second home development trends for 'regional planning with regard to providing public service, environmental zoning and land use' need to be better known. In particular it becomes important that the benefits of second homes are not lost amongst concerns for a rural idyll that never existed. Nor should it be forgotten that, in order to be effective, rural regional development needs to remain focused on people and the reasons why they either remain in or move to a region.

Part 2

Mobilities, Encounters and Meanings

Chapter 3

The 'Cottage' Privilege: Increasingly Elite Landscapes of Second Homes in Canada

GREG HALSETH

Introduction

The second home phenomenon in Canada is almost entirely associated with recreational property and vacation homes. While a number of terms are used to describe these second home properties, including chalet, cabin, camp, or cottage, I shall refer to them generically as 'cottages'. Popular literature (Gordon, 1989; Cross, 1992) and academic research (Wolfe, 1951, 1965; Helleiner, 1983; Halseth, 1998) alike highlight that recreational second home ownership is widespread across all regions of Canada. While cottage areas are almost always set within a surrounding rural countryside, to be at the cottage is to define a geographic presence in a landscape separate and removed from the rural milieu. The divide between these two very different landscapes is rooted not just in economics but also in a geographic imagination of a socially constructed symbolism intimately associated with cottage spaces.

This chapter describes the importance of cottages within Canada's rural-recreational countryside and identifies that the 'cottage at the lake' has come to assume a place in Canadian folklore. Building upon this, socio-economic differences between cottage owners and rural residents further add to a locally-constructed understanding of difference. Finally, socio-economic differences between cottage owners and the Canadian population complete the argument that cottage landscapes are elite landscapes. It is argued that the form of settlement, the geographic imagination attached to the landscape, the socio-economic distinctions between rural and cottage residents, and the demand for increasingly scarce recreational property are important in enhancing the elite status of cottage property in Canada. From this, there are social and economic implications for rural places annually 'invaded' by second home owners (Walker, 1987), and these need to be better understood if we are to contribute to community change, land use, and planning debates.

Rural-Recreational Countryside

The spatial setting in which cottage and rural property areas are juxta-posed is crucial to understanding the imagery and economics of second home landscapes. While the rural landscape in Canada is complex and diverse, this discussion is interested only in one particular cross-section, something which I will label the 'rural-recreational countryside'. In this part, I will outline some of the general distinguishing characteristics of the rural-recreational countryside, the organisation of cottage properties within that countryside, and the common tenure arrangements associated with cottages.

The rural-recreational countryside includes those rural areas that feature attractive recreational amenities. These amenities may include lake or ocean shorelines, mountain hiking or skiing opportunities, or some similar natural amenity value. To increase the potential for recreation or vacation activity, this countryside is located within weekend commuting distance of large urban places. In this respect, the rural-recreational countryside is part of a more generally understood 'urban field' (Friedmann & Miller, 1965; Friedmann, 1978) or 'city's countryside' (Troughton, 1981; Bryant *et al.*, 1982; Coppack *et al.*, 1988). The proximity and size of the urban centre, as well as the value of the recreational amenity, will influence the level of second home development pressure in any particular locality (Brunet, 1980; Jordan, 1980; Keogh, 1982; Lehr *et al.*, 1984; Wilkinson & Murray, 1991). If this potential has been exploited, the rural-recreational country-side will feature large numbers of recreational properties and cottages.

The classic volume *Second Homes: Curse or Blessing*, edited by Coppock (1977a), highlighted the fact that vacation home or cottage ownership was a global phenomenon. Chapters reported on these second home dwellings in France (Clout, 1977), Great Britain (Coppock, 1977b; Rogers, 1977), Czecho-slovakia (Gardavsky, 1977), Canada (Priddle & Kreutzwiser, 1977; Wolfe, 1977), and Australia (Robertson, 1977). Additionally, more recent reports have either added to the geographic diversity of places where cottage prop-erty has been studied or provided updates on their status in countries covered in that 1977 volume (Lehr *et al.*, 1991; Geipel, 1992; Smith & Krannich, 2000). An interesting addition to this work is now beginning to emerge from Asia, especially Japan. In the Japanese context, significant post-war urbanisation has created a community development crisis in many rural areas (Goto & Ouchi, 1996; Okahashi, 1996). To counter some of the associated economic challenges, many rural places have embraced 'green tourism' as a way to draw urban residents to countryside areas for visits, vacations, or farm or wilderness retreats (Japan, 2001). Local govern-ments, prefectural governments, and the Japanese central government have put funding and programs in place to support rural revitalisation by taking advantage of urban-recreational demands. This transient pattern of 'interchange' is now setting the foundation for 'address change' as affluent urban residents are purchasing second homes or relocating to rural communities from which they commute (physically or by telecommunications) to their urban employment (Ando, 2002).

The spatial organisation of the rural-recreational countryside is generally quite simple. The farming and rural-residential landscape is marked by large properties and a pattern of low-density development. Crossroads often mark the locations for village and service centre clusters. While a number of different patterns identify regional variations in agricultural settlement, from the dispersed farmsteads of the Canadian prairie to the linear villages of Quebec, these landscapes are clearly set off from small-lot, intensively developed, cottage property areas.

Viewed individually, a cottage along the lake may indeed appear as an isolated retreat. Cottage development, however, rarely occurs individually. Whether in clustered developments (as is common in British Columbia or New Brunswick) or in a single-tier linear band along a waterfront margin (as is common in Ontario), cottage properties represent a spatially distinct unit within the rural landscape. In either case, the individual cottage is no longer isolated but rather it is part of a collective of properties. One consequence is that development densities within cottage areas can be as high as in many North American suburbs (Halseth, 1998). Such development densities can create tremendous problems for both access and servicing, and increase the potential for environmental degradation. In the highly developed Rideau Lakes region of Ontario, for example, many jurisdictions are bringing in regulations to limit or manage waterfront and recreation uses in an effort to slow environmental damage. Parks Canada has recommended a series of development guidelines for its holdings along the Rideau Canal (Canada, 1990a, 1990b). Similarly, shoreline development guidelines based on the ecological carrying capacity of the lakes are being integrated into local land use plans and development approval processes (Rideau Valley Conservation Authority, 1992a, 1992b).

While cottage developments can be quite dense, the regional organisation of cottage areas can similarly be quite dense, to the point where cottage districts form. For example, within central British Columbia, Prince George (population 85,000 in 2001) is the principal service and supply centre. Cottagers from Prince George compete with residents of metropolitan Vancouver for access to the major resort lakes of the central interior of the province. These resort districts include the 'Canim–Bridge' lakes area near 100 Mile House, the 'Quesnel–Horsefly' lakes area near Williams Lake, and the 10 Mile Lake area near Quesnel.

There are also a large number of recreational lakes near Prince George that have developed into a rural-recreational countryside. Table 3.1 identi-

Table 3.1 Waterfront residential properties* Prince George area, BC, 1995

Location	*Total properties*
Chief and Summit Lakes	34
Cluculz Lake	736
Fraser and Francois Lakes	267
Hixon/Stoner area	9
McLeod Lake	195
Ness Lake	257
Norman and Bednesti Lakes	247
Purden Lake	79
Stuart Lake	309
Stuart/Babine/Takla Lakes	305
Tabor Lake	58
Vanderhoof (north of)	6
Vanderhoof (south of)	118
West Lake	82

* Defined as small-lot residential property, outside of municipal boundaries, along a watercourse or lake shoreline, and containing a mix of permanent and seasonally occupied dwellings.
Source: Adapted from Halseth (forthcoming)

fies nearly 2500 waterfront properties that have been developed around Prince George. More than 1500 of these properties have a dwelling unit on them. Nearly all the lakes in Table 3.1 are within daily commuting distance of Prince George, and many of these second home properties are at risk of conversion into permanently-occupied housing (Halseth, forthcoming). Since cottage area services are based on seasonal occupancy, conversion to year-round housing puts tremendous pressure on the local environment and infrastructure. Too often the costs of cottage conversion, including pollution control, road access, winter snow removal, water supply, and garbage collection, are not anticipated in cottage area planning. The costs of these services can be substantial, and may easily exceed property tax revenues. Therefore, the development of cottage lots for sale as a way of adding to local government coffers in the rural-recreational countryside needs to be critically examined (Beck & Hussey, 1989).

Two principal forms of land tenure are associated with cottage developments. The first is 'fee simple' private land tenure, where the property is owned. A key implication of fee simple ownership in Canada is the requirement to pay property taxes. These are calculated on the basis of the value of the property, and on the revenue needs of local governments and school districts. Since most cottage property is found outside of municipal boundaries, property taxation is comparatively low (Halseth, forthcoming).

The second type of cottage land tenure involves leased land (Rosenberg & Halseth, 1993). This may be either leased 'Crown' land or a lease from a private property owner. In the case of leased Crown land, the property continues to be owned by the state and the cottager obtains the right to use the land via a long-term lease arrangement. Annual Crown land lease fees for seasonal cottage property in British Columbia are approximately 3% of assessed value, with a $500 minimum. A typical lease period on British Columbia Crown lands is 15 years, with rights to renew included in the lease. Leasing from a private landholder is also common across Canada. In some cases, the owner may be a farmer who is obtaining some additional land 'rent', in other cases it may be a society, charitable group or religious organisation that gains income from its holdings. Whoever the landowner may be, the leaseholder typically pays a lease fee, has a limited term lease, rights of renewal, and a few provisions as to land uses. Lease arrangements do not come with the same protections accorded fee simple lands, and leaseholders always face the possibility of increased fees, termination with limited notice, or refusal to renew. In such cases, leaseholders have little recourse to recover their investments. As a result, chartered banks are limited by legislation from offering mortgages on leased lands and financing is generally done through credit unions or private means.

Cottage Landscape Folklore

The physical separation of cottage and rural landscapes within the rural-recreational countryside is reinforced by a socially-constructed understanding of separation and difference between these landscapes. In fact, the very 'idea' of the cottage in Canada has created a folklore that has become intimately associated with cottage landscapes. This folklore identifies the cottage landscape as something apart from the rural countryside within which it is set, and as such is a fundamental basis upon which a socially constructed and understood separation of cottage and rural areas is built. This sets the foundation for the competing geographic imaginations of the rural-recreational countryside.

Bunce's (1994) detailed study of the 'countryside idyll' clearly shows how the rural landscape has been defined and redefined over time in the Anglo-American imagination. This social geography process has shaped the way both rural and urban residents (separately of course) define, interpret, and develop an attachment to countryside landscapes. Similarly, Osborne (1988) argues that the Canadian countryside has become reified in the imaginations of urban Canadians such that it has become part of society's iconography. I would add that such images of the rural countryside are especially refined 'at the cottage'.

The 'summer cottage at the lake' is an immediately identifiable element of the Canadian countryside. The folklore now so plainly associated with cottages describes a retreat from urban settlement forms and an escape from both the physical and psychological pressures of urban life. For writers, such as Cross (1992), the essential point of the cottage is its use as a retreat. She argues that in their isolation and simplicity such places have always been havens for personal renewal, and that the journey to the cottage becomes something of a metaphorical journey along which the distractions of everyday life are stripped away. Being at the cottage is to be enmeshed in a cottage culture centred on a tradition of leisure, relaxation, and freedom from routine.

Historically, the summer house meant a physical escape from the noise and congestion of the city. The Rideau Lakes and the Muskoka Lakes regions of Ontario developed during the 1920s as summer retreats from the heat and pollution of cities such as Ottawa and Toronto. Along the Rideau Lakes, the

> Historic pattern of recreational land use and cottage development mirrors that of other central Canadian resort areas in that it was initially developed as a resort hotel destination in the 'northern' wilderness catering to an elite able to afford such distractions. (Halseth & Rosenberg, 1990: 104)

Bennett and McCuaig (1980), Brown (1984), and Kennedy (1984) all write about how the early development of cottages along the Rideau Lakes allowed upper-class families from Ottawa and Kingston to spend their summers in the countryside while the husband/father commuted to the city for the business week. Now, for Cross and others, there is a new theme of a psychological escape from the pressures of contemporary life.

But such an idyllic escape is often more a construction of the mind than of the spatial landscape in which cottages are found. One of the most insightful critiques of Canadian cottage folklore is Wolfe's (1965) commentary in *Landscape*. In that critique, Wolfe argues that the cottage is at the heart of a paradox. The often-expressed goal of cottagers is to seek a peaceful respite from the pressures of urban life, yet, in rushing to the limited number of recreation amenity locations in the countryside, these cottagers simply recreate many of the same pressures from which they sought to escape. Wolfe's characterisation of Wasaga Beach, Ontario, in the early 1950s is one where:

The traffic jams are as satisfactory as any in Toronto itself. Cars and people fill all the streets. The tourist cabins are bursting, and cars are parked in all the available space. The noise is tremendous, as [children] shout to each other, car-horns blow at them, motorboats roar on the river, and an aeroplane skims the rooftops. We are no longer in the country. We are back in the city again – or better, we are in the city away from the city. (Wolfe, 1952: 62)

Clout (1974: 102) also noted, in his classic European study, that the seasonal movements of urban residents to densely developed cottage and resort areas seems like the 'transporting [of] "the City" and its inhabitants into the countryside'; an annual process 'of a wilderness being transformed into a peculiar clone of suburbia'.

Besides the issue of retreat or escape, another part of cottage folklore in Canada centres upon the cottage as a self-contained social milieu. Both Wolfe (1965) and Jaakson (1986) highlight the separation of cottage areas within the rural landscape. Gordon (1989) wrote a best-selling humorous paperback that quite clearly enunciates this separation of cottage and rural landscapes. As seen from the cottage, the local small town is not much more than an anonymous supply depot. Adding to this imagery of cottage 'separateness' is the fact that the entry fees to cottage ownership make it a highly selective activity (Clout, 1977). In fact, Wyckoff (1990) discusses cottage and second home landscapes as one type of 'landscape of power'. For Wyckoff, these landscapes of power are part of a longstanding process whereby the affluent members of society create social and spatial exclusivity. One reason why cottages can still confer a sense of exclusivity or status is that participation is not ubiquitously available. The cost of purchasing/leasing, maintaining, and travelling to and from these second homes is considerable. The leisure time to go to the cottage must be combined with having the economic resources to afford the purchase and maintenance costs of these 'inessential houses' (Wolfe, 1965: 7).

This discussion of the geographic imagination associated with cottage landscapes highlights some critical problem areas. One of the most important involves notions of sustainable land use and environmental values. This has much less to do with the contribution of a single cottage to local pollution levels and is more concerned with the general idea of cottages. There is the serious issue of the alienation of land for use by the limited segment of the population able to afford second homes, the issue of closure of public access to large numbers of lakes ringed by a narrow band of private cottage properties (Marsh & Wall, 1982), and the issue of the environmental costs of having, maintaining, and travelling to and from these occasional-use retreats. Despite the importance of cottages in the landscape and economy of rural areas, relatively scarce attention has been paid to their form and function.

The discussion of cottages in the rural-recreational countryside also speaks to a more general, and longstanding, debate about rural change and the participation of new groups (Pahl, 1965; Pierce Colfer & Colfer, 1978; Fitchen, 1991; Smith & Krannich, 2000). Recent interest within the rural restructuring literature, for example, highlights the role of both social and economic differences in rural and small town places (Smailes, 2002; Smutny, 2002). Cloke and Goodwin (1992) argue that a form of 'commodification' of rural idylls and lifestyles has created a new theatre of consumption. Such consumption of the rural-recreational countryside can 'lead to the occurrence of "two nations" in the same rural place ... [with] a contesting of local political power ... [and] local cultural images' (Cloke & Goodwin, 1992: 331). Phillips (1993, 2002) describes this in-migration of the elite as 'rural gentrification'. While such changes are important in rural communities, they are not new. Burby *et al.* (1972: 421) long ago noted that the 'penetration of thousands of recreation-oriented households into the rural hinterlands of metropolitan areas poses a number of serious environmental and service problems' for the rural locale.

The long history of cottaging, of going to a resort landscape in the wilderness, has been important in the creation of a folklore which is now intimately attached to both the cottage and the act of cottaging. This folklore continues to define a lifestyle and a landscape clearly separate from the rural milieu within which it is set. This geographic imagination sets a foundation for understanding the rural landscape as only a picturesque backcloth, something to be passed through in travelling to the cottage. In turn, this geographic imagination also has important social and economic implications for the small-town and rural areas that thus form the 'other part' of the rural-recreational countryside.

Socio-Economic Distinctions

If cottages and cottage property are found across the Canadian rural-recreational countryside, accessibility to cottage ownership is certainly not ubiquitous. The economic costs to cottage ownership represent a further basis for constructing a distinction between cottagers and others. In this section, socio-economic characteristics are examined across two scales. The first is a comparison between cottager owners and rural residents, while the second is a comparison between cottage owners and the Canadian population. Together, these demonstrate that cottage landscapes are (re)turning into elite landscapes.

Within the rural-recreational countryside

To compare socio-economic characteristics between cottage owners and rural residents, this section will draw upon a questionnaire survey conducted in three areas across Canada (Rosenberg & Halseth, 1993). The three areas include the Rideau Lakes region in Eastern Ontario between Ottawa and Kingston, the Cultus Lake region of the Fraser Valley outside of Vancouver, and the Beaubassin Coast region of Eastern New Brunswick between Shediac and Cap Pele. Across a range of family characteristics there are some clear differences between cottage owners and rural residents. In terms of family structure, cottage owners tend to be older and to have a smaller household size with fewer children present, than do residents in the surrounding rural areas. In terms of marital status, however, both cottage owners and rural residents tend to be married.

The most marked differences between cottage owners and rural residents, however, concern socio-economic status (Table 3.2). Compared with rural residents, cottage owners tend to have higher levels of education. This is most pronounced in the Rideau Lakes and Cultus Lake regions, but is also apparent in the Beaubassin region as well. As expected, educational differences translate into household income differences. In all three regions, cottage owners report higher annual household incomes than do rural residents. Finally, cottage owners are more likely to be employed in professional rather than primary or secondary sector occupations than are rural residents. In part, this relates to educational and income levels, but it also relates to the nature of extensive land use and primary production in agriculture, forestry, and fishing that marks rural livelihoods (Cloke, 1989).

One of the interesting socio-economic characteristics in Table 3.2 pertains to 'retired' households. While a large share of rural households report being retired, the share is larger for the cottage-owner sample in each of the three regions. Given this predominance of retired households, and their typically lower income levels relative to when they were in the labour force, we can speculate that the occupational and income differences between cottage owners and rural residents would have been even more pronounced.

These findings fit well with other studies of second home property owners. Hodge's (1970) study of cottagers in Toronto's rural-recreational countryside found they were largely families with young children, and tended to have high incomes. The additional costs of second home ownership play a role in requiring these higher income levels. A study by Gill and Clark (1992) outlined a profile of second home owners in the resort of Whistler, British Columbia. Similarly, they found second home owners tended to have high income and educational levels, and tended to be employed in professional occupations. While the age profiles generated by Hodge (1970)

Table 3.2 Profiles of rural residents and cottage owners

	RIDEAU LAKES		CULTUS LAKE		BEAUBASSIN	
	Rural	Cottage	Rural	Cottage	Rural	Cottage
	%	%	%	%	%	%
Education						
Public	8.9	2.0	7.1	2.2	18.9	11.1
High school	46.5	36.9	53.5	39.7	46.7	40.00
University	40.7	60.1	35.2	54.4	34.4	7.4
Other	3.9	1.0	4.2	3.7	0	1.6
(*n* =)	(226)	(491)	(71)	(136)	(90)	(190)
Household income						
<$20,000	20.5	6.1	26.3	18.4	9.1	13.3
$20–29,000	13.4	8.9	15.8	13.2	36.4	13.3
$30–39,000	14.3	15.5	18.4	15.8	24.2	13.3
$40-49,000	12.5	12.2	18.4	15.8	9.1	21.7
$50,000+	39.3	57.3	21.1	36.9	21.2	38.3
(*n* =)	(112)	(246)	(38)	(76)	(33)	(60)
Occupation						
Professional	19.4	25.8	20.6	22.6	17.7	23.2
Service	20.4	16.7	3.5	12.8	25.9	21.1
Primary	10.7	0	7.4	0.8	1.8	0
Secondary	11.1	3.9	11.8	3.0	24.7	12.4
Other	8.3	6.0	8.8	7.5	7.1	7.6
Retired	30.1	47.3	27.9	53.4	23.5	35.7
(*n* =)	(216)	(484)	(68)	(133)	(85)	(185)

Source: Unpublished resident survey conducted by the author

and Gill and Clark (1992) showed that second home owners tended to be relatively young, Halseth (1998) points out that, while age may distinguish between different types of rural-recreational landscapes, high income remained a consistent difference between cottage owners and rural residents.

Cottages across Canada

Cottage property ownership is not widespread within the Canadian population. One of the reasons for this is the financial burden which second home ownership entails. In this section, an outline of data on the extent of cottage ownership in Canada is combined with a review of information on the economic exclusivity of cottage ownership. Unfortunately, Statistics Canada stopped collecting information on 'vacation homes' in the early 1990s.

Table 3.3 includes information about vacation home ownership from Statistics Canada's Survey of Household Facilities and Equipment (HFE). A question on vacation home ownership was included in the HFE survey intermittently from 1973 to 1992. The HFE survey makes no distinction between summer and winter vacation homes, and the data for 1973, 1980 and 1985 must be read as including all Canadian households who own a vacation home outside of Canada. In 1988, the HFE survey changed the question by specifying vacation homes owned in Canada. The data after 1988, therefore, shows a reduction of approximately 16,000, representing those Canadian households who own a vacation home outside of Canada.

Over the approximately 20-year period covered by the HFE surveys, the number of households participating in vacation home ownership increased by more than 35 percent. Given that the later data in Table 3.3 excludes vacation homes owned outside of Canada, the percentage increase is likely at least 5 percent higher. In 1992 (the last for which the data were collected), the HFE estimates that the number of vacation homes in Canada was 605,000, of which approximately 222,000 were in Ontario and 38,000 were in British Columbia. It was during the period of economic growth during the 1970s that cottage property was regarded as becoming more widely accessible.

The HFE survey also estimates the percentage share of Canadian households owning each of the range of products included in the survey. With respect to vacation homes, the HFE survey estimates show that they are owned by about 5.9% of Canadian households (Statistics Canada, 1973–1992). This share, however, has been relatively static since 1973. This is a surprising result, given the growth in numbers of vacation home owners shown in Table 3.3, and the fact that the period from 1970 to 1990 is widely interpreted in Canada as one marked by increasing wealth, leisure time, and the pursuit of recreational opportunities. Clearly, several factors (including demographics and changing preferences in leisure activity) are influencing vacation home ownership. Another explanation is the introduction of restrictions on waterfront cottage-lot creation and the resultant pressures on cottage prices. When these are combined, the effect is to further limit access to cottage ownership on economic grounds. These two trends may account for the increased vacation home ownership among upper income households.

Tables 3.4, 3.5 and 3.6 include data which highlight that cottage ownership is concentrated in the upper income segments of the population and that this concentration is becoming more pronounced. For the period from 1986 to 1990, the HFE survey estimated vacation home ownership using income groupings. In Table 3.4, the percentages indicate the share of households within each income group that are estimated to own vacation

Table 3.3 Vacation home owners in Canada

Year	Number of owners[2]
1973[1]	449,000
1974	476,000
1975	–
1976	476,000
1977	
1978	473,000
1979	–
1980	495,000
1981	–
1982	523,000
1983	–
1984	–
1985	545,000
1986	–
1987	551,000
1988	568,000
1989	552,000
1990	558,000
1991	560,000
1992	605,000

– = Vacation home question not asked in HFE survey for this year.

1 = First year vacation home question included in HFE survey.

2 = Statistics Canada estimates the percent standard error is 2.6–5.0%; no error estimate available for 1973 and 1974.

Source: Household Facilities and Equipment, Catalogue # 64-202 (Statistics Canada, 1973–1992)

Table 3.4 Vacation home ownership in Canada by income group (1986 and 1990 income years)

Average household income in Canada: 1986 = $34,261; 1991 = $46,137			
1986		*1990*	
Income	*% owning vacation homes*	*Income*	*% owning vacation homes*
Below $10,000	2.8	Below $10,000	2.6
$10–14,999	2.8	$10–14,999	2.9
$15–19,999	2.7	$15–19,999	2.4
$20–24,999	4.7	$20–24,999	3.9
$25–29,999	3.7	$25–29,999	3.9
$30–34,999	5.2	$30–34,999	5.0
$35–44,999	3.9	$35–44,999	4.7
$45–54,999	6.4	$45–54,999	7.1
$55,000 and over	5.8	$55–69,999	6.2
		$70,000 and over	10.7
National average	4.1		5.9

Source: Household Facilities by Income and Other Characteristics (Catalogue #64-202) 1987 and 1991 (Statistics Canada, 1973–1992)

homes in Canada. In 1986, approximately 4.1% of Canadian households owned a vacation home. As the table shows, while there are larger shares in the high-income categories, many income groups from $20,000 per annum upwards have close to the national average of owned vacation homes. This had shifted quite dramatically by the time of the 1991 HFE survey. For that year, it was estimated that approximately 5.9% of Canadian households owned a vacation home in Canada. While some households within all income groups reported owning vacation homes in 1990, only those with an annual household income over $45,000 exceeded that national share. For the highest-income groups, that share is well in excess of the national average.

When we compare vacation home ownership across income groups with average household income in Canada for 1986 and 1991, this period appears to mark a shift in economic accessibility. In 1986, the average household income in Canada was $34,261. Many of the income groups below this level have equivalent or more participation in vacation home ownership compared to the national average of 4.1%. By 1991, average

Table 3.5 Vacation home owners in Canada, median and average household income (current dollars)

Year	Average $	Standard error of average household income
1986	36,216	1,555
1987	47,922	3,120
1988	60,175	2,049
1989	69,236	4,353
1990	66,827	2,849

Source: Household Facilities by Income and Other Characteristics (Catalogue #64-202) 1988, 1989, 1990, 1991, 1992 (Statistics Canada, 1973–1992)

household income in Canada was $46,137. At this point, no income groups below this level have equivalent participation in vacation home ownership compared to the national average of 5.9%.

For lower-income households, several complicating issues arise in the interpretation. Included among these households are those who are now retired. As noted above, not only do retired households make up a large share of cottage owners, but they also typically have low annual incomes, even though they may have higher levels of wealth as measured by owned property and other types of securities. In addition, if cottages are 'family' phenomena, then some households may gain access via inheritance regardless of their income ability to enter this second home market.

In addition to data that show cottage ownership concentrated in higher-income categories, the data in Tables 3.5 and 3.6 illustrate that ownership may be increasingly concentrated in those high-income categories. The data in Table 3.5 are derived from Statistics Canada's HFE survey, but are reported in their catalogue on Household Facilities by Income and Other Characteristics (Statistics Canada, 1982–1985; 1987–1991). For the period from 1986 to 1990, there is a marked increase in the average household income of vacation home owners. In 1986, the average household income for vacation home owners was $36,216 compared with the Canadian average household income of $34,261. By 1990, the average household income for vacation home owners had increased to $66,827 in the HFE survey, while the Canadian census reported that the average 1991 household income in Canada was only $46,137. Over this 5-year period, the Canadian average household income increased 35% while the average household income for vacation home owners had increased 84%. Income levels reported for vacation home owners had increased at a faster rate than for the Canadian population as a whole.

Table 3.6 Vacation home owners in Canada Average household income (current dollars)

Year	Average $	Standard error of average household income
1997	53,920	1,301
1999	56,863	1,645

Source: Survey of Household Spending (Catalogue #62M0004XCB) 1997, 1999 (Statistics Canada, 1997–2001)

Table 3.6 includes more recent data on the average household income levels for vacation home owners. However, these data are from the Statistics Canada Survey of Household Spending (SHS) (Statistics Canada, 1997–2001) and involve a different survey methodology than the HFE surveys. The result is that the data in Tables 3.5 and 3.6 are complimentary, but not comparable. Between 1997 and 1999, the SHS data show that the upward trend in vacation home owner annual household income is again present.

Information on second home ownership in Canada suffers a long-standing data quality issue concerning an entity, and pattern of occupancy, where the definition has proved too malleable to operationalise in a consistent manner. Data quality issues that limit a more precise estimate of cottage impacts in the rural-recreational countryside are just one example of a continuing data dilemma for those studying change within rural Canada. While the data are not complete, the available information shows a clear pattern of increasing concentration of cottage property ownership within higher income households. In Canada, while access to second homes may have been the preserve of society's elites in the first half of the 20th century, many felt that this access had become more democratised through the 1960s as the economy and the Canadian middle classes prospered. By the end of the 20th century, however, it is clear that the increasing wealth gap in Canada is combining with the increasing costs of second home ownership to again restrict participation to high income households. In other words, cottage ownership is strongly identified with socio-economic status and cottage landscapes are increasingly elite landscapes.

Enhancing an 'Elite' Status

The demand for second home properties is putting pressure on this scarce resource in Canada, something which in turn is placing upward pressure on property prices. This demand pressure, and the associated price pressure, is contributing to the increasingly elite status of second home property. For example, McNicol (1997) has written about the town of Canmore in Alberta, and the pressures from tourism resort development. Canmore, which is located next to Banff National Park, gained global recognition during the Calgary Olympics as the site of the Nordic events. The federal government's moratorium on additional development within the Banff townsite, together with Canmore's newfound notoriety, set the stage for a relatively recent and rapid period of resort development. This type of development includes extensive second home property ownership. Local conflicts between major tourism resort projects and the conservation of natural areas create significant local debates. The influx of weekend residents into the area has been identified as a key planning problem, especially given the considerable attitudinal differences between permanent and non-permanent residents around development-versus-conservation issues (McNicol, 1997). The limited land available for development in Canmore has pushed local property values higher.

In the case of Whistler in British Columbia, Gill (2000) has documented the explosive growth of a winter resort area. Through the 1960s and 1970s, the ski slopes at Whistler were a modest yet popular recreation destination within Vancouver's rural-recreational countryside. The period from 1975 to 1995 was one that saw tremendous development and expansion to the point where Whistler is now home to one of North America's premier ski resorts. This focus on creating a world-class resort was accompanied by significant increases in housing and in property value. As argued by Gill, this 'growth machine' era was also marked by the pursuit of resort revenues at all costs with little attention being given to the needs of the community's permanent residents. This lack of attention has led to conflict between permanent and non-permanent residents. Such conflict, characterised as a set of 'community' versus 'resort' debates, is being driven by the increasingly elite status of Whistler, a status that has made it very difficult for permanent residents to afford housing or to access basic services.

Similarly, Halseth (1999) has documented second home development pressures in another part of Vancouver's rural-recreational countryside. In this case, cottage and second home property developments are blending the longstanding idyll of natural amenities with the currently marketable fad of executive golf courses. Set within a rural landscape, these developments centred on golf courses are very high-priced and cater to a very specific segment of the adjacent urban market. One reason for the recent boom in these golf-course resort developments in Vancouver's countryside is the development restrictions of the agricultural land reserve in the Fraser Valley. The land reserve is a longstanding land-use planning tool in British Columbia that is designed to protect its limited agricultural lands from urban encroachment (Halseth, 1993). Recently, there was a brief window of opportunity during which 'golf courses' were a permitted use in the agricultural land reserve. This brief window prompted a flurry of development applications. This pressure of amenity-driven second home development on prime agricultural areas has similarly been tracked in other parts of Canada (Krueger, 1978, 1980; Gayler, 1991; Halseth & Rosenberg, 1995).

Such resort-related developments continue to be significant in British Columbia. One of the most recent is the Stump Lake Cattle Company in the Nicola Valley of British Columbia's southern interior (Chow, 2002). Combining ideas of natural wilderness amenities with access to executive golf courses, the Stump Lake project also includes the novelty of a ranch-based lifestyle. Located just over two hours drive from Vancouver along the Coquihalla Highway, the Nicola Valley area has all the features that have traditionally characterised the rural-recreational countryside and these ranch-based resorts may be the first to exploit the area's development opportunities.

One of the ironies embodied within the types of development pressures just described is that, by contributing to an increasingly elite status for second home properties, these same pressures may ultimately destroy the countryside experience that first attracted urban visitors and recreation-alists. Mitchell (1998) makes a strong case that the commodification of the countryside may lead to the destruction of the rural idyll. Drawing upon an example from southern Ontario, Mitchell examines the way in which coun-tryside amenities, and especially rural heritage, have attracted retirees, second home owners, and property developers (see also Coppack, 1988; Bowles & Beesley, 1991). Through a process which Mitchell describes as 'creative destruction', amenity-driven development may ultimately turn from providing significant economic benefits for the community to a complete replacement of the very community upon which it was created. Dahms and McComb (1999) also found that amenity driven second home development could lead to a significant transformation of the host rural community. Reflective of Gill's (2000) work in Whistler and Wolfe's (1952) much earlier work in Wasaga Beach, Dahms and McComb (1999) note a replacement of basic services for permanent residents with tourist-oriented services, something which makes community life more difficult for perma-nent residents. Like Mitchell, Dahms and McComb sketch a process that involves the creative destruction of a pre-existing rural idyll and rural community.

Growth and change through second home development in the Canadian rural-recreational countryside have been significant, and now show signs of transforming into an even more intense kind of activity centred more upon high-value resort developments. This not only changes the rural place, but contributes to a social construction of difference between increas-ingly elite second home and cottage developments and the rural commu-nity within which they are set. The communities of Canmore and Whistler are grappling with this very issue at the moment, and the Fraser and Nicola Valleys may soon be grappling with it as well.

Discussion

Second homes in Canada are mostly associated with recreational and vacation property. These cottage properties occur within the rural land-scape, and yet are separate from that landscape. In the Canadian rural-recreational countryside, there is a clear separation of cottage from rural landscapes, and this chapter has introduced second homes in Canada through this theme of separation.

The foundations for this separation of cottage and rural landscapes are fourfold. In terms of spatial organisation of properties, the small-lot cottage properties are clearly distinct within the otherwise extensive land uses of rural Canada. The cottage properties also tend to be clustered close to a natural amenity feature such as a shoreline or mountainside. This clus-tering acts to increase the sense of separateness and exclusiveness.

Besides distinct physical patterning, the images and folklore associated with cottage property are also central to the creation and perpetuation of separate geographic imagination: cottages are perceived as separate from the rural landscape within which they are set. One is a landscape of leisure, while the other is a working landscape.

These issues marking a separation of rural and cottage landscapes are reinforced by a clear socio-economic differentiation of cottage owners from both rural residents and the Canadian population. The costs associated with second home ownership have long restricted cottage ownership in Canada, but pressures over the past 20 years have acted to increase the exclusiveness of these properties. Scarce recreational property is being made increasingly scarce in the market by the application of stringent envi-ronmental and infrastructure regulations on new cottage development. These regulations, required to protect against the very real pollution pres-sures of intensively developed cottage areas, have added costs and reduced potential sites. While about 6% of the Canadian population has tradition-ally participated in cottage property ownership, this is concentrated in higher income groups. Recent changes in the Canadian economy reducing the spending power of the middle classes are clearly reflected in the increas-ingly high average incomes of cottage property owners.

Finally, since such amenity locations are relatively limited, upward pres-sure has been placed upon cottage property prices. This has not only imposed further financial limitations on who can participate in cottage ownership, but has changed the patterns of development in the rural-recre-ational countryside. At present, resort development is pushing towards an increasingly elite landscape of second home properties. This trend is significantly disrupting many rural communities.

Each of these pressures by themselves creates the foundation for the very separate geographic imaginations for rural and cottage landscapes. For example, even where socio-economic differences may be minimised, the local discourse of difference based upon folklore and symbolism would be sufficient to continue pushing apart these landscapes. In addition, residential change is also coming to this landscape. In particular, this involves the conversion of second homes from seasonal or vacation uses into year-round homes. This cottage conversion not only changes the status of these second home properties, but it is introducing a new group of permanent residences into the rural community (Halseth, 1998). This new group is one whose interests have not traditionally been associated with the rural community, and as such, poses a fundamental challenge to local social cohesion and political organisation. As yet, detailed attention has not been paid to the impacts on a rural community when cottagers make it their permanent home. The work that has been done suggests that community conflict and contention is now intimately bound up with pressures caused by this change (Dilley, 1985; Halseth, 1996). As contrasting landscapes within the rural-recreational countryside collide, there are important questions for researchers interested in the multiple ways second homes can impact on the locale within which they are set.

Residential change through cottage conversion is affecting the local demographic, social, and political composition. In terms of demographic change, cottage conversion involves an older, retired, former professional, population. Social interaction between cottage and rural residents has been limited, and now cottage conversion is solidifying these patterns of separate participation. In terms of the changing political landscape, cottagers' associations have increasingly participated in local debate in order to maintain control of cottage areas by cottage property owners (*Cottage Life*, 1991, 1992, 1993a, 1993b). In some cases, this has seen the emergence of cottagers' associations as a *de facto* local government (Darroch, 1992). In these debates, the language of environmental protection serves as a metaphor for a more basic struggle for political control.

Conclusion

While cottage landscapes are indeed set within the rural countryside, to be 'at the cottage' is to construct a geographic landscape and imagination separate from that countryside. Despite the importance of the second home issues described in this chapter, research in Canada has made only tentative attempts to tie together the importance of cottage property, the accessibility of cottage ownership, and the role of cottage communities within the wider rural community into a more complex and coherent understanding of the rural-recreational countryside. Similarly, there is much work yet to be done in trying to integrate an understanding of the rural-recreational country-side into a more sophisticated model of rural Canada.

A better understanding of the rural-recreational countryside has some urgency, given the shifting economic, social, and demographic characteris-tics of this part of rural Canada. Questions need to be asked about the role of cottage property owners in local politics and local decision-making over topics such as land use, property taxation, and services to both people and property. Critical issues around environmental sensitivity, and the redevel-opment of cottage properties into year-round residences, bring the matter of second homes into larger debates such as sustainable development.

Chapter 4

The Cottage and the City: An Interpretation of the Canadian Second Home Experience

STEPHEN SVENSON

> *The summer cottage has been overlooked as a subject of serious study, in Canada as almost everywhere else. There are no statistics on it, and therefore an accurate appraisal of its importance in the geography and the social and economic life of Canada is not yet possible.*
> Roy Wolfe, 1951:10

The pioneering second home researcher in Canada, Roy Wolfe, published spatial–statistical (Wolfe, 1951), historical (Wolfe, 1962), and interpretive studies (Wolfe, 1965, 1977) of Canada's second home phenomenon, or what he understood to be the practice of 'cottaging.' Wolfe highlighted the importance of the relationship of the core to its periphery or the city to its hinterland, this relationship later being conceptualised as the 'urban field' (Friedmann & Miller, 1965). In his work, Wolfe paid particular attention to his native Toronto and the relationship of this city and its inhabitants to the place known as 'cottage country.'

While we can now say that there is no lack of academic interest in the 'summer cottage', the lack of availability of statistics on the second home (the 'cottaging' phenomenon as it is commonly known) has persisted to this day. The inclusion of a question on 'vacation home' ownership on the 1973 Statistics Canada's Survey of Household Facilities and Equipment, partly addressed this deficiency. However, while this survey's most recent incarnation (1999: Statistics Canada, 1997–2001) can determine where the households that own second homes are located (questions on 'vacation home' ownership are now part of Statistics Canada's Survey of Financial Security), it is not able to determine where these properties are located relative to the principle residence. Moreover, while access to ownership gives us some insight into the second home phenomenon in Canada, it offers little insight into who actually uses these second homes, and no insight into the social practices that 'cottagers' engage in while at their cottage. This chapter addresses the above two concerns through a spatial and statistical analysis of the Canadian Travel Survey (CTS). This analysis is based on Statistics Canada's Canadian Travel Survey Microdata, 1998,

1999 and 2001 (Statistics Canada, 1997–2001), which contains anonymised data collected in the Canadian Travel Survey. (All computations on these microdata were prepared by Stephen Svenson, and the responsibility for the use and interpretation of these data is entirely that of the author.) This chapter extends Wolfe's statistical and spatial work on the Canadian cottaging phenomenon, paying particular attention to the relation between the city and the cottage or cottage community, and concentrating on the spatial patterns and practices of cottagers as captured in the Canadian Travel Survey. The chapter then goes on to provide an account of how these spatial patterns and practices are representative of a cottaging phenomenon that is most recognisably urban. The flows of cottagers from the city of Toronto to the cottage are given life through the development of idealised 'cottager' types or social types developed from extensive qualitative interviews with cottagers from Toronto. These 'cottager' types are linked to particular cottage sites, and embody a relation to the city that is at once particular and general. The chapter concludes with a discussion of what these relations mean for the city and how these relations embody both a curse and a blessing for both the cottager and the city.

Data and CANTOURGIS

This work can perhaps be adequately conceptualised as a characterisation of the 'flows of social life' (McNaughten & Urry, 1998: 200) involved with the practice of cottaging as captured through the Canadian Travel Survey (CTS), which was a biennial survey up to 1996 and an annual survey from 1997 onwards. The purpose of the CTS is to gather information on domestic trips and travellers. It is a supplement using the Labour Force Survey (LFS) sampling frame, and collects more than 30 characteristics, which include socio-demographic information on travellers, trips and expenditures (Statistics Canada, 1997–2001: 1). To be counted in the sample, the travellers:

(1)   must be Canadians travelling to a Canadian destination;
(2)   must have spent a night in either a commercial or private cottage
(3)   they must have travelled a one-way distance of 80km to qualify as having taken a tourist trip.

The Canadian Travel Survey Microdata User's Guide defines a trip as:

> Travel to a Canadian destination at least 80 km one-way from home for any reason except: travel to and from work or school; one way travel involving a change of residence; travel of operating crew members of buses, airplanes, boats etc.; travel in an ambulance to a hospital or clinic; trips that did not originate in Canada; trips longer than a year. (Statistics Canada, 1997–2001: 13)

A useful heuristic tool in modelling and analysing these flows, particularly for the analysis of the relation between cottaging and the city, is the use of Geographic Information Systems (GIS). The quantitative analysis is complemented by qualitative data collected through in-depth interviews with cottagers from Toronto and Montréal. This chapter now turns to an exploration of cottaging using the Canadian Travel Survey and a GIS tool, CANTOURGIS (GIS software developed at the University of Waterloo by Michael Leahy and Stephen Svenson for the spatial modelling of large datasets and in particular the Canadian Travel Survey).

The Canadian Cottaging Landscape

Distribution of cottaging in Canada

Private cottages are one of the most popular types of accommodation in Canada for domestic users, after 'home of a friend or relative' and 'hotel.' From 1998 to 1999, the number of household nights in Canada remained roughly the same with only a slight increase of 0.36% (see Table 4.1). It is interesting to note that, during this same period, 'commercial cottage' and 'private cottage' nights have both experienced sharp increases of 10% and 6% respectively (see Table 4.2). According to the CTS Data Dictionary, a 'private cottage night' (PCOTNT) is defined as:

> While on the trip, number of nights spent in a private cottage or vacation home. This category includes nights the traveller spent in

Table 4.1 Travel nights in Canada and its Provinces (000s of households)

Province	1998	1999	% change
Canada	143,643	144 157	0.36
British Columbia	23,325	24,483	4.96
Alberta	18,404	18,667	1.43
Saskatchewan	7,826	7,314	-6.54
Manitoba	5,470	5,534	1.17
Ontario	45,756	44,743	-2.21
Québec	27,004	27,903	3.33
Nova Scotia	6,386	6,031	-5.56
Newfoundland	3,346	3,382	1.08
Prince Edward Island	1,231	1,312	6.58
New Brunswick	4,129	4,485	8.62
Yukon Territory	470	171	-63.62
Northwest Territories	296	131	-55.74

Table 4.2 Travel nights by type of accommodation in Canada (000s of households)

Type of accommodation used	1998	% of all accomm.	1999	% of all accomm.	% increase
Hotel	24236	16.9	24441	16.9	1
Motel	439	0.3	445	0.3	1
Bed and breakfast	967	0.6	1144	0.8	15
Hunting or Fishing	1030	0.7	883	0.6	-17
lodge resort	1128	0.8	1403	1	20
Camping/trailer	12671	8.8	11993	8.3	-4
Private cottage	14982	10.4	15928	11	6
Commercial cottage	2145	1.5	2384	1.6	10
Home of friend or relative	73595	51	74713	51.8	1
Other type/not stated/ unknown	12,450	8.7	10,823	7.1	-15
Total household nights	*143 643*		*144 157*		*0.36*

his/her own secondary residence (i.e. cottage, cabin, vacation home, condominium, or time-shared condominium) or in a residence that the traveller visited, borrowed, or rented from an individual. (Statistics Canada, 1997–2001: 48)

In Canada, the third most popular type of accommodation is the private cottage, and in Ontario it is the second most popular, after staying with a friend or relative, and the popularity of both private and commercial cottages appears to be increasing. In addition to the overall increase in household nights, both commercial and private cottage nights are also increasing as a percentage of accommodation type (see Table 4.2). Private cottaging increased its percentage of total accommodation by 0.6%, and commercial cottaging increased its share by 0.1%.

Table 4.3 indicates the relative popularity of commercial and private cottage nights on a provincial basis for 1999. A 'commercial cottage night' (CCOTNT) is defined as:

While on the trip, number of nights spent in a commercial cottage or cabin. This category includes cottages or cabins owned by a commercial establishment. These include tourist courts, motor courts, housekeeping cottages, etc. (Statistics Canada, 1997–2001: 16)

Table 4.3 Household cottage nights in Canada in 1999 (000s)

Province	Commercial	% of total HH nights for province	Private	% of total HH nights for province
Canada	2384	2.63	15928	
Alberta	119	0.64	1128	6.04
British Columbia	408	1.67	1418	5.79
Saskatchewan	85	1.16	629	8.60
Manitoba	80	1.45	756	13.66
Ontario	733	1.64	7686 (48%)	17.18
Québec	667	2.39	3618 (23%)	12.97
Nova Scotia	98	1.62	630	10.45
Newfoundland	62	1.83	201	5.94
Prince Edward Island	194	14.79	148	11.28

Ontario and Quebec together accounted for more than 70% of all private cottage nights, with Ontario at nearly 50%. Ontario also had the highest percentage of total household nights for private cottage nights at 17%, making it the most popular source of accommodation after 'home of friend or relative.'

Cottaging and seasonality

Most tourism activity occurs in the summer, and accommodation reflects this bias. However, there are some regional differences with regards to commercial and private cottaging activity and seasonality that are of some interest (see Figures 4.1 and 4.2).

Figures 4.1 and 4.2 compare commercial and private cottaging nights in Ontario and Quebec with those of Canada as a whole. What is immediately noticeable and not surprising is the dominance of the third quarter (summer) for both commercial and private cottage nights. In all instances, at least 45% of cottage nights occur in that quarter. When compared with Canada as a whole, Quebec and Ontario have a higher percentage of private household cottage nights in the third quarter, at 51% and 61% respectively compared with 45% for all of Canada. When we look at commercial household cottage nights in the third quarter, the difference is even more pronounced with Quebec at 65% in the third quarter and Ontario at 82%, compared with Canada at 45%. For both commercial and private cottage nights, Quebec does show a relatively higher percentage of activity in the first quarter relative to Ontario. This can be accounted for by

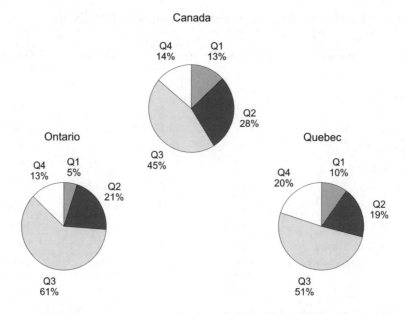

Figure 4.1 Domestic household private cottage nights by quarter (1999)

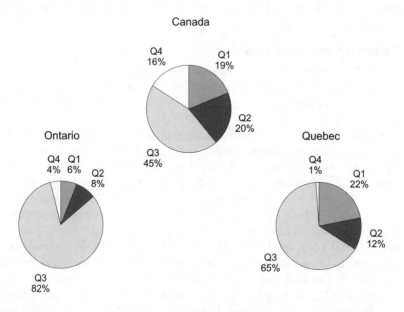

Figure 4.2 Domestic household commercial cottage nights by quarter (1999)

more winter recreation amenities, especially skiing. While Ontario's use of the private cottage in winter is only 14%, British Columbia and Quebec have disproportionately higher percentages of household private cottage nights in the winter at 24% and 20% respectively.

These observations on seasonality are directly tied in to the changing recreational practices of cottagers. Increasing numbers of 'summer cottages' have undergone winterisation, and have become a base for winter activities such as cross-country skiing and snowmobiling, as well as the regular summer fare. However, the summer bias in cottaging activity cannot and should not be understated.

Traditionally in Canada, summer is the time to be active and to move, when we are less inhibited by restrictive weather in the form of ice and snow and cold. In a word we are set free from the 'regulation' that the Canadian winter imposes on our activity. This regulation is by no means imagined, as any Canadian snowbird will attest. Their movements south are an effort to escape the restrictions that cold Canadian winter places on activity, particularly the activity of the elderly. Recreational activity that emphasises movement and mobility plays a large role in the practice of cottaging. This is captured well by the CTS, and will be examined further after a discussion of a profile of the cottagers themselves.

Who are the cottagers?

In 1999, 7% (823,000) of Canadian households owned second homes or cottages, with 77% of these households owning second homes in Canada (Kremarik, 2002: 13). The idea of the cottage as a family-motivated investment has changed slightly as well, with the process of cottage conversion (Halseth, 1992, 1998), real estate speculation, and the rise in demand for recreational property as a desirable alternative to retirement in a more expensive urban setting. According to the 2002 Royal Lepage Recreational Property Report 'demand for year round waterfront residences is growing in popularity ... The trend has been identified in Shediac; NB; Regina Beach; Qu'Appelle, and Last Mountain Lake, SK; and Haliburton, Kawarthas and Orillia, ON' (Royal Lepage, 2002: 3). What 'cottage country' is experiencing now is a pluralisation of uses and users, from seasonal residents (cottagers) to cottage converters, to retirees. This is a far cry from the post-war heyday of cottage development and expansion.

When lakeside property was cheap and plentiful, cottage purchases were in part community-motivated investments made by scores of middle-class and working-class families wanting to give their children something other than the urban life (Hodge, 1970; Wall, 1979; Kremarik, 2002). From schoolteachers to Latvian immigrants, people sought out a leisure space where they could come together as a collective. Today, the cottage owner's average age is approximately 52 years old and only a little over one quarter of second homes are owned by families with children (Kremarik, 2002: 13). However, statistics on ownership are not good predictors of cottage use as Figure 4.3, which compares family cottage ownership and family cottage use, suggests.

Figure 4.3 indicates that children do indeed have more access to private cottages in Canada than might be expected if cottage ownership and family status are the criteria used. While families with children make up 26% of those who own cottages, 37% of trips to the private cottage include children. When one further compares private cottage use and ownership in terms of education, income, and age, a much more diverse cross section of Canadian society is represented – people with more modest incomes are able to participate in the practice of cottaging (Svenson, 2002). This counters some of the claims that cottaging is an elitist activity (see Halseth, this volume), though as affordable cottage properties disappear and driving times from the city to the cottage increase, owning a cottage is becoming more and more difficult. Additionally, the costs of owning a cottage are increasing. Higher property taxes as more cottages are converted to permanent residences and increased environmental regulations that require cottage owners to upgrade facilities such as septic systems are just two examples of these increased costs. However, these costs are being offset through the renting out of private cottages, putting an unprecedented number of rental cottages on the market. Both the cottage owner and the

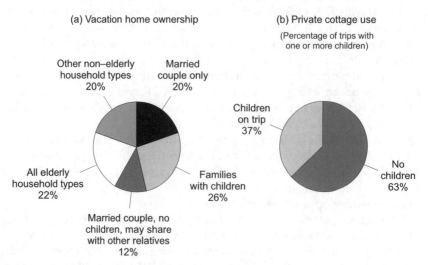

Figure 4.3 Comparison of vacation home ownership and private cottage use (presence of children)

Source: (a) Kremarik (2002); (b) Svenson (2002)

consumer would seem to benefit from this arrangement. For those families and individuals with lower incomes, the rental of a private or commercial cottage can be one of the cheaper holidays available. Tyler's Cottage Rental Directory (2002) contains more than 1400 listings, the majority of which are private cottages, some with rates as low as $Can400/week. Shared with extended family or friends, the private cottage is an attractive alternative to the marginally cheaper option of camping, and is typically much more comfortable and hassle free – especially for those families with young children. In her 2002 analysis of the Survey of Financial Security, Kremarik finds that, while income and wealth are two of the main factors that influence the ability to own a vacation home or cottage, it 'appears that many Canadians enjoy a taste of cottage life without paying the high cost of purchasing or maintaining a second home' (Kremarik, 2002: 14).

When compared with household nights spent in all other accommodation, those who stay in private cottages are generally older, have a higher household income, are more highly educated, and are more likely to have children on the trip (Svenson, 2002). Compared to these private cottagers, commercial cottagers are generally younger, less affluent and even more likely to have children with them on the trip (Svenson, 2002). It would appear that the idea of the cottage as 'for family,' persists even though the demographic that instigated the 'cottaging boom' in the 1950s and 1960s is approaching retirement. Commercial cottaging appears to cater to young people with children and lower incomes, while the slightly higher numbers of children for private cottage nights than for all other accommodation may reflect the theme of 'continuity' (Jaakson, 1986) where the grandparents introduce the new generation (grandchildren) to the cottage.

Cottagers are urban

As Canadians have become increasingly urban, the appeal of the cottage has grown. It is this urban dimension of cottaging that seems to give the practice its mystique. This mystique is explored in two recent works of fiction. *Summer Gone* (1999) by John MacFarlane and *Escape: In Search of the Natural Soul of Canada* (2002) by Roy McGregor rely heavily on the city–cottage relationship in the stories they tell, highlighting the fact that, without the comparison with the city, the phenomenon of cottaging itself would be hardly recognisable. This 'urban phenomenon' of cottaging is emphasised through the use of GIS mapping.

Figure 4.4 demonstrates the extent to which cottaging has become urban – the urban areas of Vancouver, Edmonton, Calgary, Toronto and Montréal are immediately recognisable. The figure depicts the distribution of the origin of private household cottage nights by census division in Canada for 1999 with particular attention paid to central Canada. A graduated shading scheme is used to depict relative private household cottage nights. As

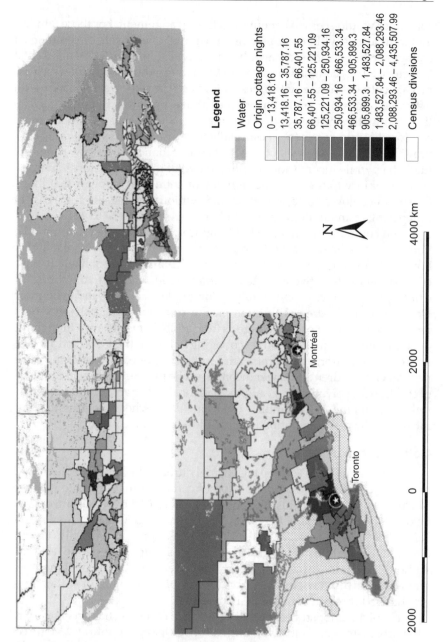

Figure 4.4 Canada: Origin of domestic cottage visitor nights

Note: The data used for this and other maps, are shown as deciles (the total numbers divided into groups of 10)

expected, the Greater Toronto Area accounts for a majority of cottagers. The destination of these cottagers is for the most part, over the 'recreational bridge' (Greer & Wall, 1979) of farmland surrounding Toronto. Across this bridge lies the Canadian Shield. The legendary Muskoka, home of the highest number of cottage nights in Canada, and 'God's Country' for Toronto cottagers, personifies the Canadian Shield and cottage life.

Figure 4.5 examines the Muskoka census division. From this example we can see that the highest concentrations of private household cottage nights are the Simcoe, Muskoka, and Parry Sound Census Divisions of Central Canada. In terms of census divisions in Canada, Muskoka has the highest number of person and household cottage nights. PCHHDE (Private Household Cottage Nights) = 1,022,000 while PCPTDE (Private Person Cottage Nights) = 2,057,000 (images derived through the use of CANTOURGIS have been modified from their original form for this chapter). In general, cottage night sources and cottage night destinations do not occupy the same census divisions to any large degree, with the one notable exception of Simcoe County.

Figure 4.6 compares the destination and source of household private cottage nights in central Canada. Simcoe County is the destination for some of the highest numbers of household private cottage nights in Canada. Simcoe is also the source of approximately 500,000 household private cottage nights, that is, movements of private cottagers from Simcoe County to other census divisions. Simcoe County is therefore an example of a former cottaging hinterland that is becoming increasingly urban.

Two things are occurring. First, Toronto's sprawl is spreading out into Simcoe County – the rapid growth of the city of Barrie testifies to this. Cheaper housing combined with a wider and faster Highway 400 allows for a tolerable commute into Toronto. Second, permanent retirement operations such as 'Lagoon City' on Lake Simcoe signify the current trend towards increased 'urban to-rural' migration by retiring baby boomers who aspire to the 'cottaging' life full time. The notion of a 'full-time' life of cottaging attests to something of value in the 'part-time' life of cottaging. An expanded analysis of the activities of cottagers can therefore take us closer to an understanding of what cottage life is about.

Activities of Cottagers

One of the main reasons why the cottage popular is that it is a staging point for a wide variety of activities. Table 4.4 outlines the percentage of people who actively participated in particular activities when person trips contain one or more cottage nights.

At the private cottage, as might be expected, swimming was the single most popular outdoor activity, followed by other water sports at 29%, and

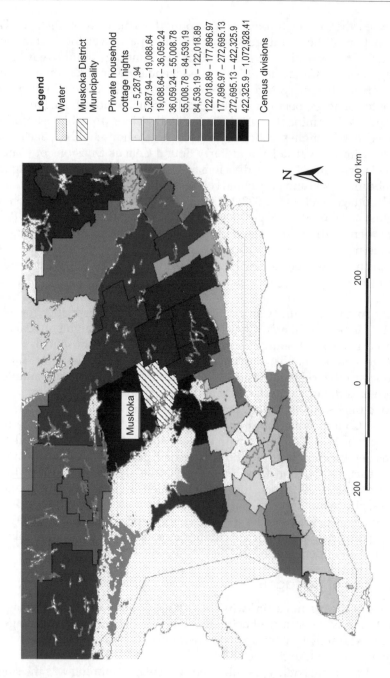

Figure 4.5 Private cottage nights: Details from Muskoka

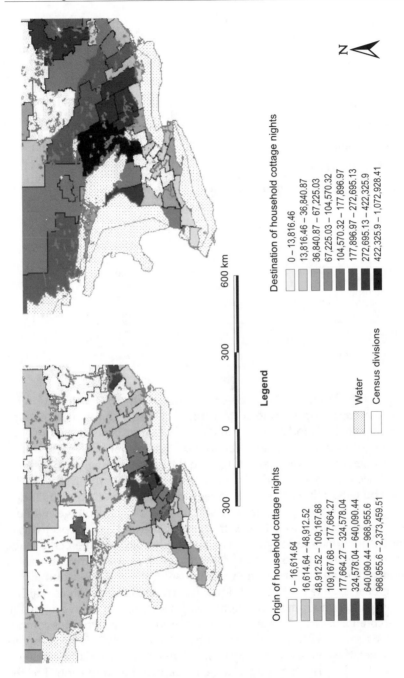

Figure 4.6 Private cottage nights: Origin and destination

Table 4.4 Activity at the cottage (1999)

Activity	Private cottage %	Commercial cottage %
Visited relatives	41.6	25.4
Visited friends	32.6	22.7
Went shopping	21.7	26.7
Went sightseeing	23.9	46.1
Went to a national park	7.9	19.5
Participated in sports or outdoor activities	74.2	78.8
Went swimming	38.2	35.1
Other water sports	28.7	18
Golfing	9.4	7.4
Fishing	18.6	18.9
Bird watching	8.6	6
Walking	38.6	39.4
Cycling	7.6	7.4
Some other sport	8.6	12.6

fishing at 19%. Walking was also very popular with 39% participation for both commercial and private cottage trips. Where a commercial cottage was used as accommodation, a considerably higher portion of trips was involved with sightseeing (46% versus 23.9%). Another interesting difference between the commercial cottage and the private cottage is the degree to which visiting friends and relatives are more significant activities at the private cottage. At the commercial cottage, 25% of the person trips included visiting with relatives compared to 42% for the private cottage, while a similar trend occurs for visiting with friends (23% and 33% respectively).

The distinction between private cottage nights and commercial cottage nights is made in order to demonstrate what on the surface appears to be a qualitatively different orientation to the use of the cottage. Commercial users appear to take part in traditional 'tourist' activities such as visiting national parks, shopping, and sightseeing to a greater degree than the private cottage users, who appear to be more engaged in activities centred at the cottage and with socialising with friend and family. For the commercial cottager, the cottage itself may be incidental to the 'tourist' experience whereas, for the private cottager, the cottage may be more central to the 'tourist' experience.

This comparison between the commercial cottager and the private cottager begins to give us an insight into differences between the private cottager and the commercial cottager, a difference that has implications for the relation of cottaging to city life. We can begin to investigate the notion of cottaging as a 'tourist' activity, or as 'travel' and explore the distinction between the 'cottager' and the 'tourist' as a way to examine what may more essentially define cottaging. At the same time we can discuss the notion of cottaging as an urban phenomenon, particularly a phenomenon of the Canadian metropolitan area of Toronto.

Cohen (1974) regarded the cottage owner as a marginal type of tourist because the cottage trip is a 'recurrent' one. 'Recurrency' then, is a particular practice that differentiates the private cottage user from the commercial cottage user. The commercial cottage user is more inclined to be non-recurrent in his/her use of the cottage, preferring to rent a cottage at a different location from year to year emphasising more of the sightseeing or touristic element of the experience. Eliminating the commercial cottager from the analysis and focusing on the long-time cottaging area of Toronto, Muskoka, can further develop these distinctions.

The significant percentages of Muskokan cottage trips that involve visiting with friends and family (45% and 36% respectively) and the high participation in sports (91%), particularly those associated with water, stand out as the two defining characteristics of cottage life (Table 4.5). Even in something as mundane as government statistics we can see a reflection of what more deeply moves the cottager: the pursuit of some form of community and the enjoyment and freedom that comes with movement, particularly movement associated with water.

While cottagers (at least the ones captured in the CTS as 'private' cottagers) have in common a return to the same place year after year, and a penchant for visiting with friends and relatives and water sports, their relation to and experience of the city can be quite different. This is reflected in experience of the cottage that is not captured in statistics. The practice of recurrency, coupled with the notion of the relation between the city and the cottage, begins to take us out of the realm of official government statistics and into the realm of lived experience.

From the City to the Cottage and Back Again

Figure 4.7 shows that, while much cottaging activity takes place within 200–300km of the city of Toronto, much of it is located further away, sometimes more than 1000km away. These distances are emblematic of broader patterns of city–cottage relations and the variable meanings of the city and the cottage. Figure 4.7 also provides an entry point into a way of talking about the relationship between the personal histories of cottagers and their

Table 4.5 Activity at private cottage, Muskoka District Municipality (1999)

Activity	Muskoka
Visited relatives	45.4
Visited friends	36.2
Went shopping	25.8
Went sightseeing	24.0
Went to a national park	8.2
Participated in sports	90.9
Went swimming	57.3
Other water sports	48.2
Golfing	12.0
Fishing	14.3
Bird watching	6.7
Walking	41.2
Cycling	8.3
Some other sport	6.4

commitments to their communities, both cottage and city. It depicts the aggregated flows of three Toronto CMA census divisions (Simcoe County, York County, and Toronto Metropolitan Municipality) both in magnitude and destination of cottage nights. The numbers 1 to 4 refer to 'cottager ideal types' that have been derived from interview encounters with Toronto cottagers and signify different of relationships with the city and the cottage. These ideal types do not purport to be exhaustive. Their intent is to capture in a meaningful way the lived experience hidden in the flows of cottage life.

(1) The cottager

The cottager is very much a stereotype of what many perceive a cottager to be. The cottager was born and raised in Rosedale, an exclusive neighbourhood in Toronto, and has spent most of his summers at the family's island cottage in the Muskokas. He is a well-educated and cultured gentleman, who desires both the city and the cottage. He retires to a condominium in the city, where winter months are filled with a variety of social engagements and cultural activities. The social circles at the cottage and in the city are similar and involvement in his local cottagers' association

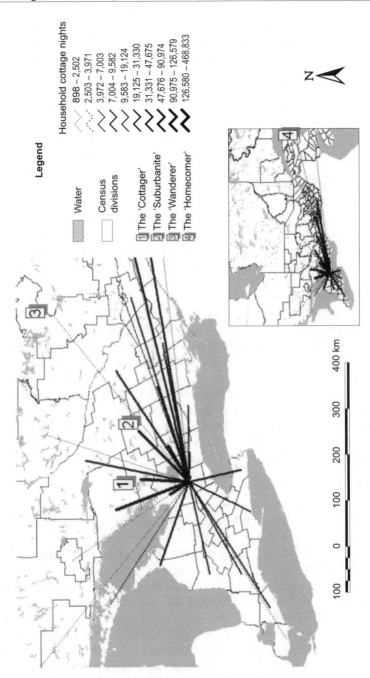

Figure 4.7 Cottaging flows from Toronto

provides particularly high levels of satisfaction. As his family has become more dispersed by the vagaries of economic opportunity, the cottage becomes an increasingly important focal point for extended family contact and renewal.

(2) The suburbanite

The suburbanite has always had an uneasy relationship with the city. In many ways she detests the city, its complexity, its diversity, its noise and stink – all of which she finds odious to her rural roots. The relationship with the city is an instrumental one. An internal migrant, she is resigned to the city for the economic benefits it endows but at the same time despises it. She has located herself as far away from the city as possible so that her children are not contaminated by it. For her the cottage is a respite from her particular notion of 'city life' and approximates closely to the remembrances of her rural past. In the future she will retire to this so-called 'cottage' (for it is not even a requirement that it be on water). What is important about the place is a particular feeling of 'ruralness' that she struggles to articulate.

(3) The wanderer

The wanderer immigrated to Canada from Europe with his family as a child. Essentially 'rootless,' he has wandered wherever work opportunities have taken him and has spent parts of his working life in the cities of Montréal, Ottawa and Toronto. He came into the cottaging culture through his work affiliations in Montréal. The cottage he shares with his network of friends is located in the Gatineau north of Ottawa. Every summer he returns to this cottage to bond again with the friends he has made in the cities where he has worked. Now approaching retirement, he is contemplating a move back to Ottawa to be in closer contact with the cottage and the social relations that it inspires and grounds.

(4) The homecomer

The homecomer travels over a thousand kilometres several times a year to the place of her birth on the Gaspé coast. Like the suburbanite, she too has rural roots. She appreciates the city for the professional opportunity it has given her but, while accepting the city, at the same time longs for home. Though the house of her birth has long been sold, she has gone out of her way to recreate it. Her 'cottage' overlooks the ocean she played in as a child. Though all her professional activities and relationships are in Québec City, Montreal, and Toronto, this is the place that has remained constant. There are still the remnants of family, some of her children even choosing that more rural existence, and there is the comfort to the eye that only a familiar landscape can bestow. Her apartment in Toronto is a shrine to the 'cottage', the place she will retire to – where she will finally return home to after her long sojourn in the city.

A final dimension to this typology of cottagers is the international one. Often, all of these actors, as they approach retirement or after retiring, have access to second homes in other parts of the world. Increasingly, the 'cottager,' the 'suburbanite,' the 'wanderer,' and the 'homecomer,' spend some or all of their winter months in southern destinations such as Florida, Arizona, Mexico and Costa Rica, mainly in what can be described as 'rural' environments. This relatively new development that further accentuates the ambivalence with which the city is treated.

Conclusion

Whether we call the place camp, cabin, chalet, cottage – whatever we call it – time spent at a second home has a strong cultural significance for Canadians and Canadian popular culture. In Ontario alone, new cottages appear at a rate of 4000 a year (Lees, 2001). As we have seen from the analysis of the Canadian Travel Survey, governments often identify travel to the second home or cottage as tourism. But what does cottaging really share with tourism, and what can be gained from distinguishing them?

We could argue, as Urry (1995) has, that the (post)modern subject engages in tourist practices most of the time, where all social practices are potentially touristic. However, this definition denies an ethical stance and an important distinction. To be a tourist is to take a vacation from commitment; it is to be in a community without being responsible to it (McHugh *et al.*, 1974). But cottaging does involve a commitment, in its strongest sense a commitment to a place, community, and future generations. The cottage, for many Canadians, is a place where extended family and friends gather together, where work is meaningful, where there is time for leisure and contact with nature, where community feels present. The 'middle landscape' of the cottage provides a space for those social practices and pastimes that we value highly yet are too often absent from the modern life we experience in cities.

'Middle landscape' is a phrase popularised by phenomenological geographer Yi Fu Tuan to describe an ideal habitat between the 'thinness' and the disorder of modern life. 'Thinness occurs when nature is reduced to pretty image and city is reduced to geometric streets and high rises,' Tuan (1998: 25) explains, 'Inchoateness occurs when nature and city have become a jungle, confused and disorienting'. The middle landscape provides an ideal habitat because it functions at a human level, with both complexity and order. Like 'the well-told story, the clear image, the well-defined architectural space, the sacred ritual, "the middle landscape" give[s] a heightened sense of self' (Tuan, 1998: 25), an awareness of being alive.

This sense of authenticity and aliveness resounds in the practices of cottage life beyond those that can be captured in a recreation-oriented survey. At the cottage we relish the simple pleasures of pottering. Whether chopping wood for the fire, replacing a few boards on the dock, or repairing Grandpa's favourite old chair, cottage work gives an immediate sense of satisfaction. Encounters with family and friends take on a richer flavour because we have the time to develop meaningful connections with one another, relationships that become forever associated with the special place of the cottage. This helps explain why the inheritance of the cottage is treated more sentimentally and with much more seriousness than the family's home in the city. Sell the house, but pass the cottage on to us: an exception to conventional priorities where real estate purchases are based on job opportunities and property values.

One of the problems that Tuan identifies with the middle landscape is that it is unstable. 'It reverts to nature, or, more often, it moves step by step toward the artifices of the city even as it strives to maintain its position in the middle' (Tuan, 1998: 27). As 'trophy cottages' continue to sprout in Ontario's Muskoka region and recreational property values soar in British Columbia's Okanagan Valley, the Canadian middle landscape may be disappearing. Second homes are taking on the value of a commodity, affordable only for the elite and based on a consumer relationship with place, the same relationship that many of us have with our cities.

In spite of these urbanising forces, the cottage continues to fill the human needs for freedom and community. It also continues to offer a powerful cultural alternative to our cities and suburbs. Cities must come to grips with the reality that they are often not chosen as communities but tolerated as economically necessary. This is not to say that the city is at fault. Second-home users could better examine their commitment to their urban homes otherwise they risk spending a large part of their lives alienated from place and community.

Commitment to the city is a difficult prospect for many Canadians, since popular, mythologised versions of Canadian culture exclude cities almost by definition (Hulan, 2002).

Incorporating an urban sensibility into what is understood to be 'Canadian culture' has a relatively young history (Niedzviecki, 1998). Many city dwellers remember the rural – and refuse to forget it. Indeed, most Canadians, following the more dominant mythology of Canadian culture, choose to orient to remembering the rural, whether or not those memories are based on experience. In relation to cottaging, this orientation to the 'rural' is both blessing and curse. It can be considered a blessing when it gives us a sense of our history and provides a space for community and freedom and a sense of place, those things that the city makes it hard to accomplish. This same blessing is also a curse. The orientation to the rural, embodied in the phenomenon of the cottage, is largely responsible for the ambivalence towards, and lack of commitment to, the City – that community where most of us live out most of our lives.

Chapter 5

Place Attachment of Vacation Residents: Between Tourists and Permanent Residents

LARS ARONSSON

The Perspective

Place attachment and mobility

In social science, place attachment and mobility are usually seen as opposite concepts (Gustafson, 2002a). In traditional society, but also during the early phase of modernity, the mobility of most people was relatively restricted. Likewise the social networks were, to a high degree, attached to place. Therefore the distinctiveness of places and place identity were clear and people could relatively easily find both meaning in a place and contacts with their roots. Place attachment is in general based on the *roots* metaphor. The term refers to a culture that is relatively homogeneous and stable and thus has a fairly unambiguous meaning. Roots imply that the individual is relatively firmly rooted in a local social environment and culture and finds identity in a place (Buttimer, 1978; Relph, 1976). In a qualitative study Gustafson (2002a: 672) found that the respondents associated roots with: 'place attachment, emotional bounds, and community'.

Modernity has changed society to a state of great mobility where many people have a social network beyond their local area. This means that both traditional values and place attachment are decreasing. The complexity and range within and between activity spaces would seem to be on the increase in present-day society, and this suggests that the importance of *routes* is also growing (Clifford, 1997; Rojek & Urry, 1997). The culture of a place seen in terms of routes suggests an unstable, changeable environment, where cultural identities and meanings form part of a mixed state. People go on a journey, for instance, and/or move to a place where they meet and separate – in these places hybridised cultures are created (Massey & Jess, 1995). In the study by Gustafson (2002a: 673) the routes theme was based 'on mobility, on travelling, on discovering and exploring new places and different cultures'. Gustafson (2002a: 674) further found that: 'The roots theme favours one or a few specific places, whereas the routes theme favours a multitude of places, in some cases also the specific collecting of places reflecting an individual life path'.

In the present fragmented 'Western' society many people seek their roots and to (re)create traditions and structures that have disappeared through modernity. The general condition for many people is complex activity spaces where living, work, leisure activities, and social relations occur in different places. This means that it is common to have multiple roots in different places, e.g. in the form of vacation homes. For the individual, routes mean that he or she is attached to a place whilst at the same time being highly mobile with wide social networks. Gustafson summarises his study on place attachment and mobility in the following way:

> Place attachment may, on the one hand, imply roots, security, and sense of place, but it may also, on the other hand, represent imprisonment and narrow-mindedness. Similarly, mobility may signify freedom, opportunities, and new experiences as well as uprootedness and loss. (Gustafson, 2002a: 680)

The concepts of roots (place attachment) and routes (mobility) are not necessary in opposition to each other. On the one hand the concepts are contradictory, while on the other people in late modern society find place attachment at the same time as they are highly mobile. Urry (2000) discusses changes in society from place-attached dwelling to one of mobility in the form of 'dwell-in-transit' as in air travel and in the car acquiring a new meaning as a personal space. From this perspective the view of space is changing to a 'flow space' and to 'mobile places'. This perspective connects to Massey's (1993) progressive place perspective, which allows for mobility as well as place identity without excluding the 'other'.

The 'Second' Home?

An extensive form of mobility in Sweden is associated with visits to, and living in, vacation homes. The vacation home resident is a kind of 'in between' – neither tourist nor permanent resident nor both at the same time. From this point of view, the vacation home is a space between the ordinary and the extraordinary, and in this context the vacation resident seeks place attachment and takes part in that place's process of change.

In Sweden it is common for the countryside houses of parents or grandparents houses to be inherited and used as vacation homes. Amongst other things, this might mean that vacation residence is deeply attached to a place, and also has strong meaning compared with common urban living. The question of which is the primary and which the secondary home then becomes central. When the norm in society is mobility, it is hard to decide which place is the ordinary and which is the extraordinary. For people living in a highly mobile society the identity that we often connect to home might be found in more than one place, while many vacation home owners may invest as much time, money, and work in their 'secondary' home as they do in their 'permanent' one. Through interviews with Swedish vacation home residents, Jarlöv found that:

> In this place for leisure and recreation [vacation homes] people are working intensively most of the time. They are building, repairing the house, building extensions, sheds for garden tools, greenhouses, and endless walls of stones. They are gardening, growing flowers and vegetables, pruning fruit-trees and harvesting the crops, collecting berries and mushrooms in the forest or fishing in the lake or the sea, preparing sailing boats. Besides being a working place, the summerhouse is also a place for close connection to what they feel 'nature' to be. For many people the lifestyle in the summerhouse also means a richer social life with more contacts with the neighbours than in town. (Jarlöv, 1999: 231)

This quote suggests what people seek through vacation home residence. It is apparent that the dominant motives are a longing to get away from the everyday urban lifestyle – a longing for the rural, nature, family life, perhaps to encounter other social relationships than the usual ones, and peace and quiet. Thus vacation residence is both an expression of escape from modernity and a longing for authenticity, roots and identity in a place. This desire might be interpreted as a way to temporarily get away from the restless and fragmented urban way of life. In a more and more placeless world, vacation residence stands out as meaningful and filled with sense of place. In vacation living the daily trajectories and projects seem to be unified and woven together. This is especially true of the family ties that knit the activity spaces together. But this does not mean that the vacation resident entirely drops the mobile urban lifestyle. Vacation living seems to be a way to temporarily and partly (re)create identity and roots in existence. At the same time vacation residence is a consequence of modernity since the development of society has given us more leisure time, higher income levels, and opportunities for greater mobility.

The Purpose

The purpose of this chapter is to study vacation residence as a form of living that presupposes both mobility and a desire for place attachment. Thus the relation between mobility and place attachment is central. For the purposes of this study, the vacation resident is seen as a category between the tourist (the mobile) and the permanent resident (usually place attached). At the same time, the activities and encounters of vacation residents in space and time are central to understanding the desire for place attachment. The empirical material is based on a study of tourists, vacation residents, and permanent residents on Smögen, an island off the Swedish west coast.[1] The study particularly focused on the activity spaces and encounters between the categories. In this chapter, the vacation residence is both placed in a societal context, and also theoretically and empirically related to the tourist and to the permanent resident.

The Earlier Study

The study was conducted in Bohuslän, a province of the Swedish west coast, and in the parish of Smögen in particular. The tourist resort of Smögen is a tiny island, about one kilometre wide and two and half kilometres long. Smögen is one of the most popular tourist resorts in Sweden and is typical of the Bohuslän fishing communities with bare, polished granite rocks, buildings clustered together and boathouses. Tourist activities in Smögen, as in the rest of Bohuslän, have traditionally been concentrated to the coastal areas with boating, fishing, sunbathing and swimming. Tourism is extremely seasonal, with a peak from about the middle of June to the middle of August.

During the summer of 1990, I conducted a qualitative interview study with 20 respondents from each of the groups: tourists, vacation residents and permanent residents of Smögen. As well as taking part in-depth interviews on attitudes to tourism, the respondents were asked to give a 'diary' of the previous day in which activities, times and places were noted. These diaries have been analysed by a time–geographical method (Hägerstrand, 1985, 1991) that permits the analysis of encounters, meeting places and aggregations of activities in time–space (Pearce, 1988). The purpose was to examine how tourists, vacation residents and permanent residents utilise time–space and to discuss issues involved in the encounters between them (Aronsson, 1993, 1997).

Time–geography's focus on the physical world encountered by people has sought to construct composite pictures of the subject in space, 'putting things (individuals and objects) together' as the components of life or to show life cycles. Over a period of time, a sequence of such moments and their content of person, activity, time and place can be related, like a diary, but also graphically. Work in time–geography has been overlooked for some time because it significantly detached what individuals did from their cultural contexts. Time–geography's perspective on actions and physical life events acknowledged only some components of human physicality – concrete, practical, intentional, objective, rational – a linear path. However, time–geography provides a valuable focus on the individual actions and encounters with space and other people.

The Changing Society: A Highly Mobile Society

Some writers characterise the present 'Western' society as a 'flow and network' society (Castells, 1996; Urry, 2000). The flows in global space consist of goods, services, people, capital, media images and information. This means an extensive and rapid mobility of material and non-material things. At the same time it is emphasised that late modern society is characterised by a coordination of flows that implies that it is a new/different organisation of society.[2]

Time–space compression is often used as a way of showing the changes in time–space relations in society. It emphasises that on the one hand the 'globe' seems to shrink through more intensive and faster interaction and on the other hand social networks tend to be more extensive in space (Harvey, 1989, 1996). A high level of mobility is thus strongly connected with economic development in modern society where increasing economic efficiency is obtained through a decreasing friction of space.

Bauman (1998) describes and analyses the stratification of society where 'global elite cultures' and different kinds of localised 'others' have come into existence.[3] It is the 'global elite cultures' that have the potential to use the mobility structures of the late-modern society – the localised 'others' do not.

The high mobility and the supply of manifold activities influence the restrictions of time in society. Thus the desire to control one's own time becomes more and more important. The experience of uncontrolled and rapid change is linked to the fragmentation of society whereby change can occur in several directions at once, which means that for many people development is hard to grasp (Hägerstrand, 1984; Elsrud, 1998). There is a trend in late modern society: in spite of the fact that we have more leisure, we also to have less 'free time'. Among other things, the expanding tourism and experience industry places demands on (or creates opportunities for) the individual to consume 'infinite' numbers of activities, and in many cases this presupposes high mobility.

Urry (1995) suggests that we in 'Western' society have reached 'the end of tourism'. In today's generally affluent world, many groups of people are highly mobile. At the same time mobility is 'built' into many people's life modes and lifestyles, both at work and leisure. Changes in the structure of society also imply changes in life modes from rural to urban. Urry's notion that we have reached 'the end of tourism' might be true whilst we all are tourists because it is almost impossible to avoid the mobility and experience-structures of today's society. Thus tourism has developed from a relatively clearly defined phenomenon to an important element in different fields and now has far-reaching influences on our life. Tourism, it might be said, has begun to 'act' on the surrounding society and has become a fundamental structure that to a great degree defines our society.

Tourism

Tourism and the experiences of tourists are manifold and complex, and different kinds of perspectives are described in the following text. However, one general theme is that we in today's society are to a great degree surrounded and influenced by the infrastructure and culture of tourism.

Traditionally, the movement in time to one or more places (which together form a destination) and back home again was seen as a basis for tourism. The tourist trip might also be seen as a process that begins the moment the decision to be a tourist is taken. Therefore one could suggest that the experience of travelling begins at home, in the idea and planning phase, and continues throughout the travel process with its real and embodied experiences for the traveller.

Tourism can also be considered from a non-material perspective or as a 'state of mind'. Such a perspective is strongly linked to the present 'Western' society with its different global systems, such as media. The fact is that many tourist trips take place through 'dreams' in front of a travel programme on TV or via a good travel story in a book or from the opportunities that information technology offers for impressions and experiences on the 'net' (Rojek, 1998). Thus there is a constant reproduction of the mobile tourist subject or one might say that the infrastructure and culture of tourism shapes the character of personality in late modern society.

The culture of consumption's central role in tourism use through which experiences and places are commodified is to be emphasised. Would tourism exist without being commodified? It appears that people have a socially and culturally created wish to travel. Thus the tourism industry creates products out of something already culturally established. At the same time one might ask what further opportunities there are for late-modern people – as by definition we all seem to be mobile. There is a lifestyle-orientated perspective implied in the discussion. In our time our identity building is partly dependent on a reflexive consumption of different lifestyles. Consumption of tourist experiences is no small part of this.

There used to be an emphasis on experiences as one of the fundamental elements in tourism. Tourism is to a great extent about people's expectations and experiences of new/foreign/different places. An experience might be defined as when a certain occurrence is experienced as extra-ordinary from some point of view, e.g. social, cultural and/or embodied. One perspective is that experiences for the 'metaphoric' tourist with tourist map in hand have replaced local knowledge. From this point of view people – the tourists – are constant foreigners who, on the one hand can orientate wherever they wish in the world but on the other hand never belong to or take part in a community. The discussion is highlighted by Urry

(1990, 1995), who notes that the tourist is looking for the extra-ordinary that is viewed with a distanced (but sometimes varied) 'gaze', and the places and experiences that the tourist encounters in general are commodified. The outcome for the tourist is that he/she above all encounters a non-authentic facade and has no possibility of engaging in 'real' community life. However, it should not be forgotten that certain forms of tourism (e.g. back-packers) to a great extent are seeking a lifestyle through travelling (Elsrud, 2001). Also other tourist groups are looking for 'real' places and experiences. However, few people have the opportunity to actually go 'back-stage' (MacCannell, 1976).

Williams and Kaltenborn (1999: 214) offer a slightly different perspective: 'Leisure/tourism is often less packaged, commodified and colonial than contemporary academic renderings seem to permit'. The perspective implies that tourism is a complex experience for tourists in which they themselves produce tourism experiences through manifold sensual and embodied activities. Thus, leisure is used by many people seeking self-fulfilment, e.g. to give expression to their identity and lifestyle, or to correct deficiencies in their everyday life. At the same time many forms of tourism contribute to changes of traditions and structures that the tourists want to experience and (re)create. As a summary, Williams and Kaltenborn (1999: 216) note the complexity and contradiction in the nature of tourism as: 'Consequently, leisure and tourism may be experienced as potentially authentic, personalised, and identity-enhancing or increasingly manufactured, commodified, and disorienting'.

The Tourists on Smögen: Encounters and Activity Spaces

The Smögen study showed that the tourists were dominated by young, relatively well-educated people generally employed in the private sector, in both blue- and white-collar professions. The 'young' age structure of the group is largely explained by Smögen's image as an in-place. The way of life of the group is mainly urban.

There are relatively few social encounters between occasional tourists and the other categories, vacation and permanent residents. The encounters of occasional tourists are generally limited to instrumental encounters in shops. Apart from these, there are sporadic meetings with other tourists, such as exchanging greetings. The exceptions are the tourists who have friends on the island. They may have a boat in the harbour, a rented apartment or a vacation home. The activity spaces of the occasional tourist are extensive and characterised by a high level of mobility (Aronsson, 2000). For this group the Smögen 'stop' is relatively short and the tourists soon return home or continue on to other places.

There is extensive private letting in Smögen. A significant number of tourists return year after year and stay for a relatively long period during summer. This group has a similar pattern of encounters to that of the vacation residents, which is described later. Even the tourists that stay for a longer period or return year after year are generally highly mobile. However, during their visit to Smögen their activity spaces are relatively local.

The Impact of Globalisation Processes on Places and People

In present society, varying global processes stand out as central. Some of them have existed for a long time but have changed in form, extent and intensity (Massey & Jess, 1995). Globalisation processes are complex, changeable and partly contradictory. On the one hand a cultural and economic homogenisation of places seems to be taking place, mainly through the effects of the market system (capital) (Relph, 1976; Shields, 1991; MacCannell, 1992; Urry, 1995). On the other hand a cultural hybridisation arises through our great mobility, e.g. through migration and tourism. Simultaneous processes of increased standardisation and increased distinctiveness (for places) and converging lifestyles and individualisation (for people) occur. Thus the distinctiveness of places is partly constructed through global interaction, between influences of economic, social, cultural and ecological character, and partly constructed by local circumstances and traditions that vary over time and from place to place. A place is inhabited by different kinds of stakeholders socially interacting, culturally-dependent and with different resources/power, e.g. this holds for women and men and for different ethnic groups. The stakeholders are linked together in space through complex local and global relationships, and every stake-holder has activity spaces with different reaches. Massey and Jess (1995) see space as constituted through social relationships, and places as localities that are the result of encounters between activity spaces with different characteristics. This implies that places are relational and open, and cannot be seen as bound points in global space. From this point of view, places are changeable but unique.

The ambiguous concepts of time and space are inseparable – activities take time, and take place somewhere. Activities and processes bring about restructuring of space. The perspective is that space, at the same time as it is an abstract concept, in its places is inhabited and 'filled' with material as well as social content. From an abstract point of view space contains structural parts as well as flows, and from a practical perspective it is experienced. People construct and produce material space as well as space filled with signs, culture and meaning.

Society, as well as its places and landscapes, is changeable. The late-modern landscape consists to a great degree of signs of consumption. The earlier more unambiguous landscape of production has more and more become a composite landscape both for production and for visual consumption and experiences at the same time (Jackson, 1989; Hägerstrand, 1991; Crang, 1998). Once again it becomes apparent that the infrastructure and culture of tourism surround our life. The surrounding world is more and more adapted to handle mobility, structures of experience and global flows. The commodification of landscape and the other environments we inhabit contribute to the organisation of mobility, such as the tourism economy's construction of experiences and the construction of places/landscapes as signals for consumption.

The 'flow society' creates new conditions for business, and reduces the importance of many places especially those with old economic structures. A reconstruction of places is therefore required in order to compete in the 'new' market economy (Castells, 1996). Thus places are looking for the right 'signs' and the right infrastructure to attract capital for investments, encourage enterprises to locate there, to attract people to move there or to create 'tourist traps' to get people to stop. Places today try to be 'stopping places' in the flow economy.

The organisation of our present society implies that from an individual perspective people largely use tourism and leisure activities as a means for establishing identity and creating meaning in their lives. Places are important starting-points in the processes of seeking identity and meaning. Places are fundamental in spite of the fact that the modern development process might be described as less friction of space, more placelessness and an increasing organisation in the form of a flow society.

The Permanent Residents on Smögen: Encounters and Activity Spaces

The permanent residents in the Smögen study were middle-aged and elderly, with a high proportion of retired people. They are poorly educated and those who are gainfully employed mainly work in the public sector rather than in the private service sector and industry. Their position in the life cycle together with the original rural nature of Smögen help to explain the low level of education and, to some extent, the current vocations of the permanent residents.

The permanent residents mainly interact with one another. At the same time there are numerous contacts with vacation residents and returning tourists in the area of the community centre. Contacts between permanent residents, vacation residents and returning tourists generally work very well. However, the study suggests that the permanent residents have a fundamental cultural identity in the place, which the other groups lack even though they may have lived there for a long time, and this probably depends on their different ways of life. The permanent residents who were

interviewed had low levels of mobility and their activity spaces were relatively clearly defined (cf. Aronsson, 2000).

Vacation Homes on Smögen

The proportion of vacation homes on Smögen is very high, about 25% of
the total number of houses. Smögen can be divided into three zones
according to the proportion of vacation homes. The first zone, the area
nearest the pier (the 'main attraction'), largely consists of vacation homes
(about 50%). Parallel with the pier's extension towards the centre of the
community, zone 1 becomes zone 2. Here there are more permanent residents, though they are still mainly elderly with no children at home. Zone 3
consists of the area farthest from the pier and closest to Smögen bridge and
the mainland. Many young families have built houses in this area, and there
are no vacation homes.

It should be pointed out that the form of coastal buildings has been
preserved even though their ownership has changed over time and they are
now used for recreational purposes. Some of the respondents in the survey
thought that the carefully restored and well-kept vacation homes turned
parts of Smögen into a museum exhibit. The survey also revealed that
Smögen's unique environment in some cases was more of a background for
the primary activity of seeking social fellowship within the framework of
an urban way of life.

Vacation Residents: Encounters and Activity Spaces

The vacation residents in the survey are mainly middle-aged and elderly
people, highly educated and employed in the service industry, particularly
in the private sector. It is this group that is able to purchase, and can afford
to live in, the relatively expensive vacation homes in Smögen. Members of
the group have an urban career lifestyle.

The vacation residents get to know the permanent residents who live in
their vicinity, as well as other vacation residents and tourists who return
from year to year, and they generally have considerable contact and dealings with people from these groups. In everyday life, the vacation residents
are highly mobile and have extensive activity spaces. However, when
visiting the vacation home they are relatively local in their activities
(Aronsson, 2000).

By far the most frequented meeting places are (for all three categories)
Smögen pier with its restaurants and cafes and (primarily for occasional
tourists and vacation residents) Vallevik bathing beach. Tourists and vacation residents in particular spend a lot of time sunbathing and swimming.
In the evenings the groups spend their time in much the same way as

regards activities on the pier. It is interesting that the permanent residents also see the pier as a big attraction.

In the answers given by the vacation residents, there is a hint of competition with the occasional tourists for the sparse environmental values. The crowding effects occur mainly in places that are heavily frequented during the summer: roads, parking places, piers, jetties and the harbour as well as service functions such as shops.

Discussion

From a tourism perspective, the development of Smögen began about hundred years ago, and has gone from 'discovery' as a summer paradise for wealthy people to the situation in the last thirty years where the place among other things is a 'stopping place' for mass tourism during summer.

The distinct categories used in the earlier study (tourists, vacation residents and permanent residents) might be questioned, because that kind of distinct grouping seldom exists in reality. Especially in today's tradition of cultural studies, there is an emphasis on the movement of people between roles, groups and categories, e.g. on other occasions the permanent residents are tourists, and vice versa. The distinction of being a tourist therefore becomes more difficult in the circumstances of more complex contemporary lives and more complex tourist practices and activity spaces.

The activities in time–space from which the experiences of the place were drawn were, from a time–geographical perspective, interpreted as objective, rational, linear encounters that privileged immediate concrete realities. There is, then, little room for the inexplicit ways in which practice confers significance of place. Geography is encountered objectively, as material for doing things. However the study shows a form of practice – an encounter between the physical space and culture (through using the methods of both time–geography and in-depth interviews). This brings the recent re-thinking of Swedish time–geography into focus, together with the recently developing work in British geography, so-called 'non-representational' geographies, adapted from broader debates in the wider social sciences (Thrift & Pile, 1995; Thrift, 1997). It seeks critically to complement interpretations of the world that prioritise representations by engaging a path through which those representations may be negotiated in everyday life. Moreover, such an approach acknowledges the increasing complexity and flows of practice and everyday negotiation rather than linear rationality. Increasingly, commentators have drawn attention to the power of individuals to negotiate and refigure views of the world through what they do themselves – in relation to, in negotiation of and with, the contexts in which they find themselves (Crouch *et al.*, 2001).

The study showed that vacation residents had surprisingly extensive social relationships with other vacation residents, with returning tourists and with permanent residents at the place. The group that has different patterns of interactions is the occasional tourists. The temporality (length of the stay and returning aspect) has therefore proved to be very significant for the development of the encounter pattern. For the occasional tourists, the study suggests that theories that tourists often encounter a facade at the visited place and seldom have opportunity to go 'back-stage' seem to be correct.

Even though there are fruitful encounters and social relations, it should not be forgotten that certain encounters are negative. These are mostly encounters between the occasional tourists and the other groups where scarce environmental values and the capacity of the infrastructure are in focus during high season.

The study suggests that the vacation residents seek self-fulfilment both in the form of place attachment and through experiences. Put another way, the group is in Smögen looking for a rural way of life at the same time as they have access to, and take part in, the urban way of life –especially on Smögen pier. Furthermore, the vacation residents put a lot of effort (time and money) into repairing and renovating their houses, which indicates that vacation residence is seen as an important (life-) project.

In comparing the activity spaces of the groups, it appears that the permanent residents with a rural way of life and roots in the place have low mobility and clearly-defined activity spaces. The vacation residents, who are characterised by an urban lifestyle, are highly mobile in their everyday life but have relatively localised activity spaces when they visiting the vacation home. The occasional tourists are generally highly mobile and also have the most mobile and extensive activity spaces during the holiday period. The latter two groups, especially the occasional tourists, might in their habits be characterised by the routes metaphor. Finally, the vacation residents seem in their encounters and activity spaces to be in a 'category' somewhere between occasional tourists and permanent residents.

Notes

1. The empirical investigation was partly carried out with a different purpose than that of this chapter. The material has been revisited and has been possible to analyse it (with advantage) for the purpose of this article.
2. Lash and Urry (1987) characterise 'Western' society as being in a transition phase from a society of 'organised capitalism' to a society of 'disorganised capitalism'. This implies, amongst other things, an increasing economic consumption market. The consumption consists mainly of diversified and differentiated services, tourism and experiences that increase in importance and extent.
3. Bauman (1998) uses 'the tourist' as a metaphor for 'global elite cultures' and 'the vagabond' as metaphor for different kinds of localised 'others'.

Chapter 6

Mobile Migrants: Travel to Second Homes

DAVID TIMOTHY DUVAL

Introduction

For Pico Iyer (2000), 'global souls' are individuals for whom travel is a way of life. For many of these travellers, 'home' is very much a dynamic and fluid concept; they may feel as much at home in the Business Class section of a Lufthansa flight crossing the Atlantic Ocean as they do in the country (or countries) in which they are required to file taxes. While Appadurai's (1991) description of global 'ethnoscapes', Urry's (2000) discussion of 'global mobilities', and Hannerz's (1996) notion of the 'global ecumene' have all succeeded in helping scholars focus their attention on the wider condition of global movement, and given the relative ease with which some 'global souls' are mobile, are there not situations in which recognition of a singular 'home' becomes problematic? More importantly, what defines home for those who, through episodes of migration and sequential (and often numerous) re-migration, are perpetually mobile? And further still, is the notion of home, for some migrants, nothing more than a spatial and temporal cognitive structural representation of place?

One could argue that the notion of home is a socially-constructed marker or signpost that is more or less designed to help align and ultimately represent an individual's allegiances and cultural comfort with a specific, although some might argue static, space. Of course, if we exclude movement that occurs for humanitarian reasons, we can make the generalisation that human mobility is a feature of those who have the economic and social means, however acquired. While movement is easier in 2002 than it ever has been, the vast majority of the world's population is relatively sedentary (Faist, 2000a; see also Tomlinson, 1999), so not everyone will necessarily recognise multiple representations of home. However, people are more mobile now than ever before, which could at least allow for the recognition that more than one home may be possible for some.

For those who are mobile, perhaps we should recognise that the concept of home is not as bounded, and thus flexes with the mobility of individuals (captured by Iyer's [2000] notion of 'global souls') and responding to shifting perceptions of space and others' perception of how they fit into it. Home is, as Douglas (1991: 289) asserts, 'located in space, but it is not necessarily a fixed space' or, as Rykwert (1991: 51) suggests, 'where one starts from.' Home is therefore cognitive, but relationally spatial and temporal within that cognition: home is ultimately where home is.

The broad purpose of this chapter is to explore a social and cultural notion of home in the context of tourism and travel using concepts such as diaspora and transnationalism (Vertovec, 1999). I argue that cultural diasporas (Cohen, 1997) present unique situations within which one might examine how 'home' is constructed and negotiated by individuals engaging in periodic sojourns to their natal home or external homeland. My argument is that multiple 'homes', connected through periodic movement or temporary migration, represent localities of significant social interaction and meaning. Such localities become interconnected through multiple migration episodes and the transnationalisation of place and locality by migrants. Furthermore, the movement between places and localities represents a unique perspective from which second homes can be studied.

Elsewhere, I have referred to the movement of migrants from locality to locality as 'return visits' (Duval, 2002), and have suggested that they are strategically used (although not necessarily consistently) to link multiple transnational social spaces (Faist, 2000b). The more immediate purpose of this chapter, however, is to provide an alternative view to some of the second homes tourism literature. It is not interested in the temporary mobility of individuals (or groups of individuals) who may own a specific piece of property outside an urban centre or, perhaps, in another geopolitical (but nonetheless still 'local') jurisdiction. In other words, towing a boat to a weekend (i.e. non-rented) cottage in rural Canada does indeed represent distinct second home travel from an operational (and definitional) perspective. But the association of second home tourism with such limited ranges of movement and cultural associations restricts a more generalised (and perhaps more 'global') perspective that would further engage issues of social representation and status, affiliation and 'rootedness' (Morley, 2000: 3; see also Tuan, 1980).

To this end, this chapter takes an interest in how the notion of 'home' works in tandem with individuals who cross geopolitical borders because of a definitive social or cultural link (or links) to a particular place or locality. Such a position follows Morley and Robins' (1990) *Heimat* metaphor for juxtaposing expression of identity in relation to (in their example) 'Europe' and 'European culture'. Also, acknowledging that some migrants may elect to refer to more than one locality as home refutes traditional approaches to migration and migrants, which often focus on the end product of the migration experience. In other words, they ignore how localities and their social significance are maintained, and indeed the voice of the migrant can be muted (e.g. Olwig, 2001). To counter this, this chapter centres on the fact that some individuals cross modern geopolitical borders in order to secure themselves in a locality that they may have at one point called (or perhaps still call) home. For them, because of migration and often re-migration, place holds significant meaning.

In order to expand the concept of home, and by extension the notion of second home tourism, I employ brief examples from several published works that demonstrate the multi-stranded identity structures that permeate many diasporic environments. In essence, I argue that maintaining connections between dual (or multi) localities of significant social meaning fits within the purview of the study of second home tourism. I then briefly discuss the relevance and meaning of 'home' to migrants from the Commonwealth Eastern Caribbean community living in Toronto in Canada, using data obtained through ethnographic investigations. I argue that a more expanded view of second home tourism would introduce complex social arrangements that span national-state designations and would ultimately force the consideration of alternative spatial metaphors to the current simple global–local or centre–margin characterisations.

Negotiating a Touristic 'Home'

On the one hand, travellers who commute from their usual place of residence to a 'second' or 'holiday' home fit quite well within the broader equation of second home tourism. We might even recognise the familiarity associated with a destination that is typified in Wickens' (2002: 841) 'Lord Byron Type' of traveller, who is defined by 'the annual ritual return to the same place and, sometimes, the same accommodation.' Wickens' (2002: 841) research from Greece suggests that some tourists – her 'homecomers' – report that Greece is a 'place [that] feels like home.' On the other hand, however, instead of the traveller who enjoys the sun and surf of a particular 'MedSun' resort on an annual basis, we need to consider the underlying meaning of cross-border travels by individuals who return briefly (perhaps even sporadically) to a locality or place of significant sociocultural importance. One situation that would incorporate such movement could involve the various diasporic populations that were initially formed as a result of migratory events, either forced or voluntary.

Following migration, it is certainly not uncommon for migrants to establish strong social and economic links in their new country of residence. In fact, many individuals who voluntarily decide to migrate often do so for economic reasons, and social cohesion with other migrants in their new home is not uncommon (e.g. Gmelch, 1992). In fact, many even consider their new place of residence 'home', yet it would not be incorrect to assert that, occasionally, two 'homes' are internalised, differing only in space and time. 'England,' one migrant could well say, 'was my home for 10 years, but now that I have returned to [insert any country here], I am truly at home.' But if that same migrant, whilst living in England, made periodic trips to the place from which he emigrated, can we not say that he is cognitive of multiple homes? More to the point in the context of this chapter, can migrants who travel temporarily to former places of residence (or even their external homeland) be considered second home tourists?

Tourism, Diaspora, Home

At issue here, then, is how tourism, diaspora and home can be conceptualised as part of a system of movement and mobility (see also Quinn, this volume). To illustrate this, we speak of transnational identities, broadly, and the 'return visit' as a transnational exercise that links two 'homes' as opposed to a 'home' and an 'away'. Let us first discuss the concept of the return visit as a mediator in the movement of an individual between two homes.

The notion of 'return visit' (Duval, 2002) borrows from Baldassar's (2001) research on Italian-Australians living in Perth. When applied to a tourism perspective, return visits can be used to characterise the return trips made by individuals living in diasporic communities who have extensive social and cultural foundations at a particular destination, which can often be their external homeland. Diasporic communities and social units are oriented within transnational frameworks because many individuals tend to retain those cultural and social patterns salient to their country or location of origin. The return visit serves as the vehicle through which transnational identity structures between diasporic communities and homelands are maintained. As a transnational *exercise*, it serves to renew and harmonise familial and social networks. It fulfils Basch's (2001: 118) suggestion that 'transnational social practices are the processes by which migrants forge and sustain simultaneous multi-stranded social relations that link together their societies of origin and settlement.'

The definitional and conceptual elements of transnationalism do not appear to be firmly grounded, or comfortably universal, in the existing literature. Transnational identity structures have attempted to make sense of the implications of concepts such as global communities (e.g. Appadurai, 1991), ethnic identities and diasporas (e.g. Basch *et al.*, 1994; Shukla, 2001) and de-territorialised and nomadic mobilities (e.g. Urry, 2000). Reference is frequently made to, for example, transnational migration circuits (Rouse, 1992), social fields (Faist, 2000b), activities (Portes, 1999) and communities (Portes *et al.*, 1999). At its most basic level, transnationalism was (and still is) utilised as a broad conceptual framework that attempts to explain the interconnected social experiences that defined the migration experience (Basch *et al.*, 1994: 5; Spoonley, 2000). Spoonley notes that transnationalism:

... is the existence of links between a community in its current place of residence and its place of origin, however distant, and between the various communities of a diaspora ... Transnationalism signals that significant networks exist and are maintained across borders, and, by virtue of their intensity and importance, these actually challenge the very nature of nation-states ... (Spoonley, 2000: 4)

Itzigsohn *et al.* (1999: 318) refer to transnationalism as a 'product of the present conditions of global capitalism and the types of relations between labour and capital that it generates'; while Albrow (1998) suggests that it was studies of international relations, particularly those in the context of non-governmental organisations, that gave rise to the use of transnationalism as a concept. Transnationalism can be seen as a broad conceptual framework that attempts to highlight the interconnected social experiences that may explain how the concept of home is translucent for some travellers. Douglas (1991) insinuates that 'home' necessarily incorporates repeated patterns of activity and structure over time. If we broaden this view and use a transnational viewfinder to explore meanings of home, then migrants who are positioned in one locality could very easily incorporate another locality into their own world view and their own construction of home. As a result, while Morley (2000: 3) argues that traditional ideas of home and homeland have been destabilised because of the vast nature of mobility patterns worldwide, transnational connections (to borrow a phrase from Hannerz, 1996) through return visits must surely reinforce some degree of place-belonging between two localities? In fact, it is the very nature of transnationalism that allows for the positioning of multiple social relationships between two localities.

Glick Schiller and Fouron (2001) note that young Haitian adults live in a social field that encompasses both the USA and Haiti. Their lives are influenced by transnational Haitian migrant experiences. Similarly:

... young people of Haitian descent living in the United States, although much more familiar and comfortable with the pace and outlook of daily life than their parents, often seek ways to identify with Haiti. They are reclaiming Haiti by strengthening their ties with their ancestral land and reaffirming their Haitian identity. (Glick Schiller & Fouron, 2001: 157)

During research among Salvadorans living in Los Angeles, Portes *et al.* (1999) interviewed the president of the pro-improvement committee of the small town of La Esperanza in El Salvador. When asked why, in the face of blatant discrimination, this fellow intended to settle in Los Angeles (LA), his response highlights how the concept of home follows migrants from one locality to another:

> I really live in El Salvador, not in LA. When we have the regular fiestas to collect funds for La Esperanza, I am the leader and am treated with respect. When I go back home to inspect the works paid with our contributions, I am as important as the mayor. In LA, I just earn money, but my thoughts are really back home. It's only three hours away. (Portes *et al*, 1999: 446)

Baldassar (2001) uses the concept of *campanilismo* (spatial self-identity) to understand how 'home' is constructed both by Italian migrants in Perth and by residents of the small village of San Fior in Italy. With respect to migrants' construction of 'home', Baldassar found that, for some, their external homeland (in particular the village of San Fior) was the central source for cultural identification, with the return visit offering special meaning for all travellers:

> The emigrants' visit 'home' is a secular pilgrimage of redemption in response to the obligation of child to kin, towns person to town. In the case of the second generation migrant, the visit is a transformatory rite of passage brought about by the development of ties to one's ancestral past. (Baldassar, 2001: 323)

From the Caribbean

One could argue that the Caribbean region presents the most intriguing case study area for the study of second home tourism with a transnational perspective, as it has long been regarded as a migration-oriented society (Philpott, 1973). As Thomas-Hope (1992) explains, colonialist ties, especially within former British colonies in the region, allowed for an intricate knowledge of Western (primarily British) society. The migration of Caribbean persons (from islands now belonging to the Commonwealth) to Britain, starting as early as the late 19th century, was therefore an exercise in 'familiarity breeding demystification' (Thompson, 1990: 43).

From ethnographic fieldwork conducted among the Commonwealth Eastern Caribbean community in Toronto, it was found that regular return visits to the external homeland fulfill the desire to maintain social connections with family members. The notion of home (which is essentially a social and cultural construction of place) was further found to be a delicate balance between Canada and the migrants' place of birth. Put simply, the association of the place of birth as 'home' determines the extent to which both social and cultural ties are maintained. In other words, migrants living in Toronto often see the Caribbean as 'home' largely because of the presence of social and familiar elements that comprise that particular destination. Walker comments on this in the context of Caribbean nationals living in Canada:

Circumstances in Canada encouraged West Indians not only to retain their Caribbean cultural traits but to maintain loyalty and identity links to their island of origin. In the Caribbean identity has been very local-ised, by territory, class and ethnicity, and this insularity and stratifica-tion continue in Canada. In larger cities there is a multiplicity of West Indian organisations whose membership is determined by island, and even in smaller Canadian cities there will tend to be separate associa-tions by ethnic origin. (Walker, 1984: 20)

For many Eastern Caribbean migrants in Toronto, however, the concept of home is a relative term. It is interchangeable when referring to a specific place and, perhaps most importantly, roughly contingent upon the level of social connection. Those who felt more integrated into Canadian (or even Toronto) culture were thus less likely to return to their external homeland. Many felt that 'home' was truly their place of birth or the place where they spent a significant portion of the childhood. For others, 'home' was both Toronto *and* the Eastern Caribbean. In some instances, the association of 'home' was dependent on the respondents' attitudes toward their initial migration episode.

The association with 'home' is allied closely with the act of the return visit as a means of maintaining social and cultural ties because it is precisely this process of maintaining ties to their homeland that triggers migrants to consider (or re-consider) the locality that they most strongly considered to be 'home'. In the words of one respondent:

I gotta[1] good life here [in Toronto], boy. Tellin' you, I made it big here. But listen, movin' here was a big mistake. I gave away all o' my stuff when I left Trinidad to all my friends. I said "Here, help yourself" to all o' my friends. I came wid nothing. I never move back, I tell you. I never will move back. I got friends here, you know. I know people. I may go to Barbados and buy a small house or someting, but not Trinidad.

Likewise, one woman, who was born and raised in St Kitts, indicated that she was thinking of moving permanently to St Lucia to be with her husband. She did, however, wish to keep a physical home in Toronto in order to have the 'best of both worlds.' For her, 'home' was admittedly a relative term; on the one hand she felt 'at home' in Toronto, yet she is conscious of the fact that St Lucia (where her husband is from) could poten-tially be 'a home'. When asked about whether St Vincent (SVG) or Toronto is his home, another migrant speaks to this balance:

Depends on who asks the question and under what circumstance. Yeh, well, there are times when Canada is home and times when SVG is home. In a sense, sometimes even now after 20 years in Canada, I could still feel homesick in relation to SVG, but Canada is always a special place. You lookin' at some sports program and you think 'maple leaf is it!' Sometimes when you feel lonely you could feel cheated that you have to beat the snow when the sun is shining in SVG, but by the same token, when you analyse the situation carefully, you can say you are richer for it for being in Canada because not many people can have two good countries to call home. I had no plans to leave SVG, but if I had to do it over again, it would be Canada.

For others, the question of 'home' is much more difficult. When one male migrant was asked about whether he considers Toronto or St Vincent to be his home he remarked that it was a 'tough question':

There are things about Toronto that I enjoy – I like my life, I have my circle of friends here ... I don' wanna say that here is home for me. Very often when I say I am going back home – home is St Vincent ... to me that is still my home. I know that one day I am gong to move back and say 'Yup, I did it, I'm back here now, there is where I'm gonna be.' One day I'll be doing that.

Irrespective of whether one individual considers his or her natal home to be either (or both) the Eastern Caribbean or Toronto, the importance of establishing community links in the diaspora is, in some cases, quite important. One migrant noted that 'in the early days,' Vincentians went to work in Aruba and Curaçao, although it was regarded somewhat as a temporary movement. In the 1960s, with the mass migration to the United Kingdom, the USA and Canada, this individual suggested that migration become more significant: 'People went to live. Some people intended to come back in ten years, maybe yes, but then they intended to be rich. So it took on a greater degree of permanency.' The result, according to this same migrant, is that adjustments needed to be made in both the homeland and the diaspora:

So now we have to adjust to this change, and how do you adjust for this change is the fact that these people are not returning, and this is what I talk about as the responsibility of the community in the foreign home.

Part of the concept of home is associated with nostalgia, but this is mixed with the degree of comfort and level of integration that the migrant has been able to achieve in the Greater Toronto Area. For example, one woman who had migrated from the Eastern Caribbean noted that, when she first moved here, she initially missed the 'freedom to walk outside' as she was living in an apartment. To her, the apartment felt like a 'prison,' especially compared with the islands in the Eastern Caribbean, where windows and doors to houses are often left open to allow for air circulation. Many shops and houses in some parts of the Eastern Caribbean follow a concept in which everything is open. In many respects, this translates into a lifestyle in which many individuals in villages would 'pass by' others' homes or shops to 'make a lime' (relax) and engage in casual conversation.

Many migrants have, of course, social connections to more than one place. One migrant, for example, suggested that her concept of 'home' might well extend beyond either Canada or her natal home of St Kitts because of her social and familial connection with St Lucia. This would suggest that 'home', as a concept, is very much rooted in how individuals organise their social space.

Olwig's (1993) historical study of migration involving the tiny island of Nevis clearly shows how migrants living abroad make periodic trips in order to maintain contact, but are expected to share their 'reputed wealth generously'. Olwig (1993: 170) reports that '... one man, who apparently found it impossible to refuse anyone, gave away all his possessions, including his jacket, and his mother told me that she had to provide him with money so that he could leave the island again.' This connection with home is further emphasised in the obligation felt by migrants to regularly send remittances. Such remittances, as we've seen above, are not forgotten when visiting, as one migrant told Olwig:

> When you go home on vacation it is almost necessary to carry a big bag of money and six suitcases of clothes. They all come and ask you right to your face to give them something. I bring something for my relatives ... I also have godchildren on Nevis, and I don't bring anything for them, but I may give them two dollars. They are fresh through, and they only want the American money. They all come to see you, when they hear that you are on a visit, and it is quite a rat race to go home. But when you go, you also get things from them. They give you fruit and provisions, which I then take back with me. (Olwig, 1993: 170)

Home involves the negotiation of identities. It often involves more than one 'place' of social importance. Travel between such places, while elsewhere (Duval, 2002) categorised as a form of VFR (visiting friends and relatives) tourism, could perhaps be further characterised as a form of second homes tourism.

Conclusion

This chapter has attempted to show that the notion of second home tourism might well incorporate broader issues of mobility (as an almost social construct) and movement in those situations where an individual maintains social connections with more than one locality. There is room, therefore, to think beyond current spatially-restricting second home tourism studies and to incorporate global migrant movements. Meaningful social arrangements made by migrants often extend beyond nation-state designations. Consequently, home becomes a fluid concept, and one that is negotiated in spatial and temporal manner. Such individuals are perhaps what Appadurai (1991) would refer to as 'deterritorialised', J.B. Thompson (1995) would call 'delocalised', and Giddens (1990) would suggest are 'displaced'.

I have argued here that the transnational nature of global movement and mobility feeds the reality of more than one locality to which an individual ascribes a relationship he or she would categorise as 'home'. It is time, therefore, to think beyond traditional, modernistic spatial constructions of global–local and, instead, revisit how 'global' and 'local' are constructed for those whose definitions of such constructions are not as clearly identifiable. In other words, perhaps we should be considering a 'local–local' approach to second home tourism. Migrants, their transnational behaviour, their maintenance of social ties with multiple localities, and their periodic movement which is designed to support such arrangements, perhaps order their own world views as multilocal, if not bilocal.

Problematic within this, however, is how an individual shifts from place to place or homeland to homeland. Iyer's (2000) 'global souls' force us to consider the multilocal nature of people, and to consider, as has Tomlinson (1999: 3), increasing 'global–spatial proximity.' In fact, we can take from Tomlinson the fact that the perception of a smaller world leads to a consideration of how people organise their social and even physical environment(s). Global–local is one way. Perhaps local–local is another.

Acknowledgements

Thanks to Paul Wilkinson, Bill Found, Bonnie Kettel, Ray Rogers, David Trotman, David Telfer and Loretta Baldassar for discussions on the broad issues raised in this chapter.

Notes

1. Where applicable, a phonetic translation of interview transcripts was used in an effort to capture the patois accent that many Commonwealth Eastern Caribbean migrants still carry.

Chapter 7

British Second Homes in Southern Europe: Shifting Nodes in the Scapes and Flows of Migration and Tourism

ALLAN M. WILLIAMS, RUSSELL KING AND TONY WARNES

Introduction

There is a long history of research on second homes. Early work peaked with Coppock's (1977a) *Second Homes: Curse or Blessing?* This reviewed two decades of growth in second home ownership in northwest Europe, which reflected increases in disposable income and the accessibility of coastal and rural areas through wider car ownership and road improvements, and also reactions to and adaptations of urban ways of life. Anglophone research focused on English-speaking countries, but there were studies of France (Clout, 1971) and Scandinavia (Bielckus, 1977). All studies in that era were concerned with intra-national mobility.

There has recently been a revival of research on second home acquisition and use, partly reflecting their internationalisation. Buller and Hoggart's (1994a, 1994b) innovative research on British property purchasers in France was an important landmark. Subsequently, detailed empirical studies of international 'amenity-seeking' migrations have multiplied, particularly on retirement-related flows from northern Europe to Spain (Rodríguez *et al.*, 1998; Casado Diaz, 1999; Williams *et al.*, 2000; O'Reilly, 2001; Salvà Tomàs, 2002). The growth of internationally-owned second homes has, however, a more widespread distribution: in several other Mediterranean countries, in the Nordic nations, and in Ireland. King *et al.* (2000) undertook a comparative study of British retirement to the Algarve, Costa del Sol, Malta and Tuscany. Flognfeldt (2002) has written about the meanings and changing geography of second-home ownership in Norway, whilst Müller (1999, 2002a) has focused on the meanings and impacts of German second home ownership in Sweden.

This chapter addresses some of the issues relating to the internationalisation of second homes. First, it conceptualises the broader framework of second home ownership in terms of 'scapes' and 'flows', and then it considers issues relating to decision making. These are explored through a case study of British retirement migration to southern Europe, drawing on the study, already referred to, by King *et al.* (2000). The conclusions consider the significance of internationalisation, and the chaotic conceptualisation that surrounds the literature on second homes.

A Conceptual Framework: Scapes and Flows

Urry's (2000) claim that mobility is the essence of modern life is hardly controversial, although the degree to which it is disembedded from material relations remains contentious. Urry proposes that the framework of 'scapes' and 'flows' is a useful way of conceptualising a 'mobility landscape'. Scapes are essentially the places and transport lines that structure the flows among the different nodes. Urry argued that: 'People, money, capital, information, ideas and images are seen to 'flow' along various 'scapes' which are organised through complex interlocking networks located both within and across different societies' (Urry, 2000: 12). Scapes include the transport and communication systems (e.g. cables, roads and satellites) for people, goods, information and social contacts across space. Their meanings, however, are to be found not only in their material construction and are constituted in four main ways (after Williams, 2002).

Communication technologies and activity spaces

Major transformations of scapes through developments in rail, road and air travel have been ubiquitous, and have brought about 'time–space compression', the greater accessibility of many places, and the extension of 'living and activity spaces' (Harvey, 1989). Such changes have been a key factor in the internationalisation of second homes. Changes in scapes have altered the relative locations of individual places and reshaped the transnational fields of migration and circulation (Vertovec, 1999). Nearly all places have effectively become 'nearer' each other, but the accessibility of some places has increased much more than others, e.g. those near to well-connected international airports. While transport accessibility may have been the most influential factor in the growth and changing distribution of second homes, electronic communication – whether by telephone lines, satellites or the Internet – has also been important. These have facilitated the geographical extension and internationalisation of home working, the ability to keep in close touch with family and friends, and the reception of native-language television programmes and information sites.

With particular reference to second homes in Mediterranean countries, the crucial technological change was the jet engine, which facilitated the growth of mass tourism during the 1960s (Williams, 2001). Cheap air travel considerably widened the search spaces of potential second home buyers, and stimulated second home ownership in foreign countries (Williams *et al.*, 2000). For example, the opening of Malaga and Faro airports in the 1960s profoundly transformed the accessibility of the Costa del Sol and the Algarve, and encouraged tourism inflows and second home ownership. Retired British people who live in these areas often cite proximity to the airport as having been a major influence on where they had purchased their second homes (King *et al.*, 2000).

Investment and development of the built environment

Investments in the technologies of domestic and settlement services and in forms of private consumption have been a key accompaniment of improved transport and communication in facilitating the spread of second home ownership. Most vital of all has been the installation of modern water and energy supply networks and health and environmental services in previously unserved or under-served areas. Tour companies, travel agents and time-share companies all paved the way for second-home growth. The economics of their operation meant that they tended to concentrate in particular regions and countries – and sometimes in single housing complexes (Williams, 2001). Estate agents and other housing market inter- mediaries have had a strong influence on the constitution of scapes. Hoggart and Buller (1994) showed that, in rural France, estate agents have a key gate-keeping role. They direct potential purchasers, through selective advertising and promotions, to particular properties and areas. Their activ- ities guided second-home seekers to particular scapes, and the occupiers and their visitors in turn reinforced and moulded the changed distribution of flows and activities. The 'circulation' patterns were both a function of and a reason for the changing structure of the scape.

Social organisation and regulation

This broad dimension of 'modernisation' encapsulates many forms of governance and regulation, from the restraint of exploitative business transactions to the way welfare states are constituted. Important elements that promote the conversion and sale of properties to foreigners as second homes are the establishment of effective land-use controls and building regulations through the local state, and the adoption by entrepreneurs, companies and trade associations of shared values in business ethics and practice – not least for property transactions and 'retail' building works.

Equally important, however, is national state regulation. Until 1981 when Greece became a member of the European Union, foreigners were not allowed to own homes in Greece. But when Greece accepted the common body of laws and practices of the European Union (*acquis communautaire*), it acknowledged that citizens of the member states had rights to freedom of movement and property ownership. The contrasting organisation of welfare and health provision in different southern European countries has also influ- enced British property purchases and retirement (King *et al.*, 2000).

Imagined places and lifestyle associations

Scapes comprise more than assemblages of material objects and frameworks of business practice and state regulation. They are also perceived, associated with imagined experiences, and are ascribed with particular values. Some of the most obvious examples of imagined scapes are the Atlantic crossing (a flow?) ending in arrival in New York harbour, or the 'romantic' associations of the Orient Express to Istanbul or Venice. But destinations themselves are also imbued with place images, often based on particular myths. Certain European rural landscapes elicit among the British a myth of a lost rural idyll, and are a potent factor in British purchases of second homes in France (Buller & Hoggart, 1994a) and Tuscany (King *et al.*, 2000). Müller (1999: 68) has written about the influence of Astrid Lindgren's writings in creating a particular image of rural Sweden amongst German second home owners: 'red-white cottages are an important ingredient in this image, as well as small towns and wooden buildings'. Other commentators have also noted that second homes can be understood as a way of reconnecting with (an often idealised) lost rurality (Jaakson, 1986; Williams & Kaltenborn, 1999). Imagined scapes comprise not only the images of the place or landscape, but also the second home and its associations. Jaakson (1986) argues that the key to understanding what second homes mean to owners is that they provide opportunities to pursue activities and a lifestyle that is the antithesis of those pursued at home. This is not just the counterpoising of leisure to work, but also for many the counterpoising of informality with formality. As with some other types of tourism experiences, second homes may be seen as a form of escape (Chaplin, 1999).

Scapes are not static, and they also cannot easily be plotted on a conventional map, because their edges are blurred even if their cores are generally discernible. But they do structure flows: for it is usually faster, cheaper – and perhaps easier and safer – to move through than outside them. Scapes may also be shaped by and for one set of users, yet be utilised by many others. Early post-war tourists from Britain to southern Europe initially utilised scheduled air flights, organised around the needs of business travellers, but later the growth of charter flights created modified scapes. In time, charters were utilised not only by tourists, but also by second home owners. When they loaned their properties to friends and families or rented them commercially, then they reinforced these scapes and structured other people's flows.

Migration, mobility and the diversification of flows

Turning from scapes to *flows*, recent research has emphasised their diversity and complexity and the ways in which migration and tourism are intertwined (Hall & Williams, 2002; Williams & Hall, 2002). As a starting point we take the thoughtful attempt by Bell and Ward (2000: 88) to locate tourism in a continuum of flows, differentiated mainly by their temporality: 'Tourism represents one form of circulation, or temporary population movement. Temporary movements and permanent migration, in turn, form part of the same continuum of population mobility in time and space'.

The continuum helps to situate tourism in relation to other forms of mobility that are differentiated in their temporality and spatiality (understood here as travel times), as shown in Figure 7.1. The earliest mass form of second homes in northern Europe were the simple houses built on allotment and garden plots in the suburbs of densely-populated cities. Second homes today are used variously for day excursions (rarely), weekend and short break holidays, longer holidays and seasonal migration (as well as family, social and financial assets). Some homes turn out to be stepping stones to permanent migration. The pattern of use may be consistent over years, or owners may shift between different forms of temporality over short periods.

It has been argued that the types and intensity of flows are shaped by scapes, as when the introduction of a more frequent or cheaper air service newly enables a second home to be used for short breaks. It is also the case,

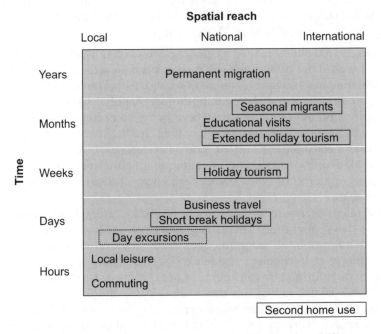

Figure 7.1 Relating second homes to a typology of mobility

Source: Bell & Ward, 2000

however, that the potential and actual demand represented by flows also alters scapes. A recent example has been increased tourism from the UK to Turkey during the 1990s. This generated new charter and scheduled flights as well as investment in regional airports in both countries. The growth of commercial and public services in these resorts, and the increasing number of bilingual workers (creating what may be termed 'economies of effort' for tourists) also became embedded into these scapes.

While flows are structured by such scapes, there are also many individually exceptional as well as mass movements, either across landscapes before imagined scapes are formed or outside the dominant scapes and flows. Thus the trickle of tourists to Tuscany over many centuries grew after 1960 and was both cause and effect of the growth of second homes. This led in time to increasingly-frequent scheduled and, later, regular charter flights to Pisa to serve the growing demand. Many tourists and second home owners were then repelled by what they considered to be the highly institutionalised travel patterns of these scapes. So they travelled outside them (perhaps overland by road), or sought to buy or rent properties outside the well-trodden Tuscan and particularly Chianti scapes in, for example, Emilia Romagna or Marche (see King & Patterson, 1998).

Over time there have been several changes in tourism-migration flows (Williams & Hall, 2002), and some have particular relevance for understanding flows to second homes. These include:

- Changes in mobility related to the fragmentation of work and leisure time, with more opportunities for short visits to second homes. The continuing cost and time constraints on international travel reinforce the importance of scapes in determining the locations of such second homes.
- A shift from migration to circulation. Increasing numbers of people have peripatetic lifestyles, whereby they circulate between different places for consumption and/or production reasons. Examples include both skilled labour migrants engaging in long-distance commuting, and second or third home owners driven by lifestyle and consumption goals.
- The relative growth of consumption-related rather than production-related migration. This is expressed both in labour and retirement migration, as migrants seek out valued environments for temporary or permanent residence (Warnes, 2001). Many of these flows are informed by considerations of climate or rural landscapes, as Salvà-Tomàs (2002) has demonstrated for the Balearic Islands (Spain), where there are significant numbers of teleworkers and semi-retired workers, as well as an exceptional presence of second home owners who seasonally or all-year round commute weekly long distances to northern Europe.

Second homes constitute significant nodes in the changing scapes that structure, but do not determine, the flows of individual second-home owners and their friends and relatives. The classic view is that they either constitute nodes for leisure recreation, or are transitional nodes (or stepping stones) in individual shifts from temporary mobility to permanent migration. As this account has shown, however, second homes play many other and diverse roles in people's working, leisure and retirement lives. The meanings and roles of second homes have changed because the nature of mobility has changed. In the next section, we examine further complexities of second home ownership and use.

Multiple House Ownership and Complex Decision Making

The second home purchasing decision has usually been conceptualised as relatively straightforward. Putting aside the locational decision, the fundamental issue has been seen as whether to purchase either for holiday purposes or as a stepping stone towards retirement residence. These are not of course mutually exclusive, and second homes may also be held for investment purposes. Some of the complexities of second home purchasing (or renting) decisions arise from their mixed functions and their change over time. Others arise from differences in the laws, customs and practice of property purchase and transfer in different countries.

Figure 7.2 presents a schematic model of the decisions to acquire and utilise a transnational second home that subsequently becomes a retirement home. It is simplified in that it assumes that an individual owns no more than two properties (in the country of origin and the destination country), and migrates only once from the origin to the destination. It therefore excludes other property ownership motivations, and return or subsequent migrations. Even with this simplification, the model emphasises the complexity of international second home ownership decisions. The model proposes three main phases in the use of second homes, related to the initial migration, to subsequent moves in the destination area, and to changes in the use of the property in the area of origin.

Several points are emphasised in Figure 7.2

(1)　Individuals usually have very *different expectations of properties used as second homes as compared to permanent homes*. Second homes are not necessarily seen as 'stepping stones' to permanent or principal homes (and therefore a 'true' migration), even amongst eventual migrants.

(2)　At the time of migration or residential re-location, all *principal homes are potential second homes*.

(3)　*At any one time a property has several different potential uses*. It may be occupied as a principal or second home, or as a source of rental income, or it may be sold to release capital, often for another principal or second home.

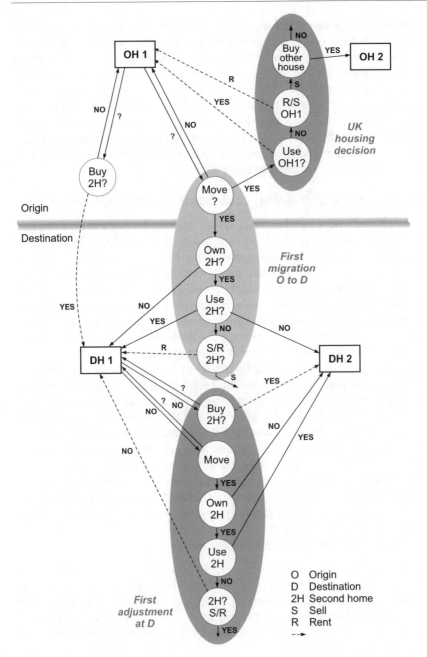

Figure 7.2 Mobility, homes and second homes

(4) There is *simultaneous decision making*. It is common for a number of decisions about the use of two or more properties to be made at the same time, particularly when personal capital is limited and the purchase of one property is conditional on the sale or rental of another. Where capital or disposable income permit, individuals may also engage in phased purchases and sales – for example, delaying the sale of a property in the origin area until the individual is satisfied with the property and associated lifestyle at the destination.

The relationship between second homes and migration is, then, far more complex than first impressions suggest, and is mediated by economic and housing conditions and changes in family and social networks as well as the availability of resources.

It is difficult to operationalise or verify this schematic or abstract model. Second homes – and especially international second homes – are poorly recorded, often for tax avoidance reasons, or because local registration processes are weak (Williams *et al.*, 1997). It will be clear that any administrative body will find it difficult to define or identify 'second' homes. There is therefore little useful official data (which, to a large extent, accounts for the weak evidence base of second homes research). However, we are able to turn to some primary survey data that was collected in connection with the authors' research on international retirement migration from the UK to southern Europe. There are a number of problems with the data. Given the absence of reliable population lists, it was mainly collected through (non-representative) purposive sampling (King *et al.*, 2000). Many aspects of the retirement location decision were considered, and in the self-completion questionnaires (and even in-depth interviews) it was not possible to collect full details of an informant's residential and property-owning histories over extended periods. Furthermore, the reliability of retrospective information about migrations and properties held years, sometimes decades, earlier is not always high.

Table 7.1 presents summary statistics about some key features of second home acquisition and retention by retired British people who became retirement residents in the four contrasting Mediterranean settings. More than one-third of the respondents (all of whom were aged at least 50 years when they migrated to their chosen retirement country) had owned a second home in the area before they migrated or moved their principal home to the country. Respondents described contrasting sequences, pathways and causalities. Some acquired the second home after they had resolved to migrate at a later date, while others took on the property solely for recreational purposes, and of course some people's original circumstances and intentions changed. The in-depth interviews found many instances of the revision of motivations and goals in relation to changed

Table 7.1 Second home ownership among British retirees living abroad
(percentages)

Characteristic and time	Tuscany	Malta	Costa del Sol	Algarve	Total
Owned or rented second home in destination immediately before migration	23	42	68	16	35
Retained second home in UK when they migrated	43	44	80	42	52
Current home was acquired as a second home	23	9	7	28	18
Had second home in UK at time of interview*	37	35	49	38	41
Sample size	109	146	138	221	614

*In response to questions on the disposal of UK and retirement-destination homes, some respondents reported owning a second home in a third country, but there was not an explicit question on their possession and the returns are incomplete.

Source: Authors' survey; samples sizes are for the first characteristic (owned before migration); sample sizes for the other questions varied slightly

lifestyle goals, experiences of other potential places for retirement, and changed marital, family and personal circumstances.

Some striking differences between the four countries are apparent. The respondents in the Costa del Sol reported an unusually high level of second home ownership before they migrated for retirement and a similarly high retention of second homes when they migrated. This probably reflects the high proportions of retired British people who had known the destination only through their holiday experiences. Only 5% of those who retired to the Costa del Sol had not taken holidays in the area, compared to 24% in Tuscany and Malta, but on the other hand only 3% had childhood or family connections with the area compared with 12% in Tuscany and Malta. Another factor is likely to have been the active marketing of holiday homes in this region by property market intermediaries.

An even higher percentage of the informants retained second homes in the UK after their retirement migration. Initially a majority did so, but even at the time of interview (bear in mind that 71% had arrived at least 5 years before the survey), 40% still had homes in the UK. The proportions were broadly similar in Tuscany, Malta and the Algarve, but higher in Spain. The UK homes were used for various purposes, including dual residence, income generation and investment, providing accommodation for relatives, and maintaining a base for a possible return. Two points can be emphasised: the 'insurance' role of retained second homes in the UK during the initial (and, for some, experimental) period of residence abroad, and their persistence as 'reverse stepping stones' for many migrants. The latter may be particularly important in later life, given the challenges associated with increasing frailty. In summary, the survey data show the overall importance of second homes for retirement migrants, and indicate some of the complexities of ownership and use. Further insights came from the in-depth interviews with a smaller number of individuals in one of the case study areas, the Costa del Sol.

Unravelling the Complexities of Second Home Ownership

The starting point of this examination was the traditional view that many second homes are stepping stones to retirement migration. While previous ownership of a second home was particularly prevalent amongst retired British migrants on the Costa del Sol, even in this group one-third did not have such a dwelling before they moved. Many of these people bought properties in the Costa and sold in the UK virtually simultaneously, while others initially rented, in some cases explicitly on an exploratory basis. Nonetheless, two-thirds of the respondents had previously owned second homes, and it became clear that their roles were diverse. Several had bought properties purely for holiday purposes. Amongst these was Robert, who responded to promotional material in the British press:

> I saw an artist's diagram of it in *The Sunday Times* and thought it looked quite beautiful. I went there on an inspection flight, liked it and put a deposit straight down on an apartment. This was before I decided to live in Spain – I bought it for holidays.

Others, such as Hilary, had used friends' second homes for holidays, and their migration decisions had grown out of these experiences:

> I had a couple of holidays in Spain. Some people I had worked with had a villa out here and they wanted a companion for their mother who was coming out. I loved the lightness, the sun, and suddenly wondered why I was staying in the cold and darkness of England.

In contrast, some had deliberately acquired second homes as stepping stones to eventual retirement migration. One example was Michael, who claimed not only that the second home was a stepping stone, but that it had precipitated his early retirement:

> My family had bought an apartment in Marbella some 20 years ago. Therefore I knew Spain well ... I retired early precisely because I knew I had somewhere to live out here.

This was rather unusual, however, and most second homes were bought a few years rather than two decades before migration. Not untypical was Peter who had identified Mijas (west of Fuengirola) as a potential location, and bought a second home there 18 months before he and his wife moved out. Sometimes, however, the role of the second home was to enable familiarisation with the destination area rather than to become the principal permanent home. Usually this was because household needs had changed since the initial purchase, or because of changes in the surrounding environment – which have been especially rapid and dramatic in many parts of the Costa del Sol. Ian's experience was typical:

> We had a holiday home near Malaga ... We had it for five years and then when I retired from the London police I decided to come to the holiday home and we found it wasn't the same. When we lived there permanently we realised that the noise was too much for us – the street was turning Spanish and there were not many foreigners left. We looked at the complete opposite – further along the coast towards Estepona and then the other way towards Almería – and eventually found this property.

Similarly, Laura sold her second home in a tourist area, and bought a home in the rural interior because she could not see herself 'socialising in the bars with the other expats'. Others had made their first Spanish property purchases as investments, usually with the specific aim of generating funds with which to buy a different property for retirement. Andrew, for example, reported that:

> I always had property at home, being in the building trade, and I decided to rent them out with a view to selling in the future. I always thought that when I retired I would come and live in Spain.

On retirement, Andrew had bought a large detached villa to live in, located on the edge of the built-up area of Mijas. This is a very different type of property and location to that of the property he rented for income.

The issue for some retirees was the type of house rather than the location. Mary, in an account of her parents' retirement, related how they had initially rented and bought a flat for holidays, and later bought the penthouse above it for their retirement. Sometimes, however, plans came to grief, and one couple found that because some of their investments had failed, they had to retire to a house they had bought to rent out and had never intended to live in. Therefore, while second homes were important in the eventual retirement of many of the British living in the Costa del Sol, they played contrasting 'experiential' and material roles in the process of retirement migration.

There were similar differences in respect of whether properties had been retained in the UK after retirement abroad – as almost one half of the survey respondents in the Costa del Sol had done. There were two main reasons for the disposal of properties in the UK. First, there were those like Graham who wanted 'a new start' and sought to sever their emotional ties with the UK:

> Some people ... run two homes. We wanted a complete break ... The only tie we have with the UK is my wife's parents and their farmhouse – we always have a base to go back to. Our children are still in the UK as well, but I couldn't imagine ever going back there.

The second reason was financial – the need to release capital to buy the new home. Peter was not untypical:

> We were not in a position where we could keep two places going. We sold our house in Cornwall, paid off the mortgage and bought the house here. It was one complete lump and there wasn't much left over. We didn't sell at a good time.

Others sold more expensive houses in the UK than they bought in the Costa del Sol, in order to release capital for investment income. Sometimes, however, there were difficulties in selling properties in the UK, and their owners unintentionally became temporary second-home owners. One interviewee, for example, almost decided to give up living abroad until she finally sold her house to a neighbour. Another took three years to sell his home, which caused financial hardship, given his relatively limited means.

In contrast, many set out to retain second homes in the UK, for both social and financial reasons. Over time, however, there was a decline in the proportion that owned homes in the UK (and only a few acquired second homes elsewhere). Some properties were disposed of after a successful trial period of residence in southern Europe, but growing financial pressures were also reported. Hilary, for example, kept her house for a while but 'I couldn't go on paying double rates. I sub-let it for a year but I don't like sub-letting'. Others responded by trading down to a smaller, cheaper and lower maintenance property. Barbara, for example, 'sold the house in Kensington but I kept a separate little flat in London for use when I came home'. One couple unusually 'kept a room in our son's house which we pay rent for. We always have somewhere to go'. Whether or not that constitutes a second home poses another interesting question.

Where capital availability was less of a constraint, houses in the UK were retained over long periods. In some cases this was purely to provide a base in the UK, usually for visiting relatives. Harry, for example, kept a house in Bolton for his annual return visits. It was looked after by a grandson, another means by which family ties were sustained. For others, the objective was purely financial, either to generate income or as an investment in the generally buoyant British property market. One respondent initially planned to sell his house in Marlow but, in the face of a depressed property market at the time, decided instead to rent to tenants.

Most retirement migrants face two basic decisions in relation to second homes: whether to move to existing second homes, and whether to retain a second home in the area of origin. But, given the changes in scapes and flows that have been described, second homes have other and more complex functions and uses for retirement migrants. First, they provide a means to escape periodically from what are viewed as increasingly difficult living conditions in the destination area. Alice, for example, lived in Calahonda, a large urbanización (planned residential neighbourhood) on the Costa del Sol, and had decided to buy a second-home in nearby Gibraltar:

> Last summer ... was a terrible time ... noisy children arrived next door here. They were absolutely terrible – young Italians. Calahonda was absolutely appalling this summer. I got into such a state by August – I had a bad reaction to living here. I admired the way Gibraltar was going ... saw a photograph of this very nice flat ... and I can't resist a bargain.

Alice thought it probable that, eventually, Gibraltar would become her principal residence, but was undecided whether she would use the newly-acquired second home or purchase a bigger flat in the same complex. Her experiences underline the continuing importance of second homes for migrants whose life stories emphasise the need to analyse individual migrations in the context of life histories of mobility.

Others bought second homes for different purposes. Pam found that her need for a second home in England increased when her younger sister had children. Having a nephew and niece made her keener to retain links with her sister, but there was no longer enough space for Pam and her partner to stay at her sister's home. They considered buying a second home in the same Sussex town. Pam reasoned that this would provide 'a fairly safe investment (and) if the day comes when we have to return to England, we would have a place there'.

Finally, Rob unusually planned to acquire a second home in the UK so that he could move from single residence in Spain to dual residence. He had retired early to Spain, and was now looking ahead:

> Once the kids are in university, or whatever, our life here will come to a grinding halt. I shall make a 100% profit on this house and we will buy a three-bedroom villa and a two-bedroom apartment in the south of England. We will spend half the year there and half in Spain.

The experiences of Rob and many other interviewees illustrate well the need for a flexible understanding of the many different ways in which second homes are used in the course of individual migration histories.

There are clearly many complex ways in which increased resources interact with changed biographies, household composition, and scapes and flows to promote second and multiple home acquisition and use. The individual experiences that we have reviewed here simultaneously illustrate, and underline the simplification of second home purchases as illustrated in Figure 7.2.

Conclusions

Second homes have been a neglected research topic in many countries in recent decades, but several factors, especially the growth in disposable income and internationalisation, have brought renewed attention. Contemporary biographies are commonly associated with sequential stages in life, from schooling through higher education and working ages to retirement (Warnes, 1992). Each stage *may* encourage relocation, and it is becoming increasingly apparent that second homes facilitate such moves, sometimes through complex investment and expenditure strategies across more than one household. Parents acquire properties in the university towns to which their children go. City-based dual income couples acquire country properties as weekend and holiday escapes *and* with a view to retirement residence. Second homes are obviously important as (reverse) stepping stones for many older migrants, as the experiences of British retirement to southern Europe demonstrate. As such, second homes represent channels for acquiring information and experiences, and for exploratory periods of living abroad. But they also have wider significance.

(1) They provide significant nodes in the flows that constitute social networks, providing a distinctive means of maintaining contacts with family and friends over space.
(2) They influence associational activity and the creation of new social networks: sustained use of a second home may create a group of friends and membership of clubs in a destination prior to migration, hence facilitating social integration.
(3) Keeping a second home in the origin country helps to maintain strong ties and may indicate an intention to return. Second homes should be seen in the context of long-term circulation and place loyalties.
(4) Second homes can have multiple purposes, and may be owned as much for income generation and capital accumulation as for personal use.
(5) Ownership of a second home is fundamentally different from other forms of (even regular) visits to a particular area, because it involves property rights and responsibilities. Property ownership usually involves a contract between the owner and local and national governments, by which specified services are received in return for property taxes. There are also, arguably, social obligations to and from neighbours.

Second homes are also significant nodes in the landscape of scapes and flows. Second home ownership is facilitated by scapes, but in turn contributes to these and facilitates further flows. Most obviously, second homes constitute accommodation nodes that help to define scapes, not only for their owners as potential migrants, but also for friends and family who use them as tourists. And where the properties are bought partly for investment, they contribute more generally to the scapes that influence the flows of migrants and tourists.

The transferable property rights embedded in second homes mean that they also have long-term significance. Jaakson (1986) emphasises the continuity represented by second homes. Many second home owners have inherited their properties, and these become places of family heritage. Whilst this association has been demonstrated principally in domestic tourism, in the future an increasing number of houses in some regions of southern Europe will be inherited by beneficiaries in other countries. If the new owners decide to retain the properties, they will create a significant addition to the stock of internationally-owned second homes, with important implications for the scapes and flows of tourism, and perhaps in the long term for migration. Or to but it bluntly, does the eventual inheritance of these second homes necessarily mean the pre-determination of an important component of future international tourism flows?

Finally, this chapter highlights the need to reconceptualise second homes. 'Home' has a very different meaning from 'house', and it is clear that many of the second homes discussed above are considered to be 'holiday' or investment properties. The label '*second* home' may also be inappropriate where individuals arrange their lives around dual or multiple homes in more than one country. There is also no simple linearity in the sequential use made of different houses. Individual properties can shift, sometimes almost imperceptibly, from being second to principal homes, or from summer holiday to winter season homes; and all such changes can be reversed. Given the many current changes in the nature of place affiliation, and with the emergence of more peripatetic life styles and long-term lifestyle planning, it is believed that an increasing share of the population is adopting residential strategies that involve complex sequential shifts in the functional use of multiple properties. The descriptively precise term 'second homes' is becoming misleading, and should perhaps be replaced with the less precise but more accurate designation 'alternative' or 'multiple' homes. They are a rapidly spreading and shifting feature in the scapes that condition flows.

Chapter 8

Dwelling Through Multiple Places: A Case Study of Second Home Ownership in Ireland

BERNADETTE QUINN

Introduction

The literature on second home ownership is by now quite extensive. While it may be also quite disparate, as Kaltenborn (1998) has claimed, identifiable areas within the general second home literature have begun to emerge. This paper focuses on one such area, that which explores the meaning of second home ownership. It re-visits one of the basic questions in the literature by asking why do people have second homes? This question has preoccupied several researchers over the past 20 years (e.g. Clout, 1972; Jaakson, 1986; Kaltenborn, 1998; Chaplin, 1999) and the ensuing literature has produced reasonably consistent findings by way of explaining the phenomenon. A number of explanatory motives have been put forward, most notably the desire to escape from routine, from home life, and ultimately from modernity itself. The second home is viewed as something of a release valve, providing a temporary escape that enables people to return to their routine lives having been revitalised and restored by their second home experiences. This chapter does not refute this basic theory, but it argues that there is a need for further refinement of the processes and meanings at issue. In particular there is much scope for considering how the meaning that people attach to different places informs the decision to become involved in second home ownership. There seems little doubt that a desire to escape is a prevalent motive, but in terms of the places selected for escaping to, the process may not be as random as the literature has generally implied to date. The growing literature on what Clifford (1997: 2) has termed 'dwelling-in-travelling' creates a useful context within which to explore how acquiring a second home creates a means of re-discovering and re-connecting with places that hold special meanings in peoples' lives, thereby serving to counter the sense of place-alienation and dislocation associated with globalisation. This chapter furthers its case using empirical material from a case study of second home owners in south-east Ireland.

Dwelling in Multiple Places

In recent times, demand for second homes has risen significantly, fuelled by growing societal affluence, an increased prevalence of the aged within society, and by technological and transport advances and the economic restructuring associated with globalisation (Müller, 2002a). Within broader contexts, both tourism and otherwise, this increasing demand is, of course, not unique. In terms of human mobility, there is now a growing awareness of how circulation between different places no longer represents an aberration from ordinary, settled life, but rather has become for many a normal part of contemporary lifestyles (Olwig, 1997). 'Many people live and spend time in more than one place, moving between locales on a recurrent basis' (McHugh *et al.*, 1995: 251). Urry (2000: 132) concurs, suggesting that 'contemporary forms of dwelling almost always involve diverse forms of mobility'. In tourism terms, globalisation has meant that places once considered to be exotic and far-flung have come within the reach of Western mass tourists. As Williams and Hall (2000a) note, connections between places are increasingly international. Less dramatically, although no less significantly, they also continue to multiply within national contexts, where patterns of movement are characterised by increasing frequency. Contemporary tourism trends clearly show that travel for leisure purposes is becoming a more regular feature of lifestyle practices. There has been a major shift away from the historic pattern of taking one holiday annually, to a preference for taking multiple but shorter holidays each year. Thus, growing movement between primary and second homes is only one example of how mobility has become an increasingly normal part of contemporary living.

For some, increasing tourist mobility is interpreted as an indication of the deterritorialised spatiality of globalisation (Scholte, 2000). This perspective finds resonance in the conceptualisation of post-modern tourists as individuals driven by a search for playful experiences (Cohen, 1995), largely disinterested in the specifics of place or the authenticity of the experience being offered. Equally, it can be linked to interpretations of tourism as a practice that illustrates how contemporary social identities are increasingly formed through consumption and play, rather than through work or professional activities (Urry, 1994). Yet, while there is increasing recognition that settled life in particular places is not necessarily a 'normal' state of being (Olwig & Halstrup, 1997), increasing mobility need not necessarily be related to decreasing attachment to place. It is useful to remember that mobility has been recognised as a constitutive part of dwelling for a very long time. Tuan (1977: 14), for example, considered place to be 'a pause in movement'. While Clifford (1997: 2) introduced his ideas about 'dwelling-in-travel' by saying that 'everyone's on the move, and has been for centuries'. Nevertheless, as Clifford (1997: 44) writes, 'once travelling is foregrounded as a cultural practice, then dwelling too, needs to be reconceived, (it is) no longer simply the ground from which travelling departs and to which it returns'. Thus basic understandings about 'home' are immediately problematised, as Harvey (1996: 246) and others have pointed out by asking 'who are we and what space/place do we belong?' In response, Williams and Kaltenborn (1999: 214) argue that home implies becoming native to a place, setting down roots and investing oneself in a place. Yet, how does this relate to contemporary assertions that we dwell in and through different places?

Massey's (1991) thoughts on a 'global sense of place' are useful in trying to conceptualise contemporary forms of dwelling, and contemporary place meanings. She calls for a recognition of the inter-connections, overlapping networks and change processes that shape and characterise all places, making them open and porous. More recently, Massey (2000: 231) has written about the 'multiplicity of histories' that make up the spatial, arguing that the histories of the places passed through permeate movement in space. These histories of place are further compounded by travellers' remembrances of times and practices associated with place, and are re-worked continuously to renew interactions and connections between places. Thus when McHugh (2000: 83) talks about people in the post-modern world having 'attachments and connections in multiple places', an obvious research task is to identify the nature of these linkages and to develop an understanding of how they come to be formed. Is there an implication that people can feel themselves to be at home in more than one place at the same time? If this is the case, then how do people forge connections with different places? The literature on second homes has not really addressed this question to any real extent.

Why Have a Second Home?

What the literature has done is to pay significant attention to why people purchase second homes. A number of researchers have produced broadly consistent answers to this question. For example, Clout (1972) found that decisions were based on the need to escape temporarily from urban centres, as an investment, for short-term enjoyment of leisure activities and as a possible retirement location. Jaakson (1986) in a detailed Canadian study reporting data gathered over a 20-year period identified and elaborated a number of key motives: routine and novelty, inversion, back-to nature, identity, surety, work, elitism, aspiration and time and distance. More recently, Chaplin (1999) in a study of British second home owners in France highlighted the escape motive, echoing Buller and Hoggart's (1994a) broader argument that Britons look to France to find a rural way of living no longer available in the UK. Based on the literature, Kaltenborn (1998: 123) usefully derives a threefold category of motives classified as: identity management (contrast to modern everyday life, status symbol), recreation and mental/psychological 'maintenance' (contact with nature, social networks), and more pragmatic reasons (fits with life phase, children, inexpensive holidays, capital investment). Kaltenborn's own empirical work identified closeness to nature, a change from everyday life, physical and psychological rest, and being with the family as the most important motives (Kaltenborn, 1998: 126)

Thus, while a great many motives have been advanced, it seems that there is a broad consensus that 'escape from modernity'/inversion of everyday life /return to nature seem to underpin people's involvement in second home ownership. As Kaltenborn (1998: 122) puts it, second home ownership could be a sign that people are seeking 'some grounding in a particular place that offers stability, a feeling of well-being and meaning in an otherwise demanding existence'. Chaplin (1999) supports this argument, positing the second home as a place where people can regain control over their lives, and escape from their routine situations where the demands of work and responsibilities can threaten to overwhelm. However, in much of the literature there is a sense that the totality of this 'escape' is not quite what it seems to be. Robertson (1977) first pointed to the irony of how 'the owners of these so-called "places to get away from it all" often encounter a considerable amount of "it" when they arrive'. He was referring to the multitude of mundane tasks and responsibilities that go along with owning a second home. Jaakson (1986: 387), too, addresses this complication quite explicitly, both in referring to the routine inherent in repeatedly returning to a second home and to the work involved while there. Both, he explains, are acceptable to the second home owner because they are subsumed within the dominant purpose of the home, which is fundamentally 'leisure-oriented', in contrast to the dominant purpose of the principal dwelling which is work-oriented. This discussion mirrors the broader tourism debate whereby the view that modern tourists seek out the exotic and the unfamiliar in order to escape routine and have themselves liminally renewed in the process (MacCannell, 1992) is countered by the argument that in reality they take much of their everyday lives along with them (Rojek, 1995).

Jackson's idea that duality 'permeates everything in what it means to be a cottager: two places with two lives, providing inversion but also merging into symbiosis', deserves further investigation. Obviously, it is not possible to have a second home without already having a primary home. Economically, this is the case, but it is also true in broader motivational terms. After all, it is the routine associated with the primary home that acts as a 'push' factor, motivating the second home purchase. Yet as Robertson

(1977), Chaplin (1999) and others have pointed out, the second home experience is also based on enjoying the familiar, the ordinary and the expected. Furthermore, as Jaakson (1986: 389) points out, attitudes to both homes 'are influenced by awareness of the certainty of returning to the other'. Thus, the implication to be drawn is that life at the second home is an extension of life at the primary home. The former complements the latter. The 'escape' to the second home revitalises home life in the primary place. Williams and Kaltenborn (1999) neatly summarise the practice as both an escape from, and an extension of, modernity. It could be viewed as a modern solution, facilitated by increasing affluence and mobility, to a modern problem: the sense of placelessness and insecurity associated with time–space compression. As such, second home ownership is part of an adaptation to dwelling in modernity that relies on multiple belongings between two, or possibly more, places of residence.

Thus, second home ownership is one modern practice that illustrates how mobility inherently informs contemporary dwelling. Rather than being understood as a process that 'displaces' or deterritorialises people, the increased mobility and circulation implicit in this practice re-affirms place rootedness, allowing individuals to consolidate attachments with multiple places. An issue that has not been specifically explored in the second home context, but one that it likely to apply, is Massey's (2000) general assertion that people's movement through space reflects a multiplicity of histories built up over time. Marshall and Foster (2002) have described migration as a process in time that relates to peoples' pasts and to their hoped-for futures. It seems likely that second home mobility patterns might illustrate a similar process. Certainly, a number of indications in the second home literature suggest that previous connections with places inform the second home location choices made by second home owners.

Attachments in Multiple Places: How Second Homes Fit in

Understanding the place connections and mobility patterns associated with second home usage can be advanced using Roseman's (1992) general typology of cyclical migration. This considers temporary movements, ranging from weekly to seasonal and to infrequent circulation over the life course, and seeks to explain movement by reference to two sets of factors: production-oriented factors (job and employment-related) and consumption-oriented factors (family and amenity-related). Viewed within this framework, tourism as a form of mobility emerges as a consumption-driven practice. Drawing on Roseman's typology, McHugh *et al.* (1995) graphically represent several examples of multiple residences associated with different stages of the life course. Some of these examples are consumption-oriented, and several are connected with tourist practices.

They include holidaying in family second homes in childhood, staying with friends and relatives, owning second homes, re-locating to sunnier climes on a seasonal basis and sometimes ultimately retiring there. Roseman's typology is useful in pointing to the clear importance that tourist practices play in creating multiple place attachments over a life course. McHugh *et al.*'s (1995) use of the typology has developed our understanding of how connections with place evolve over time through tourist practices. They found, for example, that cyclical migration patterns in their Arizona study often occurred in stages, beginning with holidays and shorter visits in midlife and progressing towards extended winter residence upon full retirement.

While there has been no methodical analysis of cyclical migration specifically in the context of second homes, some researchers have indicated that similar patterns may exist (see Duval, this volume). Burby *et al.* (1972), for example, found 'friends and family' to be a key factor determining second home locations, while Nordin (1993b) found family connections to be a common factor influencing location choice among Scandinavian second home owners. Other researchers have considered how second homes act as a forerunner to more permanent place connections. Swarbrooke (1992), for example, writing in the context of British owners of holiday homes in France, suggested that holiday homes could be bought with a view to using them as permanent residences at a later stage. A study undertaken by the Resort Municipality of Whistler (1995) in British Columbia, produced some empirical evidence in finding that 28% of holiday home owners intended retiring to live in the resort at some point in the future. More recently, Williams *et al.* (2000) noted that the purchase of a holiday home can act as a stepping stone to seasonal or permanent migration.

These findings, while tenuous, promote the idea that, in buying second homes, peoples' desire to escape is strongly tempered by an attempt both to re-connect with experiences from their past and to strive for a continuity that will stretch into their futures. Memories of places associated with childhood, with family connections or with former holiday practices, create a bank of memories that influence subsequent mobility patterns. Similar to the argument made in the section on why people buy second homes, the assertion here is that the escape in question is really an attempt to re-visit and rediscover experiences, times and places that create a sense of connectedness. Thus, second home ownership allows people to dwell in and through different places, enabling them to feel connected to more than one place at the same time. The remainder of this chapter discusses this assertion in the light of empirical findings from a case study of second home owners in south-east Ireland. It revisits the basic question of why people have a second home and explores how they integrate their holiday home into their lifestyles. It then asks how people forge second home connections with particular places and whether the multiple places that come together to create meaning in peoples' lives are connected in some way. It begins by briefly describing the historical background to second home ownership in Ireland.

Levels of Second Home Ownership in Ireland

The international literature on second home ownership demonstrates that the phenomenon has long been a part of modern tourism practices in advanced Western societies. Some countries can point to very long histories of second home ownership. Kaltenborn (1998), for example, suggests that the phenomenon of the Norwegian cabin probably dates back 100–150 years. In Scandinavia more generally, a long tradition of 'cottaging' is well recognised (Löfgren, 1999; Müller, 2001; Flognfeldt, 2002) (see also Flognfeldt, this volume). Müller (2001), for example, writes that in Sweden, legislation controlling the location of second homes in lake and seashore areas was introduced as early as 1974 in response to the phenomenon's increasing prevalence. Similarly, in France, the longevity of the phenomenon is indicated in the fact that the French population census has collected data on second home ownership since 1962 (Gallent & Tewdwr-Jones, 2000). Certainly, in a majority of Western European countries, second home ownership had become an established practice by the 1970s (Gallent & Tewdwr-Jones, 2000). Meanwhile, in a North American context, Jaakson (1986) has written about the long-established incidence of second home ownership in Canada and the historically-embedded culture that centres on the Canadian 'cottage' (the term universally used in Canada to refer to a holiday home). Since then, ownership levels everywhere have tended to show an upward trend. By the late 1980s, Go (1988) estimated that 35% of Italians owned a holiday home in their own country, the highest percentage of any European nationals to do so. Equivalent figures given for France and Switzerland at that time were 16% and 10% respectively.

The trends described above have little resonance in Ireland where, relative to the general European situation, significant levels of second home ownership are a recent phenomenon. Whereas Sweden could count half a million holiday homes (Löfgren, 1999) by the 1970s, the practice of owning a second home and using it for leisure purposes was only then beginning to emerge in Ireland. Data compiled by Gallent and Tewdwr-Jones (2000: 66) show that, out of 17 Western European countries, Ireland had the lowest percentage of households owning second homes in 1970 and 1980, and the second lowest in 1988, at just 2% for each of the given years. As Mottiar and Quinn (2003) have noted, second home ownership in Ireland had its modest beginnings in the 1970s. Initially, holiday homes were detached properties, overwhelmingly located in rural areas, with frequent locational clusters in coastal areas, relatively close to major urban areas (e.g. Wexford in the case of Dublin city, West Clare in the case of Limerick city). However, the extent of the phenomenon was relatively limited, both numerically and spatially.

The advent of the 'Celtic Tiger' economy and the economic prosperity witnessed in Ireland in the 1990s has changed this, and there are signs now that levels of holiday home ownership are on the rise. Writing in an Irish context, Suiter (1999) has commented that 'the holiday home is no longer the preserve of the fortunate few. There's an increasing amount of cash in the economy and lots of it is finding its way into the booming holiday home market'. This development has been fuelled in part by a substantial increase in the second home housing stock. A tax incentive scheme introduced by the Irish Government in 1995 to revitalise outmoded traditional seaside resorts resulted in the building of 5300 holiday cottages and apartments in 15 coastal locations around Ireland between 1995–2000. Clustered into group developments, the properties built under this scheme have been purchased either for personal holiday use or for renting as holiday accommodation.

The recentness of the second home ownership phenomenon in Ireland is easily explained relative to broader societal developments. Ireland is historically an agrarian society with one of the lowest populations densities in Europe (CSO, 2002a). Until relatively recently, it had low levels of urbanisation, and the push factors that underpin the 'desire for escape' identified in the literature were not major issues for Irish dwellers. In fact, in a European context, the Ireland of the 1970s and 1980s was for many continentals an attractive second home location, offering as it did a respite from modernity much sought after by European urban dwellers. During these decades Irish coastal towns and villages, particularly in southern and western counties like Cork and Clare, witnessed sizeable numbers of continentals buying up properties for use as second homes. The rapid economic growth and societal changes experienced over the 1990s, however, created the conditions that promoted the growth of second home ownership among Irish people, and factors such as increasing affluence, increased leisure time and increased personal mobility have facilitated the phenomenon. Throughout the 1990s and into the early 2000s, GDP and consumer spending in the Republic of Ireland have grown faster than in most other European countries (Mintel, 2002). This rising prosperity has been reflected in a multitude of ways. Car ownership levels, for example, have risen dramatically. Almost 161,000 new cars were registered in the Republic in 2001, a figure that was almost double that of 1990 (CSO, 2002a). Outbound travel from Ireland also increased dramatically, growing at an average annual rate of 10% during the 1990s. At the same time, increasing urbanisation (especially in the Dublin region), with its attendant problems of stressful living, commuting and traffic congestion, and a gradual detachment from historic rural connections, has created a need for people to re-think how they want to live. For those with means, owning a second home is a way of restoring a degree of equilibrium to their lives.

Measuring what seems to be a growing phenomenon is not an easy task, however. Müller's (2002a: 169) assertion that 'second homes are often covered in national property cadastres and thus well documented and easy to research' does not apply in the Irish case. However, Bord Fáilte, the 'national tourism organisation', gathers data, although the incidence of home ownership is thought to be under-reported, and the longitudinal data available is not comparable. Nevertheless, it would seem reasonably accurate to suggest that the role of second homes in accommodation bednights is at present modest but rising. Bord Fáilte figures suggest that they accounted for 3% of domestic bednights in 1988. Mintel (2002) figures for the 2001 season suggest that they are used by 6% of Irish holidaymakers. Certainly, the second home phenomenon has received increasing attention from the country's local authorities, which have become increasingly active in introducing planning regulations controlling the location of second homes regionally within Ireland. Much of this has been in response to the increased incidence of individuals building detached second homes on individual plots of land in rural, usually highly scenic, areas. Kerry County Council, for example, considers that the county has experienced unsustainable pressure for the development of holiday/second homes in scenic area in recent years to the extent that the visual and ecological quality of the landscape has experienced incremental deterioration (Kerry County Council, 2001). Since 1999 most of the local authorities in the coastal counties of Ireland (e.g. Kerry, Cork, Clare, Waterford, Donegal) have begun to include second home development in their county development plans. Overwhelmingly, the trend, as in the County Clare Development Plan (Clare County Council, 1999), is 'to generally not permit isolated houses for use as holiday homes or second homes' in areas under development pressure, in vulnerable areas or along scenic routes. Clear distinctions are often made between local and external populations. For the former, restrictions can be relaxed, as in the case of the Cork Plan or, their position can be favoured, as in the case of the Donegal Development Plan, which seeks to provide 'incentives for local residents in areas subject to holiday home pressure' (Donegal County Council, 2000).

Introduction to the Study Area and Methodology

The study area in question here is North Wexford, an area located some 100 kilometres south of the capital city Dublin. North Wexford is a rural area, and the largest urban settlement in the area, Gorey, has a population of approximately 7500. The south-east coastal county of Wexford has long functioned as a holiday destination for the Dublin market, drawing somewhere in the region of 50% of its domestic arrivals from Dublin each year. The Dublin region itself is the dominant source market for domestic tourists in Ireland, containing as it does, close to one third of the country's population of 3.9 million people Central Statistics Office (CSO, 2002b). In an Irish context, it is well established as a second home location. Kinsella (1982) has written that the building of holiday bungalows (as second homes) dates back to the 1970s. With its scenic coastline and fine beaches, historic towns and a warmer and drier climate than elsewhere on the island, the area has obvious appeals. Its closeness to the greater Dublin urban area is clearly a key factor. As Halseth and Rosenberg (1995) note, the rural hinterland of cities has long been used by urban dwellers for recreational purposes, and second home ownership has been one of the most important forms of recreational land use in such areas. Müller (2002a: 173) agrees, remarking that second homes are often located within the metropolitan areas' leisure peripheries, thereby allowing frequent visits.

Historically, caravans and mobile homes have been a common accommodation option for Dubliners holidaying in Wexford; but in recent years there has been a marked increase in the rise of second home developments in the area. Reflecting the national trend, the stock of second homes in North Wexford increased considerably following the introduction of the tax incentive Seaside Resort Area Scheme introduced by the Irish government in 1995. The largest resort in North Wexford, Courtown, was designated under the scheme, which resulted in some 1000 new houses being built for use as second homes or as rented accommodation for holidaymakers.

The data reported in this chapter are taken from a questionnaire survey administered to 76 second home owners in four small coastal villages/ districts in North Wexford. The largest village is Courtown, a traditional seaside resort with a history of tourism dating back to the 1860s. Courtown has a permanent population of 354 people (CSO, 1998) but in the summertime it is estimated that 3–4000 tourists stay in the resort (Webb, 2000). Other places (including Kilmuckridge, Blackwater and Curracloe) are more modest, and much more recently associated with tourism activity. The data are drawn from a larger study that also surveyed tourist and local resident populations in the four areas. The surveys were administered in the summer of 2001 on a face-to-face basis, in public places in each of the four resorts. They comprised a mixture of open and closed questions, and a series of questions that invited respondents to rank particular statements in order of importance and to compare particular factors on a number of bases.

Findings and Discussion

Profiling the second home owners

The survey began by eliciting basic descriptive information from the second home owners. It found them to be overwhelmingly domestic in origin, with 50% coming from Dublin, and 20% from Wexford or adjacent counties. Just one respondent came from outside Ireland (from the UK). This finding matches the broader tourism profile of the region as one dominated by domestic visits and having long-established associations with the Dublin market.

A clear picture emerged in respect of age profile, with 67% being middle aged. Specifically, 35–44-year olds predominated (40% of the sample), while a further 27% were aged 45–54 years. At the outer ends of the spectrum, 16% were over 55 years and 14% were aged 25–34 years. The dominance of the relatively youthful 35–44 year age group may partly explain the fact that when broken down into gross household income levels, the majority of second home owners (40%) earned mid-range incomes of between €24,000 and €40,600 (euros).

This most cursory analysis suggests that, for the sample of second home owners surveyed, acquiring a second home was a moderate, rather than a life-changing lifestyle choice. They had chosen to connect with another place within easy reach of their primary residence, at a relatively early stage in life and at a time when their household incomes were relatively modest. For a majority of individuals, holiday home ownership was a recent phenomenon. Some 60% of the sample had owned their home for a period of less than 5 years. Just 17% had owned their property for more than 11

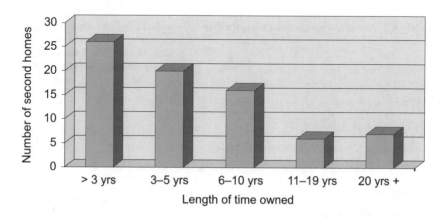

Figure 8.1 Length of time that the second home has been owned (*n* = 76)

years. The younger the age group, the more likely they were to have purchased in the previous five years.

Explaining the decision to buy a second home: Escaping or returning?

Two survey questions sought to explore why respondents had decided to buy a second home and why they had chosen the Wexford location in particular. Respondents were offered multiple reasons and asked to rank, in order of importance, the reasons that best explained their decisions. In response to the basic question about why they decided to buy a second home, it was clear that a desire to relax and to escape everyday routine prevailed (Table 8.1). 'A place to relax' was ranked by 28% of respondents as their number one reason for making the purchase. The next most popular reason was 'a place to escape from everyday routine', cited by 18% of the sample. These findings are clearly in line with existing research findings.

These motives were further elaborated by the reasons respondents gave for choosing a particular location for their second home (Table 8.2). Here there was an unambiguous preference to be close to the coast or, to be more specific, to the beach. The peacefulness and the scenic quality of the area were also important factors. These findings are again in line with existing research, indicating the extent to which the second home location is prized for its recreational and amenity value. So too were the responses elicited from the question 'what are the main differences between life here and life at your permanent residence?' The dominant response encompassed the relaxation/'getting away from it all' theme, with having more family/child-oriented time, and spending more time with nature being secondary differences noted. These responses were supported by respondents'

Table 8.1 Most important reasons for purchasing a holiday home ($n = 76$)

Reason	Instances of being ranked first	Instances of being ranked in top 3
A place to relax	21	40
A place to escape from everyday routine	14	41
A place to spend more quality time as a family	9	28
Was a regular visitor and wanted to own property here	9	20
An investment	9	16
To give the children more freedom	6	34
Plan to retire to this area	5	23

Table 8.2 Reasons for choosing the particular Wexford location (*n* = 105)

Reason	*Instances of being ranked first*	*Instances of being ranked in top 3*
Closeness to the beach	41	60
The 'price was right'	16	38
Used to holiday here as a child	7	28
Was a regular visitor and wanted to own property here	10	26
Family/friends with second home in area	9	20
Nearness to Dublin	6	38
Peacefulness of area	6	31
Scenic qualities	5	34
Family connections in the area	5	24

comments as to how the two homes differed. In this respect, dominant responses related to how life at the second home was more relaxing (31%), more stress-free (21%), was lived at a slower pace (14%) and lent itself to spending more time outdoors (11%).

However, while the desire to relax and to select a location that would promote relaxation predominated, the selection process was informed by individuals' affinities to place. For 58% of the sample, strong personal connections with the area had influenced their decision to buy a second home in Wexford. For 28%, these connections extended historically to their childhood holidays. For 18% (excluding those who had already cited the childhood holiday association), it was a case of having been a regular visitor to the area and wanting to intensify this connection. A further 24% had an affinity with the area because of family connections, while 20% were influenced to purchase a house here because friends or family already had a second home in the area. Thus the decision was clearly not founded simply on general, 'placeless' factors such as amenity value and a desire to relax. Neither was it a matter of simply 'escaping', because as the figures discussed here demonstrate, for a majority of the sample the second home represented a means of returning and of re-connecting with a place that already had special connotations for the individuals concerned.

So, where is home?

The data collected were abundantly clear on one point: these second home owners use their second homes with remarkable regularity. The circuitous movement between primary residence and North Wexford is for a majority of respondents a very regular occurrence that continues throughout the year. Geographical location promotes this extensive usage: with the exception of two respondents, all resided within a radius of 100 kilometres of North Wexford. As Table 8.3 illustrates, 70% of respondents used their second home on a year-round basis, 20% of them claimed to use it 'intensively' (meaning most weekends throughout the year), while a further 20% used it 'intensively' in summer and 'regularly' throughout the year. This means that these second homes are being used both for short-stay weekend breaks and for longer-term holidays throughout the year at times that included Easter, Christmas, mid-term and, of course, summer.

The amount of time spent in the second homes under examination here attests to the wisdom of becoming a second home owner and deciding to live life between two homes. Using the motives identified in the literature, a question was devised to explore how respondents compared life in their two homes. As might be expected, Jaakson's (1986) concept of the second home as a leisure-dominated sphere emerges unambiguously. As Table 8.4 illustrates, while in their second home overwhelming proportions of respondents feel more relaxed, have more leisure time, engage in more recreational pursuits, feel closer to nature, and think their children are more care-free. Thus, the second home is clearly fulfilling the function that respondents intended. Smaller proportions, but still a majority of the sample, claimed they felt happier, spent more time with their family and led a healthier lifestyle in their second homes.

Yet, when asked 'where they felt most at home', a small majority (32%) cited their primary home, while a greater percentage (41%) said they felt unsure, or could not answer the question. One possible way of interpreting this response is to suggest that both places have a part to play in creating 'home'. Previous research (e.g. Chaplin, 1999) has suggested that second homes may rival the primacy of the 'primary' home in the role that they play in people's lives. Indeed, the findings reported here relating to the

Table 8.3 Frequency of usage of holiday home (*n* = 68)

Frequency of usage	% of respondents
Used intensively year round	20
Used intensively in summer and regularly year round	20
Used intensively in summer and occasionally year round	30
Used intensively during summer months	25
Used infrequently	5

Table 8.4 Life at the permanent residence and the second home compared (*n* = 65)

	In permanent residence (%)	*In holiday home (%)*	*Unsure or Not applicable (%)*
Feel more relaxed	6	77	17
Have more leisure time	3	90	7
Spend more time engaging in recreational pursuits	10	80	10
Feel children are more carefree	10	67	23
Feel more 'at home'	32	27	41
Spend more time with family	22	58	20
Feel closer to nature	10	75	15
Lead a healthier lifestyle	27	48	25
Feel happier	14	49	17

intensive usage of the second home could be interpreted as supporting this stance. However, the argument favoured here is that the second home phenomenon is not founded on competition between two places or two homes. Rather it involves developing multiple associations with places that contribute to a balanced, meaningful existence such that people can feel 'at home' in more than one place. This involves blending together elements from lives in both places, to form the sort of symbiosis that Jaakson (1986) referred to and to achieve the continuity that Williams and Kaltenborn (1999) argue is achieved through second home ownership.

An insight into how this process unfolds is gained by analysing the social networks that encase the second home owners under investigation here. Respondents were asked to indicate with whom they tend to socialise while in their second home. As Table 8.5 illustrates, the largest percentage of respondents said that they socialised with the friends and relatives that they invited to come and stay with them in their second home. A further 45% said that they socialised with other second homes owners familiar to them from their lives at their permanent residences. These findings point to the stretching of social networks across space, and represent a clear instance of how second home owners seek to integrate elements of familiarity, from their primary home life and from their historic store of personal connections with the area, into their second home lifestyle. As such, they are another example of how these holidaymakers are selective in the quality of the escape that they seek. In addition, a sizeable 52% claimed to socialise

Table 8.5 Socialising while in second home ($n = 65$)

Who do second home owners socialise with?	%
Other second home owners known from permanent residence (e.g. Dublin)	45
Friends/relatives invited to visit the second home	62
Other second home owners first encountered in Wexford	52
Local Wexford residents	46

with other second home owners whom they had first encountered in Wexford. This finding suggests an image of second home owners existing as a group of incomers functioning in something of an insular manner in the midst of a broader, locally-embedded residential community. However, 46% of respondents indicated that they socialised with local Wexford residents. These findings capture the blend of the novel and the routine that characterises second home life and again suggest that what is at issue here is not a simplistic escape from ' home' life, but an attempt to enrich lives by making connections between the multiple places that are meaningful in peoples' lives.

Conclusions

As this chapter has discussed, the second home phenomenon raises fundamental questions about the nature of contemporary dwelling and about people's enduring need to seek out attachments to place. The findings that have emerged from the study reported here support existing research in identifying the second home as a leisure-oriented domain that offers a temporary release from the fast-paced, stressful and predominantly-urban lifestyles that characterise contemporary Western society. Unlike earlier research, this study stops short of using the word 'escape' to describe the practice, arguing that the concepts of return, rediscovery and renewal capture equally well the essence of what it is that second home owners are seeking to achieve. Far from being in search of the exotic, or even of difference, previous researchers have characterised second home owners as being strongly attached to the familiar and the routine. Thus, reflecting White's (1985) ideas about the ambivalence of migration and postmodernity, it is argued that the practice of living between two homes is characterised by a marked ambiguity. Second home ownership is a modern practice, devised to counter the difficulties of modern living.

Thus, as Urry (2000) argues there are many different kinds of dwellings, almost all of which involve complex relationships between belongingness and travelling. However, if 'people can indeed be said to dwell in various mobilities' (Urry, 2000: 157), the process of connecting with places *en route* is not random. It is made possible by 'a lifelong accumulation of experiences in place' (McHugh & Mings, 1996) that people draw upon to make new, and to rediscover and reform, place connections. A key finding here is that second home mobility patterns can be strongly informed by previous connections to place. These may have been forged in a multitude of ways, through what Roseman (1992) termed production and consumption factors. In this case, the latter dominated, with personal factors focused on family connections, previous holiday experiences and social networks, influencing 58% of respondent's choice of second home location.

One finding that emerged quite strikingly here was the amount of time that the second home owners spent in their second homes. Clearly, the findings are shaped by the fact that they relate to domestic second home mobility patterns. The North Wexford area offers what Müller (2002a: 173) has termed 'comfortable accessibility' for the people in question, and was thus heavily used as a weekend home. However, it was also widely used for longer holiday breaks throughout the year, which suggests that the second home can be deeply woven into people's ordinary lifestyles, complementing their life at the primary residence in an ongoing, undramatic way throughout the year. Furthermore, it may be that people are taking the decision to buy a second home more readily than in the past. Ragatz (1970a), for example, considered that two factors were necessary for the purchase of a second home: time and money. Yet, among the sample surveyed here, neither was in abundance for most of the second home owners surveyed.

The usage of second homes in this way again supports the argument that mobility is implicit in contemporary dwelling. It prompts a questioning of the historically accepted notion that the practice of holidaying and the location of the holiday destination are clearly distinguishable from the rhythms, practices and places associated with home life. There has been a tendency to think of tourist flows as a relatively uncomplicated circuitous movement, where people move between two discrete places (their home and their holiday destination) in search of difference. Always, as Burkart and Medlik's (1991) widely-accepted definition of tourism signalled, there was an intention to return *home*, to the place where the tourist was unambiguously understood not only to reside but also to belong. Certainly, there was definitional 'fuzziness' with respect to the duration of the travel involved and the variety of motivations in evidence (Cooper *et al.*, 1998). However, tourist mobility historically did not tend to inspire major theoretical questions regarding notions of belonging, nor did it question the primacy of the home place as the main source of place-based identity. The growing literature on second home ownership changes this.

These study findings cannot be generalised to a larger population, and there is no intention to imply that they should be. This is an exploratory study into an issue that in an Irish context has received no attention to date, which is something that needs redressing. Although second home owner- ship is still a minority practice in Ireland, both emerging indications and the experience of international trends suggest that it will rise. The second home mobility patterns discussed here represent domestic movements, but there are signs that rising levels of second home ownership are also informing the significant and consistent rise in outbound travel witnessed since the early 1990s. In broader cultural contexts, questions about mobility, place connec- tions and belonging have informed a significant literature on Irish identity. Writers such as Kearney (1997) have paid much attention to how mobility and connections with multiple places created largely through emigration processes have informed, and continue to shape, notions of Irish cultural identity. Recently, Nash's (2002) research on genealogical identities has shown the potential that exists for drawing on this literature to ask similar questions about contemporary tourism practices. Second home ownership represents another arena within which to usefully explore changing ideas of mobility, place connectedness and belonging, at a time when Irish society is rapidly becoming highly globalised.

Part 3

Patterns and Issues

Chapter 9

Recreational Second Homes in the United States: Development Issues and Contemporary Patterns

DALLEN J. TIMOTHY

> *It's the other half of the American Dream: no sooner do people have a decent roof over their heads than they start looking around for another roof. Not instead of, mind you, but in addition to the one they are already committed to mending and patching. They want it in a warmer place or a cooler place: a quieter place, or a livelier place. Mainly, they want it in a different place, a place where life is easier and more fun than it is at home.*
>
> Massey & Maxwell, 1993: 29

Introduction

In many parts of the world, ownership of second homes as recreational/vacation properties has a long history, dating back even before the Roman Empire. In Europe, the tradition of second homes is long, especially in the north, where in Norway, Sweden and Finland summer cottage ownership is widespread, properties are often passed down from one generation to another (Jaakson, 1986; Kaltenborn, 1998; Müller, 2002a; Flognfeldt, 2002). In most cases people who do not own a summer cottage are set on buying one. Second homes have also been an important part of social life along the Mediterranean coasts of Southern Europe (Gosar, 1989).

The tradition of second home ownership in the United States is not as old as in Europe, although today it is becoming more commonplace. Formalised second homes first developed in the United States in areas of aesthetic beauty, primarily at lakefronts, sea coasts, and in mountain regions, where there was a high 'recreational place utility' (Clout, 1970, 1972). Most summer cottages in Northern Europe provided a way of escaping the everyday environment of city, town and village life, and provided shelters while hunting and herding sheep and cattle (see Chapter 15, by Flognfeldt). While some forms of second home in the United States developed as a result of hunting and herding, most developed as a result of climatic conditions where people in hot climates built homes in higher elevations and latitudes to escape intense summer heat and people in lower latitudes and lowlands built them to escape the bitter cold of winter.

Today, second home ownership is widespread in the United States, and it has grown tremendously in recent decades as recreational housing became more affordable to a wider cross-section of society. As such, it has become one of the most important types of domestic tourism in the country, and in many locations it is the main source of tourism-related income (Brown, 1970). Regional variations in style and use have developed over the years, and several problems have arisen as recreational properties have been developed. Many early authors described the development of second homes in the United States (Fine & Tuttle, 1966; Fine & Werner, 1960; Snyder, 1967). More recently, however, few people have systematically examined recreational home ownership and its trends today. This chapter aims to remedy this by examining the second home phenomenon in the United States. First the historical development and background of recreational homes are discussed, followed by an explanation of the primary issues facing the industry in America today. Finally, some of the current trends affecting second home tourism in the United States are illustrated.

Second Homes in the United States

While many people in the United States own second homes as rental properties and financial investments, this chapter is more concerned with second homes that function as recreational or vacation properties. In most cases, recreational second homes are defined as seasonal, occasional-use housing units that are owned in addition to the occupants' primary place of residence and built for the purpose of leisure activities (Ragatz, 1970a; Deller *et al.*, 1997; US Census Bureau, 2000).

Despite the relative newness of second homes in the US, in ancient and prehistoric times, second homes and seasonal migration were part of life in North America. History reveals that American Indians commonly sought cooler temperatures and greater levels of abundance during the hot summer months and warmth in winter in locations far away from their normal abodes. The location known today as Cape May, New Jersey, for example, was a popular seaside refuge for the Leni Lenape Indians centuries before the beach homes of the 1800s were built (Massey & Maxwell, 1993: 29).

Early European settlers on the US east coast also found favour in country and mountain havens. 'Even Thomas Jefferson, the incurable workaholic, withdrew in his later years from his mountaintop home at Monticello to Poplar Forest, a small octagonal house he had built 80 miles away. There he could read and think in solitude' (Massey & Maxwell, 1993: 29). With the process of industrialisation and the subsequent growth of cities in the East and the Midwest, people became dissatisfied with urban life, for cities were becoming crowded, polluted, disease-ridden, and stressful. People with

Table 9.1 Seasonal housing in the United States by year (in thousands)

1965	1970	1975	1980	1985	1990	1995	2000	2001
1860	1746	1694	2106	2046	2931	3099	3469	3554

Source: US Census Bureau (2002)

higher-paying jobs in the cities had more money, time and motives to escape to the country (Stroud, 1985, 1995; Irvine & Cunningham, 1990; Massey & Maxwell, 1993). Thus began the rush to obtain rural properties where second homes could be built for people outside their everyday urban environments.

During the slave era of the South, wealthy landowners built second homes in the mountains to avoid diseases and the summer heat of the lowlands and built them in towns to be at the centre of commerce and social life (Irvine & Cunningham, 1990). Seaside resorts, and subsequently second homes, developed along the east coast with the advent of the steam train and expansion of the railroads in the 1800s, and later with the growth in popularity of private automobiles and a well-developed highway system. Resort villages in the hills of New York and Pennsylvania, as well as religious revival camps, also contributed to the spread of the second home phenomenon (Massey & Maxwell, 1993). Even as early as the late-1800s, the expected thrill of owning a holiday home was so great that it sparked the development of ready-made recreational properties, which were prefabricated buildings that people could order with plans and ready-cut materials from companies such as Sears Roebuck and Montgomery Ward (Massey & Maxwell, 1993: 33).

While second homes as they are known today were generally the domain of the wealthy, they became more mainstream and within the grasp of more middle-class people as venues and styles began to change and became more diversified in the mid-20th century. As changes occurred in price and accessibility, ever-larger segments of the population were able to purchase recreational properties (Ward, 1999). Table 9.1 shows the growth patterns of seasonal home ownership in the United States, which has nearly doubled in the past 35 years; today there are more than 3.5 million seasonal/second homes throughout the country. Seasonal homes are defined by the US Census Bureau (2000) as units that are intended to be occupied only during certain seasons of the year, and they are not a usual residence. The geographical distribution of seasonal homes is interesting, with the majority being located in the southeast (38%), followed by the midwest (22%), the northeast (21%), and the west (19%) (see Table 9.2).

With the obvious potential for growth, developers in the mid-1900s began to buy large tracts of land in desirable areas. These they subdivided

Table 9.2 Seasonal homes in the United States by region, 1999

Northeast	635,000
Midwest	656,000
South	1,120,000
West	550,000
Total	*2,961,000**

*This total does not reflect the total number of seasonal homes in the USA in 1999
Source: US Census Bureau (2000)

into individual plots of ground and built 'recreational subdivisions', or estates, for sale to large segments of the growing middle class. In these areas, land sales expanded during the 1950s and 60s at an extraordinary rate, and by the early 1970s, sales of sites in recreational subdivisions totalled more than $5 billion a year in the United States (Ragatz & Gelb, 1970; Stroud, 1995). With this trend, recreational properties began to take on some of the characteristics of suburbia, such as small lot sizes, paved roads, street signs, owners associations, and recreational amenities (e.g. sport centres, shopping facilities, golf courses, tennis courts) (Clout, 1970). Nonetheless, this form of second home community became quite popular, and is still one of the most prominent fixtures of the recreational landscape in the United States, particularly in Florida, Texas, the Southwestern states and along the Rocky Mountains (Stroud, 1995). Many of today's suburbs began as second home areas for the wealthy.

Problems in US Second Homes Development

Despite increased access to second homes by the broader population and rapid growth and its subsequent positive impacts on local economies through new tax revenues, consumer sales, and a roused construction industry (Brown, 1970; Deller *et al.*, 1997; Jaakson, 1986; Stroud, 1995), recreation home development has not always been seen as a positive trend in the United States. Nevertheless, as recreational subdivisions began to grow and spread throughout the country, various problems arose in terms of buildings, locations, sales/development techniques, and environmental problems. Recreational home developers became notorious for their deceitful and fraudulent sales practices aimed at selling vast tracts of raw land without being able to secure title and provide services (Stroud, 1995). Thus, many unsuspecting consumers fell victim to developers' unscrupulous sales tactics, which left them with plots of land that were difficult to build on and subsequently lay uninhabited for years.

In the rush of profit making, developers commonly chose inappropriate locations for these developments. Instead of the choice of location being based on aesthetics and knowledge of ecological capacities, sites were often chosen simply because they were located in counties where development constraints were relaxed and where land was cheap (Ragatz, 1970a; Stroud, 1995). This resulted in recreation housing of a lower standard than traditional suburban developments, which created severe structural and environmental problems later on (Stroud, 1995).

Throughout the years, second home areas and recreational subdivisions have received considerable criticism for their negative environmental impacts (Gartner, 1987). Overcrowding along lakeshores and other waterfronts, and the subsequent pollution created by widespread use of motorboats, has resulted in water and air pollution in some places, and vandalism has increased as second home visitation numbers have also increased (Ragatz, 1969, 1970a; Suffron, 1998).

Economic recessions and oil shortages in the 1970s created a drastic drop in demand for second homes (Stroud, 1995), so many subdivisions remained unfinished, and many developers went bankrupt. Toward the late 1970s, however, the situation began to improve, and to restore public trust once again in an industry fraught with negative publicity, developers changed their sales tactics and improved their building standards, which has since assisted in creating a much improved public image.

The Draw of Second Homes

After the Second World War, several socio-economic and political changes took place in the United States that enabled middle-class families to purchase second homes, which had traditionally been the domain of the wealthy.

(1) Until quite recently, property was relatively affordable. In fact, until the rapid land development efforts of the 1970s and 80s, land was still inexpensive in most rural parts of the country. In the mid-1900s, the US Federal Government even encouraged people to purchase land at cut-rate prices in more 'useless' regions (e.g. Alaska and parts of eastern Washington state), which later proved to be valuable.

(2) Increased human mobility also contributed to this growth. As mentioned before, innovations in transportation technology and the growth of the interstate highway system after the Second World War made it possible for many people to purchase land further from home.

(3) There are more dual-income families in the United States now than ever before – a trend that has developed quickly during the past two decades. In most cases, this has resulted in higher levels of disposable household income, which allows more people to make recreation/travel a higher priority and to purchase or lease of second homes

(Ragatz, 1970a). Additionally, low interest rates n the early 2000s contributed to the affordability of second homes.

(4) American society is rushed, and people are becoming more aware of the need to relax and get away from the harried lifestyle of urban living and work (Lengfelder & Timothy, 2000). This has led many people to purchase or lease second homes away from cities in an effort to 'get away from it all' and preserve their mental and physical health (Irvine & Cunningham, 1990).

(5) Tax incentives are another factor. Tax breaks were available for people to build and purchase second homes. Capital gains taxes could be avoided if a second home were purchased after the sale of another home, and tax deductions were possible for certain types of second homes for various uses (Paulson, 1989; Charski, 1998), although these liberal tax benefits have been modified somewhat in recent years.

(6) Although life is ever more hurried, people now have more free time than ever before. Leisure time has increased significantly during the past 50 years, as better transportation systems and new technology allow people to complete tasks more efficiently and work more often from home (telecommuting).

(7) Some employers have begun implementing a four-day working week, which requires more hours at the office each day but gives longer blocks of weekend time.

(8) For all the reasons listed above, there is an increased desire among American families to own recreational properties (Chaplin, 1999).

Based on research about second home ownership, Suffron (1998: 34) identified several reasons, or motives, that make recreational home ownership in the United States desirable. One can:

- find peace and tranquillity;
- enjoy nature;
- spend time with family;
- relieve stress;
- escape daily pressures;
- improve health and fitness;
- be with friends;
- escape crowds;
- get physical rest;
- be alone;
- enhance social status.

Regional variations in style and origins

A look at second homes throughout the United States reveals differences in style characteristics and origins by region (Russis, 1998). In the northeast, second homes grew to be popular in the late 1800s, as New Englanders became more affluent when urbanisation and industrialisation created employment and business opportunities. Urban conditions and other push factors led New England's more affluent residents to build summer homes along the coast and in the mountains and hills, where they could get away from the hot and humid summers of the lowlands. New England's second homes range from very elaborate coastal mansions, such as those in Newport, Rhode Island, to unpretentious simple dwellings made of boards and stone (Irvine & Cunningham, 1990). While many wealthy families still utilise mansions in the Northeast for recreational purposes, several of the homes have also become significant tourist attractions and museums. Second homes in the mountains of New England generally take the form of wood-frame structures, highly integrated into the forest environments, while the coastal houses often are of a Greek Revivalist style.

Second homes in the Mid-Atlantic region are diverse in style and origin, but some of the most common designs include lakeside rustic structures of wood (coloured a dark green to blend in with nature), farmhouse-style dwellings (in the inland interior often made of painted field stones), picket-fenced cottages along the coast with brick exteriors and balconies, and oceanfront Atlantic dune houses. Many of these often began as fishing shacks that were used by less affluent families as beachfront properties, and eventually newcomers built summer homes that imitated the shanty construction (Massey & Maxwell, 1993: 32). The Mid-Atlantic region contains several large cities (such as New York, Washington, Baltimore), which drive many residents to find solace in rural and beachfront areas. The second homes in this area generally are easily accessible by train or motor highway. Upstate New York, the inland hills of Pennsylvania, and the New Jersey coast are important destinations (Irvine & Cunningham, 1990; Massey & Maxwell, 1993).

The south-eastern United States has a rich history of second home ownership. As mentioned previously, it was typical for wealthy plantation owners to possess a house in the city to be close to commercial establishments or in the hills away from the sweltering heat of summer on the plantations. Many people of the south still spend summer holidays in the mountains, although the beach has become a more common place for second homes as well (Batie & Mabbs-Zeno, 1985; Irvine & Cunningham, 1990; Taylor & Smith, 2000). Among the most common styles of second homes in the south are fishing shacks on the Outer Banks and coastal islands, Gulf Coast-style houses overlooking the ocean, and conch houses, or Key West cottages, which are simply-designed wooden structures with a Caribbean appearance.

The Midwest is one of the most popular parts of the United States for recreational home ownership. Much of the housing stock in rural communities there comprises second homes, and much of the rural economy depends on tourism/recreation at second home properties (Ragatz, 1969, 1970a, 1977; Girard & Gartner, 1993; Green *et al.*, 1996). Recreational homes in the Midwest range from typical log cabins in heavily-wooded areas of Minnesota, Michigan and Wisconsin to the ranch houses of eastern Montana and Oklahoma. The Mackinac-Island style of house with railings overhanging the water is popular along the Great Lakes of the upper Midwest. As the towns and cities of the region grew, so did the need to get away from them, and lakefront resorts developed with individual bunga-lows incorporating porches and fireplaces (Irvine & Cunningham, 1990). Log cabins of the wooded north were largely inspired by the massive influx of Finnish and Scandinavian immigrants into the area. These people built structures in the United States similar to those found in their homelands according to their own preferences and the availability of suitable building materials (Conzen, 1990; Massey & Maxwell, 1993). The Finnish immi-grants, for example, were avid foresters carried with them the knowledge and desire to transplant many of the cultural landscape elements they left behind in Finland. For many, this included building forest cottages with saunas, hay barns and other small outbuildings (Jordan & Kaups, 1989; Timothy, 1995), many of which later became the focus and substance of summer homes in the woods.

The western United States is also home to large cities and vast rural areas, and while not as widespread and common as in the Midwest and on the east coast, second homes in the traditional sense exist in many inter-esting places. Ranches are an important part of second home ownership in the West, as are beachfront homes in California, and cabins on the coasts of Oregon and Washington and in the mountains of Washington, Idaho, Colo-rado, Montana, Utah, Arizona, and New Mexico. These locations became popular in the 1920s and 30s as hunting huts, herding shelters and rustic getaways (Massey & Maxwell, 1993). Among the most popular styles are San Juan Island bungalows in the extreme north-west, the Santa Barbara ranch house in inland California, Malibu Beach houses and cabins on the coast, and Spanish revivalist architecture throughout the south-west (Irvine & Cunningham, 1990).

Contemporary Alternatives in Recreational Second Homes

In addition to the traditional forms of second home ownership in the United States, several other recent trends should also be noted, which have either replaced customary cabins and seaside cottages, or changed the routine holidaying patterns of American families.

Timeshares

One of the largest and most recent forms of second home ownership in the United States is timeshares – the fastest-growing segment of the accommodation sector in North America, with an average annual growth rate of between 14% and 17% (Woods, 2001). Timeshares have become particularly popular in North America since the late 1970s as more affordable alternatives to traditional second homes.

While programs, plans, designs, and functions vary from one place to another and from one company to another, timeshares are basically apartment- or condominium-style accommodation units. They are normally self contained, including living rooms, televisions and video/DVD machines, laundry facilities, and kitchens with cooking utensils and appliances included – something that appeals to self-catering holidaymakers. Some of the more up-market units even contain spas, entertainment centres and fireplaces, and provide amenities such as exercise rooms, arcades, saunas, and community swimming pools.

What makes timeshares unique is ownership. Consumers purchase periods of time at a specific unit, not the property itself. Property ownership rests with the collective group of users and management companies. Most timeshare owners purchase one or two weeks in a popular destination of their choice. If they choose not to use their week in that specific location, they can exchange locations and times for a fee, and in some programs they may collect points, which can be used in exchange for upgrades, hotel stays, use of timeshares in other locations, or other travel-related products.

The timeshare phenomenon had its roots in the early 1960s at a ski resort in the French Alps where a group of young friends, who could not afford to buy individual apartments, decided to purchase one collectively, which each could use at different times. The number of weeks assigned to each person was established by how much he was able to contribute towards the purchase. Within a few years, this idea began to spread in Europe and to the United States, where the first timeshares were developed in Florida in the late 1960s (Woods, 2001) and in Hawaii in the early 1970s (Butler, 1985).

Although timesharing began in Europe and has since spread to much of the world, the United States has long been the leader in developing timeshare properties and buying and selling individual units. In 1975 timeshare sales reached US$25 million in the United States. In 1970 the number reached US$800 million, and by 1982, the US industry had achieved more than US$1.5 billion in sales (Butler, 1985). In 1998, sales in the United States were calculated at nearly US$3.5 billion, in 1999 at US$3.7 billion, and in 2000 at approximately US$3.98 billion (American Resort Development Association, 1999; Woods, 2001).

According to the American Resort Development Association (1999),

155,000 families had purchased timeshares in some 500 resorts throughout the world in 1980. In 1999, however, the number had grown to 5 million families with ownership at more than 5000 resorts worldwide. The United States' share of the timeshare supply (1600 resorts with 89,000 units and 33% of the worldwide total) was owned by three million people at the beginning of 2000. In 1998, nearly 300,000 American families purchased domestic timeshares with a continued annual average of about 250,000 purchases (American Resort Development Association, 1999; Woods, 2001), demonstrating a kind of re-birth in the growth in popularity of timeshares during the late 1990s and early 2000s.

Some 40% of the total timeshares in the United States are located in the south-eastern part of the country. Florida alone is home to one quarter of the nation's developments (Woods, 2001). Other popular regions include California, Hawaii, Colorado, Texas, and Arizona (Timothy, forthcoming). While prices range from around US$6000 for a budget villa in low season to over US$50,000 for an extravagant unit during high season, the average price for a two-bedroom unit for one week in high season was US$13,017 in 1999. For a week in shoulder season, the figure was US$9042; and for a unit in low season, the average cost was US$8125 (American Resort Development Association, 1999).

While there are many reasons why people purchase a timeshare plan, the American Resort Development Association (1999) identified the following as the most important from the industry's perspective:

- high-quality accommodations;
- opportunities to exchange locations and times
- they are a good value;
- they provide many resort-like amenities;
- the companies are credible.

In addition to these, Butler (1985) identified four other reasons for the growth in popularity of timeshare villas as an alternative to traditional recreational property ownership.

(1) The initial purchase, while seemingly large to many people, is a relatively small investment compared to the amount required to buy a regular second home.
(2) There are no renovation, maintenance, or security duties associated with timeshare ownership. These are taken care of by the developer, and are funded by members' annual fees.
(3) The buyer purchases a segment of time, which will more likely be used than property, which may go unused for months at a time if it were owned by only one individual or family.

(4) Some people have viewed timeshare ownership as an investment that could increase in value over time.

Despite these perceived benefits, the US timeshare industry is not without problems, which Woods (2001) suggests centre on marketing, image, industry regulations, strategy issues, finances, personnel training, human resources, and legal matters. Table 9.3 lists many of the most significant concerns facing the timeshare industry in the United States today. One of the primary problems concerns marketing and image. During the early years of timeshare growth, developers became notorious for their forceful sales techniques and questionable ethics. This included issues such as selling timeshares under the pretence of real estate and promising that they would appreciate in value as well or better than property. This and other dubious practices led many states to enact laws and regulations in relation to the timeshare industry to insist that timeshares cannot be sold as investment opportunities. As there is no federal-level legislation regarding timeshares, these laws, however, vary from state to state, and are often in conflict one with another (Woods, 2001).

Mobile Second Homes

Recreational vehicles (RVs) have become increasingly popular in the United States over the past 25 years. Various forms of RVs have developed since the 1950s, and perhaps the most widespread is the class of campers, trailers, and motor homes. RVs are defined as vehicles that combine transportation and temporary living quarters for travel, recreation and camping (Recreation Vehicle Industry Association, 2003). Many American families now own RVs and, for those who do not, rentals are popular. For instance, summer rentals increased approximately 40% between 2001 and 2002 (Harris, 2002). Additionally, campground reservations were at an all-time high in the early 2000s, as more and more American families began looking for alternative vacation accommodations, which they could own, but which could also be mobilised. This reflects the increasing popularity of RV rentals and ownership, which in many cases is replacing the traditional recreational second home in favour of a movable and much less expensive alternative (Timothy, forthcoming).

In 2001, almost 10% of all US vehicle-owning households owned a recreational vehicle, totalling nearly seven million households. This represented a 7.8% increase over the previous four years and a 42% increase since 1980. Approximately 7.2 million RVs are utilised throughout the United States, and there are some 30 million RV enthusiasts, including owners and renters (Recreation Vehicle Industry Association, 2003). According to the Recreation Vehicle Industry Association (2003), the following factors have contributed to the growth in RV ownership in recent years:

- They are a flexible, convenient, and hassle-free way to see America. RV travellers enjoy the freedom and flexibility to go where and when they want without the worry of tight schedules, advance reservations, airport queues and luggage limitations. RV ownership allows travellers to take their second homes with them, instead of being limited to a specific location.
- With fully self-contained kitchens and baths, rooms that slide out, air conditioning, heat, running water, TVs, VCRs, stereo systems, and more, RVs provide travellers with all the amenities of home while on the road.
- RVs appeal to the family market. 'RVing' is a uniquely enjoyable way to travel as a family. According to some studies, frequent RV vacations as a family can foster an increased sense of togetherness and help improve familial communication.
- RV vacations are sometimes more affordable than travel by personal car, commercial airline or cruise ship. Since food preparation and sleeping are done in the RV, some estimates suggest that families can save up to 70% on travel expenses by using RVs. Likewise, recreational vehicles are nearly always less expensive than second homes (US$5000 to over US$100,000), and even some of the more expensive and luxurious RVs are less expensive than many stationary recreational houses.
- The lure of the outdoors leads many people to purchase RVs. Travellers can enjoy beaches, mountains, parks, small towns, famous tourist attractions, cities, and rural areas without leaving 'home'.
- RVs are also highly versatile. In addition to travel, camping and outdoor recreation, RVs are being used for a wide variety of other purposes, such as shopping, tailgate parties, and sporting events.
- Rental availability is another important appeal. Hiring or leasing an RV is a popular way to 'try before you buy'. The RV rental sector is a US$191 million industry and growing, according to the US Census of Retail Trade (Recreation Vehicle Industry Association, 2003).

Houseboats are another type of recreational vehicle that is also a form of accommodation and second home in the United States (Ragatz, 1970a). While these are very expensive to purchase compared with caravans and other smaller-scale wheeled 'seasonal homes', rentals and purchases of houseboats have become more popular in recent years (Jaakson, 1986), particularly in mountain lakes and in desert reservoirs where water-based recreation has become especially fashionable (Stroud, 1995; Rose, 2002).

Urban locations

Traditionally, the ideal location for second homes was far enough away from one's primary residence to be psychologically detached, but close enough to access by car in a relatively short span of time. Ragatz's (1970a, 1977) research found that most vacation housing in the United States in the 1970s was located approximately 150 miles (245 kilometres) from the central city. This distance meant that city dwellers had to travel a couple of hours to reach their destinations (Freedman, 2000). Distance has long been an important consideration in choosing locations because the use of second homes is restricted by time and distance of weekend travel (Jaakson, 1986: 369). When the children were out of school on summer breaks, families began to spend entire summers at second homes, and holiday weekends became popular for travelling to not-so-distant recreational properties in the countryside (Irvine & Cunningham, 1990).

Today, however, more and more rural residents have opted to purchase second homes in and near urban areas to be close to nightlife and cultural attractions (Stroud, 1995; Freedman, 2000). This pattern follows tradition, as in the past many farmers in rural America built small 'Sunday houses' in town that they used at weekends for social Saturday nights and church on Sunday morning before returning to their distant farms for the remainder of the week (Irvine & Cunningham, 1990: 3).

Seasonal migration and permanent residence

The primary reason for second home ownership, and even more so with seasonal migration, is physical comfort – escape from winter's cold and summer's heat (Irvine & Cunningham, 1990). Seasonal migration has become a common trend in the United States, the most noteworthy pattern being retirees who spend springs and summers at their primary places of residence and winters in the warmer states of the south-east and south-west. Among these so-called 'snowbirds' the most popular destinations for winter migration are Arizona, southern California, Florida, and Texas, primarily owing to their warm and temperate climates during the winter when the weather in the northern states is cold. Arizona, California and Texas are also popular destinations because of their proximity to Mexico, where older Americans can purchase pharmaceutical products and dental and medical services at a considerable discount compared with prices in the United States.

While seasonal migration in the United States has traditionally been seen as the province of retirees, today even younger Americans are travelling to second homes on a seasonal basis if their careers allow it. For instance, it is not uncommon for schoolteachers who teach from August to May to spend summers living at a second home working at a summer job or not working at all. According to Deller *et al.* (1997: 689) the pull of seasonal dwellings is drawing people into retirement earlier than normal, and recent estimates suggest that some 10 million American baby boomers, or 13%, will own second homes by the time they reach 65 (Stern, 1994).

A frequent pattern for people who spend time at second homes is to end up living there on a permanent basis. Most commonly, recreational dwellings become permanent homes when people retire (Godbey & Bevins, 1987), but natural amenities, such as climate and scenery, established social networks, familiarity with the culture and environment, employment opportunities, and nearness to family cause many people to move permanently to their former recreational home destinations before they officially retire (Groves & Timothy, 2001). Thus, a personal attachment to place develops which persuades people to make their seasonal home their permanent home (Cuba, 1989; Marshall & Longino, 1988; McHugh, 1990; Groves & Timothy, 2001).

Such place attachment, according to Groves and Timothy (2001) and Timothy (2002) can be explained as a process. The first step is when people become exposed to a location as a short-term vacationer, perhaps in conjunction with second home ownership. This often results in an individual travelling to the same place on a more long-term basis later in life, say for the winter season, after he/she retires. Finally, as mentioned above, people will often move permanently to their original vacation destination, especially if they already own a home there. Other authors have observed similar patterns (Godbey & Bevins, 1987; Cuba, 1989; McHugh, 1990).

Ownership abroad

Although the majority of American-owned second homes are in the United States, there has been a notable growth in ownership abroad (Chaplin, 1999). Many Americans are now buying second homes in foreign countries, most notably in Mexico, Canada, Italy, France and Spain (Go, 1988). Americans have long owned vacation homes in Mexico, particularly in the central and southern parts of the country around Acapulco, Puerto Vallarta and Lake Chapala. But more Americans have begun purchasing vacation homes closer to the border, particularly along the Baja coast and in budding new tourist resort communities such as Puerto Peñasco (Rocky Point), which lies only 100 kilometres from the US border and is a very popular beachfront location for residents of Arizona, California and Texas to build their vacation homes (Heltsley, 1997; Kelly, 2000).

In many parts of Canada, especially the Rocky Mountains of Alberta and British Columbia and along the lakeshores of Ontario, Americans comprise a large proportion of second home owners (Jaakson, 1986). This has become even more the case since the early 1990s, when the US dollar gained strength against the Canadian dollar, and Americans began crossing the border to 'shop' for summer cottages, which were considered inexpensive in relation to the cost of second homes in similar environments in the United States (Timothy, 2001).

Conclusions

Spending time at a second home has long been the desire of many Americans, and as the quote at the outset of the chapter attests, some commentators (e.g. Massey & Maxwell, 1993) have argued that it is a part of the American dream! Whether or not this is truly the case, the fact remains that second home ownership in the United States has grown to enormous levels during the past 40 years, with notable regional variations in style and concentration.

While the modern concept of second homes in the United States developed more recently than in Europe, it appears to have gone through a rather quick three-part evolutionary process during the 20th century, which has not occurred in some other parts of the world.

(1) Vacation properties in the US originally developed from structures that had utilitarian purposes (e.g. fishing shacks, hunting shelters, places of commerce in towns, and herding huts), were often physically isolated (e.g. in mountainous areas), and which the original owners kept in their families as seasonal destinations. Many of them were improved and passed down to other generations.

(2) Next came the development between the 1950s and the 1980s of quick and prefabricated dwellings in second home neighbourhoods. These were nearly always built for recreational purposes in high-amenity areas following the Second World War.

(3) The final trend is marked by the temporary nature of some second homes. Mobile second homes and timeshares dominate the latest trend, which grew in the 1960s–2000s and the 1970s–2000s respectively. These provide a more affordable alternative for millions of Americans, allowing them to possess a 'second home' for at least part of the year.

Of course each subsequent phase did not replace the previous one, for each trend continues even today. However, each phase increased in popularity over the previous one. Today, for instance, many more American families own motorised holiday homes than owned isolated cabins/cottages and recreational subdivision homes of the past.

The second home industry in the United States has been fraught with conflict and negative images since the 1960s, but this began to change with legislation that aimed to protect consumers, local communities, and environments from the unscrupulous tactics of developers. Alternative forms of vacation dwellings grew laregly as a result of these issues, and organisations that deal specifically with these alternative forms are thriving.

Another trend that appears to be on the increase is increased international travel by Americans. US residents are travelling abroad more now than ever before (Goeldner *et al.*, 2000). This may yet be another less expensive and more flexible alternative to owning fixed recreational property close to home. This is particularly so now that high-amenity acreage in much of the United States is increasingly expensive, particularly in the areas that have traditionally attracted second home developments (e.g. Florida, Arizona, California, Colorado, and the upper Great Lakes region). In some of these amenity-rich places, prices reach as high as US$200,000 to $500,000 for less than half a hectare. These inflated prices, which have far exceeded growth in average earnings, preclude many people from ever being able to afford recreational properties in these places, and have necessitated the development of alternative forms and developments in cheaper and less appealing locations.

Chapter 10

Recreational Second Homes in the South West of Western Australia

JOHN SELWOOD AND MATTHEW TONTS

We like the place as it is (or was), and dislike the notion of supplied
electricity, which will bring added expense and perhaps other undesirable
things such as a shop, or perhaps, god forbid, a tavern
Windy Harbour Respondent 45[1]

There is enough land for cheap second homes and (they) should be
encouraged rather than lock the whole coast up. Creates Employment.
Windy Harbour Respondent 15

Introduction

One of the strongest traditions in Australian society has been the so-called 'Great Australian Dream' of home ownership. Currently, around 70% of Australians own or are purchasing their homes (Beer & Badcock, 2000). Many Australians have also invested in second homes used for recreational purposes, such as holidaying or hobby farming (see Robertson, 1977; Wild, 1978; Selwood *et al.*, 1995; Curry *et al.*, 2001; Tonts & Grieve, 2002). This chapter discusses the development and widening distribution of second homes in Western Australia, which is particularly interesting in light of its relative isolation from the rest of the continent and, indeed, the rest of the world. We provide several examples of some of the more distinctive holiday home communities in the State and identify the most controversial issues confronting them as they evolve from modest facilities offering a relaxed getaway for primarily local populations to more fully developed entities servicing an increasingly diverse market.

Historical Perspectives

For more than a century, segments of the Western Australian population, be they rural or urban based, have invested in recreational second homes, predominantly in coastal locations. A century or so ago, for example, the newly-rich of Perth were building lavish second homes on the coast at Cottesloe, now almost in the heart of the city. But it was not until after World War 1 that the ownership of recreational homes became rather more common, when a buoyant economy and growing population saw a number of localities close to Perth become popular second home destinations. During the interwar period, other settlements emerged, such as City Beach, Scarborough, Trigg and Marmion, all within 30 kilometres of the central city and now well within Perth's urbanised area. Sporadic, but similar developments (such as Safety Bay) also sprang up south of Perth around Cockburn Sound. Small, two- and three-bedroom fibro-asbestos cottages were once prevalent in these areas, but most of them have now been demolished and replaced by much more substantial homes occupied by permanent residents. Further afield, a number of coastal towns made accessible by rail or by improved roads (such as Albany, Busselton, Rockingham and Mandurah) became popular summer resort communities that also catered to holidaymakers from Perth (see Figure 10.1). The city people were joined by increasing numbers of holidaymakers from rapidly-expanding agricultural regions that were also enjoying a high level of prosperity during the 1920s. Local residents provided temporary holiday accommodation for most of the visitors, although a number of holidaymakers acquired a second home at their favourite resort. Other holidaymakers elected to camp, and many coastal recreation reserves and private campgrounds catering to this demand were established during the inter-war period. Association, 1995; National Parks and Nature Conservation Authority, 1999; Selwood & May, 2001).

While the Great Depression and World War 2 saw a slowdown in second home development, the post-war economic boom was accompanied by a rapid expansion in the ownership of such properties. Strong commodity prices permitted many rural residents to acquire a second home in established coastal towns or in Perth, while other farmers of the state's central and south-western districts 'bush-bashed' their way to the coast to establish a number of more informal second home settlements at sheltered anchorages that offered good recreational fishing. They were joined by increasing numbers of salmon harvesters and crayfishermen, who were seeking more convenient access to their fishing grounds as demand for their products increased. As with the settlements closer to Perth, these more remote communities usually had their origins as campsites, and were frequently located on Crown reserves created for that purpose. However, the camps gradually became more permanent as holidaymakers began to construct basic shacks and cabins in order to avoid shipping in all of their gear each season.

Although they were illegal, state and local authorities initially tolerated development of the squatter settlements, and the shack owners soon began to improve the comfort and quality of their accommodation. Despite the lack of basic services, such as sewerage and electricity, the shacks were often well appointed and became notable for their vernacular architecture, generally distinguished by corrugated iron construction and water tanks made of the same material. Many of the more inaccessible squatter shack communities still survive, primarily because of a lack of resources to deal with them, and a relatively *laissez-faire* attitude in government, many of whose officers have themselves been shack owners (Selwood & May, 2001). However, many of the former squatter settlements have disappeared as state and local authorities became concerned about their proliferation. A

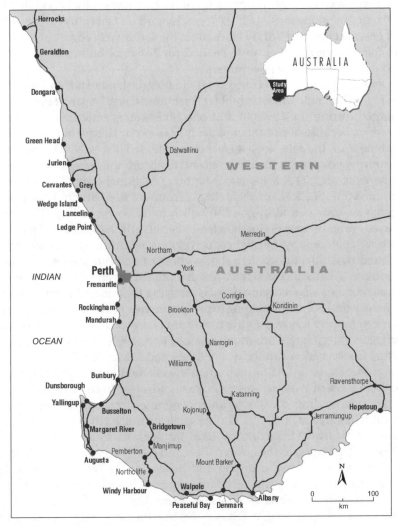

Figure 10.1 Second home communities in south-western Western Australia

few were upgraded to legal townsite status, and the squatters were encouraged to relocate on to properly surveyed lots with freehold title. As a result, a number of holiday towns serviced with appropriate infrastructure were established during the 1960s, such as Lancelin, Cervantes, Jurien Bay, and Ledge Point (Clark & Selwood, 1970). During the 1990s, there was another round of eradicating squatter shack settlement and of expanding townsites, with the squatter era being commemorated by the erection of 'heritage' signboards at former sites. Townsites generated out of the squatter communities still contain high proportions of second homes (Selwood & May, 2001). At other locations, such as Horrocks north of Geraldton (Cole, 1991), and Peaceful Bay and Windy Harbour in the south-west corner of the state, less formal communities were created for seasonal homes on leasehold land managed by local government.

One example of a surviving coastal squatter settlement is the community at Grey, on the State's newly dubbed 'Turquoise Coast' north of Perth. Grey emerged during the 1950s and at one time was gazetted as a townsite. However, because of a number of delays caused by debate over the appropriateness of the site, lots were never released for sale. The eventual outcome was to cancel the townsite and to absorb the area, which by then contained over 200 shacks, into Nambung National Park. The squatters were given notice to clear their shacks from the site, although they were given a six-year period of grace in which to do so. Since then, they have enjoyed annual extensions of their leases because the locality is still virtually inaccessible except by four-wheel drive vehicles. Although several of the squatters have abandoned their shacks, most are still clinging on in hopes of a reprieve. The local community association, led by an articulate group of people in professional occupations, is lobbying for this on the grounds that the association is thereby helping to protect the area from vandalism and that their community is now a tourism attraction because of its uniqueness and heritage value (Grey Community Association, 1995; National Parks and Nature Conservation Authority, 1999; Selwood & May, 2001).

Another example of a former squatter settlement is Peaceful Bay, on the southern coast of Western Australia. Pastoralists who ran their cattle down to the surrounding coastal scrub for summer grazing opened up the Peaceful Bay area in the 1930s. The camping areas used by these pastoralists were subsequently taken up by local farmers, many of them from the wheat–sheep region to the north of Peaceful Bay, who would trek down to the coast for a holiday, camping and fishing at the relatively-protected anchorage. When the local road board upgraded the track into the campsite in 1954, some of the regular visitors began erecting shacks and this, in turn, resulted in the creation of a 'Class A' reserve for camping purposes and a subdivision plan to regulate the allocation of lots. By 1963, some 90 lots had been released on 10-year leases. Additional lots were released through the

1960s. Services and infrastructure were also upgraded during this period, with significant improvements in water supply, drainage works and road construction. These improvements were partly funded by a State Tourism Development Authority grant designed to improve tourist facilities in the district and to exert more control over coastal development. Since then, the proportion of people from metropolitan Perth who have second homes at Peaceful Bay has risen quite dramatically, especially since the recent addition of another subdivision offering a 25-year lease on the lots. The more extended leases are helping to transform the settlement into a more up-market community featuring brick-and-tile homes instead of the less obtrusive, vernacular corrugated iron, fibro-asbestos, or timber-clad shacks of the earlier generation (Selwood *et al.*, 1995).

Westward of Peaceful Bay, the district north of Windy Harbour was first opened up in the 1920s, based on the timber industry and farming. Windy Harbour became a popular place for camping and fishing soon after the district was settled and this led to a recreation reserve being established there. As happened elsewhere, in the late 1940s a number of locals began to construct squatter shacks on the reserve. Since there was no formal planning of the settlement, shacks were simply constructed on sites that appealed to the builder. This is reflected in the oldest part of the settlement, which is widely referred to as Chinatown because of its haphazard, but appealing layout and vernacular architecture. By the mid-1950s, about 80 such shacks had been constructed (Evans, 1992). Government authorities became increasingly concerned about the development of illegal shacks and from about 1953 began to 'regularise' the settlement. This included surveying blocks, formalising streets and establishing a system of annual one-year leases for the second home owners. The settlement continued to expand slowly during the second half of the 20th century, and by 2002 consisted of around 220 second homes.

Alongside the development of squatter settlements, the growth of Western Australia's established coastal towns was particularly rapid during the post-war period. Towns such as Mandurah and Busselton were transformed from sleepy coastal settlements into thriving holiday centres containing significant numbers of second homes. This growth was fuelled by a number of factors.

(1) The rapid growth and prosperity of the Perth metropolitan area created a population with the financial capacity to purchase a second home. Major contributors to this were the minerals boom of the 1960s and 1970s, and the increasing amount of capital that became available during the 1980s as superannuation funds began to mature.

(2) The Australian taxation system has provided a number of tax breaks for people owning investment properties, including recreational second homes.

(3)   A strong agricultural sector meant that an increasing number of farmers invested in established towns, as well as the squatter settlements described above.

(4)   An increasing number of prospective retirees began to invest in recreational second homes with a view to migrating permanently to coastal locations.

(5)   Improvements in road construction and transport technology meant that many coastal areas became increasingly accessible.

Over the past 20 years or so, there has also been a growth in second homes in inland areas, particularly the wetter and more scenic and accessible parts of the State. The Avon Valley, some 80–100 kilometres from Perth is a case in point. A combination of accessibility, affordable property, historic towns and local planning regulations has stimulated the subdivision of larger farms into smaller hobby farms. The area has become a haven for those looking to escape the city, although in this area significant numbers of people now commute to Perth on a regular basis. Even in more remote parts of the south-west of the State, the number of people owning second homes in inland areas has increased significantly. One reason for this has been the large number of farm properties created through Premier James Mitchell's ill-fated Group Settlement Scheme of the 1920s. This scheme was designed to establish closer settlement in the heavily forested areas of the south-west, converting the forests into small dairy farms that would reduce the State's reliance on imported foodstuffs, would increase population and would contribute more generally to the state economy. Ironically, the group settlers were frequently the people who first established the coastal resort settlements now so much in demand. However, for the most part, mainly due to circumstances beyond their control, they failed as farmers, and their partially cleared holdings are now considered prime targets for country living (Curry *et al.*, 2001). An obvious attraction of owning a hobby farm is that, if it has an annual turnover of more than $20,000, and meets all the other criteria of the Australian Taxation Office for a legitimate agricultural venture, the owner is eligible for a range of tax breaks and discounts.

Geographic Linkages

There is a strong and changing geographical dimension in the ownership and use of second homes in Western Australia. For much of the 20th century, second homes tended to be located relatively close to the primary residence of the owner. Given the state of many local roads and the capabilities of early motor transport, this is not surprising. For people living in Perth during the 1920s, this meant constructing second homes in places such as City Beach, less than 20 kilometres from the city centre, but which at that time still presented the challenge of navigating the rudimentary 'plank' road across sand dunes to the beach (Selwood, 1981).

A similar situation existed in rural districts. For example, at Windy Harbour second homes were built mainly by people living in the nearby communities of Northcliffe, Pemberton and Manjimup, all of which are within 80 kilometres of the settlement. Much the same geographic linkages are evident today, although to a lesser extent. In 2002, of a total of 220 second homes in the settlement, only 62 (28%) are owned by people from outside these three communities. Ownership patterns thus still reflect the importance of Windy Harbour as an affordable and accessible holiday destination for local residents. Another reason why there is a low proportion of owners from outside of the immediately surrounding district is the settlement's relative isolation. Windy Harbour is still around seven hours' drive from Perth, which is a relatively long haul, even over a long weekend.

It is clear, however, that for a number of coastal settlements, the ownership patterns of second homes have become increasingly dispersed over the past two decades or so. Significant improvements in the road network and transport technology have made many coastal locations more accessible to a larger population and particularly to residents of the metropolitan area. Extensive areas of the State, including many scenic parts of the countryside, have now been incorporated into Perth's urban field. The result has been an influx of second home owners into localities that had once been regarded as too isolated to attract such development. This process is akin to Blumenfeld's 'tidal wave of metropolitan expansion' and is typical of the peripheral expansion of tourism destinations as inner zones reach capacity or are priced out of the reach of most holidaymakers (Blumenfeld, 1954; Lundgren, 1989: Selwood, et al., 1995; also see Chapter 1).

A very good example here is the area around the town of Denmark on the south coast. For much of the period after World War 2, the Denmark region was important as a holiday location for people living in nearby rural communities and as a summer camping destination for holidaymakers from Perth. However, improvements in transport and the 'discovery' of the area in the 1970s, 1980s and 1990s by a larger urban population have seen it experience a rapid expansion in second home development. Much of this development has occurred in existing coastal settlements, such as Peaceful Bay, Walpole and the Denmark townsite, although second homes are being constructed further and further inland on small rural blocks and hobby farms. Most of the newer development is driven by people from Perth. A recent survey of 236 second home owners in Denmark showed that 158 (67%) had their primary residence in the Perth metropolitan area, about 400 kilometres away. Whereas 30 years ago it took 8–9 hours by car to get to Denmark, improvements in the transport have seen this reduced to a little over four hours.

This expanding urban field has not only had an impact on smaller communities such as Denmark, it has also contributed to development in larger, more established vacation centres. For example Albany, 50 kilometres east of Denmark, is a major port town and regional centre with a population of more than 20,000 people that has become an increasingly popular location for second homes. As of the 2001 census, it was estimated that around 900 (12.5%) of Albany's 7240 dwellings were second homes. While a combination of scenic coastal and inland environments, a mild climate, good swimming and fishing and the availability of services have long made it an attractive holiday and retirement destination, Bradley (2002) suggests Albany has become an increasingly popular place for Perth residents to invest in second homes, largely as a result of it's good highway linkage with the metropolitan area.

Improvements in accessibility have also contributed to the expansion of second home ownership in inland agricultural districts. In a study of the growth of hobby farms in Chittering Valley region of Western Australia, roughly an hour's drive north-east of Perth, Edmonds (1998) found that the improved accessibility of the area had encouraged a number of Perth residents to establish 'weekender' recreational, rural retreats. Most of these are located within 100 kilometres of their owner's permanent residence. Other factors in the purchase decision were the scenic environment and the low cost of land relative to Perth.

The Question of Overdevelopment

Increasing pressure for development over recent years has frequently contributed to substantial local economic, social and environmental change in the affected areas. Former wilderness or farming areas are being converted into extensive rural retreats (Tonts & Grieve, 2002). At Eagle Bay, which until a short time ago was virtually deserted, luxurious second homes now dominate the landscape. Outside Denmark, the pristine Nullaki Peninsula has been subdivided into 20-hectare land parcels that are being marketed into Japan for second homes. A number of towns are now being rapidly transformed from relatively modest localities for inexpensive holidays to upmarket and highly commercialised resorts. Denmark, Peaceful Bay and Windy Harbour are but three minor examples of a much wider trend. Sanders (2000) has shown that the process is much further advanced in the more accessible resorts such as Prevelly, Gracetown and Yallingup in the Leewin-Naturaliste Region. In the coastal town of Busselton, the local authority has been actively encouraging the development of international standard resorts. Very recently, a major developer has sought approval for the massive expansion of Jurien Bay townsite on the 'Turquoise Coast', north of Perth. The proposal, contingent upon completion of the planned coastal highway, envisages the present community of 1200 growing to 25,000 over the next 40 years to become the northern equivalent of Dunsborough to the south (Buggins, 2002). However, as Butler (1980), Mitchell (1998) and others have pointed out, these developments can destroy the very attributes that make a place attractive.

A recent survey by the authors of 442 second home owners in four rural localities (Bridgetown, Denmark, Hopetoun and Windy Harbour) indicated that there are numerous concerns about the impact of excessive development in those communities. For example, the following comments were offered by second home owners in Denmark:

> Over recent years there has been too much emphasis on progress which is aimed at tourism which in turn puts much pressure on the fragile environment, when more attention should be given to retain the real atmosphere of peace and tranquillity. (Denmark Respondent 57)

> Not against development in Denmark, but some proposed (and existing) developments are out of character with the area. If we wanted a soulless suburban block we would have bought in one of the many developments in Perth. Denmark has a unique identity which is slowly being whittled away as land is carved up by opportunistic money grabbers. (Denmark Respondent 53)

A number of respondents drew comparisons with the nearby towns of Margaret River and Dunsborough, which have experienced particularly rapid growth over the past 15 years and are no longer low-profile centres for local holidaymakers, but places of mass tourism and extensive commercial development:

> Denmark is a unique and special area, that hopefully will not become another 'Dunsborough or Margaret River'. Overcrowded and overdeveloped. We would like to see Denmark retain its quaintness and yet developed enough to attract sufficient tourists to maintain funding to keep the area pristine. (Denmark Respondent 167)

Second homes in Dunsborough have led to overdevelopment which has destroyed much of the value Dunsborough had so that the once close knit community is now swallowed up by the excessive crowds that visit so that now the country atmosphere of Dunsborough has gone together with many of its scenic beaches ... Upmarket resorts have pushed out the family holidaymaker.. I would hate to see Denmark go the same way due to developmental greed. (Denmark Respondent 192)

These comments highlight one of the key challenges facing localities that are experiencing second home and tourist development: the challenge of promoting development that maintains the character of an area and, at the same time, retaining the fundamental economic, social and environmental characteristics that make it attractive. One of the problems is that there are inevitably demands for further development in second home localities. Furthermore, these often stem, not just from commercially driven motives, but from second home owners themselves. A very good example rests in the small settlement of Windy Harbour. The townsite has no shops, only the caretaker's cabin where a few emergency supplies can be obtained. The only other service of any significance is the volunteer sea rescue, which operates during the holiday season. Furthermore, the community has no electricity supply, with most homes powered by privately-owned diesel generators that must be switched off by 10pm each evening. A number of second home owners in Windy Harbour argue that much of the settlement's charm and attractiveness was associated with its remoteness and lack of modern facilities: that the absence of electricity discourages development, and that this is important if the place is to retain its character.

> Windy Harbour is more than just a holiday home for us, it is a way of life, no phones or electricity have kept the community spirit alive and made it a wonderful place to bring the children for holidays. (Windy Harbour Respondent 51)

> We like the place as it is (or was), and dislike the notion of supplied electricity, which will bring added expense and perhaps other undesirable things such as a shop, or perhaps, god forbid, a tavern. (Windy Harbour Respondent 45)

These views, however, tend to be in the minority. Many second home owners in Windy Harbour are convinced that the provision of electricity and other services would contribute to economic development and generate employment in the area. Some of the responses included:

There is enough land for cheap second homes and (they) should be encouraged rather than lock the whole coast up. Creates Employment. (Windy Harbour Respondent 15)

> I would like to see the following: (1) Windy Harbour get power; (2) make it the newest town in Western Australia; (3) open up more blocks; (4) find a better water supply. I think Windy Harbour could be the saviour of the Manjimup Shire after the failure of our timber industry. Job creation e.g. caravan park, tavern, proper jetty for fishermen, shop, coolrooms for salmon, tourist guides (Windy Harbour Respondent 27).

Similar development pressures exist in virtually all of Western Australia's coastal second home localities and, in many instances generate considerable political conflict (Selwood & May, 1992, 2001; Sanders, 2000; Priskin, 2001). Tonts and Grieve (2002) identified similar conflicts inland around the town of Bridgetown. Located on the Blackwood River, some 270 kilometres from Perth, Bridgetown has an abundance of heritage architecture and is surrounded by an attractive farming landscape. Many of Bridgetown's second homes are located on small rural holdings. In some parts of the district, the traditional agricultural landscape has been radically altered by subdivisions, suburban-style housing, access roads and electricity pylons. The concern of many permanent residents and second home owners alike is that this type of development is not only ruining the landscape but, in the long run, will undermine property values and tourism development potential. The challenge facing local and state authorities is to ensure that development is sustainable.

Regulating Second Home Development

One of the characteristics of the Australian planning system is that much of the responsibility for land-use planning is devolved to the level of local government. While this means that local authorities are in a strong position to guide development, it can also result in a lack of consistency in planning guidelines throughout the state. In the context of second homes, this means that there is little uniformity in the way in which development is regulated. One local government may be pro-development and encourage the subdivision of new second home sites, while a neighbouring authority's aim might be to restrict development and preserve the social and environmental character of a particular locality.

In a number of the larger coastal settlements, planning tends to have been driven by pro-growth sentiment. At Busselton, for example, the local authority has encouraged the subdivision of old agricultural lots to cater to the demand for second homes and the development of international standard resorts (Sanders, 2000). In towns such as Mandurah, Busselton, Yallingup and Kalbarri, property developers have begun to provide for increasing numbers of large condominiums, suburban-style subdivisions and resort complexes for wealthier segments of the local market and, in some cases, international second home owners. Golf courses and other sporting facilities, health clubs and marinas are just some of the infrastructure that can accompany these newer high profile developments.

In contrast, a number of other local authorities have attempted to maintain the low-profile character of second home localities. The Shire of Manjimup, for example, which is responsible for the management of Windy Harbour, has developed a strategy to maintain the integrity and character of the settlement as a family holiday destination. Its 1999 Management Plan for the settlement contains guidelines seeking to prevent over-development and destruction of the area's cultural heritage. Some of the guidelines include: restrictions on the use of bricks, concrete and clay tiles in constructing housing, with a preference for the use of timber or other similar construction materials; limiting the height of buildings to one storey; and preventing individual leaseholds from being fenced off.

Authors of the Management Plan also assert that maintaining property under lease, rather than converting to freehold, will be a powerful tool in controlling land use, regulating building development and thereby retaining Windy Harbour's character. Despite this, the shire is bowing to pressure from leaseholders and gradually shifting from 1-year leases to 21-year leases contingent on the dwelling meeting higher standards, particularly with regard to building safety and sewage disposal. Ironically, while the Windy Harbour Management Plan aims to preserve the character of the settlement, the upgrading requirements and their associated costs will pressure the shire to allow further development. Currently, the political balance within the shire is towards a 'preservationist' approach. However, a shift in this political balance has the potential to bring major changes in planning guidelines and the nature of development. The situation facing Windy Harbour is not unique, and characterises a number of Western Australian local governments (see, for example, Tonts & Grieve, 2002).

Conclusions

The record of second home ownership in Western Australia goes back for more than a century, but it was not until after World War 2 when rapid population growth, prosperity and increased mobility began to put pressure on higher-amenity localities. It was only then that any need to address the issue became apparent. Prior to that time, those who wished to spend a holiday at some favourite location could readily find themselves a place to stay, whether it be rental accommodation, a second home, or a spot to camp. Camping was virtually unrestricted on Crown land for many years, to the extent that the freedom to do so was perceived by many to be a right. This attitude was responsible for the proliferation of holiday squatter settlements in the 1950s and this led, in turn, to the creation a number of coastal townsites designed primarily to service the demand for second homes. Although much of the demand for second homes was subsequently absorbed by coastal townsites, squatter settlements continue to exist in localities not readily accessible except by four-wheel-drive vehicles. Scenic inland locations have also become increasingly attractive to second home owners. Indeed, the factors contributing to increasingly dispersed patterns of second home ownership are identical to those that have given rise to counter-urbanisation – the more permanent migration of people from urban to rural regions. Explanations for counter-urbanisation include:

(1) the emergence of an increasingly affluent society able to act on their preferences for rural living;
(2) area-specific factors, such as high quality amenity landscapes;
(3) reduced distance friction associated with improved transport technologies, which has permitted an extension of the urban field into widely-dispersed networks that are nonetheless generally still metropolitan-focused (see Hugo & Smailes, 1985: 12; Hugo, 1994: 15).

One of the more interesting characteristics of second homes in Western Australia is the diversity in the type and value of dwellings. Whereas some of the earliest homes were quite large and luxuriously appointed, most were typically modest, ranging from the corrugated iron squatter shack, through the rehabilitated timber-worker or group-settlers' timber cottage, to the pattern-built, fibro-asbestos home. Over the past two decades, in some localities however, there has been a proliferation of larger, more upmarket second homes that are indistinguishable from the standard suburban house. Other purpose built-second homes run the gamut from the caravan permanently parked on-site in a caravan park, through the small, self-contained condominium, to the palatial country mansion on its landed estate. In part, the selection of newer generation second homes styles and their location has been the resident's choice. However, the regulatory authorities will play an increasingly important role in determining the future, especially as they drive up development standards and more tightly manage and protect the state's higher amenity areas.

Note

1. The quotes in this chapter are from second home owners in the rural localities of Denmark and Windy Harbour who took part in a survey conducted by the authors. To preserve their anonymity, the respondents were identified by numbers only.

Chapter 11

A Hidden Giant: Second Homes and Coastal Tourism in South-Eastern Australia

WARWICK FROST

Introduction

Venus Bay is a small coastal town, 170 kilometres south-east of Melbourne, Australia. At the most recent census (1996), it had a resident population of 385. It also contained 978 private dwellings, of which 795 were unoccupied at the mid-winter date on which the census was conducted. There are also nearly 2000 vacant blocks zoned for residential development. Venus Bay has four real estate agents and two restaurants, but has no petrol retailer, post office, bank, school, doctor, water supply, sewage system or rubbish collection service. House designs, block sizes and street patterns generally follow the conventions of Melbourne's outer suburbs. However, most houses are surrounded by native bush, 30-kilogram wombats burrow underneath and 1.5-metre kangaroos may be seen in streets and gardens at sunset.

Venus Bay is a town of second homes (or holiday homes, as they are typically known in Australia). It is one of a series of second home towns that form a belt along the coast between 80 and 200 kilometres either side of the city of Melbourne (population 3 million). Whilst in some of its characteristics it is an extreme example, the unusual features listed above occur to varying degrees in most of these second home towns.

In terms of scale, second homes are a major component of domestic tourism in Australia. In 2000, nearly 4 million visits and 12 million nights by domestic holidaymakers were at second homes. At 5% of visits and 8% of nights, this was the fifth largest category of accommodation for domestic holidaymakers (BTR, 2001). For 2000–2001, the gross value added of second home tourism was estimated as $A1605 million, or 6% of all tourism gross value added (ABS, 2002). This was nearly double the output of travel agency and tour operator services and greater than casinos, gambling, libraries, museums, arts and other entertainment services combined.

Second homes were particularly favoured by intrastate rather than interstate visitors. In 2000, only 2% of interstate visitors used second homes, in contrast, 7% of intrastate visitors used them. The highest level of second home usage by intrastate visitors was in Victoria, where there were nearly 1.2 million visitors to second homes (9% of all Victoria's intrastate visitors). Indeed for Victorian intrastate visitors, second homes were the equal third most popular form of accommodation (BTR, 2001).

Significant local and regional variations are masked when we consider state averages. As discussed in more detail below, the second home belt on the coast near Melbourne may contain at least 15,000 second homes, and these accommodate 10–30% of domestic visitors to these areas. Even the latter figure underestimates the scale of second home usage, on two counts. First, as an annual figure it ignores seasonal highs such as summer school holidays. Second, it does not count visits to the second homes of friends or relatives.

However, despite its gigantic scale, the second homes sector is generally ignored in discussions of Australian tourism. While researchers have considered second homes in Western Australia (see Chapter 10 by Selwood and Tonts), there are no similar studies for the eastern states. Second homes in the south-east have been briefly discussed in historical surveys of tourism (Inglis, 1999; Frost, 2000) and in works concerned with coastal protection (Branton, 1977; VPIRG, 1977). However, second homes are generally absent from the mainstream of the Australian academic tourism literature. Nor are they considered in the various national and state tourism strategies. They have been mentioned in some regional plans, but usually only to acknowledge their existence, size and lack of appropriate information (e.g. Department of Infrastructure, 2001; Parks Victoria, 2001). Furthermore, it is surprising that the method of estimating the output of second homes adopted for the national Tourism Satellite Accounts has stimulated little debate – see Frost (2003) for a discussion of these calculations. Finally, while geographers and economic historians have studied the urban and suburban growth of Melbourne and the rise of the post World War 2 consumer society in great detail, they have stopped short at considering how second homes relate to these developments.

We can only speculate on the reasons for this lack of interest in second homes, for those researchers who fail to mention them do not give any reasons for their omissions. However, the most likely explanation is that second homes are seen as sitting outside the conventional tourism industry. They are not commercial operations, their owners are not tourism businesses, they do not engage with tourism associations or destination marketing authorities, and they do not appear to generate employment or other direct economic effects. As such, it is easy to overlook them and their impact.

The purpose of this chapter is to reveal the hidden giant that is the second home belt on the coast of south-eastern Australia. The chapter is divided into four sections. The first examines the dynamic nature of the second home belt as the pressures of suburbanisation and residential tourism have forced second homes further and further away from Melbourne. The second attempts to measure the scale of this second home belt at the current time. The third describes the main features of second home towns and usage, drawing on Venus Bay as an example. The fourth considers the problems of providing services (and paying for them) to areas with growing numbers of second homes.

An Expanding Belt

Today, the belt of second homes that surrounds Melbourne is not where it was a hundred years ago. Historically, it has undergone changes, not only in location, but in form and usage patterns. In simple terms it has been expanding, being pushed further and further out by the pressure of Melbourne's urban growth.

In the 1860s, second homes tended to be on Port Phillip Bay, within 5–10 kilometres of the city centre. With the economic boom of the 1880s, second homes shifted further along the shores of the Bay, in particular to the fashionable resorts of Queenscliff and Sorrento, which were 60 kilometres by boat from Melbourne (Inglis, 1999). For historian Andrea Inglis, this leap illustrates how visiting the beach in the 19th century was concerned, 'not so much with pleasure and amusement as with ... the demonstration of status and class' (Inglis, 1999: 22). Initially, second homes were monopolised by the elite, who described their accommodation grandly as, 'marine villas' and 'summer villas'. They were willing to locate themselves some distance from Melbourne in order to distance themselves from day-trippers (Inglis, 1999).

Late in the 19th century, railway expansion down the eastern side of Port Phillip Bay opened up a large area to a new type of second home owner. Middle class office workers and shopkeepers found they could afford seaside blocks where they could build simple shacks. Visits were mainly confined to weekends (hence 'weekender' as another term for second home) or owners could even commute daily by train during the summer (Brady, 1911). By the beginning of the 20th century, most second homes were 20–40 kilometres from the city, though they finished abruptly at Frankston, where the railway left the coast (Brady, 1918). The effect as described by travel writer Edwin Brady on his 1911 adventure of driving a motor car around Port Phillip Bay was, 'mile after mile of beach and bower, charming seaside suburbs, restful marine resorts, out of town houses, weekend cottages and camping grounds' (Brady, 1911: 33).

In addition, after World War 1 there was a boom in second homes in the nearby mountain ranges. High profile owners of mountain second homes included the Prime Minister Billy Hughes and the painter Arthur Streeton. As with the coastal belt, second homes in the mountains appealed to a wide cross section of society, even the gangster Squizzy Taylor holidayed in one (Frost, 2000). A further category was the grand country houses of the wealthy, where the owners could pretend to be English squires. Mount Macedon, where the Governor had his second home, was particularly popular.

As Melbourne grew, the second homes migrated further away from the city. In 1918 Brady described the coast from Beaumaris to Mordialloc (20–25 kilometres), as having, 'an atmosphere half country and half suburb'. His comment that, 'the weekender has not yet destroyed their quaintness' revealed his worry that they soon would (Brady, 1918: 306–8). The primary concentration of second homes was now between 25 and 40 kilometres out, 'from Mordialloc to Frankston the sun-loving Australian has found a curve of congenial shore whereon to erect hundreds of little bungalows and weekend places' (Brady, 1918: 308). As development grew, concerns were raised about the environment. In 1928 the bushwalking writer Robert Croll wrote that the scrub was now full of houses and, 'the astounding growth of settlement between Mordialloc and Carrum threatens seriously the fine tea-tree [*leptospermum*] tract that edges this perfect beach' (Croll, 1928: 39–40).

The economic boom after World War 2 transformed this second home belt into suburbia. The surge in population, the rise in car ownership and the development of an industrial zone in the south-east combined to make this land too valuable for second homes. A shortage of new building materials in the late 1940s and early 1950s encouraged many to buy cheaply-built shacks for permanent homes.

The second home belt was pushed further down the bay, to Rye and Rosebud (70–80 kilometres out), on to the Bellarine Peninsula on the western side of the bay (100 kilometres out) and to resorts facing the ocean such as Torquay, Barwon Heads, Ocean Grove, Flinders and Phillip Island (90–140 kilometres out). Previously these towns had been fairly small, for they lacked rail connections, but the spread of car ownership now made them accessible.

The rapid post-war spread of the second home belt was accompanied by significant social and cultural changes. Employees typically were given two weeks' paid leave, generally just after Christmas, which resulted in massive population peaks at second home towns during this period. Many new second home towns had surf beaches, and these proved popular for swimming and the new sport of surfing. Along the west coast, particularly at Torquay and Bells Beach, an American-influenced surf culture took hold. Recreational fishing became popular. In contrast to the growth of these new second home towns, the elite resorts of Sorrento and Queenscliff declined, their conspicuous consumption villas now seen as old fashioned and impossible to run now that servants were too expensive to hire.

As this new second home belt filled up, developers subdivided farmland for new *estates*. This was the case at Venus Bay. While there was a long history of small parties camping at Venus Bay, because there was no public access, they typically were friends of local farmers (Charles & Loney, 1989).

In 1960 the Evergreen Estate, which consisted of four dairy farms, was sold to a developer. This was subdivided into 1500 blocks, which was later increased to 2800 (Charles & Loney, 1989). Development was slow at first; between 1960 and 1972 an average of only nine building permits a year were approved (Branton, 1977: 3).

As second homes expanded rapidly, there was a reaction, primarily due to their environmental impact (Branton, 1977; VPIRG, 1977). The Victorian Government acted by protecting large areas of coastal land, particularly through the creation of the Angahook-Lorne State Park (1987, currently being upgraded to a National Park), Point Nepean National Park (1988, expanded to the Mornington Peninsula National Park in 1995), French Island National Park (1997) and Cape Liptrap Coastal Park (1997). In 1985 the Victorian Government froze private land sales at the Summerland Estate on Phillip Island and began a buy back scheme with the intention of removing all second homes and so protecting the adjacent Penguin Parade.

The second home belt is now in turn ringed by a belt of National and State Parks. New estates will have to come from farmland rather from than bush land, which may increase the potential for tensions within local communities. This reduced supply of new second home sites, coupled with increasing suburban pressure and continued demand for second homes, has resulted in significant price increases in the last few years (*The Age*, 2001, 2002).

Measuring the Second Home Belt

Measuring the extent and growth of second homes in Australia is difficult, as governments do not distinguish them from primary houses (compare this with other countries, such as Sweden, as outlined in Chapter 16 by Müller). In particular, local government makes no distinction between first and second homes for purposes of planning zoning or levying property taxes. In 1986, the Federal Government did collect data on second homes as part of the Census of Population and Housing. However, even though this 1986 information is used to calculate the production value of second homes for the Tourism Satellite Account (Frost, 2003), it has not been collected since.

Two statistical collections do provide data on second homes. Individually they have some limitations, but combined they provide a reasonable idea of the extent and location of second home usage. Furthermore, being national collections, their results are available for other parts of Australia. They are the data on unoccupied dwellings from the five-yearly Census of Population and Housing and accommodation at own properties for domestic overnight visitors in the annual National Visitor Survey.

The Census of Population and Housing is conducted on a weeknight in the middle of winter. The rationale behind this is to maximise the number of informants at their primary home and minimise those travelling or at second homes. Population figures for second home towns therefore reflect their permanent inhabitants rather than their holiday peaks.

The Census does record whether a private dwelling was occupied or not. In the 1996 Census, 10% of all private dwellings in Victoria were unoccupied (calculated from ABS, 1998: 28). Accordingly, second home towns should record levels of unoccupied dwellings well above the state average. Table 11.1 lists for Victoria the 14 towns of more than 500 dwellings that had 50% or more of their dwellings unoccupied.

At 81%, Venus Bay had the highest level of unoccupied dwellings. All of the 14 towns were coastal towns. They included 13,000 unoccupied dwellings and, when smaller towns are also counted, this suggests at least 15,000 second homes in the coastal belt. Some 13 of the towns were in the second home belt between 75 and 170 kilometres from Melbourne. Indeed 10 were in a smaller radius of between 110 and 145 kilometres. We may hypothesise that at less than 110 kilometres from Melbourne there were sufficient commuters to compete for houses. At more than 145 kilometres, the distance from Melbourne was too great and potential second home purchasers were discouraged. The exception was Loch Sport, where the attractions of boating and fishing on the Gippsland Lakes were sufficiently strong to encourage second homes.

For non-coastal areas, the only comparable rates were for the old gold towns of Blackwood (57%, but with less than 500 dwellings), Daylesford (30%) Bright (25%) and Maldon (22%) – calculated from ABS, 1998: 28–37. As these are all popular tourism destinations, it is assumed these high rates do indicate second homes rather than just vacant housing. Another area of possible second home usage is the snowfields. However, snow resorts such as Mount Buller were not counted as urban centres in the Census.

The National Visitor Survey records the type of accommodation used by domestic overnight visitors. It is published for a number of large regions. Unfortunately, the sheer size of some of these regions, while improving reliability, often reduces the specificity of the data (Frost & Foster 2002; Zanon & Frost, 2002). However, it is possible to reprocess the unit records (i.e. raw data) to calculate data at the level of local government areas and even sections of these. Table 11.2 lists 13 of these smaller areas, the number of overnight visits they received in 1999, and the main types of accommodation used.

The highest level of second home usage was 26% in the southern section of the Mornington Peninsula. The Shires of Surf Coast and Bass Coast recorded 17% and 18% respectively, and South Gippsland and the Bellarine Peninsula recorded about 10%. Combined, these five areas cover the second home coastal belt around Melbourne. Furthermore, analysis of sections of these municipalities showed that, on Phillip Island, 33% of

Table 11.1 Unoccupied dwellings in urban centres of coastal Victoria, 1996

Urban centre or locality	General location	Kilometres by road from Melbourne	Population	Total private dwellings	Unoccupied private dwellings	% Private dwellings unoccupied
Venus Bay	East of Phillip Island	170	385	978	795	81%
Loch Sport	East Gippsland	280	791	1319	933	71%
Indented Heads	Bellarine Peninsula	110	453	785	554	71%
Airys Inlet-Fairhaven	Great Ocean Road	121	761	1035	719	70%
Cape Paterson	East of Phillip Island	141	593	755	502	67%
Cowes	Phillip Island	142	3060	3941	2665	67%
Newhaven	Phillip Island	125	1091	1351	891	66%
Anglesea	Great Ocean Road	111	1995	2340	1520	65%
Coronet Bay	Near Phillip Island	115	482	621	386	62%
Flinders	Mornington Peninsula	87	501	583	354	61%
Lorne	Great Ocean Road	142	1082	1417	936	60%
St Leonards	Bellarine Peninsula	115	1226	1489	903	60%
Somers	Mornington Peninsula	77	963	973	569	58%
Inverloch	East of Phillip Island	145	2448	2540	1377	54%

Calculated from ABS (1998: 28–37)

Table 11.2 Domestic overnight visits, accommodation type for selected local government areas, 1999

Local government area	Towns and areas included	Domestic overnight visits '000s	Motels and hotels %	Caravan parks and camping %	Friends and relatives %	Second homes %
Mornington Peninsula – southern section	Portsea, Rye, Flinders	936	9	13	41	26
Surf Coast	Lorne, Torquay Anglesea	529	16	17	34	18
Bass Coast	Phillip Island, Inverloch	698	14	21	32	17
South Gippsland	Venus Bay, Wilsons Promontory	189	14	28	29	12
Greater Geelong, Bellarine section, Queenscliff	Bellarine Peninsula, Barwon Heads	536	11	25	39	10
Colac-Otways, southern section	Apollo Bay	258	28	21	21	6
East Gippsland, Western section	Bairnsdale, Lakes Entrance	411	30	20	28	6
Alpine	Mt Hotham, Falls Creek	413	34	22	17	6
Campaspe	Echuca, Kyabram	454	37	27	24	2
Albury–Wodonga	Albury–Wodonga	611	55	6	34	1
Greater Bendigo, Bendigo section	Bendigo	500	31	13	50	1
Warrnambool	Warrnambool	329	46	20	21	1
Greater Ballarat	Ballarat	576	38	14	42	0

Source: Zanon & Frost (2002: 8, 13)

domestic visits were to second homes; for the western half of the Surf Coast (Anglesea to Lorne), 27% were to second homes (Zanon & Frost, 2002: 13). This indicates that the highest usages of second homes were equally distributed in a ring around Melbourne at approximately 80–140 kilometres. In addition this belt attracts between 70% and 90% of its domestic overnight visitor nights from Melbourne (Zanon & Frost, 2002: 10).

Further away from Melbourne, the rate of second home usage fell away, even on the coast. At Apollo Bay (190 kilometres west) and Bairnsdale-Lakes Entrance (300–330 kilometres east) it was 6%. At Warrnambool, a popular coastal resort 270 kilometres east of Melbourne, only 1% of domestic visitors used second homes. At major inland centres with high volumes of tourism, including Ballarat, Bendigo, Albury-Wodonga and Echuca-Moama, second home usage ranged from less than 0.5% to only 2%. In the Alpine Shire, which includes most of the snow resorts, second home usage was 6%.

Some Characteristics of Second Home Towns

The lack of research into second homes in Australia makes it difficult to generalise about their characteristics. Accordingly, the comments in this section tend to be more speculative and indicative of the need for further research. One approach to understanding the coastal second home belt is to consider it in a negative context – in other words, what it is not, and what it is lacking. By utilising this approach, some social and economic features appear.

Elsewhere in the world there is much concern about social tensions arising from second home owners squeezing out established communities (see Chapter 2). This seems to be far less of a characteristic of the Melbourne second home belt. The currently growing second home towns either have a long history of tourism or are purpose-built estates on former farm or bush land. Venus Bay is an excellent example of the latter. Established in 1960 on a former dairy farm, it has no established community to feel dispossessed. Nor is there a flow of returning former residents (see Chapter 6, by Duval). If anything, it is the spread of Melbourne's suburbia into former second home territory that may be creating feelings of loss amongst those who had second homes in the past.

However, there may be significant tensions between residential tourists (typically known as 'permanent residents' or 'permanents') and second home users. The biography of Kath Pettingill, matriarch of a well-known Melbourne crime family who settled in Venus Bay, paints a detailed and attractive portrait of the co-operation between the permanent residents (Tame, 1996: 272–6). However, it is also significant that the community described is entirely permanent and appears to have little contact with second home users.

Anecdotal evidence from Venus Bay and other towns indicates a common tendency for permanents to create what Hobsbawm (1983) termed 'invented traditions' – permanents are creating their own societies with distinctive social practices and traditions, and excluding second home users, who are characterised as mere tourists. Given that most residential tourists are themselves relative newcomers, such developments may seem strange. However, as Hobsbawm argued, this trend towards the rapid creation of communities and traditions has been common throughout history. Whenever society has gone through rapid changes (in this case, the rapid growth of residential tourism in coastal towns), there has been the impetus to invent traditions that have the purpose of, 'establishing or symbolising social cohesion or the membership of groups, real or artificial communities' (Hobsbawm, 1983: 9). In addition, there is anecdotal evidence of second home users inventing their own traditions (for example, visiting at the same time each year); and there is also a suggestion that some second home users may see themselves as established (or 'local') in comparison with newcomers or other tourists.

Tourism in these second home towns is strikingly non-commercial, and this contributes to second homes often being overlooked as a social and economic force. As shown in Table 11.2, at least half of the accommodation for domestic visitors was non-commercial (second homes, or visits to friends and relatives) in the main second home municipalities. This charac-teristic is well-illustrated at Venus Bay, which has only a caravan park and four small bed-and-breakfast operations. There is no motel and no holiday apartments. Nonetheless, there is a strong commercial tourist traffic it just lacks visibility as it flows through non-commercial institutions. The main accommodation providers are the real-estate agents. They field enquiries, take bookings and advertise Venus Bay as a destination. In return they receive 10% commission, which may comprise a major part of their busi-ness. Most of their properties are normal second homes, which are offered for rental on a part time basis, generally during peak periods. In addition, second homes may also be rented opportunistically through informal networks, such as friends or fellow employees.

The economic benefits of second homes are often hidden, for they may occur some distance away. Loans for second homes are typically taken out with Melbourne banks (usually as an extension of the mortgage of the primary home rather than as a new loan), and petrol and food are often purchased in Melbourne where they are cheaper. Expenditure may leak into the local economy, but it is often through businesses at established (even non-tourist) towns. Venus Bay does not have a butcher, a hardware store, a petrol station or a post office. These are located five kilometres inland at the farming town of Tarwin Lower (whose population is half of Venus Bay's). The hardware at Tarwin Lower, in particular, is much larger than what would normally be expected in such a small town. Its clientele is mainly second home owners from Venus Bay. Similarly, the nearby large town of Wonthaggi, is well serviced with two large supermarkets and other shops, partially fuelled by Venus Bay and other nearby second home towns.

The Service Dilemma

The nature of Melbourne's second home belt produces a dilemma for government planners. If there is no legal distinction between second and primary homes, how can appropriate levels of services be determined? If second homes are eventually overtaken by residential tourism and suburbia, when should services be upgraded and who will pay for them?

Venus Bay lacks many services. Table 11.3 outlines a range of facilities and services for Venus Bay and two nearby inland towns (Tarwin Lower and Fish Creek) that service predominantly agricultural hinterlands. Even though Venus Bay has double the resident population of the other two towns, *plus* a much larger peak population, it has fewer shops, facilities and services. These nearby towns may be characterised as 'free riders', gaining economic benefits from their proximity to second home towns. Indeed, they may even be viewed as benefiting at the expense of second homes.

Table 11.3 Facilities and services at selected country towns in the Shire of South Gippsland, 2002 (X indicates existence)

	Venus Bay	*Fish Creek*	*Tarwin Lower*
Population 1996 Census	385	under 200	under 200
Year established	1960	c1880	c1875
Petrol station		X	X
Hotel		X	X
School		X	X
Butcher			X
Supermarket		X	
Newsagent		X	
Hardware store		X	X
Post office		X	X
General store	X	X	X
Restaurant	X	X	
Recreation ground and sporting facilities		X	X
Country Fire Authority station	X	X	X
Medical		X	X
Rubbish collection		X	X
Community centre or hall	X	X	X
Bus connection to Melbourne		X	

Certainly, they provide shopping facilities that are viable only because of second home users and other tourists. For residents at Venus Bay, the local school and post office are located at the smaller town of Tarwin Lower.

In the early decades of Venus Bay, the local council saw its development as a potential source of revenue for expenditure elsewhere in the shire (Branton, 1977). Such logic held only as long as most property owners were second home users, visiting for only a portion of the year and willing to accept a limited range of services. However, the development of residential tourism threatens to change this. At the 1996 census, Venus Bay recorded a population of 385, twice that of the nearby farming towns. Recent estimates have put its current population at 500 (*The Age*, 2001; Parks Victoria, 2001) and these may be too low. The recent property boom, with prices doubling in two years (*The Age*, 2001), may also have changed expectations of services.

As Venus Bay grows and changes, there may well be greater demand for government expenditure. In 2002, the local council responded to residents' pressure by holding a plebiscite as to whether or not a weekly rubbish collection should be introduced. Other changes may be forced upon government. At present each house in Venus Bay has an individual septic tank system. At some stage population pressure will force government to introduce a town sewerage system. As the resident population consists mainly of retirees, there is likely to be strong future demand for medical and other services for the aged. Owing to the low level of government services in the past, so there may well have to be a significant increase in expenditure to make up the difference.

Conclusion

Second homes form a major component of domestic tourism along the coast near Melbourne. For nearly 150 years they have been a major part of the city and its recreational facilities. There are at least 15,000 second homes currently located within a belt of between 80 and 150 kilometres from Melbourne. In a number of towns, second homes account for more than 50% of all private dwelling. These second homes accommodate up to 30% of all domestic overnight visitors in this area.

However, despite its size this belt of second homes has often been over-looked. This is probably due to the non-commercial nature of second homes. The shifting nature of second homes, particularly the way they have been forced further and further away from the city by increasing suburbanisation, also contributes to this lack of knowledge. Accordingly, there is a lack of information about second homes, which may have a negative impact on planning and development decisions. Such a pattern is not unique. As shown elsewhere in this book, underestimating second homes and their impact is a common problem.

Chapter 12

Second Homes in New Zealand

DONNA KEEN AND C. MICHAEL HALL

Historically, second homes have been an integral component of New Zealand lifestyles (Thompson, 1985). The second home is colloquially known as a 'bach' (in the North and Upper South Island) or a 'crib' (in the lower South Island). From one perspective the traditional second home is an eyesore, something that diminishes the intrinsic value of the land on which it is built, possibly taking away the enjoyment of the area from other recreational users (Public Access New Zealand, 1994). In comparison, second homes, particularly the traditional bach, can be seen as an icon of New Zealand culture and a definition of how New Zealanders best spend their leisure time (Thompson, 1985). Second homes in New Zealand are represented through a number of different styles, and characteristically illustrate a vernacular style of architecture. However, second homes, by virtue of their location, tourism significance, and various features of design and use, have substantial implications for environmental, economic and social planning. This chapter provides a discussion of these planning issues with respect to three different case studies of second home development in New Zealand. However, before examining the case studies a brief overview of second homes in New Zealand will provide the context within which such second home development occurs.

Despite their recognised significance within New Zealand culture and landscape there is little research on second homes in New Zealand, particularly with respect to planning issues (Lister, 1977; Washer, 1977; Shearer, 1980; McMillian, 1982; Montgomery, 1991). Nevertheless, the role and character of second homes in New Zealand have changes significantly since the first recognised second home developments in the 1890s although several themes continue through to the present day (Table 12.1).

The earliest census figures record bach numbers in 1926 at 6716, which equated to roughly 2 % of the housing population (McMillian, 1982). It was not until post 1945 that bach numbers increased, so much so that by 1951 bach numbers were as high as 15,615 (Table 12.2). Chapple (1988) attributes this increase to post-war optimism and increasing mobility owing to greater ownership of automobiles and improved infrastructure for travel. Further contributing to this growth was the belief that second homes were a means of recreation available to the average New Zealander – a belief that

Table 12.1 Trends in second home development in New Zealand

Period	Characteristics
Late 1890s to 1945: basic bach construction	• Roughly constructed, built on public and private land, often with 'loose' agreements for settlement. • Substantial concentration on second development in coastal areas.
1945 to mid-1960s: boom in bach building	• Continuation of pre-war trends with increased developments owing to growth of personal mobility through car use and greater disposable income. • Characteristics of baches still very basic.
Mid 1960s to present: 'refined homes' and environmental considerations	• Trend toward planned second homes as part of subdivisions, often for 'lifestyle' developments. • Changes related to shifts in New Zealand society with respect to leisure and holiday behaviours, and greater planning and environmental restrictions. • Availability of second homes in some areas related to rural restructuring and other economic changes. • Strengthening of relationship between second home purchase and retirement as well as amenity migration. • Increased development of second homes in inland areas, particularly near alpine recreation areas.

resulted in the spread of ramshackle structures along the coast, river and lake edges of New Zealand (Mitchell & Chaplin, 1984). Indeed, the nature of much second home housing in New Zealand meant that many of them would not have been included in official census returns, and the official statistics did not show the true number that existed. Furthermore, current census data is not reliable, as second home numbers are noted only if they are occupied on census night.

Prior to the 1996 Census, second homes were recorded as both occupied dwellings (on census night) and unoccupied dwellings. Census New Zealand changed the data recording for two reasons. First, it was felt that a separate category within 'unoccupied dwellings' for baches and cribs raised a number of concerns over reliability of data, as the decision to designate a building as a bach or crib was down to individual data collectors. Second, Census New Zealand did not believe there was an end use for this information. Subsequently, second homes that are unoccupied on census night are no longer distinguished from other types of unoccupied dwellings and the baches and cribs recorded in census data are only those that are occupied as a second home on census night.

Despite the inadequacies of census data, information can be estimated

Table 12.2 Number of second homes in New Zealand

Year	Number	Percentage of households
1926	6,716	2.0
1936	8,435	2.2
1945	10,975	2.5
1951	15,615	3.0
1956	19,899	3.3
1961	26,997	4.0
1966	29,534	3.9
1971	32,446	4.0
1976	33,143	3.5
1981	37,100	4.3
1986	40,950	
1996	2,565*	

* On the census night 2,565 holiday home dwellings had occupants (6,021 people). In total 113,388 dwellings were listed as unoccupied. These included dwellings where residents were temporarily away, and baches and holiday homes defined as empty dwellings

Source: Statistics New Zealand (2001)

based on the number of unoccupied dwellings. Table 12.3 illustrates the proportion of unoccupied to occupied dwellings on census night for semi-rural areas. For many locations, the proportion of unoccupied dwellings is disproportionate because of the high use of the area as a tourism destination, and so these figures can be taken to represent the high number of second homes in that region. Though this means of accounting for second homes lacks accuracy, it remains one of the best ways of accounting for second home numbers except where specific councils maintain records themselves. Councils can estimate second homes based on the number of owners with contact addresses outside the region; but this data is difficult to source.

Evidence of the value of second homes as a tourism product is illustrated through the New Zealand Domestic Travel Survey (Tourism Research Council, 2000). Tables 12.4 and 12.5 present findings from the Domestic Travel Survey 2000. Table 12.5 indicates that holiday homes/baches account for 7.9% of the total accommodation used, though this figure does not include the use of second homes owned by someone in the extended

Table 12.3 Minor urban areas in New Zealand by unoccupied dwellings, 2001 (areas above average total for unoccupied dwellings for minor areas)

	Total occupied dwellings	Residents away	Empty dwellings	Total unoccupied dwellings
North Island				
Taipa Bay-Mangonui	735	81 (7.9%)	210 (20.5%)	288 (28.2%)
Russell	399	75 (12.8%)	111 (19.0%)	186 (31.8%)
Snells Beach	1233	99 (6.2%)	264 (16.5%)	363 (22.7%)
Waiheke Island	3234	465 (9.7%)	1107 (23.0%)	1575 (32.8%)
Raglan	1086	258 (17.4%)	138 (9.3%)	396 (26.7%)
Whitianga	1374	123 (5.5%)	750 (33.4%)	870 (38.8%)
Whangamata	1785	537 (13.4%)	1686 (42.1%)	2223 (55.5%)
Tairua	660	495 (37.3%)	171 (12.9%)	666 (50.2%)
Waihi Beach	810	261 (19.1%)	297 (21.8%)	555 (40.7%)
Mangakino	507	21 (2.8%)	210 (28.5%)	231 (31.3%)
Turangi	1296	126 (6.9%)	414 (22.6%)	537 (29.3%)
Ohakune	492	249 (24.6%)	267 (26.4%)	519 (51.3%)
Raetihi	363	6 (1.4%)	69 (15.6%)	78 (17.7%)
Waiouru	465	30 (4.6%)	153 (23.6%)	183 (28.2%)
Foxton Community	1932	96 (4.0%)	402 (16.5%)	498 (20.5%)
Martinborough	573	69 (9.1%)	117 (15.5%)	183 (24.2%)
South Island				
Picton	1665	171 (8.6%)	150 (7.5%)	324 (16.3%)
Kaikoura	897	69 (6.1%)	174 (15.3%)	240 (21.1%)
Hanmer Springs	324	12 (1.6%)	399 (54.3%)	411 (55.9%)
Twizel Community	459	21 (2.2%)	468 (49.4%)	489 (51.6%)
Cromwell	1113	96 (6.7%)	228 (15.8%)	327 (22.7%)
Wanaka	1446	165 (6.4%)	957 (37.3%)	1119 (43.6%)
Arrowtown	690	126 (12.2%)	216 (20.9%)	342 (33.1%)
Queenstown	3480	708 (15.3%)	453 (9.8%)	1161 (25.0%)
Te Anau	750	48 (4.3%)	321 (28.7%)	369 (33.0%)
Riverton	702	81 (8.5%)	171 (17.9%)	255 (26.6%)
Total, minor urban area (n = 99)	*122,469*	*7716 (5.3%)*	*15,312 (10.5%)*	*23,025 (15.8%)*

Source: Statistics New Zealand (2001)

Table 12.4 Accommodation types used in 2000

	Total (000s)	*Share (%)*
Private home of friend/relative	25,581	51.3
Holiday home/bach	3,921	7.9
Camping ground:	5,114	10.3
Tent space	2,315	4.6
Cabin	967	1.9
Caravan space	1,832	3.7
Licensed hotel/motel	5,414	10.9
Unlicensed hotel/motel	5,056	10.1
Other:	4,804	9.6
Backpackers	994	2.0
Rented	1,316	2.6
Other	2,494	5.0
Total	*49,890*	

Source: Tourism Research Council (2000: 25)

family nor permanent caravan second homes. For holiday and leisure purposes, holiday homes/baches account for an even greater portion of the accommodation types used (13.9%). These are significant figures given the relatively uncommercial and un-promoted nature of second homes. The use of rented accommodation should also be considered as contributing to the role of second homes as accommodation providers. If this facet of second home use is included, the value of second homes as a feature of the tourism product becomes even more pronounced (Barton, 2000).

Second Home Types

An alternative way of understanding second homes, given the lack of statistical data, is to distinguish second homes types. Arguably, three key types of second homes exist in New Zealand, these are

- *vernacular*: traditional 'do-it-your-self', minimalist second home;
- *re-use*: second home communities that have sprung up in areas where the discontinuation of other industries has left redundant housing that has provided infrastructure for second home communities;
- *contemporary*: the purpose-built second home in resort areas.

Table 12.5 Percentage of holiday homes/ bachs used for accommodation given motivation of holiday/leisure

	% used for holiday/leisure
Private home of friend/relative	34.0
Holiday home/bach	13.9
Camping ground:	17.6
Tent space	8.0
Cabin	3.0
Caravan space	6.6
Licensed hotel/motel	10.3
Unlicensed hotel/motel	11.2
Other:	13.1
Backpackers	2.5
Rented	4.2
Other	6.4

Source: Tourism Research Council (2000: 25)

Though not exhaustive of the different types of second home communities and their variant, grouping them in this way provides a possible avenue for planning and segmenting these distinct communities for planning purposes.

Vernacular second home

As with the Nordic countries, vernacular second homes are intrinsic to New Zealand's national identity. Baches represent a form of both tangible and intangible heritage (Butts, 1993). Early baches were built around coastal areas and lakes, and were close to urban areas (Thompson, 1985). Often they were built on land that was leased or where the landowners had given permission. In some cases, baches were built on public land, specifically legal paper roads (roads that legally exist on a map, but have not been constructed), without the express permission of the relevant authorities (Thompson, 1985). One of the distinctive features to note about the early baches is the way in which they represent a particular style of vernacular architecture (Nelson, 1994). Baches prior to 1965 are a recognised style of New Zealand architecture (Nelson, 1994), and this has added to the awareness of the their heritage value. The heritage feature of second homes has become more pertinent as pressures for alternative development and increasing housing regulation have threatened baches. The second aspect of bach heritage is intangible – they are a key feature of the New Zealand cultural landscape. This cultural landscape is created and represented by the prominence of second homes in many artistic genres such as film, literature and music. This image of second homes is also heavily reinforced through popular media such as the periodic articles that appear in New Zealand magazines such as *The Listener, North and South,* and *House and Garden.* These articles embody the simplicity of second home life, as evidenced by titles such as: 'Sea Change' (Neville, 2002) and 'Bach to Basics' (Shopland, 2002b). Arguably, the representation of second homes in such a way has encouraged an awareness of their place in New Zealand.

Butts (1993) observed that in New Zealand there is a growing need to protect this cultural heritage, yet there is a dearth of appropriate legislation. Since the mid-1990s many of the articles written about second homes have mentioned, if not entirely focused on, the potentially endangered classification of the vernacular second home. Despite attention being given to second home development in the popular media, within local government there is no coordinated response to second homes. The pressures placed on bach settlements by development and local government pressure are documented in a number of places (Thompson, 2000; Ansley, 2002).

Heritage protection agencies have become increasingly active in their advocacy for the protection of this type of second home. According to the International Council on Monuments and Sites (ICOMOS), baches 'can say more about New Zealand's cultural and social identity and development than can grander gestures' (ICOMOS, 2000). ICOMOS argues that efforts should be made to protect this heritage by developing inventories of archetypal baches and by encouraging the protection of vernacular second homes at the local government level.

The New Zealand Historic Places Trust (NZHPT) has also been influential in campaigning for the protection of second homes (NZHPT, 1995; New Zealand Heritage, 2002). For example, the NZHPT has recently registered a bach settlement on the edge of the capital Wellington City as part of New Zealand's heritage. The reason given for this registration is that:

> Baches are arguably one of the few indigenous forms of New Zealand architecture. Those at Red Rocks and Mestanes [location of registered baches] were particularly important to Wellington in the early to mid 20th century as a retreat for Wellingtonians to enjoy leisure time and solitude. (New Zealand Heritage, 2002: 47)

Re-use second homes

Within New Zealand, issues of rural depopulation have resulted in an excess of housing stock. These redundant houses are often used as second homes. Second home owners convert old farm buildings, former churches, schools and houses. In many cases this creates a situation whereby second home owners represent a vast proportion of the community. A number of issues arise from this representation, relating to the retention of services and the dynamic that is created by the opposing views of the permanent community and the seasonal residents. However, the level of impact that these residents create arguably depends upon the location itself and the value that second home owners can add to the area.

A further feature of re-use second homes is the adaptive use of historic buildings. In Southern New Zealand, goldmining during the late 19th and early 20th century resulted in villages with substantial infrastructure, specifically Victorian heritage. A number of these villages have large numbers of second homes. Similarly, a number of hydroelectric scheme settlements from the 1960s and 1970s have been converted for second home use. From one perspective, the use of these buildings ensures the buildings are looked after. However, anecdotal evidence illustrates that often members of the community or people with interests in the preservation of heritage are upset by the structural changes that owners may make to such buildings (see below).

Contemporary/purpose-built second homes

Table 12.2 showed that, since the 1960s, both changes to society and increasing environmental regulations have influenced the development of this type of second home. As a reflection of this change, highly-planned and highly-regulated beach communities such as Pauanui in the Coromandel are becoming increasingly popular (McMillian, 1982; Aronson, 2000). In comparison to those built in the previous decades, second homes in the 1960s and 1970s began to resemble 'miniature family homes' (Mitchell & Chaplin, 1984: 21). As Chapple (1988: 14) notes 'what developed was the holiday suburb, its roads wide and beautifully curbed and channelled, its houses perfect examples of compliance to the building codes'. Cox (1995) even suggests that perhaps we are better to call the houses built in these 'holiday suburbs' beach houses or holiday homes instead of baches. Even though modern second homes are generally located in resort settings, some are built in remote locations just like their vernacular forebears. But, unlike their forebears, they are built following architectural blueprints and include everything needed for luxurious living. Nevertheless, what defines a bach is arguably more than what it is made from, its style of architecture or its historical value; instead a bach is defined according to the holiday ethos that has been created since the development of vernacular baches in the early 1900s.

A number of issues arise from the development of these 'modern' second home communities. In the case of Raglan on the Waikato coast in the North Island, Barber (2001) describes how permanent residents now often feel alienated, with land prices and rate increases being pushed beyond their means as a result of growing numbers of second homes. In Raglan the population changes from a resident population of 3070 to 15000 at its peak, thereby having an impact on the water supply and sewage systems, the roads infrastructure and the social structure of the community (Barber, 2001). Similarly, in the case of Banks Peninsula in the South Island, second home migration has also been noted as having substantial social impacts in relation to the permanent community particularly with respect to issues of development control (Fountain & Hall, 2002).

Planning Issues

Second homes, regardless of whether they are vernacular, re-use or contemporary, have a number of planning issues associated with them. While vernacular second homes are seen as the most archetypal, it should be noted that many of the holiday oriented motivations and benefits associated with their use are similar to both re-use and contemporary second homes. However, the second home is still used for relaxation, escapism and the opportunity for the mythical 'bach' lifestyle.

The key economic issue relating to second homes within New Zealand is arguably the rising cost of ownership. The perception exists that second homes are an accepted and available means of recreation for the majority of New Zealanders. Indeed, this perception was true during the first phase of bach building. As already noted, second homes in New Zealand were relatively inexpensive to acquire (Thompson, 1985). During the 1950s and 1960s, Heeringa (2001: 74) noted that 'you could capitalise your family benefit into a lump sum, buying a bach or at least a section at the beach was a reasonable middle-class expectation'. Thus the experience of the second home was available to a greater socio-economic demographic (NZHPT, 1995).

The increases in the value of second homes in New Zealand have been significant. Heeringa (2001) notes that the average cost of lakefront sections in Taupo, Mid North Island, was close to the average yearly wage during the 1950s and 1960s. Similar properties are now four times the average wage. Myriad other costs have also become associated with owning a second home. For example, Watts (2002) notes that insurance companies associate a greater risk with second homes, as they are unoccupied. The second home has transformed itself to such a degree that now it must be considered not just for its inherent recreational value but as an investment property; this issue is obviously related to the increasing values for both purchase and maintenance.

In some ways economic constraints affect the social prescriptions of the

New Zealand second home. Heeringa (2001) notes that the increases affect the ability of most New Zealanders to experience second home life. Rising costs mean that owning a second home is beyond the 'average' New Zealander in many parts of the country that either have high amenity values or are close to major urban centres. With increasing economic constraints, using a second home purely for the purposes of the owners' holidays is increasingly a luxury available only to the wealthy or those fortunate enough to have retained a second home within the family. Second homes ownership is increasingly a form of holiday available only to a select few (Cumming, 2002).

In planning terms, second homes are the responsibility of local government. Second homes provide local councils with planning problems similar to those of first homes, particularly infrastructure development. However there are also distinct tourism-related considerations associated with issues of seasonal utilisation, host-community conflict, user group conflict, and contribution to regional economic development.

One of the key problems to local government involvement in second home tourism in New Zealand is simply that local governments do not identify second homes as tourism. Conversely, they do not see second homes as being different from the homes of permanent residents (Aronson, 2000). Tourism officials in local government sometimes even fail to see the tourism dimension of second homes. For example, Tourism Coromandel's chief stated 'People who go to their daddy's bach in the Coromandel and take 20 friends with them are not tourists' (Aronson, 2000). Nevertheless, it must be stressed that not all local governments in New Zealand fail to identify the significance of second homes to tourism (King, 2000). In 2000, Tourism Central Otago estimated that second homes accounted for 178,875 bed nights compared with the estimated 189,000 bed nights from commercial establishments (King, 2000). Possible explanations for local government's failure to include second homes as features of tourism include the difficulties in identifying second homes (given lack of effective data recording at a national level), and the level of spending and influence that second home owners have on the area. However, despite possible confusion at the local government level, there is a need for second homes to be subject to the same degree of planning as any other feature of the tourism industry.

Before the 1960s, local government in New Zealand showed ambivalence to many of the buildings that fell below the official expected housing standard. For example, the *Housing Improvement Act of 1945*, enacted to set standards for housing in New Zealand, was ignored when it came to baches (Thompson, 1985). However, during the 1960s local councils began to exert authority over many of these dwellings, for a number of reasons. For one, the standard of housing was no longer ignored; the lack of effective waste disposal and the poor and untidy construction of houses meant that baches were identified as an environmental problem. Second, Thompson (1985) believes the changing local government attitude was connected to a change in perceptions of what constituted a holiday.

In 1970, baches were officially identified as a problem by local councils. In that year, the New Zealand development conference expressed a concern over bach and crib development, particularly the lack of planning (Shearer, 1980). The effect of these voiced concerns was a change toward planning restrictions on second homes. Second home owners must now apply to local government for consent to alter or build on to bachs (*Westport News*, 1998 in PANZ, 1999); prior to the 1960s, extension to second homes was at the discretion of the owners themselves. Connected to this issue was the alternative usage of land that the houses were built on. The land was seen as possessing other more lucrative usages; the land the bach was built on might be used for something else or the bach could negatively reduce the enjoyment of that site (Shearer, 1980; Thompson, 2000).

Regardless of the impact of legislative changes mentioned above, local government involvement with second homes tended to be as an aside to planning that was primarily targeted at housing in general. For example, the 2001–2003 review of the *Local Government Act (1974)* proposed a number of changes that have serious implications for second home owners (Local Government New Zealand, 2001). The main change was the right of second home owners to vote in local elections in the district in which they pay rates. The review of the *Local Government Act* proposed to remove the right of 'Non-residential ratepayer electors' – the right of second home owners to vote in local elections. The change is rationalised on the beliefs that this right is costing too much money and also that large numbers of people are not utilising it. In areas with large concentrations of second home owners, this change will effectively take away the right to have a say in the way in which an area develops and changes. In Queenstown, for example, a former councillor estimated that this would affect half of the ratepayers (Somerville, 2001).

To plan for second homes, councils need to understand the role of second homes, and to develop planning policies and effective implement strategies. The following section provides three case studies of second home development in the South Island of New Zealand, with each identifying the specific planning issues associated with each location (Figure 12.1). Each case study is related to a specific type of second home development according to the categorisation outlined earlier in the chapter. Each case study was developed on the basis of research conducted between 2000 and 2003.

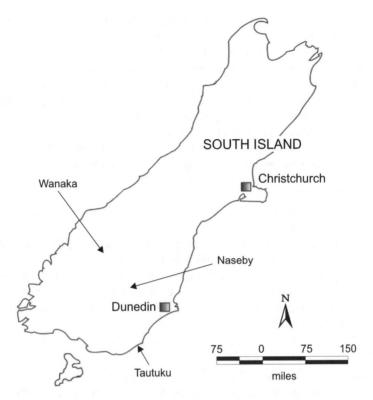

SOUTH ISLAND

Wanaka

Christchurch

Naseby

Dunedin

N

75   0   75   150

Tautuku

miles

Figure 12.1 Location of second home case studies

Case Study 1. Tautuku Peninsula: Vernacular Second homes

I guess it is fair to say that Tautuku is a bit of a forgotten outpost and we don't physically administer it because it's inaccessible and not one of the buildings over there comply with the building code of the day. So we turn 'Lord Nelson's' eye to it and we have nothing to do with it. (Planning Officer, Clutha District Council)

The Tautuku Peninsula is located on the Catlins Coast, on the southeastern coast of New Zealand's South Island. The Catlins is an area high in scenic and recreational values. The cribs are built on a peninsula that juts out from the southern edge of the Tautuku Beach. Access to the peninsula is difficult because a tidal river cuts off the peninsula from the land access. The peninsula can be accessed at low tide either by wading through or in a heavy duty vehicle.

The first cribs were built on the peninsula during the 1940s. The settlement at the Catlins consists of 31 cribs situated either on Road Reserve Land (public land) or on land owned by a Maori Land Trust, Tautuku A. Of these cribs, 23 are built on a legal paper road or on road reserve, and a further 8 are on land belonging to the Tautuku A Land Trust. There is also a community hall on road reserve land. The cribs are basically constructed, following many of the archetypal building styles of early vernacular second homes. Invariably they are also characterised by each being in a number of different colours. This 'ramshackle' appearance is often a reason for complaints against vernacular second homes (Ansley, 2002).

All the cribs are built on the 'Leeward' side of the peninsula to avoid the worst of the coastal weather. Though they are not easily accessible physically, the cribs can be seen from the beach and the road. They can all be seen from the Tautuku Beach and from the main Catlins Road. This road is a main vantage point for Tautuku Beach and affords one of the most spectacular views over the coast. Most of the owners of the cribs come from the Otago and Southland Districts, primarily Invercargill and Balclutha. There is a very strong community feeling within this settlement, and the crib owners have formed the Tautuku Crib Owners Association as a form of advocacy for any issues that may arise. Within the settlement itself, crib owners have also constructed a 'Community Hall', which acts as a common meeting place for crib owners.

Issues

> The time will come when we have to take a hard look at these cribs and either arrange some more secure tenure or make them subject to building control and requirements but at this stage we are just talking about it and haven't done anything. But it is sad that the days of the Kiwi holiday at the riverside at the crib are gone. (Planning Officer, Clutha District Council, 2001)

As with many vernacular crib or bach settlements around New Zealand, a number of issues arise relating to the ownership of the land on which the cribs are built. In the 1940s, licenses were issued to 23 of the crib owners by the Clutha County Council allowing for the occupation on council road reserve land. These crib owners pay the Clutha District Council a rent of NZ$20 per year. A further 8 have been built on adjoining land owned by the Tautuku A Lands Trust.

Since the 1990s, there have been varying degrees of conflict over the rights of the crib owners to access both this land and the road reserve land. In 1998, the Tautuku A Lands Trust took the issue to the Maori Lands Tribunal. The trust wanted the paper road to be dissolved and included within their land ownership. This change would effectively have made the position of a greater number of the crib owners even more tenuous because the land would then fall out of public ownership and become privately-owned land. The paper road remained publicly owned, mainly for reasons far wider than the crib ownership. However, to settle any dispute over the access of the crib owners and the right to effectively trespass on privately-owned land, the crib owners now pay the trust a rental of NZ$360 per annum (Paterson, 1999). The crib owners have also signed an agreement not to add to existing cribs or to build new ones, and have agreed to certain restrictions on how they use the land. The local council's role appears to have been as a mediator and the council has not planned for the eventual removal of the cribs.

Clutha District Council noted that one of the threats to the second home settlement was from the national Department of Conservation (DoC): increasing pressure 'to retain the natural environment' could result in the loss of cribs. However, the DoC stated that the land on which the cribs are built is not DoC land and hence is not part of its jurisdiction. However, the DoC does administer the adjacent beach and the land behind it. As the Catlins area experiences increasing tourist growth, the resulting pressures of the tourists' expectations and land use could have a greater influence on the way in which DoC views this area. However, tourists to the area noted that they did not see the cribs as detracting from the natural environment but rather, as Wolfe (1977) noted, the cribs added to the physical environment.

The cribs at Tautuku typify the situation of vernacular second homes around New Zealand that could best be described as existing in a state of flux. They are increasingly becoming recognised by planning authorities as being in countenance to the planning laws and bylaws. However, the cribs represent a strong part of New Zealand identity and as such cannot be dealt with as normal housing. Instead, any dealings must consider the opinions of the second home users, the users of the land surrounding, and the local community. Key planning considerations for vernacular second homes include:

- the effect on the natural environment;
- the value of the second homes as part of heritage;
- the role of second homes as part of the identification of the area;
- the rights of 'legal' land owners;
- potential issues of negligence;
- possible land use;
- creating legislation or guidelines for non-legitimised buildings.

Case Study 2. Naseby: Re-use Second Homes

The Maniototo area is characterised by a large plain used for extensive grazing surrounded by three main mountain ranges; this creates a land-scape that is unique for Southern New Zealand and a key dimension of tourism promotion (Keen, 2002). Historically, industry was based on goldmining and agriculture. The gold rush lasted throughout the 1880s and 1890s and, though not long in duration, was important in developing the cultural heritage of the Maniototo. Agriculture still remains the principle industry of the region. However, the industry has changed since the 19th century to much smaller farms and a diversification from sheep farming to horticulture, dairying and tourism.

The village is located only two hours away from Dunedin, New Zealand's eighth largest city. The proximity to Dunedin has made Naseby a popular destination for the local market (Topham-Kindley, 2000). In terms of Müller's (1999) (see Chapter 1, Table 1.2) conceptualisation of second home use, Naseby can be seen as a weekend home destination. Currently, Naseby is experiencing a period of growth due to tourism and agriculture (Hepburn, 2002). The increase in visitor numbers and in the length of time they stay in the village has provided more customers for the existing businesses, community craft shops and museums in the area (Keen, 2002). As a result of the rising number of tourists, property prices in the village have increased. Whereas in 2000 many properties had been on real-estate agents' listings often for years, the market of available land and housing is now limited. Further development is planned, with a lodge and conference centre, a restaurant and an international curling rink.

Naseby was once the centre of a large goldmining boom within the Maniototo. The end of the goldmining boom left a large number of redundant buildings, and these have been utilised as second homes since the 1950s. Prior to the tourism developments in the late 1990s, tourism in Naseby was centred largely on second homes. They are a still a key component of the tourism industry in the region, albeit one that is not recognised by relevant authorities. Table 12.6 shows that, on Census night 2001, 80% of the houses in Naseby were empty; a large proportion of these are second homes. The permanent population of Naseby is around 90, in the peak summer period (when second home owners are in residence) the population of the village is close to 1000.

Second home owners represent a significant proportion of the community in this village, and have historical ties similar to those of many permanent residents. The second homes in Naseby, particularly those that use

Table 12.6 Naseby: Permanent vs. empty dwellings, Census night 2001

Location	Permanent dwellings	Empty dwellings	Total	Percentage empty dwellings
Naseby	51	210	261	80%

Source: Census data, Statistics New Zealand (2001)

heritage buildings, provide a strong link with the past. For example, one second home owner noted that using his home in the winter season and experiencing difficulties such as frozen water and cold made him feel as if he was getting a taste of the way that life was lived during the pioneering days. Another second home owner, in Naseby, said that the holiday home 'Becomes part of your heritage and roots' (Smith in Dungey, 2003).

A further motivation is the opportunity to experience a quieter way of life, while still having a range of potential recreational opportunities. The entrance to the village reads 'Welcome to Naseby: 2000 feet above worry level'. Second homes within the village provide people with an opportunity to get away from it all. A Naseby second home owner noted that a second home contributed to 'a person's sanity, great when children are young and provides families with happy memories to bolster spirits when they are low' (Smith in Dungy, 2003). Furthermore, a second home visitor noted 'And so we farewelled Naseby – a little wiser and with a few less worries' (Topham-Kindley, 2000).

Issues

In the summer months, the village changes from a sleepy little hamlet to a bustling seasonal tourist destination. Second homes provide a supply of visitors through second home owners, visiting friends and relatives, and people who rent out second homes. This benefits the businesses in the village, particularly the local service shops and the pubs. An owner of one of the local pubs highlighted the importance of second home owners to the viability of their businesses. He mentioned that it was important to recognise and understand their role and importance in the village. He also noted that businesses need to understand that they could not rely on the second home owners, whose their impact was generally seasonal. Indeed, one of the main objectives when he and his partners took over their business was to develop other means of business so as not to be reliant upon the second home owners.

In addition to the contribution to local business, demand for second homes has also boasted the local property market. Property values in Naseby have increased by more than 75% between 2000 and 2003 (Townsend in Hepburn, 2003). The local real estate agent attributes this growth to two factors (Townsend, 2003, personal communication). First, the development of a Rail Trail has attracted people to the area and helped to develop an awareness of the area. Second, he believes the popularity of a local artist, Grahame Sydney, has increased the attraction of the area. Further contributing to this growth is the growing cost of real estate in other central Otago towns such as Wanaka and Queenstown, while Naseby is still a location where people can afford a second home (Dungey, 2003). Such reasons exhibit strong parallels with Müller's (1999) research on German second home owners in Southern Sweden. However, Townsend notes that this growth is limited by the lack of land for subdivision and the enclosure of the village by forestry (Hepburn, 2003). Since 1998, Townsend (2003, personal communication) noted that only two new houses had been built. She states that this building boom is in part due to the Resource Management Act. In order to have resource consent to build, water must be available but it is a scarce resource in the area. A further obstacle is that there are few sections for sale, and most are owned by locals who are unwilling to sell (Townsend, 2003, personal communication).

Second home owners account for a significant proportion of Naseby's community (as much as 80%). Therefore, they can substantial impacts on the permanent population. In many respects the dynamic of second home owners and permanent residents could be viewed very much as one of 'them' and 'us' (e.g. Jordan, 1980). Community members have mentioned the role that second home owners have played in community matters. One local mentioned that local people were unhappy with a recent change to the main street; they argued that it was not in keeping with the heritage of the town and blamed second home owners for the change. Yet, regardless of their potential to impact in the way mentioned above, second home owners are not officially recognised by the local government as part of the community. One community member noted that the local council fails to acknowledge the importance and rights of second home owners in the village. The lack of recognition was also highlighted by the failure to find anyone in local government with any detailed knowledge of second homes in the village.

One of the reasons for the failure of local government in Naseby may be the difficulty in distinguishing between second home owners and permanent residents. Yet with the increasing development of Naseby, both in terms of tourism and agriculture/forestry, the role of second home owners needs to be better understood, as they have a significant influence on the overall well-being of the community.

The re-use of housing in rural areas as second homes is a crucial feature in many tourism destinations in New Zealand. The example of Naseby can be seen as indicative of many locations around New Zealand where industry change has left a redundant housing stock. With the increasing interest in the development of rural areas, the role of second home owners needs to be understood as part of this dynamic. Key planning and management issues include: identifying the heritage component of re-use second homes;

- from a destination development perspective, tourism organisations need to understand the economic utility of second homes;

- understanding the inter-relationship between community and second home owners;
- real estate development of second homes;
- local government responsibility;
- response of second home owners to development.

Case Study 3. Wanaka: Contemporary

Wanaka is an alpine resort in the Southern Lakes District of Otago. It is located about half an hour from the major resort of Queenstown and was a service centre to the farming community. Tourism in Wanaka was originally centred mainly on second homes of Otago and Southland residents. With the development of recreation infrastructure, other forms of tourism have developed in response to the number of natural attractions it offers.

Tourism contributes an estimated NZ$80 million to Wanaka (Smith, 2002a). Wanaka has a range of natural attractions, which make it a destination in both winter and summer. In the winter season, Wanaka is a main ski destination, with two major ski fields and one nordic/cross-country field. The range of summer facilities includes the lakes and rivers and the range of activities offered in the nearby Mount Aspiring National Park. Wanaka also has a range of events throughout the year, including the 'Warbirds over Wanaka' festival held every two years at Easter. In addition there are a growing number of adventure and rural activities, including bed and breakfasts, wineries, and farmstays.

Second homes in Wanaka account for a significant proportion of the housing population. As Table 12.7 indicates, 40% of the dwellings in Wanaka were empty on census night 2001. Though there is no specific research, anecdotal evidence suggests that a number of the second homes in Wanaka now have international owners. Some domestic owners have noted that they still keep their holiday home in Wanaka for investment reasons (Dungey, 2003) and potential retirement, but they now find the place too crowded. Increasingly, the style of second homes is becoming more sophisticated in design and it is difficult to find the humble holiday house.

Table 12.7 Wanaka: Permanent vs. empty dwellings, Census night 2001

Location	Permanent dwellings	Empty dwellings	Total	Percentage empty dwellings
Wanaka	1449	957	2406	40%

Source: Census data, Statistics New Zealand (2001)

Issues

One of the main issues in relation to second homes in Wanaka is their role as rental accommodation. Second homes are an important component to the accommodation provision in the Wanaka area. Lake Wanaka Tourism estimates that this accommodation is at least equal to, if not greater than, the legitimate accommodation sector in Wanaka (Lake Wanaka Tourism, 2002, personal communication). Therefore, these second homes arguably provide a much-needed part of the infrastructure for the development of tourism. However, there is pressure from formal accommodation providers for the identification of private home owners who rent out homes and have them pay greater local rates (Jamieson, 2002). Recently this pressure has led the tourism organisation to make plans to investigate the impact of home rentals and their contribution to tourism and infrastructure funding.

Smith (2001) noted that the 'median section price had leapt from $41,500 in 1992 to $116,000 in 2001', also ratepayers have had a rates increase of 12.3% (Smith, 2002b). Wanaka was once a traditional New Zealand summer retreat, but new baches there are now too expensive, and New Zealanders have had to go into the surrounding areas (*Otago Daily Times*, 2002). As the previous case study noted, this is now resulting in greater interest in rural areas such as Naseby. As well as leading to the displacement of potential second home owners, rising real estate and rental prices means that accommodation for workers and permanent residents is difficult (Thomas, 2002).

Wanaka is a characteristic contemporary second home development, with 'its roads wide and beautifully curbed and channelled, its houses perfect examples of compliance to the building codes' (Chapple, 1988: 14). However, there are a number of social and environmental issues related to the development of second homes in these resort locations. One of the difficulties facing local government is that the size of many of these resorts means that addressing the issues that arise from second homes becomes highly complex. The development of tourism as a whole frequently means that the issue of the contribution of second homes to the economy and the impacts that arise from them is not addressed. For example, in Wanaka little is known about the specific impact of second home owners. Yet, in relation to this type of settlement, local government must understand the contribution of second homes to the economy and their role in the social dynamic of the community as a whole. Key planning and management issues for local government include:

- the need for effective subdivision control;
- the displacement of 'local' second home owners;
- the displacement of local buyers;
- the impact of second home owners on local economy
- the changing dynamic of ownership;
- a need to consider seasonal usage.

Conclusions

This chapter has provided a brief description of second home development and planning issues in three distinct case study regions in the South Island of New Zealand. Although these case studies all share some common characteristics, there are obvious differences that illustrate the need for local government to address second home planning issues according to the needs of specific locations (Table 12.8). However, these findings should be used for reflection and contrast with other situations.

In social terms the bach and the crib have an important place in New Zealand culture that is only recently becoming recognised – possibly as a response to the loss of 'traditional' second homes and the holiday lifestyles that are associated with them. Perhaps even more significant is the failure

Table 12.8 Case study findings

	Tautuku Peninsula	*Naseby*	*Wanaka*
Type	Vernacular	Re-use	Contemporary
Host community	No permanent residents	Small percentage (10%)	Substantial host permanent population
Location	Remote coastal	Rural	Resort
Tourism use	Second home users	Increasing domestic tourism	Major international and domestic destination
Motivations	Escapism Community	Community Rural	Recreation Investment
Major issues	Properties on tenuous lease No building guidelines High value natural area Representation of New Zealand 'Bach/Crib' Heritage	Seasonal occupation Two communities Substantial economic contribution to village Rental income	High property value Displacement of locals Rental income Adds to general concerns of tourism growth
Planning considerations	Enforcement of housing standards Length of leasehold	Housing standards Subdivision growth Spokesperson role	Subdivision growth Tourism growth Affordable housing
Examples	Falls Dam Taylors Mistake Rangitoto Island	Twizel Cromwell Clyde Otematata	Pauanui Queenstown Te Anau

of many regional and local councils to recognise the development and planning significance of second homes. Table 12.9 shows some of the key issues for second homes in New Zealand in relation to the analysis, planning and implementation of planning at local government level. Under each of the three sections factors necessary for effective planning have been identified. However, given the history of second home development in New Zealand, it is likely that these planning issues will be acted only on in a reactive fashion in light of pressures at specific locations.

From the perspective of local government, planning should not deal solely with housing regulations and resource consent nor with the negative issues associated with second homes, but should also be created to effectively gain the most benefit now and in the future. The current importance of regional development, particularly to rural New Zealand, and the overall importance of domestic tourism, increases the significance of second homes in many jurisdictions. However, the lack of understanding of/and research on second homes makes effective planning and policy setting extremely difficult.

The results of this research suggest that second homes are perceived by New Zealand's local governments as both a curse and a blessing, and increasingly contribute to the development of elite landscapes in many parts of the country. In order to provide effective planning, local government must recognise the inherent uniqueness of second homes as a housing and tourism factor, as well as their implications for regional development. However, in New Zealand the planning and development of second homes is still ad hoc rather than strategic in nature. The long-term consequences of such a situation may mean that the economic, environmental and cultural benefits of what has long been an important component of New Zealand society may not be maximised to the benefit of those who still desire to holiday at the bach.

Table 12.9 Planning issues for second homes in New Zealand

	Factors	*State of knowledge in New Zealand*
Analysis	Operational definitions	No clear definition. Lack of local government understanding of the characteristics of second homes
	Maintenance of statistics	No specific statistical information, what there is as a result of census data through unoccupied housing
	Research	No research from local government perspective
Key planning issues	Motivations	Part of New Zealand way of life
	Social impacts	Displacement of permanent residents
	Environmental impacts	Infrastructure
	Economic impacts	Identified as important to local government
	Tourism influence	Slightly acknowledged but generally seen in relation to second home rental. Second home owners not seen as tourists
Implementation of policies	Type of second home development	Case studies have identified obvious differences for planning between second home types
	Use of second homes	Linkage to location, motivations
	Culture	Meaning of second homes, i.e. cultural identity
	Location	Important in terms of impacts, regional development

Chapter 13

Second Homes: Reflections on an Unexplored Phenomenon in South Africa

GUSTAV VISSER

Introduction

The issue of second home development has been the focus of considerable debate in tourism and migration-related research since the 1990s. In particular, the linking of these traditionally unrelated fields of interest has portrayed second home development as a form of both migration and tourism, which defies many of the categorisations and descriptions of either tradition individually. Notwithstanding (or perhaps because of) this, second home development has become one of the most researched interfaces between tourism and migration (Williams & Hall, 2000a: 19). Indeed, as Williams and Hall (2000b) observe, tourism expansion has long been interdependent with that of particular forms of migration. It is argued that, quite apart from the fact that tourism itself constitutes a form of migration of varying duration, it has generated two distinctive flows of migrations: that of *labour migration*, and that of *consumption-led migration systems*. The focus of this chapter is on consumption-led migration systems that have developed something akin to a symbiotic relationship with tourism flows, as part of the redefinition of the practices of consumption. This phenomenon may, as Williams and Hall (2002b: 2) assert, assume several forms, depending on the duration of the migration, the motivations and property relationships which include second home development, seasonal migration, lifestyle migration and retirement migration. Whereas the analysis of these complex and varied relationships has been the focus of a burgeoning academic literature (as mentioned elsewhere in this volume), these concerns have not been explored within the South African context.

Although large numbers of towns and villages along the South African coastline, and increasingly in the interior, have grown significantly as a result of consumption-led migration, the South African Geographical, Tourism Studies, as well as Town and Regional Planning research discourses, remain mute concerning second home development. Indeed, second home development as a topic of investigation has remained invisible to the South African scholarly gaze. In part, this deafening academic silence can be attributed to the research context in which it functions. Considering a milieu of multiple societal challenges and transformations, research attention has in large part come to focus on the extraordinary dilemmas of everyday survival and the myriad complexities that apartheid social engineering conferred upon the South African space economy (Visser, 2003a). Furthermore, in the context of a social science tradition that was ridiculed for its 'lily-white' research focus, and its rather insensitive and unconcerned engagement with the histories, lives and experiences of the majority of the country's citizens (Beavon & Rogerson, 1981; Rogerson & Browett, 1988), second home research seems rather out of place in South Africa's day-to-day realities. Moreover, research areas such as tourism have only very recently emerged as a serious field of investigation in this country (e.g. Rogerson, 2002). Nevertheless, whatever the reason for the 'invisibility' of the second home phenomenon to South African researchers, the fact of the matter is that at present no systematic academic reflections have been forthcoming in this context.

Given the void in academic reflection on second home development in South Africa, the task of this chapter is twofold. The first objective is to provide some insight into the dynamics of second home development in this country, and the second is to sketch an outline of the types of issues that second home development affords researchers in this uncharted terrain of investigation. These concerns are explored in five uneven sections.

First, some observations are made relating to the development of real estate in South Africa, particularly in its traditional tourism and recreation regions. This section serves as a backdrop to three specific processes – holiday, weekender and retirement migration – which are interpreted as underpinning the current expansion of second home development in this country. In turn, this provides the focus of the three sections that follow. Consequently, the second section focuses on established tourism migration patterns and their linkages to second homes as holiday accommodation. The third section explores the growth of a number of rural hamlets and villages that have developed as locations for second homes that mainly serve as weekend retreats away from South Africa's main metropolitan areas. The fourth section briefly draws attention to the complex second home development trends linked with retirement migration. The final section reflects on the types of issues these observations highlight, and seeks to provide a research agenda that could serve as a framework for the systematic exploration of second home development in the South African context.

Second Home Development in South Africa: A Historical Sketch

The development of second homes, whether for holiday purposes, retirement, weekend recreation or leisure, is certainly not a new phenomenon in South Africa. Indeed, a number of towns and villages along its coastline were established or developed as a direct result of such use. Perhaps the oldest of these are those on the Cape Town pleasure periphery of False Bay (Figure 13.1). Here the small fishing villages of Muizenberg and St James became holiday and weekend retreats for the Victorian and Edwardian Capetonian gentry, as well as a host of 'Rand Lords' (mining magnates from the Witwatersrand goldfields) escaping the dreaded dust storms of the Johannesburg mine dumps. Luminaries included Rudyard Kipling, Cecil John Rhodes, as well as Prince and Princess Natale Labia. Similarly, along the south coast of present-day KwaZulu-Natal, the landed gentry of the sugar-cane industry – including the Campbell, Chennels, and Hullett families, to name but a few – built weekend and holiday retreats in seaside hamlets and villages such as Park Rynie, Scottburgh and Pennington (Figure 13.2). Over the next half-century, second homes were developed further along the KwaZulu–Natal coast, with Margate, Ramsgate and Port Shepstone among the popular destinations with tourists from the interior. Muizenberg and St James, on the other hand, were systematically absorbed into the sprawling urban hinterland of Cape Town and in the process ceded

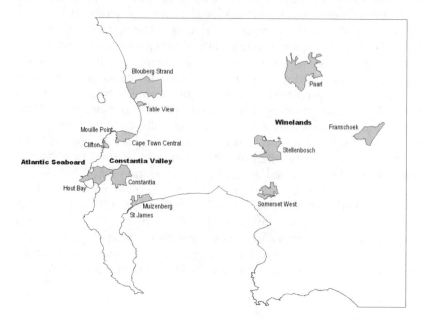

Figure 13.1 Selected second home locations in Cape Town

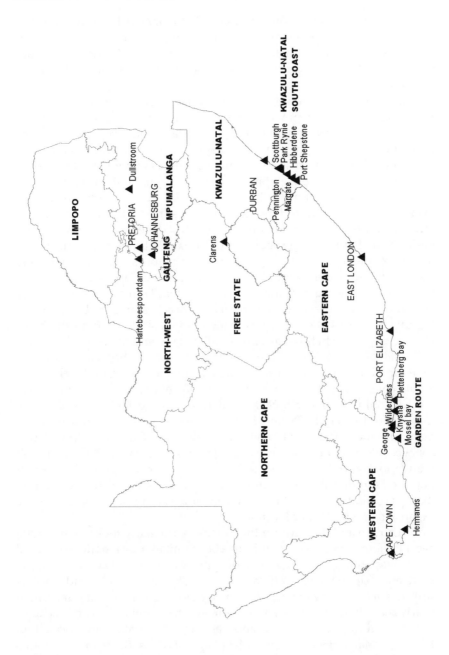

Figure 13.2 Selected second home concentrations in South Africa

their former exclusivity. The key trend that emerged from the outset of second home development was, however, that the fortunes of those towns and villages, and others that were still to be 'discovered', tended to be intimately linked to developments in the economic heartland of South Africa – the Gauteng region.

South Africa's economic boom from the late 1950s to the early 1970s led to the large-scale development of its three main metropolitan regions: Cape Town, Durban and Johannesburg/Pretoria. More important to the present discussion, higher levels of disposable income and discretionary time would lead to large-scale second home development along the country's coastline. This development was, however, not even, with the KwaZulu–Natal coastline at that time enjoying considerable precedence over that of the Cape. In large part this was linked to the fact that the transportation systems in the country were best developed between Johannesburg and South Africa's main port, Durban. This meant that the trip to the KwaZulu–Natal coast was only six to seven hours' drive, in contrast to the near two-day trek, either by car or train, to the Cape south coast and Cape Town. Other factors included the fact that Durban was historically also an established seaside resort city, its beaches and facilities family-friendly, whilst its warm winters made it an ideal escape from the harsh Highveld winters. In time the once-small villages and hamlets to the north and south of this city, initially reserved for the wealthy, became more accessible for middle class families. Perhaps the greatest spurt of development would emerge with the large-scale development of time-share units along the KwaZulu-Natal south coast, and to a lesser extent its north coast, throughout the late 1970s and 1980s. Moreover, it may be argued that in many instances the development of these loci of domestic travel was connected to apartheid South Africa's increasing isolation from the rest of the world, as well as the increasing control over foreign exchange that impacted significantly on the more affluent classes. It is also to this period that the current concentration of second homes can trace their large-scale expansion and particular location.

As Durban and the surrounding towns, particularly those to the south, became more populated with middle-class families, vast amounts of capital were invested in the development of appropriate holiday accommodation such as budget hotels, self-catering holiday apartments and endless stretches of timeshare units. Indeed, in terms of timeshare accommodation nearly 300,000 South Africans now own timeshare units. Most of these were acquired during this period and the largest number are located in KwaZulu–Natal (Heath, 1990; Mabotja, 2003). As these areas became increasingly frequented by the middle classes, they lost their appeal for the elite of Johannesburg and Pretoria. Furthermore, Durban as a resort city was experiencing typical processes of resort decay, whilst the province itself was increasingly becoming the focus of apartheid political violence (Visser & van Huyssteen, 1997, 1999). This in turn stimulated a move into more underdeveloped and remote regions in the country.

It was in the late 1970s and early 1980s that the archetypal second home locations in South Africa (such as Plettenberg Bay, Knysna, and Hermanus) started to develop along the south coast of the Western Cape Province. Plettenberg Bay is probably the textbook example. In this case, the establishment in 1972 of an upmarket hotel, and an airfield servicing it, made this lush coastal woodland area accessible to well-heeled folk from Johannesburg and Pretoria. Moreover, the fact that soon after this a well-connected Johannesburg landowner parcelled off his seaside farm and sold it to the country's elite classes gave it immediate appeal for those seeking a new exclusive holiday home location. In this way a whaling-station of no more than a few hundred people developed into a town of more than 70,000 inhabitants, and some of the most expensive real estate in South Africa. Systematically, towns further south on the so-called Garden Route became the focus of attention for property developers, and the old forest station of Knysna soon emerged as a playground for the wealthy. As the 1980s drew to a close, a host of changes in the political system of South Africa would emerge that would in turn lead to the current spate of second home development mushrooming along the country's coastline and increasingly dotting its interior.

In the wake of the opening up of South African urban areas to all its citizens (rather than being the preserve of 'whites only'), the greatest re-working of the South African property market is to be found in the late 1980s and early 1990s. The demise of apartheid and its convoluted legislative apparatus underpinned the emergence of a range of popular discourses as to which areas of the country were desirable for both permanent and semi-permanent residence. First, urban areas such as Pretoria and Johannesburg were increasingly perceived as dangerous and unstable locations. Furthering this view was the fact that the emergence of an increasingly post-industrial economy was finding spatial expression in the physical form of industrial cities such as Johannesburg (Rogerson, 1998, 2000; Visser, 2002, inpress b). The accompanying spatial restructuring of this urban space was dramatically witnessed in the economic, social and cultural decay of its central business areas and immediately adjacent neighbourhoods (Dirsuweit, 1999). Moreover, well-rehearsed dinner-party conversations on crime statistics had the chattering classes of Johannesburg and Pretoria reeling with fear of murder, rape and pillage (Dirsuweit, 2002). In this context a broader-ranging movement away from central city areas, ever deeper into the suburban sprawl of Johannesburg and Pretoria, began to be apparent. A wave of emigration ensued, which has only recently begun to subside, along with a semi-migration of wealthy individuals to cities and towns interpreted as less vulnerable to black urban in-migration, physical transformation and economic restructuring. It was in this context that Cape Town became the main beneficiary of white and wealthy southward migration for both permanent and holiday purposes, which in the process caused Johannesburg and Pretoria to experience some of their worst property slumps. For those who could not 'escape to the Cape', the reality of permanent residence in Johannesburg led even those of relatively modest means to invest heavily in places that were not deemed as dangerous and risky in terms of both personal safety and return on property investment. In the wake of such thinking, the south coast of the Western Cape Province has enjoyed a decade-long real estate boom. This is a process that is still in motion, with 10% of all bonds issued by South African banks estimated to be for second home development (Fife, 2001: 46). Despite such claims, no data currently exist that could provide an accurate indication of the real number of properties involved. However, ample media coverage allows for the identification of a number of trends in second home development in South Africa. Perhaps the clearest of these trends is the fact that both the developers and uses of second homes are varied, as are their spatial imprint and impact upon the communities in which they are located. It is in this context that the focus now turns to some recent trends in second homes as the loci of holidaying, weekend retreats, and retirement residences.

Second Homes as Holiday Homes

Although many second homes in South Africa are utilised as holiday homes, I must hasten to add that, as demonstrated in much of the international research on second homes, any differentiation between second homes as holiday, investment, weekend or retirement properties is close to impossible. The concentrations of second homes highlighted here can fulfil the role of one or all of these functions; and these functions might, and do, change over time. Nevertheless, the second homes briefly investigated here mainly fall within the realm of holiday homes, with a clear investment role.

The most popular and well-known second home area in South Africa is the Western Cape coastline. The region of about 800 square kilometres can, however, be divided into different regions that fulfil holiday home functions in different ways. As mentioned earlier the expansion of second home development in these areas can in the main be attributed to changes in the type of spaces sought for leisure consumption in the late 1980s and early 1990s. Indeed, in some ways this era might be viewed as a first wave of development, with the second wave currently under way. The establishment of Plettenberg Bay as the key holiday destination for the superlatively well-heeled folk of Gauteng, ushered in a period during which the Cape south coast began to be viewed in a substantially different manner. In part, better road links along the coast, particularly between Mossel Bay and Port

Elizabeth, contributed to the improvement of accessibility. Moreover, through aggressive tourism marketing of the region, a larger grouping of people became aware of the exceptional natural beauty of the region and the fact that it was largely an underdeveloped area.

The first wave of development is closely linked to domestic holiday home investors in Plettenberg Bay, along with increased tourism flows through the region. The fact that this village developed from a limited number of allotments that were first released to the wealthy, well-connected contingent of society, and that it did not have many local residents, meant that exclusivity could be built into the fabric of the town from the outset, securing its rise to 'second home fame' – the location of consumption owned and controlled by the extremely wealthy. In less than a decade, all 1000 sea-facing allotments had been developed, mostly with mansions costing several million Rands. However, the fact that the supply of land was restricted and that the point of holidaying there was the seaviews, meant that inevitably there were limits to how many properties could be developed. Indeed, investor interest in the town started to wane in the face of a shortage of available housing stock. This led to investors seeking out opportunities elsewhere in the region.

Subsequently, the development of the region commenced in a southward direction, towards towns such as Knysna, Sedgeflied and Wilderness. These towns were small and secluded holiday retreats for a handful of individuals for over a century, but they were not particularly popular. However, Knysna, which was located between a dramatic coastline, a stunning inland lagoon and the large indigenous Tsitsikama forest, was ideal for second home development. Initially, quaint cottages and old family homes were bought up and renovated. Later some plots of land were made available on the outskirts of the town; on these were built properties of enormous proportions and value, between R1 and R5 million (US$125,000–625,000). Finally, a host of property developers started to build luxurious marinas along the lagoon (e.g. see Keenan, 1999). Further south traditional holiday towns such as Hermanus, historically a favoured destination for retired apartheid-era political elites and for wealthy Boland farmers, also developed out of all proportion.

After a period of slower growth in the mid-1990s, the areas are again receiving attention. Three new trends are, however, underpinning this expansion. One relates to the increased development of smaller towns and hamlets near the initial focus of second home development; a second relates to the movement towards holiday homes in the larger towns and particularly Cape Town; and a third relates to increased international involvement. Firstly, the brief hiatus in second home development was closely linked to a major lack of domestic investor confidence in the core economic regions of South Africa during the transition to post-apartheid democratic rule.

However, although holiday homes accordingly briefly lost their lustre as an investment opportunity, the subsequent growth in second homes, not to mention the growth in value, has consistently averaged between 10 and 35% (Muller, 1999a: 47). Moreover, the development of these second home areas has impacted on the upper-middle classes who, through aspirational consumption, also seek out a second home, although mainly for investment purposes, rather than for pure holiday use. As a result, almost every month over the past four years popular financial magazines have published articles under enticing headings such as 'How to find that little home in the country' (_Financial Mail_, 2001: 26) or 'Your family's dreams ... an affordable reality' (_Finance Week_, 1998: 69) or 'Tomorrow's Clifton and Plet' (_Finance Week_, 1999: 52). In the light of such suggestions, numerous developers have targeted undeveloped land in close proximity to the highly fashionable locations of the first wave of second home development. The consequence is that ever-larger tracts of land are being developed between these established second home core areas (_Finance Week_, 1998: 62; Muller, 1999b: 52). This trend is clearly demonstrated in a selection of investment remarks summarised in Table 13.1 (Fife, 2001: 46). It also increasingly provides property developers and market-wise estate agents with the opportunity to re-market and remake holiday destinations that lost their second home appeal in the late 1980s. Indeed, since the late 1990s cities such as Durban, Port Elizabeth and East London, as well as numerous towns between them, have received countless 'value for money' accolades (see for example _Finansies en Tegniek_, 1997: 47–59).

The demise of apartheid not only led to a range of changes in South Africa's cultural, economic, political and social structures, it also ushered in a massive expansion of the tourism system. At first the novelty of visiting the once-forbidden shores of South Africa generated elevated international tourism interest (Visser & Van Huyssteen, 1997). Subsequently, an exceptionally affordable currency and an extensive tourism resource-base, have increased the number of South Africa's overseas tourists from 50,000 in the mid-1980s to 1 million in the late 1990s and more than 2 million in 2003 (Visser, 2003a: 4). A result of such increases has been greater interest in the South African property market by those who have been impressed by the exceptional value for money the region has to offer. The region that has benefited most from international tourism expansion has been the Western Cape Province, which in turn has acquired an enhanced profile as an area in which to invest in a second home (Visser & Van Huyssteen, 1999).

The location of second homes as holiday property in the Western Cape Province is concentrated not only along the coastal 'holiday belt', but also in many of the major towns, although Cape Town is undoubtedly the focus of attention. Indeed, some (see Muller, 1999a) have suggested that the 'discovery' of urban property in Cape Town as second homes for holiday and

Table 13.1 Examples of second home development advertising

'... But status and pleasure far outweigh the problems of most South Africans as they discover the joys of a home at the beach, mountain, trout stream, village, game farm or smallholding ...'

'...You do not have to be a billionaire to own a piece of South Africa's (SA) most fashionable locations. For instance, a beachfront mansion in Hermanus might cost R10m, but you can watch the sun set over the sea from your veranda down the road at Sandbaai for R179,000. You can buy a riverfront three-bedroomed home within walking distance of billionaires' row in Plettenberg Bay, Beachy Head, for R1m. And you can still talk about your little place among the rich ...'

'... South Africans are spoilt for choice in second homes for less than R1m. What about a beachfront flat in Umhlanga Rocks: Done, for R795,000. Perhaps one of those rural ghettos for the rich in KwaZulu–Natal? Bosch Hoek in Balgowan starts at R1.8m, but homes at Sakabula estate near Howick start at R450 000. A home at the fifth tee in a golf estate? You can buy a three-bedroomed house for R450,000 at Dolphin Creek, Great Brak River, between George and Mossel Bay ...'

'... Perhaps the least discovered coastal area is the Eastern Cape. Most holidaymakers know Port Alfred, but few have heard of Riet River, Kleinemond, Mtati, Mjwalana and Birha. A four-bedroomed home in Birha will cost R600,000. But you can get a luxury house with spectacular sea views for R920,000 (probably negotiable below R900,000) in Kliemond ...'

'... Kleimond and Birha have only 300 properties each, with prices starting at R300,000. Mtati has only 20 wooden homes and Riet Rivier is a company-owned resort in which you can buy shares. But you can still buy at Port Alfred Marina for R550,000 ...'

'... You can go further up the coast between East London and Port St Johns, but most of the area is tribal land and there is little freehold ownership. Down the coast, at St Francis Bay, the thatched houses on the beachfront and up the Krom River remind you of Hermanus 50 years ago. You might just find a home there at R1m, but most are well above that. Holiday cottages outside the prime area cost R350,000 upwards ...'

'... Another area for value is on the coast near George. You can find a home in Sedgefield for between R200,000 and R500,000 ...'

'.... Down the coast towards Mossel Bay, at Rheebok, Fraai Uitsig, Little Brak and Tergniet you can get a three-bedroomed home with wonderful sea views for R350,000. At more upmarket Hershan and Herold's Bay, prices start at R550,000 ...'

'... The Cape West coast between 30 minutes and three hours north of Cape Town also offers value for money ...'

'... Closer to Gauteng, a R3m home at Hartbeespoort Dam's Pecanwood might be outside your budget, but a cottage in nearby Cosmos, on the edge of the dam, can be had for less than R1m. A townhouse will cost less than R500,000. You can buy a 2 ha site at Letama, a game farm just 35 minutes from Sandton, from R250,000. A share in a trout farm at Dullstroom can still be had for under R1m, but rather buy a complete farm on the Mooi River in the midlands for the same money ...'

Source: Fife (2001: 46)

investment purposes was causal to the drop in second home development along the Cape south coast during the mid-1990s. Furthermore, the increased popularity of Cape Town and its immediate hinterland, for domestic and international tourists, has been central to the increase in the number of second homes in this city.

There are a number of locations in Cape Town that have been the focus of second home investment. In particular, Cape Town's Atlantic seaboard has emerged as the 'upmarket Mecca' for both local and foreign investors. The most sought-after suburb in this region is undoubtedly Clifton, with its mountain-hugging houses. These spectacular properties have all the elements of a Mediterranean villa, but at a fraction of the cost. Notwithstanding their supposed affordability, average prices have risen from R630,000 (US$78,700) in 1994 to R4.7 million (US$587,500) in 2002 for a two-or three-bedroom apartment. The average house price for a standalone property is R11.3 million (US$1,412,500) (Fife, 2003). The neighbouring suburb of Gantry Bay has experienced similar growth, with average prices rising from R410,000 to R3.6 million in the same period. Even the (until recently) far less desirable Falkland of Mouille Point has seen properties with prices averaging at R2.2 million. Perhaps most interesting is that only 50% of all these home owners reside permanently at these residences (Fife, 2003). Of the non-residential owners, half are from abroad and the other half from Gauteng (*Business Day*, 2001a, 2001b). For those seeking a more rural ambience, the Constantia Valley and Hout Bay have been most popular, and prices there range from R1–R6 million (*Business Day*, 2003). Other properties that are keenly sought out as second homes are the security-gated golfing estates in Cape Town (Atlantic Beach, Steenberg, Sunset Links, Ruyteplaats) and the immediate interior, such as Paarl (Boschenmeer), Stellenbosch (Zevenwacht) and Somerset West (Erindale) (*Finance Week*, 1998; Muller, 1999c). This trend is indeed starting to extend to other golf estate developments along the Western Cape coast. Popular locations include Arabella near Hermanus, and Garden Route estates such as Fancourt (George) and Sparrenbosch (Knysna) (*Finance Week*, 1998).

Currently, the Cape Town property market is receiving even greater attention and is in the throes of a further real estate boom, largely owing to a range of international trends:

(1)   the current 'safe haven' status of South Africa as a tourism and investment destination is stimulating further investment;

(2)   the instability of investment returns on the global stock markets has led to a return to the relative safety of real estate;

(3)   the high rate of tourism growth to the region has stimulated further interest in the Cape Town property market, whether for retirement, investment or holidays;

(4)   to gain access to the increased tourism revenue flows, many investors
      are investing in property that has tourism development potential .

International second home investors, whether seeking out property for
semi-permanent retirement purposes, as investment property, or for
holiday homes, are starting to display distinctive trends. Undoubtedly the
British market is most prominent in the region, and covers a large range of
properties in terms of both location and price range, not only in Cape Town
or the Western Cape Province, but across South Africa. In large part the
close historical linkages between South Africa and Britain mean that these
investors have a far broader knowledge of and affinity for the country
(d'Angelo, 2003a). Indeed, the fact that nearly 1.5 million South Africans
have British passports makes this nearly inevitable. Currently, the second
most important second home-owner category is that of German nationals.
In the main these investors focus their attention on properties in the
R1–5 million range. The Dutch are the third most important investor category, generally investing R1–2.5 million mainly for retirement, and also
investing in bed-and-breakfast establishments in many cases. An increasingly important investment community is that of Ireland (d'Angelo,
2003b).

This is not to say that all second homes are in these rather expensive price
categories. The largest estate agencies in South Africa (Pam Golding and
Seeff) (according to *Business Day*, 2003) have noted that quality security
cluster development in the middle ranges is increasingly receiving interest.
Again the main overseas investors are British, Dutch and German, with
ownership of up to 15% of all property in the northern coast suburbs of
Table View (the neighbourhood has a view of Table Mountain from across
Table Bay – the quintessential postcard view of Cape Town). The greatest
difference in this trend is that these are middle-class investors who often
acquire property jointly as a group of friends or family members. The properties are then made available to members of this consortium throughout
the year. Increasingly, too, the properties are rented out as tourist accommodation to visitors from their respective countries of origin. This has led to
large-scale development of this area. Whereas the area had 7800 houses as
recently as 1996, it now has 10,000; and approved development will see this
total rise to 17,000 within the five-year development period. Typically
properties are priced in the R300,000 to R400,000 (US$37,500–US$50,000)
price range, which is approximately the average price a South African
middle-class family is expected to pay for a compact residence.

Weekenders and Second Homes

Relative to second homes that serve as holiday homes, often with investment returns in mind, the number of regions that are exclusively or more

closely associated with weekend leisure consumption is smaller and much more difficult to identify in the South African context. In the main, such properties are located, as one might expect, close to the main metropolitan regions. The prime weekender-generating region is undoubtedly that of Johannesburg and Pretoria, which is the locus of nearly 50% of the country's Gross Geographic Product, with the secondary regions being Durban and Cape Town. What makes it difficult to identify weekend second homes in the case of the latter two regions is the fact that these zones of development are inevitably located in the same areas as those that are popular amongst holiday second home developers. For this reason, the discussion only briefly considers the impact of weekend leisure consumption on second home development in the immediate hinterland of Gauteng (Figure 13.2). This hinterland might be defined as those places within a three-hour driving distance of Johannesburg.

Within a one- to two-hour drive from this massive concentration of urban and industrial development, are to be found an extraordinary array of different natural landscapes, ranging from subtropical forests and the Drakensberg escarpment to numerous rivers and large dams. Two established destinations and one emerging destination for weekenders may be identified as this urban metropolitan region's 'pleasure periphery' (see Rogerson, 2002). Dullstroom, about two hours' drive from Johannesburg in Mpumalanga Province, as well as Hartebeespoort Dam, located about an hour from Johannesburg in the North-West Province, have both developed rapidly since the mid-1990s. The developments at Dullstroom were highly regulated and were linked to the trout fishing industry of the region. As such, Dullstroom was and remains a retreat for those who seek to escape the city. During this time, however, Hartebeespoort Dam became the favoured weekend getaway, particularly among the financial services sector and stock market millionaires, interested in water sports and golf. One of the first gated inland golf estates, Pecanwood Estate, saw property prices rise immensely and was regarded as 'the' place in which to invest (Muller, 2003). Indeed, this development attracted so much interest that water-fronted property prices doubled within three years, and property in this area became the most expensive real estate in the country (Muller, 2003). Subsequently, a host of developers has followed suit. This process has, however, led to the classic problems of over-development, and this is reflected in the decreasing popularity of this market. Whereas a small undeveloped lot cost R400,000 (US$50,000) three years ago, such lots are now available at R230,000 (US$28,750). In the main, the investors' view is that the area has lost its tranquillity through overdevelopment, the water quality of the dam has been degraded by overuse, and the road infrastructure is poor – largely because the roads linking the area to Johannesburg were never intended to carry that much traffic. The latest trend for weekend homes is a movement towards the south of the province to the Vaal River. This is supremely ironical in that this area was and remains a favourite recreational area for the working classes, with historically little 'snob' value.

Located three hours' drive away from Johannesburg, a new emerging area of weekend second home development is Clarens, in the sandstone mountain ranges of the eastern Free State. Many in the real estate market have referred to this village as 'the next Dullstroom' (*Property24*, 2002). In the main, this comparison has been made in order to avoid any negative association with the over-development issues witnessed at Hartebeespoort Dam, amongst other localities. Whereas development has until recently been largely focused on the renovation of the much-sought-after sandstone cottages and other good property, new houses are increasingly being developed. Indeed, real estate developers are descending upon the opportunity that property development holds in terms of weekend, retirement or investment homes. However, these developments might soon dwarf the original 500 properties, housing around 3000 permanent inhabitants. Several projects have recently been launched that include 42 new stands in the town itself, as well as an 89-stand gated golf estate, on the town's border. Furthermore, 10 one-hectare stands, with 4 fly-fishing dams, along with another smaller golf course, are being developed (*Property24*, 2002).

Retirement and Second Homes

It is often argued that retirement migration constitutes a special case of the more general category of consumption-led migration. Williams and Hall (2000a: 18–19) suggest that retirement migration, within the over-arching context of differentiating tourists from migrants, poses some of the greatest definitional challenges. A number of approaches such as those of King *et al.* (2000) and O'Reilley (1995) have been put forward to deal with the conceptual issues of how to consider retirees in the context of migration, and their role in second home development. These are considered in more detail elsewhere in this volume; suffice it to say here that they have not been considered in the South African context.

Of course, retirement migration in South Africa is nothing new. Many of the locations already mentioned have been popular among retirees over the years. Indeed, many have retreated from their primary residences in the cities to holiday homes along the coast. The demographic shift to an increasingly ageing population, particularly among the wealthier white classes, underlies a natural process of expansion in housing developments for this cohort, as the structure of families has changed to one in which parents and their grown-up children live independently. As a result a number of locations in South Africa have experienced retiree growth in coastal towns such as Hermanus, Wilderness, George and Plettenberg Bay. Another area that has traditionally been popular among retirees from the interior is the KwaZulu–Natal south coast, including towns such as Hibberdene, Margate, Scottburgh and Ramsgate, to name a few. Moreover, there has for a long time been a trend among the farming communities of the Free State Province, Northern Cape Province and North-West Province in the interior, for people to retire to the main towns in the region, migrating between the *dorpshuis* (town house) and the farm for varying periods of time. Furthermore, similar trends have been experienced both historically and currently, on a continual basis in the Western and Eastern Cape Provinces. The most important trend in retirement migration and its reflection and impact on second home development in South Africa has little to do with domestic retirement migration, but relates rather to the migration of international retirees.

Although there has for many years been a significant presence of foreign retirees in South Africa, mainly from Britain, the issue of their presence has only recently emerged in public discourse. This is with good reason, for a large number of British retirees live in second homes in South Africa. As the country emerged from its apartheid isolation, views about more permanent settlement in the country have changed dramatically. As a consequence, literally thousands of mainly British, but also other Europeans (mainly Germans), have retired to South Africa over the past decade to take advantage of the favourable exchange rate, which enables them to enjoy a higher standard of living than in their home country, and to experience the warmer South African climate. Generally, these retirees are 'swallows' coming to South Africa for four or five months a year. Currently, it is estimated that up to 10% of all property transactions by international investors in the Western Cape Province, and as many as 15% of all property transactions in Cape Town itself, are carried out by this investor category (d'Angelo, 2003a).

Some Impacts of Second Home Development in South Africa

In the context of these brief observations, a range of issues can be teased out as potentially important areas of investigation into second home development in South Africa. The task of this section is to provide an outline of some impacts currently associated with second home development, whilst also providing a potential future focus for more systematic considerations of this phenomenon in the South African context.

In the first instance the impact of second home development, whether for holiday, weekend or retirement purposes, cannot be properly understood before basic and general information regarding the number, location and ownership-base of these properties has been quantified. Currently, there are simply no clear and reliable statistical data that can elucidate the prevalence of second homes in South Africa. It is not even possible to have recourse to significantly improved census data, as no questions regarding the use of other properties are included in the survey. It is also important to note that second properties are plainly not a reality for most South Africans – South Africa is after all a country that has a housing shortage of between 1.5 and 2 million units. This is not to say, however, that second home development is not important. On the contrary, it is the very fact that shelter is so scarce that makes the study of second homes in South Africa so crucial.

Recognition of the impact that second homes, and the various cohorts of people involved in this complex system of consumption-led migration, hold for host communities is starting to attract attention at the highest levels of South African governance. The emergence of such investigation is partly explained in the context of the recent Zimbabwean land-grab fiasco, with many questions currently being asked about who owns what type of property, where, and for what purposes. It has to be noted that under the South African constitution there are no restrictions on land ownership, and there is no intention of banning foreign ownership of land. However, the Deputy President, Jacob Zuma, was recently compelled to make a public statement that the Land Affairs Department 'is conducting research into the matter of foreign ownership of land ... with comparative study of countries facing similar challenges' (Pressley, 2002: 1). Perhaps one of the most burning issues to emerge from current parliamentary debates relates to the fact that the sale of land to foreigners is leading to house price hikes that are beyond the reach of many South Africans. The point is that second home development in this country is currently largely connected to foreign home ownership and not to second homes *per se*. Indeed, the issue of foreign land ownership has been most clearly focused on the European retirees. Whereas they are welcomed by tourism authorities because of their normally high spending over a long period of time, and the concomitant induction of VFR tourism, many locals feel cheated out of property. Indeed, the Department of Home Affairs (whose proposal is not supported by other national government departments) has suggested that changes to the Immigration Act are required.

These debates are focused in particular on the Western Cape Province and Cape Town in particular. The heavy involvement of foreign investors in the Cape Town property market is reshaping large parts of this city (for an example, see Visser, 2003b). On the surface this seems desirable, especially in a country where urban areas, particularly the more central parts thereof, have been in decline for some time. Cape Town has been undergoing radical changes in its Central Business District. Increasingly, international consortiums are buying up abandoned office blocks, with an Irish property development firm being the latest investor to buy up two-street blocks adjacent to the Houses of Parliament for tourism-related

functions such as hotels and housing units. Needless to say, these investments are closely linked to increased tourism flows to this city and the very
buoyant international demand for second homes.

Nevertheless, irrespective of the proportions of international investors,
both foreigners and South African nationals are investing very heavily in
second home properties. The result, echoing countless experiences interna-
tionally, is that Cape Town property is increasingly being priced beyond the
means of local residents who lead normal every-day existences. Whereas
investment in second homes in areas of the really wealthy is of lesser
concern, the impact is mainly felt lower down the socio-economic ladder.
The issue is not that property is expensive in Clifton, but rather that this has
a knock-on effect throughout the city property market. The first to feel these
impacts are the middle classes. Although population growth in this cohort
is stable, there is an increasing shortage of housing in the middle-income
housing range of R300,000 to R600,000. As mentioned earlier, increasing
numbers of international buyers are targeting this market segment. In
response, the middle classes are moving into formerly less desirable neighbourhoods, setting off a range of urban-renewal processes that in turn
thwart the spread of lower classes into formerly lower-middle class white
areas, and this in turn frustrates processes of racial desegregation in residential areas. Indeed, the buying power of the emerging black middle class
– which currently accounts for 10–20% of (middle class) property buyers in
South Africa – cannot keep pace with these rising property values. As a
result they are restricted either to far less desirable lower-class neighbourhoods or to the township areas (Fife, 2003: 71). Thus, the indirect impact of
second home development and acquisition in Cape Town is retarded residential desegregation and a fortification of the spatiality of the race-class
status quo.

Whilst these impacts are important, foreign ownership is not the real
issue, as indeed most of these properties are locally owned. Moreover, Cape
Town is hardly the only focus of such development. On the contrary, there
are literally hundreds of kilometres of second home developments along
the South African coast, that hold a range of environmental and economic
impacts that we currently do not know or understand. The case of
Hartebeespoort Dam highlighted a number of issues that are important
elsewhere in the country. Over-development or inappropriate development, particularly in an ecologically fragile environment such as that of
South Africa, has to be considered. Whereas in some ways it is probably too
late to totally remedy the situation at Hartebeespoort Dam, developments
elsewhere might be carried out in more appropriate ways. These concerns
are relevant to Clarens. For example, the town is on the border of a
newly-declared transfrontier park, and has a unique mountain ecology.
The development of trout fishing, four-wheel-drive and mountain biking

trails could endanger the very resource that currently makes the town so desirable as a weekend second home retreat. Such concerns are not only of issue in Clarens but are relevant to large stretches of coastline areas in South Africa, which are being developed in even more ecologically sensitive areas. In this context, a range of issues focusing on the physical impacts of second home development needs to be investigated.

In the Clarens context, however, conflicts have arisen in terms of the economic and spatial development of the town. For example, the second home owners have contended that, with the exception of the main road through the town, all other roads should remain untarred, as they feel the surfacing of the roads will compromise the rural character of the town. Whereas the poorer segments of this community, restricted to the township, aim to see infrastructural and economic development that provides integrated formal urban spaces and employment, the second home owners are lobbying for the curtailment of local economic development beyond art galleries, restaurants and the like. Similar questions are relevant to scores of coastal towns and villages in South Africa. Indeed, many issues arise when the different communities of a particular town or village have irreconcilable visions of what development should entail. Consumption-led, migration-associated second home development just does not always offer a sufficient range, or permanency, of employment opportunities, to meet the needs of what are often poor and low-skilled host communities. This points to a host of issues surrounding economic, social and planning questions that are currently not being asked, let alone being answered.

Conclusion

This chapter has set out to plot some of the current trends and issues associated with consumption-led second home development in South Africa. It has argued that, whilst second homes as a phenomenon are not new to this country, the phenomenon is nevertheless one that has for a number of reasons remained invisible to the scholarly gaze. The discussion provided a brief geography of where second home development has been taking place and the different types of consumption-led migration systems that underpin these developments. On the whole such second home development in South Africa is, as is so often the case elsewhere, concentrated along its coastline. It was noted that a number of regions have experienced the impacts of such development, with large concentrations found in the Western Cape and KwaZulu–Natal Provinces. What is clear from this discussion is that second homes are, at least for the time being, properties that fulfil a holiday function, with weekend homes and those associated with retirement seldom being the main reason for such developments. Indeed, second home development in South Africa is mainly linked to the family holiday home. Although these properties are mainly owned by South Africans, a discernible increase in foreign interest in second homes in this country is starting to emerge. This, it was argued, has led to a range of impacts, many of which are not desirable to the host community. Whilst there is currently a remarkable silence concerning the impact of second homes, the issue of foreign ownership might focus attention on the broader issues surrounding this phenomenon.

Chapter 14

Second Homes in Spain

MARIA ANGELES CASADO-DIAZ

Introduction

Increased leisure time, greater affluence, increased mobility and income growth are some of the factors that explain the growth, over several decades, in the demand for second homes in Spain. Greater wealth, particularly among the retired, has provided people with the means to buy holiday homes abroad, and the Spanish coast has proved to be one of the most popular destinations for both national and international retirees in search of a second home. Tourism development in Spain has been intrinsically linked to the construction sector and the further urbanisation of the territory. In many cases such developments have formed the basis for the development of tourist areas along the coast (Vera Rebollo, 1987; Navalon, 1995), but development has also spread towards rural areas previously used for farming purposes (Salvå & Socias, 1985).

Recent research has focused on the study of second homes as a seasonal form of migration or semi-migration (Flognfeldt, 2002; Gustafson, 2002b) and has linked this phenomenon to the wider issue of 'consumption migration' (Williams & Hall, 2000a), particularly in later life, when the obligations of work are no longer an important residential constraint. Furthermore, second home tourism has been defined as 'an intersection between tourism and migration', and given as an example of 'the complexity of current mobility' (Müller, 2002c: 83; also Chapter 1, this volume).

Müller (2002c) provides an interesting discussion about second home tourism in the tourism–migration continuum, pointing out the difficulty of assessing the limits of what is considered to be a permanent or temporary move to a second home. According to Müller (2002c), the traditional administrative term 'second home' and the 'time–space' approaches have proven to be insufficient to establish the real meaning of the second home for its owner. Müller (2002c) proposes the use of 'place attachment' approaches to achieve a greater understanding of this concept.

Other authors have noted that, for most second home owners, the second home provided a sense of place, of 'roots', a sense of community, and also a sense of being one of an elite (Jaakson, 1986: 380). Jaakson (1986) also pointed out the 'social distance' between second-home owners and

215

local residents, mainly in terms of their above-average income, their higher educational background, and their greater age (Shucksmith, 1983). Second home owners were defined as a form of 'permanent tourist' in a perpetual state of travel anticipation (Jaakson, 1986: 388) and were visibly different from year-round residents in terms of status, values, behaviour and attitudes. Müller (2002d) has characterised cottage owners as 'leisure gentrifiers', pointing out their perception of the countryside as a recreational resource ready for consumption and their characteristic seasonal circulation. He also suggests that the social distance between second home owners and local residents increases if the properties are in a country different from their own.

The impact of such differences on the socio-economic and demographic structure of the local population has been the subject of many studies (Shucksmith, 1983; Jaakson, 1986; Barke, 1991; Girard & Gartner, 1993). Apart from altering the socio-demographic structure of local communities, second home developments also have an impact on the provision of local services. The findings of Girard and Gartner (1993) revealed the relationship between the life cycle of second home communities and the quality and quantity of services provided to seasonal and permanent residents. During periods of rapid growth, pressure on community services can cause quality of life perceptions to decline, which can lead to the decline of the second-home community (Girard & Gartner, 1993). It has become apparent that there is a lack of appropriate legislation to mitigate the negative impacts of these developments on host communities. According to Gartner (1987), the extent and type of environmental impacts were a function of the location of second homes and the length of stay of second home owners (1987). However, as Müller (2002c: 67) has pointed out 'the way in which second home owners perceive and conceptualise their situation influences substantially the assessment of the impacts of second homes'.

Other authors have also analysed the effects of second home developments on the housing market (Shucksmith, 1983; Instituto Nacional de la Vivienda de Portugal, 1991), highlighting the conflict between local residents and second home owners that results from competition for second homes and the local demand for housing. In many areas, second-home owners had competed with local residents for cheaper existing housing stock. To resolve this conflict Shucksmith (1983) proposed various policy options to local planning authorities, such as preserving the necessary land for public housing or reducing the number of second homes through planning controls.

This chapter analyses the growth of second home developments in Spain, and explores the links between residential tourism and international and domestic retirement migration. It is divided into four sections. The first section reviews the existing literature on second home developments. The second section discusses the official statistical data available for the analysis of residential tourism in Spain. The third section provides an overview of the extent of residential tourism in the Spanish Mediterranean coast and examines the geographical origin of national second-home owners. Finally, the main characteristics of foreign second-home owners in the case study area (Torrevieja, Spain) are discussed in the last section.

Second Home Research in Spain

Despite the large number of second homes, few studies of Spanish second-home communities have been undertaken. Most studies have tended to examine the patterns of location of seasonal residences and their main morphological characteristics (Miranda, 1985; Barke, 1991; Fraguell, 1996). Nevertheless, more recent studies have examined the actual and potential impacts of tourism development on the socio-demographic structure of local populations and the future housing needs of these elderly populations (Casado-Diaz, 1999, 2001; Huber, 2000; Rodríguez *et al.*, 2000).

Barke and France (1988) studied the growth of second homes in the Balearic Islands. They pointed out the dual structure of home ownership and the different spatial distribution of the two types. Foreign owners and tourists tend to be located in the main tourist centres and coastal areas, whereas the inland areas were the principal location for permanent residents of the Balearics (Barke & France, 1988). Barke also carried out a study of the distribution of second homes and their changing pattern in Malaga, and noted the extensive urbanisation of the coast during the last 30 years and the sustained demand for vacation homes by foreigners, with large proportions of these second homes being purpose-built. He also pointed out the importance of residential tourism, where people live in the area for at least part of the year – usually foreign second home owners (Barke, 1991). Further research revealing the importance of second home tourism and the difficulties involved in the analysis of this type of tourism has been conducted, particularly in the regions of Catalonia (Fraguell, 1996; Priestley & Mundet, 1998) and Valencia (Miranda, 1985; Hermosilla, 1992; Vera Rebollo, 1995; Casado, 1999, 2001).

The movement of older people from northern European countries towards southern Europe is not new, and for decades many of those with the necessary financial resources have moved from the colder and wetter European regions towards areas with a warmer and drier climate, such as the Mediterranean coast. Although retirement migration represents a small (but significant) percentage of migration flows within Europe, it has become very important since the early 1980s, particularly in countries like Spain, Portugal and Italy. During the last decades, international retirement migration has experienced a rapid growth owing to an increased life expectancy, greater wealth among older people, higher levels of education, more people taking early retirement, changes in lifestyle (such as more experience in travelling and working abroad), easier international travel, and easier and cheaper communications (Gober & Zonn, 1983; Cuba, 1989; McHugh, 1990; King *et al.*, 2000; Williams *et al.*, 2000; Casado-Diaz, 2001; Rodríguez, 2001; Müller, 2002a; Salvá Tomás, 2002; Truly, 2002; Williams & Hall, 2002). All these factors have given large numbers of retirees access to new leisure and residential alternatives in search of a better quality of life.

In Spain, regions such as Costa Blanca, Costa del Sol and the Balearic and Canary Islands have become the favourite locations for both permanent and temporary European older age migrants. The extensive urbanisation of the coast since the early 1970s and the sustained demand for vacation homes by foreigners, with large proportions of these second homes being purpose built, have produced important changes in the urban structure of municipalities with residential tourism. In the Costa Blanca, and especially in municipalities such as Torrevieja, the unplanned growth of a large number of settlements is one of the major features of tourist development, and most of the settlements have been characterised by the lack of facilities and services (Vera Rebollo, 1987; Navalon, 1995; Torres Alfosea, 1995).

International retirement migration in Spain is linked to the rapid growth of second home developments along the Mediterranean coast, and second home ownership has proven to be a very important factor in deciding where to migrate in later life, either on a temporary or permanent basis (Casado-Diaz, 2001).

According to Cuba (1989) prior tourist visits to the destination areas might strongly influence the future decision to move. Thus, the accumulated knowledge acquired through repeated visits to the same destination, together with the formation of new social networks, play an important role in the migrant's decision-making process. Furthermore, the tourist nature of some of the most important retirement destinations and the existing provision of leisure services and recreational facilities provide the necessary infrastructure for the settlement of amenity-led migrants. Similarly, other authors have established the strong relationship between temporary mobility and permanent migration and how the former might act as a precursor or substitute for the latter (Bell & Ward, 2000; McHugh, 1990; Williams & Hall, 2000). Gustafson (2002b) has also shown the importance of seasonal retirement migration along the Spanish coasts and discussed the differences between seasonal older migrants, tourists and local residents in terms of social distinction and authenticity.

Methodology: The Problem of Data

One of the most important problems both in second-home developments and international retirement migration research is how to obtain accurate estimates of their extent. In the case of measuring the extent of second-home ownership, this is due to the poorly measured statistics and the different definitions of 'second home' given by institutions and researchers (Shucksmith, 1983; Barke, 1991; Fraguell, 1996). Fraguell identifies the lack of reliability of statistical data as one of the main problems analysing residential tourism development. One of the most common mistakes is to consider the second home as unoccupied housing or vacant dwellings (Barke, 1991; Fraguell, 1996). Demographically, another important problem is the fact that these new 'residents', who usually spend a long period of time in their second homes, are not normally recorded in the Census of Population. Therefore, the population size of many tourist resorts is usually underestimated in local and national statistics.

A similar problem exists with the information provided by the buildings census. There is no distinction between dwellings built in order to be primary residences and those built to be second homes. This contributes to the lack of information provided by official sources. There are many definitions of second home and there is no 'typical' type of dwelling associated with them. Generally, conceptualisations of second homes are based on physical character and temporary use. However, in a large number of second home communities, this temporary use is more commonly becoming a year-round use.

Similarly, the lack of accurate official records of the number of migrants makes research in this field extremely difficult (Rose & Kingma, 1989; Age Concern, 1993; Rodriguez *et al.*, 1998; King *et al.*, 2000; Casado-Diaz, 2001; O'Reilly, 2001; Casado-Diaz & Rodriguez, 2002). The most important reason is the reluctance of the expatriate community to be recorded, both because of time-consuming bureaucracy, and in order to avoid taxes from both the original and the destination countries. There is also no obligation for migrants to register with the municipality unless they spend more than six months in the destination area.

Despite the problems of quantification mentioned above, several official sources of information are commonly used to analyse the growth of second homes in Spain. This analysis draws on three main official sources of information:

(1) *Frontur*, the Spanish annual official survey of international tourism in Spain (Frontur, 2003);
(2) *Familitur*, the annual domestic tourism survey that provides information about the flows of Spanish journey-makers between the various Autonomous Communities and of those going abroad (Familitur, 2001);
(3) the 1981 and 1991 Spanish Census of Dwellings, produced by the Spanish Ministry of Development (1998) containing information about the stock of second homes.

(4)   finally, the analysis of the seasonal mobility patterns of foreign second
       home owners in Torrevieja, Costa Blanca, is based on the findings
       from a research project of northern European retired migrants living
       in Torrevieja, based on a questionnaire survey and in-depth face-
       to-face interviews with key informants and the migrants themselves.

The definition of second home used by the Familitur and Frontur
surveys is:

> a property other than the common dwelling (and located outside the
> usual municipality of residence), whatever may be the tenure arrange-
> ment (owned, rented for more than six months a year or lent) and
> designed to be used at least once a year for spending therein one or
> several days.

With a total sample of 10,800 households, the Familitur survey allows for
the information provided to be representative and comparable at both
national and regional levels. However, it is important to mention that the
available Familitur data refers only to 'short trips to second homes' (four
nights or less), as opposed to 'long duration second home trips' (more than
four nights), which are included in the total number of tourist trips. Frontur
is an official survey to determine the number and main characteristics
(destination areas, type of accommodation used, means of transport,
reason for travelling to Spain) of the international tourism flows to Spain.

Spatial Distribution of Second Homes in Spain: The Growth of Second Homes

According to the *Statistical Atlas for Housing* (Ministerio de Fomento,
1998), in 1981 there were 1,899,759 second homes in Spain. In 1991, the
number of second homes reached 2,628,817, an increase of nearly 28% over
ten years.

Figure 14.1 shows the growth of second homes in the Spanish provinces
from 1981 to 1991. Those provinces that have experienced more than 75%
growth during the decade analysed are located in mainland regions
(Extremadura, Andalucia and Castilla La Mancha) and in the region of
Catalonia. However, most Mediterranean provinces have also witnessed a
very sharp increase (50–75%) in the number of second homes located in
their territory. That is the case of the provinces of Alicante, Murcia and
Castellón. Generally speaking, only a low number of Spanish provinces have
experienced low levels of growth compared to the whole country (Table 14.1).

Barke (1991) examined the pattern of spatial distribution of second
homes in Spain in the 1970s and 1980s. He reported that most second homes
in Spain were to be found along the coastline, particularly in the Mediterranean provinces, and in mainland provinces near to large metropolitan areas

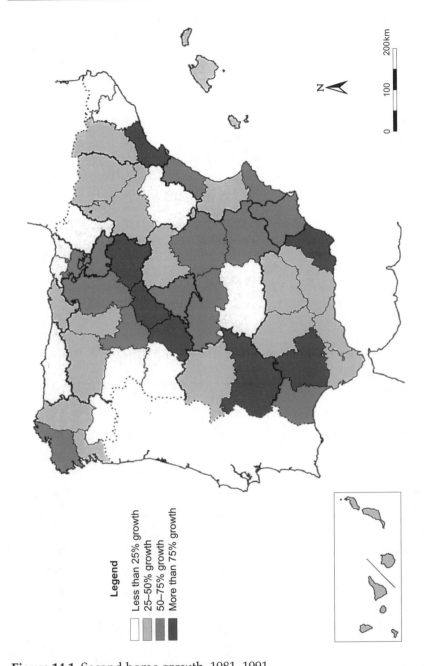

Figure 14.1 Second home growth, 1981–1991

Source: *Statistical Atlas for Housing* (Ministerio de Fomento, 1998)

Table 14.1 Second homes in Spain (1991)

	Total housing stock	*Secondary homes*	*Secondary homes as % of total*
TOTAL	17,160,677	2,628,817	15.31
ANDALUCIA	2,830,028	409,615	14.47
Almeria	213,916	38,694	18.08
Cádiz	390,517	61,772	15.81
Córdoba	280,877	26,154	9.31
Granada	345,864	57,647	16.66
Huelva	194,2 88	47,415	24.40
Jaén	261,570	29,259	11.18
Málaga	572,776	113,403	19.79
Sevilla	570,220	35,271	6.18
ARAGON	574,011	91,085	15.86
Huesca	108,437	26,681	24.60
Teruel	91,904	27,121	29.51
Zaragoza	373,670	37,283	9.97
ASTURIAS, PRINCIPADO DE	462,283	46,628	10.08
BALEARS, ILLES	414,035	82,093	19.82
CANARIAS	581,037	69,475	11.95
Las Palmas	278,380	31,717	11.39
Santa Cruz de Tenerife	302,657	37,758	12.47
CANTABRIA	225,789	40,789	18.06
CASTILLA - LA MANCHA	819,427	184,537	22.52
Albacete	157,578	22,763	14.44
Ciudad Real	201,990	32,658	16.16
Cuenca	118,661	34,412	29.00
Guadalajara	100,941	38,491	38.13
Toledo	240,257	56,213	23.39
CASTILLA Y LEON	1,269,443	268,450	21.14
Avila	119,897	47,475	39.59
Burgos	187,797	46,626	24.82
León	247,183	35,532	14.37
Palencia	87,357	16,947	19.39
Salamanca	173,437	32,882	18.95

Segovia	85,314	25,299	29.65
Soria	60,450	17,136	28.34
Valladolid	195,680	22,361	11.42
Zamora	112,328	24,192	21.53
CATALUÑA	2,748,541	414,047	15.06
Barcelona	1,900,389	166,891	8.78
Girona	336,666	102,210	30.35
Lleida	163,924	25,498	15.55
Tarragona	347,562	119,448	34.36
COMUNIDAD VALENCIANA	2,087,123	496,804	23.80
Alicante	788,780	229,068	29.04
Castellón	268,982	78,612	29.25
Valencia	1,029,361	189,124	18.37
EXTREMADURA	470,055	80,247	17.07
Badajoz	264,208	35,052	13.26
Cáceres	205,847	45,195	21.95
GALICIA	1,132,559	122,387	10.80
La Coruña	446,404	41,033	9.19
Lugo	167,506	15,518	9.26
Orense	186,760	30,548	16.35
Pontevedra	331,889	35,288	10.61
MADRID, COMUNIDAD DE	1,928,940	144,720	7.50
MURCIA, REGION DE	478,870	98,933	20.65
NAVARRA, C. FORAL DE	202,041	17,756	8.78
PAIS VASCO	773,986	37,544	4.85
Alava	105,760	9,475	8.95
Guipúzcoa	244,811	9,427	3.85
Vizcaya	423,415	18,642	4.40
RIOJA, LA	128,346	23,394	18.22
CEUTA Y MELILLA	34,163	313	0.91
Ceuta	18,250	106	0.58
Melilla	15,913	207	1.30

Source: Adapted from the 1991 Population and Dwellings Census. INE. Mº de Economía y Hacienda (National Statistics Institute, 1991)

with a history of rural-urban migration, and he highlighted the growing importance of 'residential tourism' in the Spanish coast.

Müller (2002a) argues that second homes are usually located within the leisure peripheries of the metropolitan areas' thereby allowing frequent visits. This is also the case for most Spanish second home owners who bought their properties in the same region of residence. According to the Familitur survey (2001), nearly 4 out of 10 Spanish second home owners own a secondary residence in the same region of residence, and they tend to visit this during weekends and short vacations.

According to the figures provided by Familitur (2001), 63.6% of all tourist journeys conducted by Spanish households in 2001 were short trips (4 days or less) to second homes. A common feature of Spanish tourist behaviour is access to second homes, and in 2001, nearly 27% of all Spanish households had access to a second home. Five out of 10 households had access to a second home owned by a friend or relative, while 48% owned a second home. Figure 14.2 shows the proportion of Spanish households with access to a second home according to region of residence (Familitur, 2001).

The Spanish regions with the highest percentage of households with access to a second home are Madrid (45.1%), Pais Vasco (38.6%), Aragón (31.4%) and Asturias (29.7%). In Valencia and Catalonia, at least 25% of all households also have access to a second home (Familitur, 2001).

One of the most important spatial characteristics of second home tourism in Spain is the intra-regional character of most trips to second homes. The journeys tend to take place within the same autonomous region, except in the case of Madrid and Pais Vasco, where locals have traditionally moved to the coast during the summer months and Easter vacation (Familitur,2001). Table 14.2 shows the total number of Spanish households with access to a second home by region of residence, and the average distance from main residence to second home.

According to the Familitur survey (2001), a total of 3,488,069 Spanish households had access to a second home in 2001. Those regions with the highest number of households with access to a second home were Madrid (42%), Pais Vasco (27%), Asturias (24%) and Catalonia (22%). The average distance to a second home within the region of residence is only 43.6 kilometres. Of those who own or have access to a second home outside their usual region of residence, the average distance to the second home increases to 348 kilometres.

Those regions with a higher proportion of households with access to a second home within the same region are Canarias, Baleares, Murcia, Cantabria, Galicia, Valencia, Asturias and Navarra y Andalucia. One common feature for most of these areas is their coastal location. By contrast, the regions with the greatest number of households with access to a second

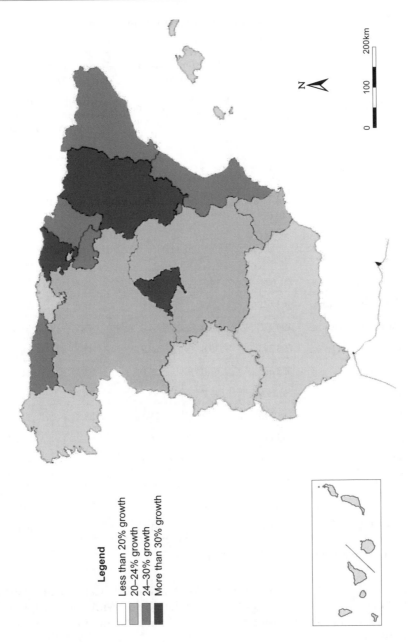

Figure 14.2 Proportion of households with access to a second home in 2001 by region of residence

Source: Familitur, 2001

Table 14.2 Location of second home and average distance from main residence to second home

Autonomous region	Total Access to a second home	Location of second home		Average distance to second home (km)	
		Within the same region	In another region	Within the same region of residence	Outside the region of residence
Total	3,488,069	37.7	62.3	43.6	348.0
Andalucia	394,130	51.1	48.9	42.8	236.5
Aragon	132,997	42.0	58.0	65.7	254.7
Asturias	110,629	55.1	44.9	65.1	456.2
Baleares	53,244	67.4	32.6	27.9	632.7
Canarias	108,939	75.7	24.3	45.4	1,313.9
Cantabria	31,600	64.7	35.3	43.5	311.7
Castilla-La Mancha	131,612	29.0	71.0	47.2	239.2
Castilla y Leon	194,275	46.0	54.0	43.1	341.2
Cataluna	608,593	30.8	69.2	42.0	381.2
C. Valenciana	333,689	61.0	39.0	32.4	319.5
Extremadura	56,263	49.7	50.3	58.7	411.9
Galicia	147,543	61.9	38.1	38.1	312.4
Madrid	780,110	13.2	86.8	50.2	350.7
Murcia	78,760	65.6	34.4	49.4	838.6
Navarra	42,388	52.3	47.7	53.4	374.3
Pais Vasco	258,394	12.7	87.3	29.5	319.8
Rioja (La)	24,904	48.2	51.8	37.3	294.9

Source: Adapted from Familitur (2001)

home in another region are Pais Vasco, Madrid, Castilla la Mancha, Catalonia, Aragón, Castilla-León and La Rioja. With the exception of Catalonia, these regions are located on the Spanish mainland with no access to the sea.

When the analysis is conducted at a more local level, the high concentration of second homes in specific municipalities becomes obvious, particularly those located in the Mediterranean provinces of Alicante, Tarragona, Barcelona and Valencia (Figure 14.3).

Those municipalities with the highest proportion of second homes in relation to the total housing stock are shown in Figure 14.3. The data reveals that the proportion of second homes is higher than 60% in certain municipalities, such as Benicasim in Castellon, Calafell and Salou in Tarragona, and Calpe and Teulada in the province of Alicante.

With regard to international tourism, one of the most important characteristics is the high degree of geographical concentration in the Spanish coastal regions. According to the Frontur survey (2003), in 2002, 92% of the total number of foreign tourists to Spain were found in six autonomous regions. Catalonia accounted for 22.4% of all tourist visits, followed by Canarias (20.6%), Baleares (18.5%), Andalucia (14.3%) and Valencia (9.5%) (Frontur, 2003). These figures revealed the attraction of Spanish coastal destinations for international tourists, especially from the United Kingdom or Germany.

The data regarding the type of accommodation chosen reveal the importance of foreign second home owners in Spain. According to the Frontur survey (2003), 19.1% of all international tourists in Spain stayed in non-paid -or accommodation, mainly second homes (Table 14.3).

These figures also reveal the importance of visiting friends and relatives (VFR) tourism associated with the access to a second home owned by a

Table 14.3 Number of international tourists according to type of accommodation used in 2002 (%)

Total tourists	% of total	Inter-annual variation (%)	Average stay (days)
Hotel accommodation	64.8	0.9	8.0
Non-hotel accommodation	34.9	8.0	15.5
Non-paid-for accommodation	19.1	0.6	15.5
• Second home of friends/relatives	9.6	16.9	11.8
• Own second home	8.9	-11.4	19.4
• Time-share	0.6	-18.6	17.1
Rented accommodation	9.5	16.3	17.5
Other accommodation (campsites, caravanning ...)	6.3	22.1	12.6

Source: Adapted from Frontur (2003)

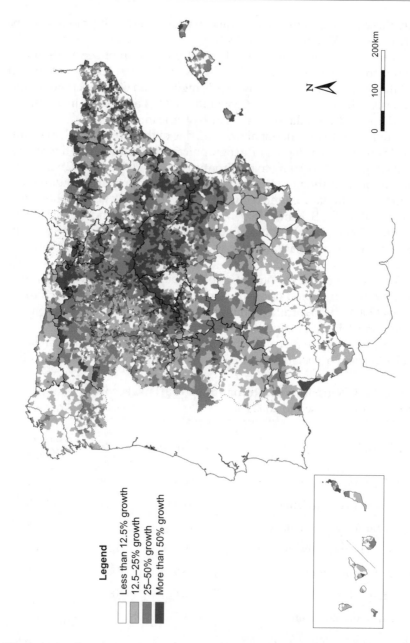

Figure 14.3 Proportion of second homes as a percentage of the total housing stock in Spain (1991)

Source: *Statistical Atlas for Housing* (Ministerio de Fomento, 1998)

friend or a relative. It is likely that these second homes are used when the older seasonal migrants go back to their countries of origin during the warm summers, and return to Spain for the winter. Compared with the figures for 2001, accommodation in properties owned by friends or relatives has experienced an annual growth of nearly 17%, indicating the increasing importance of this type of tourism and its close relationship with second home tourism and seasonal migration among older people.

Residential tourism, both domestic and international, has become a very important feature in most coastal Spanish regions, particularly in the Mediterranean regions of Catalonia and Valencia. According to the Frontur survey (Frontur, 2003), 22% of all foreign tourists arrived in the Valencian region, and 17% of those visiting Murcia stayed in their own second homes.

A Case Study of Northern European Second Home Owners in Torrevieja

Relationships between second home tourism and seasonal retirement migration

Müller (2002c) notes that, for a great number of people, 'circulation' (visiting a number of different places on a regular basis) is now more common than permanent migration to a single place. The author argues that, with regard to mobility among second home owners, a distinction should be made between circulation (frequent visits during weekends) and seasonal migration (use of the second home for longer periods once or twice a year) – see Chapter 1. This seasonal migration among second home owners has also become apparent in a recent study conducted among a sample of Northern European retirees in Torrevieja on the Costa Blanca (Casado-Diaz, 2001).

Although the author's survey did not look specifically into second home ownership, the patterns of stay and the frequency of the visits to the country of origin suggest that seasonal migration was an important characteristic of those interviewed. This research revealed that previous holidays in Spain (51%), ownership of a second home (23%) and friends or relatives already spending their holidays there (14%) were among the most important reasons for choosing Torrevieja as a place to retire (Casado-Diaz, 2001).

Müller (2002c) establishes three categories of second home owners.

(1) *the traditional second home owner*, who bought a second home for leisure purposes;
(2) *the incidental migrant*, who originally bought a second home for the same reasons but after a period of time decided to move there on a more permanent basis;

(3)   *the conscious migrant*, whose ultimate goal is to migrate to the country
       where the second home has been purchased.

According to the survey carried out by Casado (2001), in the case of
Torrevieja we can distinguish between:

(1)   those who spend less than 27 weeks a year in Torrevieja and owned a
       property in the region of origin;
(2)   those who spend most of their time in Torrevieja but visit their country
       of origin on a regular basis and have usually kept a home there;
(3)   those who live most of the year in Torrevieja, hardly ever visit their
       country of origin, and do not own a property there.

The study by Williams *et al.* (2000) concluded that nearly two thirds of
their sample of foreign residents followed some kind of peripatetic lifestyle
between the region of destination and their country of origin. They also
pointed out the fact that this pattern of mobility was facilitated by the
ownership of a second home in the area and discussed the implications in
terms of 'visiting friends and relatives' tourism (VFR) from the United
Kingdom to Southern Europe. As shown in Table 14.4, in Torrevieja, 51% of
those interviewed stated that they spent more than nine months a year in
the destination area showing the attachment to their 'second home', as
opposed to their residence in the country of origin. However, the frequency
of visits shows that most people visited their country of origin at least once
or twice a year, to some extent maintaining the contacts with their relatives
and friends.

The smaller numbers of people in Torrevieja with peripatetic lifestyles,
when compared with those found in Williams *et al.* (2000), are linked to the
restricted financial resources of those choosing this Spanish destination.
Many of these 'residential tourists' were forced to sell their homes in the
country of origin in order to purchase a property in Spain, and this obviously had an impact on the frequency of the visits to their countries
(Casado-Diaz, 2001). Those who live less than six months a year in
Torrevieja account for nearly 30% of those interviewed, while the percentage
of people who live in Torrevieja between six and nine months a year is 19%.

Table 14.4 shows that the frequency of visits to the country of origin is
much higher among the first group (those who spend less than six months
in Torrevieja), with one-third of them travelling three or more times
between the two countries. The second group tends to travel to their place
of origin once or twice a year. Finally, those in the third group (who spend
more than nine months in the destination area) tend to follow the same
pattern and visit at their home countries least once or twice, with the exception of those spending practically all year round in Torrevieja, who tend not
to visit the home country at all or just once. The average number of weeks

Table 14.4 Number of weeks spent in Torrevieja and number of visits to country of origin (%)

Weeks in Torrevieja	Number of visits to country of origin					
	None	*1*	*2*	*3*	*More than 3*	*Total*
< 27	7.9	38.2	21.1	10.5	22.4	29.3
27–39	8.2	36.7	38.8	10.2	6.1	18.9
40–44	0.0	42.1	42.1	5.3	10.5	7.3
45–49	0.0	54.2	29.2	12.5	4.2	18.5
50–52	32.8	49.3	11.9	4.5	1.5	25.8
Total	12.4	44.0	25.1	8.9	9.7	100.0

Source: Author's survey

spent in the home country was 10 weeks a year, and in terms of type of accommodation used 53% stayed in their own homes, while 41% stayed with friends or relatives.

With regard to ownership of a property in the home country, the survey results show that 5 out of 10 have retained a property there, while nearly 9 out of 10 own a home in Spain. These results, together with the analysis of the frequency of the visits to country of origin and number of weeks spent there, reveal the importance of seasonal migration in the destination area.

Conclusions

This chapter has examined the growth and spatial distribution of second homes in Spain during the last two decades, focusing on the differences between national and international second home owners. The analysis of second home growth in Spain has revealed the sharp increase in the number of second homes in mainland Spain, such as Extremadura, Andalucia and Castilla la Mancha, where the percentage of growth was above 75%. However, the demand for second homes in popular tourist destinations has also risen considerably in the Mediterranean regions of Catalonia, Valencia and Murcia, where residential tourism is a basic component of the tourist industry. As argued earlier, the importance of residential tourism is especially significant in some coastal municipalities where the proportion of second homes with respect to the total housing stock exceeds 80%. It is in these municipalities where the impacts of second homes are particularly important, particularly in terms of socio-demographic and spatial changes (Casado-Diaz, 1999).

The official figures show that most Spanish domestic tourist trips are short trips to second homes. Nearly 3 out of 10 Spanish households either own a second home, or have access to a second home owned by friend or a relative. In regions such as Madrid and Pais Vasco, however, this percentage reaches 40%. Another important characteristic of second home tourism in Spain is the preference for second homes located within the region of residence. Thus, in the Valencia and Murcia regions, for example, the percentage who own second homes within the region is more than 60%. In terms of international second home owners in Spain, the results reveal the importance of residential tourism, as nearly 20% of all international tourists that arrive in Spain in 2002 stayed in non-paid accommodation, mainly second homes owned by themselves or by friends or relatives. Following Müller's (2002a) typology, most Spanish second home owners could be characterised as 'circulating' second home owners, rather than foreign second home owners – 'seasonal migrants' who visit their secondary residences in Spain less frequently, but stay there for longer periods. The increasing importance of circulation as opposed to migration in the context of consumption-led mobility, suggests the need for more research on the tourism–migration continuum and the links between residential tourism and seasonal and permanent migration.

Chapter 15

Second Homes as a Part of a New Rural Lifestyle in Norway

THOR FLOGNFELDT JR

The Norwegian economy is one of the most prosperous in Europe. Five weeks of paid holiday, extending to six for those over 60 years old, and the opportunity of exchanging overtime work for extended weekends, means that there is plenty of time available to spend in the second home. In addition, a high proportion of families have two full-time jobs with a corresponding significant level of disposable income. It is therefore not surprising that second homes are a major form of housing investment for many Norwegian families. Nevertheless, second homes, especially in the form of *hytte* (mountain or seaside cabin) have long held a special place in the Norwegian way of life. In 2002 more than 360,000 dwellings were classified as second homes (SSB, 2002). This is double the number of second homes that were officially registered in 1970, but these figures cover only purpose-built second homes. In addition, there are 40,000 official registered second homes owned by Norwegians in other countries (*Dagens Næringsliv*, 2003). However, this figure does not include long-term rental properties. As of 2002, every second family in the country, therefore, had access to at least one second home, with access deriving from either direct ownership or, very often, from homes owned by older family members that are regularly lent out for free to other family and close friends.

Growth in the number of and access to second homes is not the only change in the Norwegian second home market. The location and building standards of second homes have also undergone rapid change. The first locations for second homes tended to be close to summer farms in the mountains or near to steamship and railway terminals in coastal areas. Changes in transport and recreational activities have therefore also influenced new location patterns. In addition, changes in household economy have meant that second homes have been transformed from modest cabins without conveniences such as electricity, water supply or sewerage to, in some cases, new second homes built to higher standards than most family houses. This is particularly the case for second homes at alpine ski resorts or at attractive sites along the southern coastal shores.

Changes in building construction and levels of disposable income have

also been followed by changes in usage patterns. The development of electronic communication technology such as mobile phones and the Internet
has meant that, for some, more and more work can be undertaken away
from the office. In addition, many of the resort environments are regarded
as better places to live in for families with children than the cities are, and
this has therefore meant that some families have considered using the
second home as the primary home.

This chapter begins with a brief discussion of the second home concept
in Norway. This is followed by a historical overview of second home developments in Norway, with special attention being given to second homes in
the alpine regions. The conclusion presents some ideas regarding planning
for multi-site living that is a feature of second homes. In this connection
challenges for different bodies, such as local government, tourism industry,
site developers and second homeowners are examined.

The Concept of Second Homes in Norway

In Norway the concept of *hytte*, meaning a cabin or in some cases a
cottage, has for many years been taken to approximate the concept of a
'second home'. There were, of course, other types of second homes, but they
were not that common or else belonged to special interest groups, often for
purposes such as fishing or hunting. Unlike other European countries,
Norway does not have a historical legacy of country or hunting estates.
Examples of other types of second home that were once of some significance include trade union cottages that catered for the holidays of trade
union members and their families and were often located close to train and
steamboat transport nodes for ease of access. Perhaps more significantly
summer farms have long held an important place in Norwegian agricultural and social practice.

Owing to the scarcity of arable land and grassland in the valleys, most
farms in Norway have an additional summer farm up in the mountains. For
many years these summer farms were multipurpose production areas
during the summer season – milking and cheese-making, wild berry
picking, trout fishing and providing accommodation to hikers were all part
of the income base. During the 1950s, this economic base was altered by the
increased accessibility for both agricultural produce and tourists, thanks to
the development of new roads and milk trucks that had seating for
passengers. This therefore provided opportunities for the establishment of
mountain lodges and hotels that competed with the informal accommodation provision of the summer farms. Nevertheless, the function of summer
farms as second homes was reinforced from the 1960s onwards as, when
children left the farm for the cities either for education or work, small
second homes for these children were often added on to the summer farms.

Later new detached second homes were built in the surroundings of the summer farms (Langdalen, 1965) (Daugstad and Saeter (2001) provide an excellent review of summer farms in Norway.)

Second Home Zones in Norway

Arguably there are two important zones for second home development in Norway: a *national* zone based on markets in the Oslofjord area, and a series of *regional* zones based on much shorter trips out from the urban areas around the country. Most of these zones can be divided into a coastal and a mountain zone, since most urban areas in Norway are located close to both coast and mountains.

Initial developments in coastal second homes took place when the main cities started growing and steamship routes were developed along the coast. As communications and roads improved, new areas farther away from the cities and towns became attractive, and buyers purchased either old houses or vacant lots on which to erect their second home. After the state license system of car ownership disappeared in 1960, new areas along Norway's southern coastline were opened up for second home development although the implementation of the1965 Building Law meant the introduction of more rigid planning controls on second homes. Hansen (1969) described the development of second homes in the coastal community of Eidanger, which is located just outside the Oslofiord. As early as 1965, this municipality had 1100 summer cottages, mostly owned by residents from the nearby towns of Porsgrunn and Skien. When the weekend commuting zones reached Telemark and Agder counties, even parts of Sweden became an attractive option for residents of the eastern part of Norway. Indeed, much of the Bohuslän part of Sweden has significant Norwegian second home ownership. Such developments may be expected to continue in parts of western Sweden with high amenity values as the development of coastal second home sites along the southern Norwegian coastline is now very restricted by lack of available land, and in many coastal areas older houses are being restored or replaced by new homes.

As noted above, in Norwegian mountain areas there is a long tradition of using second homes that originated as seasonal working places in connection with cattle, goat and sheep grazing. Some wealthy people built recreational second homes as early as the national Romantic period of the 19th century. However, the first large-scale development phase began in the1920s and derived from the growth of outdoor recreation and improved access to the mountain areas, mostly through a combination of train and bus transport, but later by the extended ownership of private cars. There were many similarities between the Norwegian cottage holiday experience at this time and that of Sweden (Löfgren, 1999; see also Chapter 16, this volume).

Langdalen (1965) described the development of cottages in relation to summer farm sites as follows:

(1) good grazing conditions motivate the establishment of a summer farm;
(2) a good summer farm (because of good grazing) motivates the building of a road;
(3) improved car access and the idyll of a summer farm makes the summer farm area attractive for second homes;
(4) more second homes motivates a better road system;
(5) a better road attracts more traffic and encourages further building development;
(6) easy access and increasing traffic encourage the establishment of one or more commercial tourism businesses (e.g. accommodation);
(7) the commercial tourism business expands, and provides a basis for the development of even better roads, possibly a through road linking to other summer farm areas. This might also increase the use of the accommodation in the low season;
(8) the reason for the initial utilisation of the area (summer farming) is now reduced because of the heavy development of second homes, tourism businesses and heavy traffic. Some summer farms will, therefore, be closed down.
(59 the conditions that motivated the first round of second home development – close contact to summer farming and nature, and easy access to small roads – are no longer present.

Langdalen made these observations almost 40 years ago, and in many areas some new phases have occurred. Nevertheless, the overall development pattern remains relevant to the present day. However, the main difference is that since the early 1990s there has been a new development pattern in some localities, with several designated second home areas being developed in connection with alpine skiing resorts (Flognfeldt, 2002). Figure 15.1 seeks to illustrate the relationship between the market (potential developer) and planning authority (municipality) in different locations from A (bottom of a valley/township area) to D (the high mountain area) (Langdalen, 1992). It also shows the three activity zones for golf, alpine skiing and cross-country skiing and mountain hiking that have become a feature of more recent recreational activities related to second homes.

During the late 1990s some resorts, mostly those with access to alpine skiing, embarked on a master plan to design both alpine ski lifts and slopes and also housing and shops. Mountain resort areas such as Trysil, Hemsedal, Beitostølen and Hafjell have all been through such processes, which will result in a new type of resort with greater focus on elements of

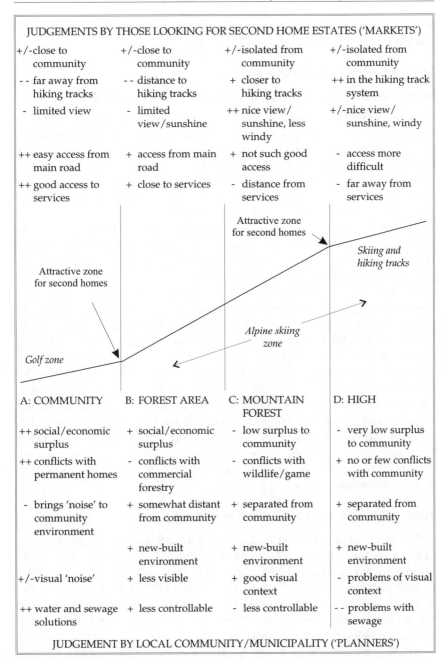

JUDGEMENTS BY THOSE LOOKING FOR SECOND HOME ESTATES ('MARKETS')

+/-close to community	+/-close to community	+/-isolated from community	+/-isolated from community
- - far away from hiking tracks	- - distance to hiking tracks	+ closer to hiking tracks	++ in the hiking track system
- limited view	- limited view/sunshine	++ nice view/ sunshine, less windy	+/-nice view/ sunshine, windy
++ easy access from main road	+ access from main road	+ not such good access	- access more difficult
++ good access to services	+ close to services	- distance from services	- far away from services

Attractive zone for second homes

Attractive zone for second homes

Skiing and hiking tracks

Alpine skiing zone

Golf zone

A: COMMUNITY	B: FOREST AREA	C: MOUNTAIN FOREST	D: HIGH
++ social/economic surplus	+ social/economic surplus	- low surplus to community	- very low surplus to community
++ conflicts with permanent homes	- conflicts with commercial forestry	- conflicts with wildlife/game	+ no or few conflicts with community
- brings 'noise' to community environment	+ somewhat distant from community	+ separated from community	+ separated from community
	+ new-built environment	+ new-built environment	+ new-built environment
+/-visual 'noise'	+ less visible	+ good visual context	- problems of visual context
++ water and sewage solutions	+ less controllable	- less controllable	- - problems with sewage

JUDGEMENT BY LOCAL COMMUNITY/MUNICIPALITY ('PLANNERS')

Figure 15.1 Location of second homes in mountain areas

the urban way life than the former sole cottage in mountains or forests. This issue is discussed in the following section.

Second Homes in Alpine Areas

From 1945 to 1965: A period of democratic development

When World War 2 ended, the need for building material for housing and industry in Norway was immense, and recreation houses were not considered an appropriate demand. There was, however, one way of building second homes, and that was to re-use old wooden material. Most people were eager to remove symbols of German occupation, mainly wooden soldiers' barracks, and the wooden panels and other construction material were often offered to second home builders.

As noted above, in most of the mountain areas, and even some sites along the coast, at the time there was no requirement for building permits to erect a second home. Some of the work force had periods of seasonal unemployment, especially during the winter, and many of these people possessed some construction skills, and building a simple hut was regarded as a good way of using the spare time. Some of these huts were sold and others were kept within families. These second homes was usually located close to the main home, not only because of transport accessibility but also because the unemployed had to collect their benefits once a week.

In 1962 the Norwegian government appointed a committee headed by Professor Sømme to discuss the regulation of the use of mountain areas (Sømme, 1965; Ouren, 1965). Until 1965 the location and design of second homes was a private agreement between the landowner and the potential home buyer. The erection of the building could proceed without any intervention or regulation from the local authorities. However, after the passing of new building laws in 1965 the local municipality assumed regulatory control of building and siting practice.

1965–1990 The second home planning period

The 1960s might be described as a period of the introduction planning permission for building in Norway. The Building Act of 1965 meant that building of small cabins in mountain and coastal areas had to go through a formal planning process. In fact this meant both a slow down in the development of second homes, and also a rise in building quality of those second homes that were erected. Most cabins, however, were still without electricity, indoor water supply or sewage systems.

In some areas the planning process proceeded more professionally, with the development of 'cabin villages' being a chief aim of the new planning regime. However, from the perspective of central government, this process was implemented too slowly and in the 1980s the Brundtland government appointed a Second Home Commission to examine second home development within the context of 'recreational dwellings' (Miljøverndepartementet, 1981). The report noted an imbalance between the demand and supply of recreational dwellings and stated that:

> ... the National Government has a special responsibility for making more second home plots available for those groups who want to buy one. To do this the government must engage in more land-use planning at the municipal level to make more plots available. Better instructions for land-use planning, information and even stimuli for such planning issues, are proposed. On nationally-owned land, a more active planning phase should begin. (Miljøverndepartementet, 1981: translated by the author)

However, even after the report of the Second Home Commission the growth of second homes did not take off. One reason might be the recession of the late 1980s; another was that the development possible sites did not provide the developers with opportunities for building in the way that the markets were seeking. In retrospect it seems that there was a gap between what it was possible to build and what the markets really wanted.

In some areas, however, the development continued, in areas close to alpine ski venues. The developments were inspired by what happened in the Swedish mountains from the mid-1980s, but Norway did not fall into the 'time-share trap', as many Swedish projects had. Single ownership of flats and cottages was the rule, even when the privately-owned accommodation was rented out by commercial firms for most of the holiday season.

The Winter Olympics at Lillehammer 1994: A turning point for a new standard of second home in rural areas?

One of the key factors in the improvement of the quality of second homes in Norwegian alpine areas was, ironically, the Green opposition to the hosting of the 1994 Winter Olympics which sought to 'green the Games'. The development of environmental quality standards for the Olympic Games facilities and infrastructure led to dramatic improvements in sewage and waste-water treatment. A modern sewage system was built for the Hafjell alpine skiing venues near Lillehammer, and a 30-kilometre pipeline was constructed down to a cleaning plant near the shores of Lake Mjøsa. Up to this point, only a few cottages in the Hafjell area were supplied by electricity; most were not. Almost none had a proper water supply, bathrooms or a connection to the sewage system. The Olympic investment therefore opened the area up for the construction of a new type of cottage in the mountain slopes between zones C and D in Figure 15.1.

As a result of the successful Olympic bid some new areas for second home development were planned close to the alpine skiing slopes. The hope was to sell these lots in the years prior to the Olympics and that the owners should invest in property to be used during the Games. This was a far greater success than anticipated, and a stock of high-quality cottages was very quickly established. This naturally raised the question of whether or not this demand would still exist after the Olympic flames had been extinguished.

Post-Olympic development

Even though the trend started some years earlier, the choice of Lillehammer as a destination for the 1994 Winter Olympics might be regarded as a turning point for the development of high-standard second homes in non-coastal Norway. The main reason was the need for accommodation for journalists, which was partly catered for by building new cottage projects either in the immediate surroundings of Lillehammer itself or close to the alpine venues at Hafjell 20 kilometres away. As noted above, new high-capacity water and sewage systems were built, not only for Hafjell, but also to the already highly developed cottage areas of Sjusjøen and Nordseter (Flognfeldt, 2002). Most of the buildings were pre-fabricated and, during the Olympics, had more or less functioned as provisional hotel accommodation.

After the Olympics, many high-quality cottages were rebuilt for sale on the open market. This rebuilding meant, in most cases, that most bathrooms were taken away and replaced by other facilities, such as a kitchen. Some bedrooms were also changed – walls were taken down so that two or three former bedrooms became a living room. Since the rebuilding was pre-planned, the developers were able to take care of the 'Olympic accommodation market paradox' in that during the Olympics there was a strong need for hotel-type accommodation, but afterwards there was only a market for self-catering dwellings. Many commentators thought that the price of these new high-standard second homes was far too high, and the media were often eager to report that these cottages would never be sold at the prices asked. However, in the eight years following the Olympics, most of the second homes have at least tripled in value.

Of course, the demand for older types of second homes has not completely disappeared (Table 15.1). The existing supply of such units, however, seems to be sufficient to cover the day-to-day demand, apart from continued pressure in some of the southern coastal zones. However, the hosting of the Olympics is only a partial explanation of the new stage in second home development. Demand for modern high class cottages spread to many places in Norway very quickly; reasons for this growth include:

Table 15.1 Comparing traditional (1950s) and new (1990–2002) second homes in Norwegian mountain areas

Traditional Norwegian Mountain cabin	Mountain second Home – Hafjell type
No water supply and no sewage system	Full water and sewage system – including shower(s) and sauna
No electricity – modernised by small solar cell for reading lights	Full electricity, even including central heating and permanent outdoor lights
Primitive summer road access	Full year-round road access, garage included
30–60 square metres	100–250 square metres
Land on lease (just the building plot)	Preferably ownership of land and the surrounding areas
Outdoor sitting area (some with roof and some sort of pavement)	Wooden balconies with roof and fences
Often self -built (with a little help from friends)	Built by craftsmen, designed by architects
	Office space included – sometimes also meeting space
Often in zone D (Figure 15.1)	Most often in zones B, C (Figure 15.1) preferably close to alpine ski venues

- the state of the Norwegian economy;
- the restructuring of traditional rural economies;
- better communications, road systems, meaning quicker access to potential cottage areas during weekends;
- new technologies allowing parts of the weekly workload to be done outside the traditional office

The combination of these factors has led to the growth of new types of second home villages with architects, planners, builders and estate brokers all eagerly embracing this new business.

The Future of Second Homes in Norway

Over the last ten years second home development in Norway has seen something of a gold rush. Prices and standards of buildings have mostly been at the top end of market demand. Plots for privately building a cottage, in the way that most cottages were built during the 1950s and 1960s, are hard to obtain at the new integrated and planned locations. Those who want a cottage to fulfill their do-it-yourself craftsman dreams must either buy an old one and refurbish it, or accept a lot in more remote or unpopular locations, often with less accessibility to electricity and sewage systems.

Perhaps the main development question today is: *how long will this extreme demand continue?* Some signs suggest that the demand for very up-market cottages, of NOK5 millions and upward, is decreasing, with the stock of expensive second homes growing far more quickly than the demand. In the middle-range, from NOK1.5 to 3 million, there is still a demand for both new and older second homes. Changes to this demand structure will mainly depend on:

- sale after inheritance, with the money for each heir possibly providing the assets for the purchase of new second homes;
- sale following divorce or moving away from the weekend zones;
- sale following changing tastes for holiday accommodation within the owner's family;
- the development of new resorts such as golf resorts or integrated alpine and golf resorts;
- the development of new types of coastal second home development;
- second homes becoming the primary residential location with a small flat being kept in the cities primarily for business use; and
- second homes being used for business meeting places, in competition with hotels.

The changes of the 1990s meant that second home ownership turned from a hobby and family activity into a professional real estate business. For the local communities, this change has created a new level of issues and challenges with respect to second home development. This is particularly the case with respect to new patterns of demand from second home owners for the provision of municipal services because of their extended use of second homes, as well as similar demands from the resorts themselves (Flognfeldt, 1999; Flognfeldt, 2000).

For some people staying in their cottage might be regarded as 'living in an alternative home' either because of family relationships to the cottage area or the desire to fulfill a sort of a 'back-to-nature dream' (Kaltenborn, 2002). Such a situation may have substantial implications for land use. Indeed, some concerns have been expressed that the growth of high-value cottaging communities may lead to restrictions on traditional grazing activities in some areas (Flognfeldt, 2002). This might mean more fences in the second home areas thereby reducing access for all visitors. In some areas this has already created some conflicts. However, in most cases second home owners fit well into local environment.

The last question to ask is: what about the many traditional second homes or hytte? Will there still be a demand for buying such properties?

Arguably, this will partly depend both on location and the possibilities of renewal and inclusion of electricity and water supply. But at some locations traditional homes will remain in their old state, perhaps used for only a few nights of the year. Any rental market for these properties will need to be extended to other European nations and to focus on nature lovers and dedicated environmentalists. However, these market segments seems to be a very unstable, and may not provide long-term security for the traditional Norwegian second home.

Chapter 16

Second Homes in Sweden: Patterns and Issues

DIETER K. MÜLLER

Second Homes Revisited

The increasing mobility within certain sections of the industrialised world and the new emerging geographical patterns of production and consumption have led to renewed interest in second homes (Müller, 2002a; Williams & Hall, 2002). This is also important in the Swedish context, where second homes have always been a prominent issue owing to the importance of second homes within Swedish family life and culture (Bielckus, 1977). Recent second home development in Sweden has, therefore, increased concern and debate, particularly with respect to foreign second home purchases (Müller, 1999, 2002a) and to second home developments in the archipelagos outside the metropolitan areas. Within the public debate, second home development has held to be the reason for population displacement and rural decline. Given this context, a new examination of second homes and their impact on rural change in Sweden is almost mandatory.

The purpose of this chapter is to provide an overview of second home ownership in Sweden during the 1990s. The chapter also discusses to what extent issues raised in the 1970s are still valid for second home tourism and development in the 1990s and beyond. To achieve this, the chapter revisits several issues raised in Coppock's (1977a) seminal book *Second Homes: Curse or Blessing?* and relates them to the Swedish situation in the 1990s. In particular, the chapter addresses changes in the geographical patterns of second home tourism and highlights impacts on the property market on the outskirts of metropolitan areas, in peripheral areas and in areas demanded by foreign tourists.

Analysis is limited to rural second homes that form the vast majority of second homes in Sweden. This approach implies that second homes are all those properties that are regarded and thus registered as second homes in the Swedish cadastre, i.e. that second homes are of villa type and considered second homes by their owners. The data of the analysis is taken from a comprehensive database on second homes located at the Department of

Social and Economic Geography, Umeå University, and covering data for more than 500,000 second homes and their owners for the period 1991-1996.

Social Change and Second Home Development

Second home research has always addressed a variety of issues. But the peaking of interest in second homes during the 1970s was mainly due to the conflicts caused by second home tourism, not least in the Welsh country-side where English-owned second homes attracted considerable opposition (Coppock, 1977c; Shaw & Williams, 1994; Gallent, 1997; Gallent & Tewdwr-Jones, 2000). Phillips (1993) argued that second home development was a form of class colonisation of the countryside rather like the migration into the countryside by the middle class. Although this perception of second home development might be mainly seen as a British phenomenon, there is evidence in many parts of the world that second home owners often come from professional and managerial groups and from those with above-average incomes (Bielckus, 1977; Clout, 1977; Wolfe, 1977).

Even more important for the interest in second homes was the prediction by Berry (1970) that in the future *telemobility* would allow people to bring experiences to them instead of visiting the experiences themselves. Second home growth was perceived by Rogers (1977) as an early result of this development which implied a substantial change for the countryside. Although the *invasion* of second home owners never occurred to the extent feared by Berry (1970) and Rogers (1977), the perception of second home ownership as problematic to rural sustainability remains to the present day.

The argument that second home ownership causes displacement of permanent residents is still fashionable and is still used to explain rural decline and out-migration. The argument can be heard in Great Britain and is also put forward regarding foreign second home purchases in Sweden where second home owners were accused of displacing the traditional rural population in the Swedish archipelagos (Müller, 1999; Gallent & Twedwr-Jones, 2000).

Of course, second home ownership is interrelated to processes of rural change. On the one hand second home development facilitates rural change in terms of the socio-cultural composition of the countryside, the rural property market, and the landscape. On the other hand, second home development is also a result of rural change, particularly the impact of economic restructuring on the rural arena and out-migration. Out-migration means that migrants convert former permanent residences into second homes. Alternatively, out-migration may cause a change of ownership and purpose. Nevertheless, the perception that many rural out-migrants are forced away from the countryside by to the influx of second home owners is too simplistic. It fails to acknowledge recent research findings on migration which show that the majority of migrants are consumption-led rather than production-led and, moreover, are usually satisfied with their residential relocation (Garvill *et al.*, 2000).

The conversion of permanent homes into second homes can also be the result of demographic changes in the area. Households living outside the rural area can inherit former permanent homes independently whether or not they are interested in keeping and maintaining these houses. Communities of heirs can be forced to keep the property because if a lack of demand for it on the rural property market. Hence, out-migration implies a conversion of the former permanent home into a second home, not necessarily because it is the owner's wish, but simply because of a lack of demand. Therefore, the rural property market forms a powerful constraint that affects the potential use of rural housing.

In contrast, permanent residences may also be converted into second homes because of an outside demand; purchases of rural homes in France and Sweden by English and German households respectively, attracted particular attention during the 1990s (Buller & Hoggart, 1994; Müller, 1999, 2002a). In both countries commentators argued that the traditional rural population was displaced because of foreign demand. However, Müller (1999) argues that there is no evidence available to prove this. Rather, it seems that, compared with the domestic market, foreign households require different qualities from a property. Foreign customers consider peripherality attractive, whilst domestic customers do not share that view and choose areas that match their expectations more closely. The expectations towards the property can, however, differ radically because of different cultures and experiences (Müller, 1999). Differing motives and, in particular differences between consumption-led and production-led ways of reasoning can contribute to opposite appraisals of locations and landscapes. Even though these contradictions are most apparent in an international context, differences between urban and rural requirements can also be significant at a national level.

Second Homes as Markers

In some rural property markets the use of the term second home is also somewhat questionable. In peripheral areas with low demand, properties may be registered as 'second homes', even though they are used only very occasionally or not at all. In contrast, where substantial demand exists, second homes may of course become a significant part of the rural property market. Still, in many countries administrative practices force households to decide on a usage for the property. In Sweden, the taxation procedures oblige people to choose whether the property is a second home, a permanent home, or an agricultural property which, by definition, requires certain incomes related to the property ownership (Müller, 1999). Property statistics and registers generally fail to reflect true conditions and usually neglect the actual use of the properties in terms of frequency and length of visits. Hence, second home development can be considered as a marker for various other developments.

Disappearing regions

Second homes can mark disappearing regions where the property supply is greater than the demand for them. Population decline and demographical ageing characterise what may be termed 'disappearing regions'. Accordingly, it can be expected that assessed property values mirror the situation on the property market, at least if they are assumed to represent housing standards and commercial demand. Disappearing regions have a high number of second home properties with low assessed property values and an assessed property value development that is below the national average. Moreover, because of their origin in the original rural settlement structure, second home patterns are generally more dispersed. In contrast, purpose-built second homes are more concentrated to places with scenic qualities or recreation opportunities.

Although second home ownership is sometimes underrated with regard to its economic impact on the regional economy (Müller, 1999), disappearing regions contain less-used houses and so the economic impact of second home tourism is rather low. Nevertheless, it is important to realise that the opposite scenario is not that the houses are used as permanent homes. Rather, the houses are not used at all and thus, the economic impact of second home tourism can be small; but still it means that at least some money is spent that can contribute to sustain local shops and services (Müller, 1999).

Hot spots

Second homes can also mark regions that are highly attractive, where the demand for second homes is greater than the supply. The attractiveness can derive from the scenic quality of the region, from the imaging and re-imaging of the area, from opportunities for certain activities, from a positive location in relation to a major metropolitan area, or from a status provided by the presence of certain celebrity residents. These areas are here called 'hot spots', to highlight the fact that the attractiveness of these areas is constructed and hence, likely to be limited in time.

Second home development in hot spots is a particular issue of debate. The conversion of permanent homes to second homes is interpreted as a reason for displacement. It is argued that assessed property values increase thanks to the growing demand and the high prices paid for the second homes. Subsequently, former owners are forced to move out, simply because they cannot pay the increased property taxes. Hence, the formerly lively countryside is converted into a countryside that is deserted for large part of the year and flourishes only during some short summer months.

An alternative interpretation departs from the notion of a permanently changing countryside. Employment opportunities in agriculture, forestry, fishery and manufacturing industry disappeared owing to economic restructuring (Butler, 1998; Hall & Jenkins, 1998; Jenkins *et al.*, 1998). The resulting new patterns of production and consumption imply that once-productive areas now turn to new ventures such as tourism. However, these changes also imply mobility to and from the area, with some people looking for employment and education outside the area while other households seek amenity-rich environments in the emerging tourist and lifestyle areas (Fountain & Hall, 2002; Williams & Hall, 2002). Although, both interpretations are based on the same observation, they certainly differ in their assessment of the underlying processes. In any case hot spots, should be identifiable by an increase of assessed property values, a relatively high turnover rate of properties, and in-migrants and second home owners coming from rather affluent groups within society.

Second Homes in Sweden

In the following sections some examples of second home development in Sweden are presented and briefly discussed. First, an overview focuses on changes in second home ownership between 1991 and 1996. Then, three cases are offered that represent both second home hot spots and disappearing regions.

Second home patterns

Although second home development occurred before 1900 (Pihl Atmer, 1998), more common access to a second home is an achievement of the Swedish welfare state. During the 1960s and early 1970s, the number of second homes increased significantly (Nordin, 1993b). However, between 1991 and 1996 the total number of second homes in Sweden decreased from about 530,000 to 500,000. This was because small properties vanished from the statistics for several reasons, but mainly because they were converted into permanent residences on the outskirts of the Swedish metropolitan areas.

Other changes also distinguished second home areas in Sweden from one another. The assessed property value of the second homes, which is expected to mirror the market value, is unevenly distributed across Sweden. Higher assessed property values occur in coastal locations, in the Swedish *fjäll* (the mountain area along the Norwegian border) and in the interior parts of southern Sweden. This of course mirrors the distribution of the population and the location of the most popular tourist resorts. However, the average change in assessed property values is smaller in the interior of Northern Sweden than in those areas mentioned above. This could be read as a turn towards a more touristic validation of the second home, which implies a greater demand for second homes in scenic areas.

Other indicators reinforce this pattern. As shown above, patterns of change in the distances between second home and permanent residence between 1991 and 1996 provide evidence for the characteristics of the disappearing region. Even increases in the incomes of second home owners can be used to distinguish second home hot spots from disappearing regions (Müller, 2002b).

In conclusion, during the first half of the 1990s, second home ownership in Sweden underwent significant changes towards a more touristic use. The result is a more segregated second home pattern featuring decreasing demand and lower income households in northern Sweden –disappearing regions named earlier (Figure 16.1). At the same time, areas on the outskirts of the cities and popular tourist areas in Southern Sweden and in the mountains experienced a significant increase in both assessed property values and long-haul visitors and can thus be considered second home hot spots.

Stockholm's archipelago

Second home development in the country's archipelagos is a hotly-debated issue. Second home owners are accused of displacing the archipelagos' permanent population by causing assessed property values to increase. The Swedish National Development Agency demands powerful action against this development in order to sustain the archipelagos' communities (Glesbygdsverket, 2001). To counteract the conversion of permanent residences into second homes, the agency proposes a legal obligation for the owners to register and live in the communities. This section focuses on one of the country's archipelagos outside Stockholm.

The number of second homes in the Stockholm archipelago increased in most of the parishes between 1991 and 1996 (Figure 16.2). For example, the parish of Värmdö in the central archipelago experienced an increase of 255 second homes in that period. However, patterns are not homogenous, showing decreased development in nearby parishes. Still, it cannot be shown empirically that second home development is related to population development, as the entire county has a positive population development. In order to be able to see differences, another geographical scale has to be chosen.

Although property taxation values are rising more than average, it is not obvious that assessed property values are increasingly significantly more in areas in the central archipelago. Instead, it is possible to see an increasing

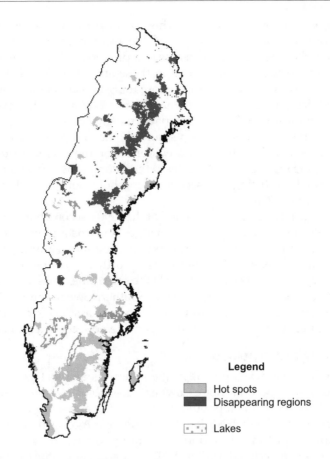

Figure 16.1 Second home regions in Sweden, 1996

Hot spots are defined by an above-average development of disposable household income and of assessed property values within 20km; disappearing regions are defined by a below-average development.

variance between second homes in the outer archipelago in terms of assessed property values (Figure 16.2). This indicates that there is a more heterogeneous stock of second homes. Indeed, certain second homes obviously have increasing property values, while others do not.

One may conclude that the Stockholm archipelago forms a popular second home region with an increasing number of second homes. Because of the strong overall population growth in the Stockholm region, it is not possible to find evidence that second home owners have replaced the permanent archipelago population, at least at the parish level. It is also obvious that the outer archipelago is an area of great change, where second home tourism takes different forms – there are second homes that are clearly very much improved in terms of their physical condition. This situation provides evidence for a certain turnover of second homes that can be seen in relation to the emergence of new patterns of production and consumption.

The northern periphery

The remote parts of northern Sweden have suffered considerably from depopulation, an ageing society, loss of employment opportunities and a shrinking service sector. The need for change is comprehensively accepted and tourism development, in particular, is seen as a means to improve the current situation. However, the long distances between attractions and communities provide a difficult situation for tourism development. Given the extent of vacant housing stock in the area, second home tourism has been considered a viable option for tourism development.

This case study focuses on Lycksele, a municipality in the interior of Northern Sweden and part of the area that was earlier identified as a disappearing region. Between 1991 and 1996 the population in Lycksele dropped from 14,231 to 13,838 as a result of negative natural population change and out-migration. In the same period the mean age in the municipality increased considerably. The regional centre of Umeå with about 106,000 inhabitants is 140 kilometres away.

For the study the second home owners in the municipality were distributed into three different categories reflecting the permanent homes of their owners. The first category contains the households living within the municipality. Second home ownership among these households does not imply an inflow of consumption into the municipality. The second category refers to households from the municipality's adjacent areas. Second home owners from these areas are assumed to use their second home rather frequently, but primarily during short breaks and weekends. Thus, a lot of provisions and commodities are simply taken from the permanent home (Bohlin, 1982a, 1982b; Nordin, 1993a). This area was defined as a 100 kilometre zone around Lycksele municipality. The third category comprises those failing outside the two previous categories.

During the period 1991–96, the total number of second homes in the Lycksele municipality decreased from 1099 to 971 houses, mainly because of a decreasing number of local citizens owning a second home. The number of second homeowners with permanent residence outside the municipality decreased from 430 to 413.

The characteristics for the different categories of second home owners are only slightly different. Owners living outside the municipality are on average some years younger and better educated. Moreover, they own on

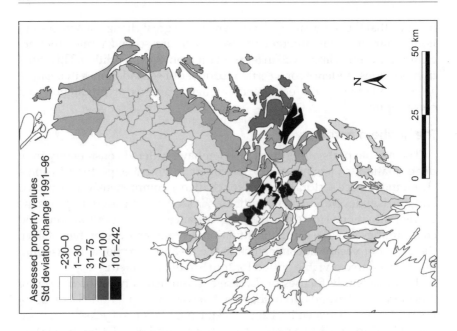

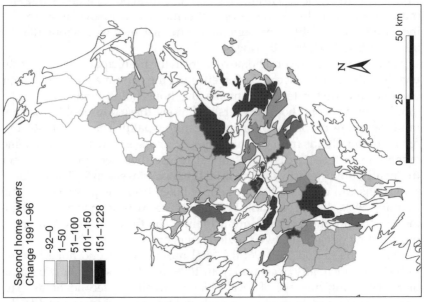

Figure 16.2 Changes in second home numbers and assessed property values in Stockholm County, 1991–96.

Source: Umcobase (1996)

average less valuable properties than the local population. This points at a less intensive use of the second home and locations in less attractive areas within the municipality. Thus, to a great extent second home owners from outside the municipality seem to be persons with emotional links to Lycksele. The decreasing population of course challenges the future of second home tourism in the Lycksele municipality by undermining the basis for emotional links with the municipality.

A closer inspection of the assessed property values shows that a high number of second homes have rather low property values (Figure 16.3). It is obvious that residents from outside the municipality own many of these second homes. A possible interpretation is, of course, that these households inherited the second homes (see Chapter 17). This affects also the usage of the second homes. In contrast to the local population, who often own second homes with higher assessed property values, the non-local house-holds probably visit their properties only occasionally. It is, however, remarkable that more than 50% of all local second home owners dispose of second homes with an assessed property value below SEK40,000.

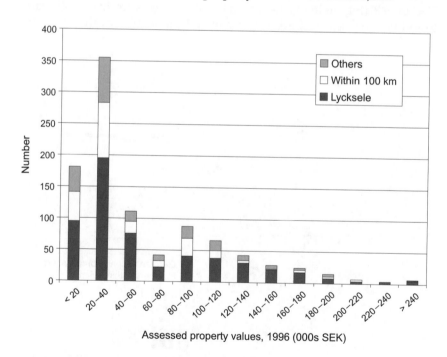

Figure 16.3 Assessed property values in Lycksele

Source: Umcobase, 1996

The changes in second home ownership also implied that the municipality attracted only a relatively small amount of consumption. This shows that Lycksele has, until now, managed to maintain a steady turnover from second home tourism. It is, however, clear that a change towards a more touristic demand of second homes challenges this fragile balance.

In conclusion, it is apparent that many of the so-called second homes in Lycksele are not used as second homes, in fact they tend not to be used at all. Only the second homes that serve the local demand are maintained and even improved. Hence, second home tourism in Lycksele does not seem to be real second home tourism. Instead, it can be assumed that the second homes are mainly used as destinations for the local population's everyday and weekend mobility.

The internationalisation of Southern Sweden

During the early 1990s, Southern Sweden was discovered by German second home buyers (Müller, 1999), and over a five-year period the number of German second home owners in Sweden trebled from 1526 in 1991 to 5587 in 1996 (Figure 16.4). The reasons for this process are, of course, many. In addition to reasons related to German unification, the devaluation of the

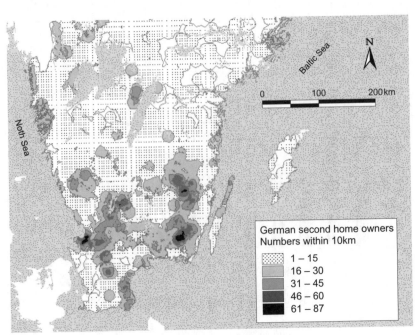

Figure 16.4 German second home ownership, 1996

Source: Umcobase, 1996

Swedish currency obviously contributed to German purchases (Müller, 1999). In 1992 the value of the currency decreased by about 25% within just a few weeks and transformed Sweden overnight into an almost-cheap destination.

The German tourists in Sweden soon became aware of the changed situation and the relatively low property prices in Sweden. The activities of German-speaking estate agents towards the German market made the Swedish property even more accessible to German customers. However, even before the devaluation of the Swedish currency, property prices constituted no serious obstacle to purchase as in 1991 there were already more than 1500 German second home owners in Sweden. Indeed, even in relation to the German consumer price index the prices of the second homes decreased during 1992. Prices then increased and in 1995 reached almost the same level as in 1991. In other words, considering the German inflation rate, at the 1995 year's Deutsche Mark value the actual amount paid for a second home in 1995 was almost the same as in 1991.

The actual price can be related to the annual increase in second home purchases. The 1992 price decline was followed by an increase in purchases the following year. The increasing prices in the following years were accompanied by a declining increase of purchases (Table 16.1). Thus, it seems that the price development had at least some impact on the rate of diffusion of German second home ownership in Sweden.

However, the price decline for second home ownership is but one important feature of the total Swedish situation. The population redistribution in Sweden and the resulting concentration of the population in certain areas form an additional contribution to a reasonable explanation for German purchase patterns. In addition, the distance between the German first home and Swedish second home is important to an understanding the geograph-

Table 16.1 Mean second home prices, 1991–1995

Year	Average prices			Number of dated sales
	SEK (current value)	DM (current value)	DM (1995 value)	
1991	277,000	76,000	67,000	127
1992	236,000	63,000	58,000	159
1993	299,000	63,000	61,000	440
1994	303,000	64,000	62,000	562
1995	330,000	66,000	66,000	620

Source: Umcobase (1996)

ical development of German second home ownership. Most cottagers perceived the utility of a second home nearby as greater, and so a majority purchased second homes within 300 kilometres of the ferry harbours that provided access for the German market.

Moreover, German second home owners preferred remote properties in secluded localities within the forests (Müller, 1999), and most of the properties can be characterised as rather unattractive to a Swedish market. The destinations for the German second home owners are also in parts of the Swedish countryside that are suffering from depopulation and an ageing society.

In conclusion, it can thus be said that, despite the increase in German second home purchases, it is likely that few or no Swedish households were forced to leave the areas where Germans bought their second homes. The Germans bought second homes for a particular price and adapted their purchases to price changes. The regions where Germans bought their second homes did not become hot spots because there was no competition between the local population and domestic second home tourists. Instead, the demand from Germany itself was the only one to put pressure on the property market. Nevertheless, according to the estate agents, the winter season renewed the supply on the property market and so access to second homes seemed to be almost infinite.

Still, the German presence does not necessarily imply an economic boost, although German second home owners contribute considerably to the maintenance of local businesses thanks to their long stays in Sweden and their obvious attachment to the Swedish countryside. Many of the second home owners are keen to maintain the areas in their traditional state and so are rather hostile towards tourism and other development (Müller, 1999).

Conclusion

This chapter has shown that there is reason to revisit second home tourism and development, since there have been considerable changes in second home development in recent years. The perception of second home owners displacing the traditional countryside population is not realistic at a time when large parts, at least, of Sweden's rural areas are suffering from depopulation and ageing societies. Economic restructuring has eroded the basis for making a living in large parts of the countryside, and the cities attract many of the young to gain education, jobs and entertainment.

A look at the periphery shows that the impact of Berry's *telemobility* (1970), which became a real option when the Internet provided a link with other parts of the world, was greatly overestimated. The peripheral areas of Sweden register a negative permanent in-migration and the second home market is characterised by decreasing relative property values and a mainly-local interest in second homes. Some areas, such as Småland in the south of Sweden, were, however, integrated into the growing hinterlands of cities in the north of Germany. Although Småland can be considered peripheral from a domestic point of view, it has recently become an integral part of the functional surroundings of Berlin and Hamburg, satisfying needs of the citizens of these cities for recreation and leisure environments. The same is true for the scenic archipelago close Stockholm where a growing number of urbanites invest in rather expensive second homes, even though cheaper second homes are still available.

The case studies also make clear that the concept of the second home is not a perfect one. It fails to highlight the differences between second home development in different settings and different areas. The processes in the northern periphery are different from those in the Stockholm area, even though they are interlinked and are the result of the same process of restructuring. These differences are highlighted by the use of the concepts of 'hot spots' and 'disappearing regions'. Of course, the northern periphery will not decline simply because of a negative development in second home tourism. However, it is clear that the second home development in the area is a marker for decline, leaving the second homes as a visible sign of obsolete physical structures. The situations in Småland and the Stockholm archipelago are similar. Both areas are within the recreational hinterlands of large metropolitan areas. The vicinity of the archipelago and the city put heavy pressure on the property market and hence result in an increase in the number of second homes and growing market values. However, Småland is on the outer edge of the recreational hinterlands of Hamburg and Berlin, and so the German second home purchases do not have the same dramatic consequences.

Second homes are usually considered to be tourist accommodation, and most probably are. But there are many so-called second homes that are not homes at all, but deserted inherited houses. The national statistics do not however include a depressing function like that and so in the statistics these houses are 'converted' into second homes. Moreover, national statistics also prohibit that second home owners from living in two places at once; so many second homes are described as second homes simply because their owners have to choose where they spend most of their time. Still there is no possible way of verifying the validity of these statements, and it may be assumed that house owners tend to state their first home at places with lower taxation rates. And thus, people in the Stockholm archipelago are not considered true inhabitants although they may have the opportunity to spend the larger part of their time in the second home.

The question as to whether second homes are a curse or blessing to the receiving communities is still rather difficult to answer though it depends both on structural and perceptual issues. It is, however, obvious that the processes involved are more complex than expected during the 1970s. Second home development has to be seen in terms of economic restructuring and changing geographical patterns of production and consumption, but also in changes in working life allowing for more flexible use of space and time. The areas in the functional hinterlands of the metropolitan areas have thus become important zones for recreation and part-time living. Hence, second homes are essential elements of this at least partly new function. Peripheral areas on the other hand are isolated and hence, second homes are marking decline and no renewed interest.

Part 4

Future Issues

Chapter 17

Second Home Plans Among Second Home Owners in Northern Europe's Periphery

BRUNO JANSSON AND DIETER K. MÜLLER

Second home ownership is today an almost self-evident achievement of the Nordic welfare states. Although definitions vary, official statistics and research suggest that Sweden has 500,000–700,000 second homes (Müller, 1999), Finland 450,000 (Statistics Finland, 2001), Denmark 220,000 (Tress, 2002), and Norway 360,000 (Statistics Norway, 2001). This suggests that there are about 10–15 persons per second home, although the commonality of shared ownership within an extended family implies that a majority of households have access to a second home. Second home tourism is thus a core component of the domestic tourism in the Nordic countries, with second homes in the region increasingly attracting investments from Germany (Müller, 1999).

Despite the present situation, there is reason to challenge the assumption that second home ownership tourism in the Nordic countries will continue more or less unchanged. Changes in population distribution, population composition, family structures and tourism preferences all affect the future second home tourism. Today, the occurrence of second homes does not necessarily imply that an area is a popular tourist destination. Instead, second homes can mark a surplus on the regional housing market (see Chapter, 2).

A problem in this context is that scrutinising ownership patterns and characteristics does not explain the factual use of the second homes and, hence, provides only limited insights into how second home tourism works in practice. Assessing the future of second home tourism therefore requires surveying the current use of second homes and the future plans of their owners. However, such research is addressed only infrequently (Velvin, 2002; Müller, 2004). The aim of this chapter is to fill this gap.

Life Course and Second Home Ownership

Consumption and mobility vary during an individual's course of life, the 'life course' (Boyle *et al.*, 1998). Usually the concept of a life course is used to explain the varying propensity to migrate at different stages of life; although there is no *one* life course that all households pass through. Individual events structure the life course: acquiring an education, establishing a family, getting a first job, the nature of a professional career, and other events during the life course influence migration choices and usually occur at particular ages or stages in life.

Tourism is also influenced by these changes through the life course, partly because of the development of households' consuming powers and changing interests. It is certainly reasonable to argue that there is no singular life course regarding tourism. However, it can be claimed that there should be common characteristics for tourism demand for different stages of the life course. For example, small children do not make their own decisions about where to go on a holiday, though it can be assumed that parents consider their interests. Teenagers are usually still dependent on their parents although they may travel on their own or with a group of people. Later on, travel decisions can be expected to depend on the time, budget, economy, and knowledge of tourism destinations. After retirement, time constraints change yet again and hence, for those with sufficient income, there is potential for more time to be spent outside the everyday environment.

The above discussion implies that interest in second homes should also follow the life course, simply because different stages in the life course imply different opportunities for purchasing and using a second home (Godbey & Bevins, 1987). Households that are well established on the labour market and the housing market often purchase second homes. In many cases the household members are 40 years of age or older – their children have left the household or at least arrange their leisure independently. Consequently, such households dispose of surplus capital that can be invested in increasing consumption of capital products (Malmberg & Lindh, 2000). The absence of children within the household also provides more available leisure time that can be used for new individual projects. In this context, second homes provide a popular platform from which to conduct a variety of activities and can form a new common family project substituting for the raising of children.

Family Second Home Ownership

Access to second homes influences the patterns that result from the tourism life course. In cases where second homes are inherited, they can form permanent stations in the tourists' life courses, especially given the place attachment of many second home owners (Jaakson, 1986; Kaltenborn, 1997a, 1997b, 1998, 2002; Williams & Kaltenborn, 1999). This is particularly the case when second homes represent family heritage or 'roots'. Family ownership of second homes also implies that visits to the cottage are a tradition maintained during the entire life course (McHugh *et al.*, 1995).

According to Jaakson (1986) this gathering of the family is one of the main motives for second home ownership. The cottage is a common project for the entire family providing an arena for the family members to engage in various activities. In contrast, Jarlöv (1999) argues that second homes are mainly male projects that put construction work into focus. However, evidence from Sweden demonstrates that second home tourism engages all members of the family, even if activities at the second home can be gendered. The male owner often works with house improvements and the female owner is engaged in gardening and interior design (Müller, 1999; Jansson & Müller, 2003). Second home owners also report that their relatives and particularly their children visit them in their second homes. Hence, Jaakson's (1986) argument seemed to be strengthened. Second homes appear to be places for families to meet that cross generational boundaries. Motives for family second home ownership therefore reach beyond individual reasons and sometimes cover even future generations. This is especially so for inherited second homes that are maintained as a common property for the entire family. Indeed, some households purchase second homes so as to establish such family-centred places for future generations.

Second Home Use

Different perceptions of the meaning of second home ownership are mirrored in their patterns of use. In particular, family second home ownership involving several generations means that second homes are used by members of different generations at the same time. It may also imply that second home improvements are undertaken so as to fit the requirements of future generations. Nevertheless, plans for the future use of a second home are made in great uncertainty. Obviously, children's future plans may differ from the expectations of their parents. Moreover, the restructuring of the economy has caused comprehensive domestic and also international population redistribution, sometimes creating large physical distances between the different generations of a family. However, Kaltenborn (1998) argues that this condition in fact enhances interest in second homes, with the second home becoming a permanent place to return to during an otherwise rapidly-changing life course. Indeed, recent changes in the working life arising from more flexible forms of production and weaker attachment to certain places of production mean that an increasing number of households have more time to spend away from their everyday environment (Williams & Hall, 2000). Nevertheless, such changes may mean that second homes cannot be used often, and so family reunions occur less frequently. In addition, some second homes may not be used at all, particularly in cases of multiple ownerships where properties are located in the periphery and outside amenity-rich areas. These issues are dealt with in more detail in a study of the Kvarken area in northern Finland and Sweden detailed below.

The Kvarken Study

The geographical focus of this study is on five regions in an international area in northern Scandinavia, known as Kvarken (Figure 17.1). The municipalities of Ähtäri, Korsholm, Robertsfors, Lycksele, and the Tärna parish have all identified second home tourism as a field where tourism development can take place in the future.

Two of the municipalities had recent experiences of inbound demand for second home living. In Ähtäri, a national second home trade fair was organised in 1998 that entailed the construction of luxurious up-market second homes. The resulting properties attracted wealthy buyers both from other regions in Finland and from abroad. In Lycksele, a Norwegian company specialising in second homes in Sweden had bought up a housing area built in the 1970s and converted more than 50 apartments into second homes for the Norwegian market.

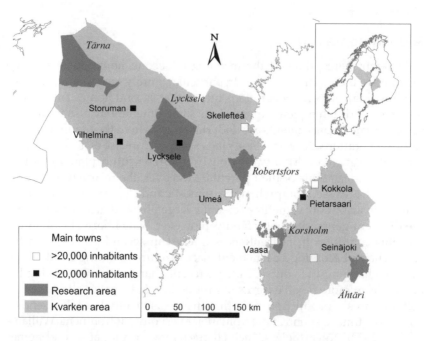

Figure 17.1 The study area, Kvarken in northern Finland and Sweden

Before putting further effort into the development of second home tourism, the municipal authorities decided to investigate the use of all second homes in the area (Jansson & Müller, 2003). The idea was that extensively used second homes could form the resource base for future second home tourism. Hence, in 2001 questionnaires were designed and sent to a random sample of second home owners in the municipalities. A selection of results clarifying current use of second home and future plans is presented in this chapter.

The survey

The survey of second homes owners in Kvarken comprised 1271 questionnaires, of which 730 responses were received. Of these, 672 could be processed in full, giving a response rate of 52.8% with a variation in response rate from 44.3% in Korsholm to 66% in Robertsfors.

The second homes were acquired in three main ways: built by the owner, bought on the market, or inherited – sometimes in combination with investment from relatives. It is important to remember these three different types, since the type of acquisition may be important for future second home planning. The survey also revealed quite a number of reasons for having a second home (see Table 17.1). Each respondent was invited to give the three most important reasons for having the cottage. Even though not all respondents gave three answers, 2,188 reasons were recorded. The three most important reasons were to have a place providing an easy *access to nature* (31%), to have *a place just to relax*(25%), to maintain *contacts with the native district, the landscape of childhood* (10%).

As mentioned above, it is often claimed that families acquire second homes for their children, in order to provide them with a place to stay during the summer. Therefore it is perhaps surprising that few owners who said that the second home is part of catering to children's needs (3.9%). There were also differences between the surveyed areas. In particular, in the Tärnaby area contacts with the native district were less important than for the other Swedish municipalities. Sports activities, such as downhill skiing, were also one of the most important reasons for having a cottage. This indicated that these second homes are more in use during the winter than the others in the survey. Significantly, children's needs are more important for these families than in the other areas. In this context it must also be noted that the typical age for the acquisition of a second home is in the 40s when the children are teenagers with just a few years more to stay in the parents' home.

Just over 4% of responses indicated inheritance as the major reason for having a second home. Approximately 10% of responses indicated that one of the most important reasons for having a second home is to keep up the *contacts with the native district*, as the landscape of childhood.

Table 17.1 Reasons for having a second home (%)

	Tärnaby	Lycksele	Robertsfors	Korsholm	Ähtäri	Mean
For the children	5.3	3.1	3.3	3.1	4.5	3.9
The cottage is inherited	6.0	5.0	3.0	3.5	3.4	4.3
We see it as an investment	0.7	1.0	2.1	2.3	0.3	1.3
For keeping up the links with native districts	6.0	19.0	14.6	5.7	11.3	10.4
For contact with nature	35.1	23.3	25.2	37.2	34.2	31.8
To have a place just to relax	22.8	18.1	31.9	29.0	23.6	25.0
For sports activities	14.0	1.0	0.6	0.7	0.7	4.2
To do manual work	1.6	4.0	8.5	7.8	4.1	5.1
Miscellaneous answers	0.2	1.2	0.6	0.9	0.3	0.6
No answers	8.4	24.5	10.0	9.9	17.5	13.3
Total (%)	100	100	100	100	100	100
Number in sample (n)	570	421	329	576	292	2188

Second homes have changed over the years, from simple summer huts in the 1930s and 1940s to the recently-built high-quality houses that well insulated and equipped for permanent living. Building costs have increased and today the trend towards bigger houses and higher standards suggests that only wealthy people will be able to afford to build new second homes in the years to come. Building activities in this sector have also declined, and environmental restrictions make it increasingly difficult to build new second homes in really attractive sites. A number of different types of houses are used as second homes in the Kvarken area:

(1) second homes that are built specifically for this purpose;
(2) permanent homes that have been converted to second homes, including houses that have been divided off from a farm;
(3) former farms;
(4) apartments (in Lycksele).

By far the largest group is the second homes that have been built just for the purpose of being a second home. However, there are differences in the geographical distribution of different types of houses. The former farmhouses and former permanent homes are most frequently found in Lycksele in Sweden. Modern second homes of a higher standard are found in Tärnaby, Robertsfors and Ähtäri. Many of these houses were erected in the 1980s. The Korsholm second homes are often small and poor-quality houses situated on islands or along the coast, and a substantial share of these have problems with fresh water and electricity supply. Most of these houses are used only during the summer.

The distance between the first and the second home also varies considerably between areas. The owners of the second homes in Tärnaby have to travel long distances between home and Tärnaby, which means that the cottage will tend to be used less often but for longer periods. The other areas present a different picture. Robertsfors and Korsholm's cottage owners mainly live in nearby cities. Lycksele and Ähtäri present an intermediate position. Second homes in Lycksele and Robertsfors to a greater extent than the other areas tend to be former permanent dwellings or farmsteads converted to second homes. Using a limit for daily visits to the second home of 60 minutes each way and 5 hours for a weekend trip, gives the spatial distribution of owners shown in Figure 17.2. The Norwegian-owned holiday flats in Lycksele form a special case, where all owners live in Norway but mostly within the weekend zone.

The Korsholm and Robertsfors cottages are most often situated at a convenient distance from the owners' homes. Most of the owners live in the neighbouring towns, Umeå in Sweden and Vaasa in Finland. Between 80% and 90% of respondents have their second home in the daily visit zone. Most interesting is the distribution of the Tärnaby houses with less than 5% in the daily-visit zone and less than 60% under the upper limit of the weekend zone. Some 20% of the respondents in Lycksele and Ähtäri are

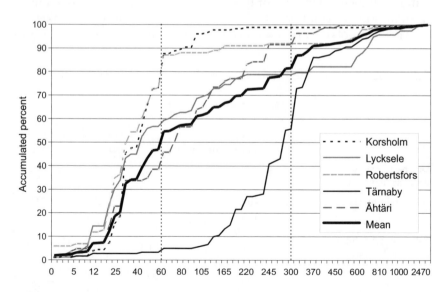

Figure 17.2 Distance between home and second home measured in time

located in the vacation zone more than 5 hours away from their permanent home. This means that distance makes it difficult to use the second home in Tärnaby for shorter visits. So the cottages in Tärnaby and to some extent in Lycksele are typical of second homes in problematic rural and remote areas where the distance prevents more frequent use, and where substantial parts of the cottages are converted from former permanent buildings when the previous owners either died or moved out of the area.

Future Plans

Between them, the second home owners in our survey expressed numerous ideas about what will happen to their property in the future. Of 730 responses, 11.5% expressed no plans at all. The remaining responses (653 answers) are shown in Table 17.2. It seems that most owners want their children and grandchildren to take over when, because of old age or other circumstances, they no longer able or willing to use the property. However, it is interesting to note that as many as 15% of the former farms and about 12% of former permanent dwellings are more or less expected to be abandoned when the present owners become very old, which will happen in the near future. These properties are often older small dwellings of low standard and with a limited market value.

The former farms that today are converted to second homes seem to have lesser emotional value for the owners, and 40% of the respondents plan to sell them. Only 35% of the former farmhouses are expected to be taken over by the children. This can probably be explained by weakening links to their roots over generations. These old farmsteads are often beauti-

Table 17.2 Plans for the future ownership of second homes in the study area (%)

	Earlier use					
Plans	Diverse	Farm-steads	Permanent dwellings	Flats	Purpose-built second homes	Total
Diverse transfers within the extended family	5.6	10.0	6.0	0.0	3.2	3.7
Sold on the market	22.2	40.0	31.3	28.6	23.2	24.7
Stays mainly unused	5.6	15.0	11.9	0.0	2.2	3.7
Taken over by children or grandchildren	66.7	35.0	50.7	71.4	71.3	68.0
Total %	100	100	100	100	100	100
Number in sample (n)	18	12	67	14	534	653

fully situated in the landscape, but far away from the owners' present dwellings and are often even further away from the homes of their sons and daughters. The responses tot he survey also indicate that quite a substantial proportion of the former farmsteads are co-owned with sisters and brothers as a result of previous divisions of the estate. A sale would then also solve possible problems arising from the joint use of the property by a number of owners.

A clear majority (82%) of all second homes in the study was built as second homes or summerhouses (a more common term in the area). The owners have built a substantial share of the houses (40%). However, about 26% are purchased on the market. The third group (just over 29%) are acquisitions through family transactions or inheritance.

One of the most common activities in the use of the second home is maintenance. Relaxing, which is given as one of the most usual motives for acquiring a second home, often seems to be the equivalent of maintenance work (Jansson & Müller, 2003). The second home thus plays an important role in family activities and the families, who have put a lot of effort into the house and garden, really become attached to it. The second home created and maintained by the owners is something they would like to hand over to the coming generation. Interestingly enough, only about 4% of the houses are acquired and kept '*for the children*' and another 4% for '*sports activities*'. This contrasts to the average of 68% who expect to hand it over to the children when they themselves do not want to use it any more. These owners are thus planning for their children, but there could be serious doubts whether or not the children plan to be the future owners of these properties.

Many of the houses, especially the former permanent dwellings, are inherited and/or kept for the sole purpose of keeping up contacts with the owner's childhood landscape even though they now live a considerable distance from the cottage and use it only occasionally. Furthermore, as society becomes more mobile, many heirs to these second homes may lose their specific place attachment and become less interested in keeping up links to a society of which they, as second or third generation out-migrants, have only scant memories. The diminishing attachment to the native landscape or the parents' childhood landscape is illustrated in Figure 17.3 showing that over time, in principle, that contacts in the present overtake the contact fields of the past.

Thus, the owners plan for their children. Our research, however, indicates that teenage sons and daughters often do not want to go with the parents to the cottage, and as adults they seldom visit the family's second home. Thus, when the sons and daughters have shown little interest in the cottages for a long period, the properties that the parents plan to hand over to the next generation may well end up not only as an economic but also a psychological burden to the heirs. Little-used houses in distant places cost

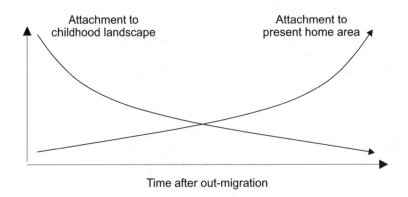

Time after out-migration

Figure 17.3 Changing attachment to 'place' after out-migration

Source: Jansson, 1994

money regardless of how frequently they are used. Property taxes and insurance are only two of these costs, but if one wants a property to maintain its value, regular maintenance is necessary. Psychologically, inherited property in the families' home territory carries a set of expectations and feelings for what parents and grandparents have created and passed on to the next generation these properties cannot easily be given up. Nevertheless, a substantial number of second homes will be placed on the market after the present owners have stopped using them. They will be sold according to views expressed by some of the owners, or after being inherited by children or grandchildren who often live far away and are less attached to the families' home places. After some time they may decide to sell to relieve the economic and psychological burdens.

Middle-aged people (30–50 years old) mostly acquire second homes because they are in a position in society that gives them substantial economic means. The next generation will inherit in 30–60 years' time – a time span that gives the presumed heirs plenty of time to acquire second homes for themselves, better situated in relation to their own homes and/or better in line with their lifestyle. At the time of the survey many of the second home owners had already reached the age of 60 or 70. Thus, the first wave of changes has already started.

Extended Use of the Second Homes

Since many owners use their second home only occasionally, the possibilities should exist for an extended use of the properties. Two types of more intensive use of the cottages were examined. If the properties were to be used just two weeks more each year, the local population would benefit greatly from the additional money spent during these weeks.

One type of extended use is cottage-renting. However, the only place where there was any interest in renting out the houses for shorter periods, was in Tärnaby in the Swedish mountains, where a small cottage-renting service operates locally and the effects can be seen in the number of houses that are let for shorter periods. Another reason for the rental activities to be greater in that area than in others is the age of the houses. They were built recently, and renting out for some weeks of the skiing season was part of the financing package by which the cottages were developed. In the rest of the study area, the owners were strongly against letting their property, and presented a multitude of more or less reasonable arguments for not letting it even though they often used it for only a couple of weeks during the season. Cottage renting on a larger scale therefore seems to be out of question under present ownership considerations.

Since a number of the second homes in the area are of high quality and could be lived live in all-year round, a substantially increased use of the properties would be of interest to the local communities which are often badly affected by out-migration and depopulation. New inhabitants would be an important addition to the local community, bringing with them more purchasing power and thus increasing the possibilities for continued service in the region. However, two-thirds of the respondents stated that a move to the second home as a permanent base was unlikely. Only 5% thought it was probable and about 17% said that it was a possibility in the future, mostly in connection with retirement. Thus a sale is far more probable than a conversion to permanent living.

Concluding Remarks

Second homes in the study area are mainly of two types. First, most of them were built (either by the present owner or a previous owner) solely for the purpose of being a second home or *sommarstuga* ('summerhouse' in Swedish). Second, there is a considerably smaller group of previously-permanent dwellings that have been converted to second homes. These are farmhouses on farms that have been closed down or houses that, for other reasons, have become redundant because of out-migration or other changes in the local communities. The number of second homes in sparsely populated areas will probably increase in peripheral areas because of economic changes. In fact, the number of properties converted to second homes can be seen as a problem indicator. Nevertheless, the survey showed that in most cases the present owners are convinced that the children or grandchildren will take over the property when the time comes.

Previous research on second homes (Kaltenborn, 1997a, 1997b, 1998,

2002) states quite romantically that they are gathering places for meetings across generation boundaries, especially where they represent the family's roots. It is also argued that second home ownership is a reaction to internationalisation and globalisation. In that context it must be noted that second homes often are only one of the nodes of family leisure patterns. It seems that the second homes are increasingly becoming more a refuge for the adults in a family where they can escape the stressful everyday life to enjoy nature and quietness. When, at a later stage, they want to move on with their lives, the second home can be sold. It is not always a lifetime commitment. Even if the present owners claim that the cottages were acquired *'for the children's sake'*, children may not be so interested in going there when they would prefer to be with friends somewhere else.

However, these inherited cottages, although beautifully situated, are often not in contact with what are considered to be good leisure areas. They are often in troubled, remote, and sparsely-settled areas with high levels of out-migration. So, if one wants to seek one's roots in the form of relatives one may have to search widely. In today's mobile society it will be more of a rule than an exception that children move away to other places distant from family and relatives and even further from the second home. The subsequent changes in family structure also prepare the grounds for a restructuring as far as the second home is concerned. Inheriting a remotely-situated second home may, under these circumstances, come as both a physical and an economic burden for today's young people. The present owners are reluctant to extend the use of their second homes, and our prediction is that a change in ownership could be the necessary measure to bring about a more modern view of the use of second homes. A break in the chain of heritage would thus be a good thing.

Finally, the number of permanent dwellings converted to second homes can be expected to increase owing to changes in society including a depopulation of the countryside, growing internationalisation, smaller household sizes, and an increasingly mobility. At the same time, the building of new second homes can be expected to remain at a low level owing to high building costs and the present environmental protection regulations that make it very difficult to build on the attractive sites on or near the water. Therefore, the future use of these second homes will be influenced by changes in society, and individual plans for the second home – often based on emotional reasons – may be seen as only wishful thinking.

Chapter 18

The Future of Second Home Tourism

DIETER K. MÜLLER AND C. MICHAEL HALL

This volume has emphasised that second homes are not an issue of the past, but are an important element of contemporary lifestyles, mobilities, tourism and regional development. This has meant that since the early 1990s the growing interest in second home tourism has been shared across the social sciences but particularly by those interested in the changing natures of rural areas and human mobility. As demonstrated in this volume, there are several reasons why second homes are significant. New forms and patterns of production and consumption now enable an increasing number of households to spend time away from traditional working and production environments, and in preferred locations with high amenity values (Williams & Hall, 2000a, 2002). Although this may be related to broader movements of counter-urbanisation and the development of a post-productivist countryside (Ward, 1993; Halfacree, 1994), second homes also indicate the development of new, more fluid, patterns of mobility and place affiliation. These, rather than setting the 'rural' and the 'urban' as opposing categories, position them as part of an interrelated and networked whole.

Another important factor with respect to second home development is the growing quantity of retirees in the Western world with their disposable spare time and consuming power adding significantly to the number of households that can make use of a second home. As of 2000, 11% of the world's population was aged 60 and above. By 2050, one out of five will be 60 years or older; and, by 2150, one out of three persons will be at least 60 years old. However, even the older population is ageing. Between 1950 and 2050, the number of very old people (aged 80+ years) is projected to grow as much as 8 or 10 times on the global scale. On current trends, by 2150, about a third of the older population will be 80 years or older (United Nations, 1998). Such a demographic shift will clearly have substantial implications for second home tourism. Not only may particular types of tourism (such as cruising) geared towards retirees continue to grow in popularity, but second homes that go on to become a seasonal or even permanent retirement homes may become increasingly important in destination development strategies. For example, a number of places in parts of

Mediterranean Europe and the Iberian Peninsula, Queensland's Gold and Sunshine Coasts, and the south-western United States and Florida are already subject to substantial seasonal and permanent retirement migration – much of it international in nature (Williams *et al.*, 1997, and also Chapter 7 in this volume). Therefore, for those with the economic and social capacities, second homes are an important expression of locational decision-making in terms not just of spatial mobility but also of temporal mobility over the term of a person's life. For the localities in which retirees choose to purchase second homes, which may then become a component of a seasonal or even permanent migration strategy, such demographic shifts will have a range of implications for service provision in the short term and economic and social development in the longer term. Just as important, such second home mobility will have development and infrastructure implications for the locations in which the 'first homes' are located.

As has been well demonstrated in this and other volumes, second home tourism may also be embedded in national leisure and cultural traditions. The cottage is much a part of the national folklore of Canada (Halseth, Chapter 3) as is the Swedish 'stuga' (Aronsson, Chapter 5; Jansson & Müller, Chapter 17), the Norwegian 'hytte' (Flognfeldt, Chapter 15) or the New Zealand 'bach' (Keen & Hall, Chapter 12). Increased international mobility may have interesting implications for the place of second homes within national cultures and identities. For example, immigrants from parts of the world where there is no tradition of second homes may not be particularly interested in a summer cottage or a weekend home, although they may desire a vacation home in their country of origin (Duval, Chapter 6). Other immigrants may well embrace second homes because second homes are a part of the host country's culture and they seek to 'fit in' to that host community. Nevertheless, it is apparent that the continuation of some of the historical traditions of second home tourism being tied in to connections with places of origin can no longer be taken for granted. One reason for this is the large and increasingly diverse immigrant populations in places like Sweden, New Zealand and Canada; another is the overall growth in personal mobility that make relationships with 'traditional' family-connected second home locations much more difficult for some individuals and households.

The location of second homes as being a distinct expression of a national identity that takes place within national boundaries has therefore also clearly changed. Müller's (1999, 2002a, and Chapter 16) research on German second home owners in Sweden for example, clearly indicates the transnational nature of second home ownership in Europe, a situation clearly reinforced by the work of Williams *et al.* (Chapter 7) on second home and retirement migration in southern Europe. Such transnational second home movements are not uniquely European. In North America, 'snowbirding' (Timothy, Chapter 9) is the term given to the seasonal migration of many Canadian retirees (as well as American retirees from the northerly states) to Florida, the south-western United States and, increasingly, Mexico. In Australia, the Gold and Sunshine Coast resort areas near Brisbane both receive significant numbers of New Zealand retirees during the New Zealand winter in an Antipodean version of snowbirding. Undoubtedly, such large-scale movement has significant longer-term implications for national and transnational identities that are only beginning to be recognised (Duval, Chapter 6). Yet many of the broader agreements surrounding free trade and human mobility, such as those found within the European Union or the Asia Pacific Economic Consultation Forum (APEC), are serving only to encourage further transnational second homing. It is therefore likely that, even given the increased regulation of human mobility for some nationalities as a result of security concerns, the capacity of wealthier individuals in the developed world to engage in transnational second homing will not only continue relatively unhindered, but may even be further encouraged by some regions seeking inward investment.

The mobility implicit in the notion of second home tourism challenges established practices and institutions at both local and national levels. Assuming that an increasing number of people reside in several places, it is doubtful whether current administrative practices are sufficient to consider the interests of the mobile. In many countries, democratic rights are traditionally exercised at one home only. Accepting multiple homes therefore also entails a significant challenge for national governments. Examples from Finland (Leppänen, 2003) show how second home owners have been invited to establish a local association that enables them to act as a partner for the local authorities in planning issues. In the case of New Zealand, Keen and Hall (Chapter 12) noted how, in one example, second home owners had created an organisation to identify common interests and represent these to local government. However, it is also noticeable that in New Zealand, where the local government laws had provided for local voting rights on the basis of land ownership, such a provision was under review because of the supposed costs of such democratic exercises.

Another major issue to emerge in this volume is the extent to which second homes actually make a positive contribution to rural regions. Yet, the role of second home tourism for the countryside depends on the national and regional context. The question of whether second home tourism is a positive contribution to the rural economy primarily depends on whether or not second home tourism has entailed a displacement of the rural population. Except in areas of extremely high amenity value, this seems however seldom to be the case. Instead, second home tourism often tends to fill the vacancies caused by rural out-migration or to develop in ways that are not invasive of the surrounding rural landscape. Therefore, second home tourism often forms an important contribution to the local economy and particularly to the local service supply (Jansson & Müller, 2003). However, the local tourism authorities rarely acknowledge this role of second home tourism, and mainly make efforts to attract more high-profile tourists. Nevertheless, this is not to deny that, in certain highly sought after, high value amenity locations, second home development adds to the pressure on local housing stock and land prices. However, given the overall importance of such amenity values both for tourism and for permanent migration to such regions, second homes should not be singled out for blame. Instead, governments need to develop integrated planning and development strategies that seek to address the needs of permanent inhabitants as well as the needs of temporary mobile tourists and second homers. Indeed, one of the most significant dimensions of second home tourism, and one that makes it different from many other forms of tourism, is that second home owners make an ongoing financial commitment to a location on the basis of their decision to purchase a second home there. Such place commitment clearly offers substantially positive possibilities for the second home destination that could be harnessed for the common interests of permanent and temporary inhabitants alike.

The social role of second home owners for rural society will also be different depending on the regional context and on the composition of the second home stock. Converted second homes often provide better purchasing opportunities than purpose-built second homes outside traditional settlements. Both Quinn (Chapter 8) and Flognfeldt (Chapter 15) report that second home owners socialise with the local population and act as ambassadors for the rural areas in which their homes are located, promoting their produce and virtues. Flognfeldt (2002, Chapter 15) has also observed the value of second home owners for helping with entrepreneurial start-ups, the creation of business networks and opportunities, and the replacement of intellectual capital that had previously been lost through rural depopulation and out-migration. However, in contrast, Halseth (1998, Chapter 3) argues that second home landscapes are islands in the rural landscape. Such contrasting perspectives clearly provide opportunities for further research on the cultural and locational context within which second home development occurs and in the barriers and opportunities for the creation of economic and social networks.

The final issue that we address is the ongoing accessibility of second homes. Are they still widely accessible, or have they become the domain of the rich? As with many of the issues surrounding second homes that this volume has raised, the answer depends on the socio-cultural, economic and political context in which second home development occurs. At least in the Nordic countries, second homes have been an important achievement of the welfare state, guaranteeing access to second homes for a large proportion of the population (Nordin, 1993b; Tress, 2002; Jansson & Müller, Chapter 17). As in other parts of the world (eg. Keen & Hall, Chapter 12; Selwood & Tonts, Chapter 10; Visser, Chapter 13) there is, however, reason to question the future opportunities for maintaining this situation. Besides the demographic changes and new patterns of demand resulting shifts in population (see Jansson & Müller, this volume), changed regulatory regimes have had a dramatic impact on the availability, and hence the accessibility, of second homes.

Perhaps ironically, given the commitment of many second home owners to environmental amenity values, environmental protection issues have emerged as a major constraint on second home development. In the Nordic countries, environmental protection policy has made the availability of second homes along shorelines a limited resource. In Sweden the political desire to protect lakes because of their role in biodiversity actually prevents authorities in peripheral areas from developing new second home areas. Hence, because of their rarity value, amenity-rich second home areas are increasingly converted into exclusive and segregated spaces (Müller, 2002e). Halseth's notion (Chapter 3) of an increasingly elite second home landscape therefore gains some validity within the Nordic context where second homes had previously been a common ground. Similarly, in the case of New Zealand, Keen and Hall (Chapter 12) report how housing regulations and the championing of a particular notion of aesthetic landscapes which removes or reduces human presence from some coastal and mountain areas has also constrained second home development. This is, of course, not to argue that second home development should be unregulated. Clearly there are significant concerns over sewage disposal and environmental quality. Nevertheless, in many jurisdictions within which second homes occur, housing and environmental regulations have served to limit accessibility to the development of second (as well as first) homes rather then to meet social access concerns.

The selection of the term common ground in the title of this book is not only meant to refer to the ideal of common access, but also reflects broader cultural attitudes to accessibility to land in a number of the countries in which second homes are significant. In the Nordic context and in the historical context of Australia, New Zealand and, arguably Canada and South Africa, public land was traditionally seen as available for the development of holiday and fishing shacks and summer huts that often served the dual purpose of leisure and work. Over time, the leisure purpose came to dominate and provided for holiday access for many of the less wealthy members of society as well as for those who sought to maintain connections with the places of their childhood and their family. However, these relationships to place are often being constrained (and in some cases completely cut off) by the commodification of land and the development of values based more upon real estate development and speculation than the notion of a common good that includes rights of access for recreation, including second homes. Such commodification practices are implicitly and explicitly related to the regulatory regimes created by government. In much the same way that government intervention can restrict second home development and thereby pave the way for the development of elite landscapes, so intervention can also create opportunities for second home access. The decision is a political one that, arguably, reflects broader attitudes towards welfare and the public good.

In the mobile developed world, the landscapes of second home development are more of a blessing than a curse for many regions, particularly in peripheral areas. But, as with all things, much will depend on the specific context within which second homes occur. Nevertheless, this volume has highlighted the fundamental role that second homes play in regional development, as well as some of the potential social and economic implications of such mobility. Ironically, much government activity, particularly at the local level, is spent trying to attract mobile capital and people, such as that represented in second home development, in order to achieve growth-oriented economic and social-policy objectives. Yet despite such policy-setting, government tends to have a poor understanding of such mobilities, and demographic and economic instruments remain set for a time of relatively static populations that has long since passed, if it ever really existed. In many parts of the developed world, second homes constitute a greater potential number of bednights for travellers than the formal accommodation sector. Second homes create significant short-term and long-term economic, social and political relationships between their owners and the communities in which they are situated. Second homes also have highly significant functions with respect to collective and individual notions of heritage, sense of place and even identity. Yet, in terms of contemporary understanding of leisure-oriented mobilities, including tourism, and the regulation of these mobilities, the nature and significance of second homes has been poorly understood by government and academia alike. It is hoped that this book represents a contribution to furthering such understanding.

References

ABS (1998) *Census of Population and Housing: Selected Characteristics for Urban Centres and Localities, Victoria.* ABS catalogue no. 2016.2. Canberra: Australian Bureau of Statistics.

ABS (2002) *Australian National Accounts: Tourism Satellite Account, 2000–1.* ABS catalogue no. 5249.0. Canberra: Australian Bureau of Statistics.

Age Concern (1993) *Growing Old in Spain: Older British People Resident in Spain.* London: Age Concern England.

Albarre, G. (1977) Second homes and conservation in southern Belgium. In J.T. Coppock (ed.) *Second Homes: Curse or Blessing?* (pp. 139–146). Oxford: Pergamon.

Albrow, M. (1998) Frames and transformations in transnational studies. Working paper (WPTC-98-02). Transnational Communities Research Programme, Institute of Social and Cultural Anthropology, University of Oxford. On WWW at www.transcomm.ox.ac.uk/working_papers.htm.

Aldskogius, H. (1968) Studier i Siljansområdets fritidshusbebyggelse. *Geografiska regionstudier 4.* Uppsala: Department of Geography.

Aldskogius, H. (1969) Modelling the evolution of settlement patterns: Two studies of vacation house settlement. *Geografiska regionstudier 6.* Uppsala: Department of Geography.

American Resort Development Association (1999) *State of the US Vacation Ownership Industry: The 1999 Report.* Washington, DC: ARDA.

Ando, M. (2002) Interchange between rural and urban Japan. Paper presented at annual meeting of Canadian Rural Revitalization Foundation, Mirimichi, New Brunswick, October 29.

Ansley, B. (2002) Home away from home. *Listener,* 18 February, pp. 16–21.

Appadurai, A. (1991) Global ethnoscapes: Notes and queries for a transnational anthropology. In R.G. Fox (ed.) *Recapturing Anthropology: Working in the Present* (pp. 191–210). Santa Fe: School of American Research Press.

Aronson, C. (2000) Tairua, Pauanui subdivision capped after spill of sewage. *New Zealand Herald,* 29 September.

Aronsson, L. (1993) *Mötet. En studie i Smögen av turisters, fritidsboendes och bofastas användning av tid och rum.* Högskolan i Karlstad: Gruppen för regional-vetenskaplig forskning, Forskningsrapport 1993, 1.

Aronsson, L. (1997) Tourism in time and space: An example from Smögen, Sweden. In D.G. Lockhart and D. Drakakis-Smith (eds) *Island Tourism. Trends and Prospects* (pp. 118–136). London: Pinter.

Aronsson, L. (2000) *The Development of Sustainable Tourism.* London: Continuum.

Baldassar, L. (2001) *Visits Home: Migration Experiences between Italy and Australia.* Melbourne: Melbourne University Press.

Barber, F. (2001) 'Raglan's new wave'. *The New Zealand Herald Online.* On WWW at www.nzherald.co.nz/storyprint.cfm?storyID=113722. Accessed 30.4.01.

Barbier, B. (1965) Logements de vacances et résidences secondaires dans le Sud-Est méditerranéen. *Bulletin de L'Association Géographes Francais* 344–5, 2–11.

Barke, M. (1991) The growth and changing pattern of second homes in Spain in the 1970s. *Scottish Geographical Magazine* 107 (1), 12–21.

Barke, M. and France, L.A. (1988) Second homes tourism: Balearic Islands. *Geography* 73 (2), 143–145.

Barton, C. (2000) Searching for a slice of heaven on the web. *The New Zealand Herald Online*. On WWW at www.nzherald.co.nz/storyprint.cfm?storyID+156620. Accessed 30.04.01.

Basch, L. (2001) Transnational social relations and the politics of national identities: An Eastern Caribbean case study. In N. Foner (ed.) *Islands in the City: West Indian Migration to New York* (pp. 117–141). Berkeley: University of California Press.

Basch, L., Glick Schiller, N. and Szanton Blanc, C. (1994) *Nations Unbound: Transnational Projects and the Deterritorialized Nation-state*. New York: Gordon and Breach.

Batie, S.S. and Mabbs-Zeno, C.C. (1985) Opportunity costs of preserving coastal wetlands: A case study of a recreational housing development. *Land Economics* 61 (1), 1–9.

Bauman, Z. (1998) *Globalisering*. Lund: Studentlitteratur.

Beavon, K.S.O. and Rogerson, C.M. (1981) Trekking on: Recent trends in the human geography of southern Africa. *Progress in Human Geography* 5, 159–89.

Beck, R.L. and Hussey, D. (1989) Politics, property rights, and cottage development. *Canadian Public Policy* 15 (1), 25–33.

Beer, A. and Badcock, B. (2000) *Home Truths: Property Ownership and Housing Wealth in Australia*. Melbourne: Melbourne University Press.

Bell, M. (1977) The spatial distribution of second homes: A modified gravity model. *Journal of Leisure Research* 9, 225–232.

Bell, M. and Ward, G. (2000) Comparing temporary mobility with permanent migration. *Tourism Geographies* 2 (1), 87–107.

Bennett, C. and McCuaig, D.W. (1980) *In Search of Lanark*. Renfrew: Renfrew Advanced Ltd.

Berry, B.J.L. (1970) The geography of the United States in the year 2000. *Transactions of the Institute of British Geographers* 51, 21–53.

Bielckus, C.L. (1977) Second homes in Scandinavia. In J.T. Coppock (ed.) *Second Homes: Curse or Blessing?* (pp. 35–47). Oxford: Pergamon.

Blumenfeld, H. (1954) The tidal wave of metropolitan growth. *Journal of the American Association of Planners* (Winter), 3–14.

Bohlin, M. (1982a) The spatial and economic impact of recreational expenditures and sales in the Pigeon Lake area of Alberta. *Forskningsrapporter från Kulturgeografiska institutionen vid Uppsala universitet* 77. Uppsala: Kulturgeografiska institutionen.

Bohlin, M. (1982b) Fritidsboendet i den regionala ekonomin: Vart fritidshusägarnas pengar tar vägen. *Geografiska regionstudier* 14. Uppsala: Kulturgeografiska institutionen.

Boschken, H.L. (1975) The second home subdivision: Market suitability for recreational and pastoral use. *Journal of Leisure Research* 7, 63–75.

Bowles, R.T. and Beesley, K.B. (1991) Quality of life, migration to the countryside and rural community growth. In K.B. Beesley (ed.) *Rural and Urban Fringe Studies in Canada. Geographical Monograph No. 21* (pp. 45–66). Toronto: York University.

Boyle, P., Halfacree, K. and Robinson, V. (1998) *Exploring Contemporary Migration*. Harlow: Longman.

Bradley, M. (2002) Sustainable transport in Albany. Unpublished BSc (Hons) thesis. Department of Geography, The University of Western Australia.

Brady, E.J. (1911) *Picturesque Port Phillip*. Melbourne: George Robertson.

Brady, E.J. (1918) *Australia Unlimited*. Melbourne: George Robertson.

Branton, M. (1977) *A Resort Despoiled: A Study of Inverloch and Venus Bay.* Melbourne: Conservation Council of Victoria.

Brown, H.M. (1984) *Lanark Legacy: Nineteenth Century Glimpses of an Ontario County.* Perth: Corporation of the County of Lanark.

Brown, R.N. (1970) *Economic Impact of Second Home Communities*. Washington, DC: US Department of Agriculture.

Brunet, Y. (1980) L'Exode urbain: Essai de classification de la population exurbaine des cantons de l'Est. *Canadian Geographer* 24 (4), 385–405.

Bruxelles, S. de (2001) Exmoor to ban second homes. *The Times*, 5 September, p.1.

Bryant, C.R., Russwurm, L.H. and McLellan, A.G. (1982) *The City's Countryside: Land and its Management in the Rural–Urban Fringe*. London and New York: Longman.

BTR (2001) *Travel by Australians, 2000: Annual Results of the National Visitor Survey*. Canberra: Bureau of Tourism Research.

Buggins, A. (2002) Developer puts plan for bigger Jurien Bay. *The West Australian*, 17 October.

Buller, H. and Hoggart, K. (1994a) *International Counterurbanization: British Migrants in Rural France*. Aldershot: Ashgate.

Buller, H. and Hoggart, K. (1994b) The social integration of British home owners into French rural communities. *Journal of Rural Studies* 2, 197–210.

Bunce, M. (1994) *The Countryside Ideal: Anglo-American Images of Landscape*. London: Routledge.

Burby, R.J. III, Donnelly, T.G. and Weiss, S.F. (1972) Vacation home location: A model for simulating the residential development of rural recreation areas. *Regional Studies* 6: 421–439.

Burkhart, A.J. and Medlik, S. (1991) *Tourism, Past, Present and Future*. Oxford: Heinemann.

Business Day (2001a) Gauteng recovery boots Cape residential market. On WWW at http://www.bday.co.za/bday/content/direct/1,3523,854234-6132-0,00.html. Accessed 16.08.02.

Business Day (2001b) Demand drives strong Natal revival: Gauteng recovery boots Cape residential market. At http://www.bday.co.za/bday/content/direct/1,3523,985519-6132-0,00.html. Accessed 16.08.02.

Business Day (2003) International buyers spark a boom. On WWW at http://www.bdfm.co.za/cgi-bin/pp-print.pl. Accessed 19.05.03.

Butler, R. (1980) The concept of a tourist cycle of evolution: Implications for the management of resources. *The Canadian Geographer* 24, 5–12.

Butler, R. (1998) Rural recreation and tourism. In B. Ilbery (ed.) *The Geography of Rural Change* (pp. 211–232). Harlow: Longman.

Butler, R.W. (1985) Timesharing: The implications of an alternative to the conventional cottage. *Loisir et Société/Society and Leisure* 8 (2), 769–779.

Buttimer, A. (1978) Home, reach and the sense of place. In H. Aldskogius (ed.) *Regional identitet och förändring i den regionala samverkans samhälle*. Uppsala: Uppsala universitet.

Butts, D.J. (1993) Institutional arrangements for cultural heritage management in New Zealand: Legislation, management, and protection. In C.M Hall and S. McArthur (eds) *Heritage Management in New Zealand and Australia: Visitor Management, Interpretation, and Marketing* (pp. 169–187). Auckland: Oxford University Press.

Canada (1990a) *Rideau Canal Management Planning Issues: Recreation and Tourism.* Ottawa: Environment Canada, Canadian Parks Service.

Canada (1990b) *Rideau Canal Management Planning Issues: Shoreline Land Use.* Ottawa: Environment Canada, Canadian Parks Service.

Casado-Diaz, M.A. (2001) De turistas a residentes: La migración internacional de retirados en Espana. Unpublished thesis. Universidad de Alicante.

Casado-Diaz, M.A. (1999) Socio-demographic impacts of residential tourism: A case study of Torrevieja, Spain. *International Journal of Tourism Research* 1, 223–237.

Casado-Diaz, M.A. and Rodriguez, V. (2002) La migración internacional de retirados en Espana: Limitación de las fuentes de información. *Estudios geográficos* LXIII (248–249), 533–558.

Castells, M. (1996) *The Rise of the Network Society. The Information Age. Economy, Society and Culture* (Vol. 1). Oxford: Blackwell Publishers.

Chaplin, D. (1999) Consuming work/productive leisure: The consumption patterns of second home environments. *Leisure Studies* 18 (1), 41–55.

Chapple, G. (1988) Bach boom. *Listener*, 16 January, pp. 14–15.

Charles, R. and Loney, J. (1989) *Not Enough Grass to Feed a Single Bullock: A History of Tarwin Lower, Venus Bay and Waratah.* Geelong: Rod Charles.

Charski, M. (1998) Second homes for sale. *US News and World Report*, 28 September, p. 70.

Chow, W. (2002) Meanwhile, back at the ranch. *The Vancouver Sun*, 7 September, E1, E5.

Clare County Council (1999) *County Clare Development Plan 1999–2004.* Ennis: Clare County Council.

Clark, R. and Selwood, J. (1970) Lancelin townsite: An urban study. *Australind* 3, 25–34.

Clawson, M. and Knetsch, J.L. (1966) *Economics of Outdoor Recreation.* Baltimore: John Hopkins Press.

Clifford, J. (1997) *Routes: Travel and Translation in the Late Twentieth Century.* Cambridge: Harvard University Press.

Cloke, P.J. (1989) Rural geography and political economy. In R. Peet and N. Thrift (eds) *New Models in Geography: The Political Economy Perspective* (Vol. 1, pp. 164–197). London: Unwin Hyman.

Cloke, P.J. and Goodwin, M. (1992) Conceptualizing countryside change: From post-Fordism to rural structured coherence. *Transactions of the Institute of British Geographers* N.S.17, 321–336.

Clout, H.D. (1969) Second homes in France. *Journal of the Town Planning Institute* 55, 440–443.

Clout, H.D. (1970) Social aspects of second-home occupation in the Auvergne. *Planning Outlook* 9, 33–49.

Clout, H.D. (1971) Second homes in the Auvergne. *Geographical Review* 61, 530–533.

Clout, H.D. (1972) Second homes in the United States. *Tijdschrift voor Economische en Sociale Geografie* 63, 393–401.

Clout, H.D. (1974) The growth of second-home ownership: An example of seasonal suburbanization. In J.H. Johnson (ed.) *Suburban Growth: Geographical Processes at the Edge of the Western City* (pp. 101–127). London: John Wiley and Sons.

Clout, H.D. (1977) Résidences secondaires in France. In J.T. Coppock (ed.) *Second Homes: Curse or Blessing?* (pp. 47–62). Oxford: Pergamon.

Cohen, E. (1974) Who is a tourist: A conceptual clarification. *Sociological Review* 22 (4), 527–555.

Cohen, E. (1995) Contemporary tourism, trends and challenges. Sustainable authenticity or contrived post-modernity? In R. Butler and D. Pearce (eds) *Change in Tourism, People, Places, Processes*. London: Routledge.

Cohen, R. (1997) *Global Diasporas: An Introduction*. Seattle: University of Washington Press.

Cole, J. (1991) A coastal management plan for Horrocks Beach, Western Australia. Unpublished BA (Hons) thesis. Department of Geography, University of Western Australia.

Conzen, M.P. (ed.) (1990) *The Making of the American Landscape*. London: Unwin Hyman.

Coppack, P.M. (1988) The role of amenity. In P.M. Coppack, L.H. Russwurm and C.R. Bryant (eds) *Essays on Canadian Urban Process and Form III: The Urban Field, Publication Series No. 30* (pp. 41–55). Waterloo: University of Waterloo, Department of Geography.

Coppack P.M., Russwurm L.H. and C.R. Bryant (eds) (1988) *Essays on Canadian Urban Process and Form III: The Urban Field, Publication Series No. 30*. Waterloo: University of Waterloo, Department of Geography.

Coppock, J.T. (ed.) (1977a) *Second Homes: Curse or Blessing?* Oxford: Pergamon.

Coppock, J.T. (1977b) Social implications of second homes in Mid- and North Wales. In J.T. Coppock (ed.) *Second Homes: Curse or Blessing?* (pp. 147–154). Oxford: Pergamon.

Coppock, J.T. (1977c) Second homes in perspective. In J.T. Coppock (ed.) *Second Homes: Curse or Blessing?* (pp. 1–16). Oxford: Pergamon.

Cottage Life (1991) From the President: Keep up the pressure on property tax. *Cottage Life*, July/August, pp. 93–94.

Cottage Life (1992) From the President: Lake stewardship programs are a promising first step. *Cottage Life*, June, pp. 89–92.

Cottage Life (1993a) John Sewell cites cottagers as leaders for the environment. *Cottage Life*, April/May, pp. 107.

Cottage Life (1993b) Looking for loopholes. *Cottage Life*, September/October, pp. 13–14, 16.

Cox, N. (1995) At the bach. *New Zealand Geographic* 25, 34–52

Crang, M. (1998) *Cultural Geography*. London: Routledge.

Cribier, F. (1966) 300,000 Résidences secondaires. *Urbanisme* 96–7, 97–101.

Cribier, F. (1973) Le résidences secondaires des citadins dans les campagnes français. *Études Rurales* 49–50, 181–204.

Croll, R.H. (1928) *The Open Road in Victoria: Being the Ways of Many Walkers.* Melbourne: Robertson and Mullens.

Cross, A.W. (1992) *The Summer House: A Tradition of Leisure*. Toronto: HarperCollins.

Crouch, D., Aronsson, L. and Wahlström, L. (2001) Tourist encounters. *Tourist Studies* 1 (3), 253–270.

CSO (1998) *Census of Population*. Dublin: Central Statistics Office.

CSO (2002a) *Ireland North and South: A Statistical Profile*. Dublin: Central Statistics Office.

CSO (2002b) *Census of Population (Estimates)*. Dublin: Central Statistics Office.

Cuba, L. (1989) From visitor to resident: Retiring in vacationland. *Generations* 13, 63–67.

Cumming, G. (2002) Coastline moving beyond our reach. *The New Zealand Herald*. On WWW at www.nzhearld/storydisplay.cfm?thesection=news&thesubsection=&storyID=209856. Accessed 24.04.03.

Curry, G., Koczberski, G. and Selwood, J. (2001) Cashing out, cashing in: Rural change on the south coast of Western Australia. *Australian Geographer* 32, 109–124.

D'Angelo, A. (2003a) European retirees and swallows welcome to settle. *Business Report*. On WWW at http://www.../br_newsview.php?click_id=345&art_id= 1044517863661N234&set_id=6. Accessed 06.02.03.

D'Angelo, A. (2003b) Irish are the latest to catch the property-buying bug in SA. *Business Report*. On WWW at http://www.busrepco.../print_article.php? fArticleID=146901&fsectionID=566&fSetId=30. Accessed 19.05.03.

Dagens Næringsliv (2003) Bonanza for feriehus i utlandet [Bonanza of Norwegian owned holiday homes abroad]. *Dagens Næringsliv,* 30 April.

Dahms, F. and McComb, J. (1999) 'Counterurbanization', interaction and functional change in a rural amenity area: A Canadian example. *Journal of Rural Studies* 15 (2), 129–146.

Darroch, K.A. (1992) An assessment of the Otty Lake Association and a recommendation for future provincial policy on lake planning. Unpublished master's thesis. School of Urban and Regional Planning, Queen's University.

Daugstad, K. and Saeter, S. (2001) *Seterliv [Life at Summer Farms]*. Oslo: det Norske Samlaget.

David, J. (1966) Résidences secondaires et structures fincières dans le Val de Bourget. *Revue de Géographie Alpine* 54: 489–503.

David, J. and Geoffroy, G. (1966) Les résidences secondaires en Chartreuse isérois. *Revue de Géographie Alpine* 56: 65–72.

Deller, S.C., Marcouiller, D.W. and Green, G.P. (1997) Recreational housing and local government finance. *Annals of Tourism Research* 24: 687–705.

Department of Infrastructure, Victoria (2001) Great Ocean Road Region, towards a vision for the future. Discussion paper. Department of Infrastructure: Melbourne.

Dilley, R.S. (1985) Local government, public expectations and planning policy in a rural recreational area. Paper presented at International Conference on Management of Rural Resources: Problems and Policies, Guelph.

Dirsuweit, T. (1999) From fortress city to creative city: Developing culture and the information-based sectors in the regeneration and reconstruction of the Greater Johannesburg area. *Urban Forum* 10 (3), 183–213.

Dirsuweit, T. (2002) Johannesburg: Fearful city? *Urban Forum* 13 (3), 3–20.

Donegal County Council (2000) *County Donegal Development Plan*. Lifford: Donegal County Council.

Douglas, M. (1991) The idea of a home: A kind of space. *Social Research* 58 (1), 287–307.

Dower, M. (1977) Planning aspects of second homes. In J.T. Coppock (ed) *Second Homes: Curse or Blessing?* (pp. 155–164). Oxford: Pergamon.

Dungey, K. (2003) Buying that place in the country. *Otago Daily Times*, 17 January.

Duval, D.T. (2002) The return visit–return migration connection. In C.M. Hall and A. Williams (eds) *Tourism and Migration: New Relationships between Production and Consumption* (pp. 257–276). Dordrecht: Kluwer.

Edmonds, C. (1998) Chittering's rural restructuring: The economics and politics of land use change. Unpublished BA (Hons) thesis, University of Western Australia, Perth.

Elsrud, T. (1998) Time creation in travelling: The taking and making of time among women backpackers. *Time & Society* 7 (2), 309–334.

Elsrud, T. (2001) Risk creation in travelling: Backpacker adventure narration. *Annals of Tourism Research* 28 (3), 597–617.

Evans, H.D. (1992) *Windy Harbour Settlement*. Windy Harbour: Windy Harbour Sea Rescue Group.

Faist, T. (2000a) *The Volume and Dynamics of International Migration and Transnational Social Spaces*. Oxford: Clarendon Press.

Faist, T. (2000b) Transnationalization in international migration: Implications for the study of citizenship and culture. *Ethnic and Racial Studies* 23 (2), 189–222.

Familitur (2001) *Movimientos Turisticos de los Espanoles*. Instituto de Estudios Turisticos.

Fife, I. (2001) How to find that little home in the country. *Financial Mail*, 7 December, p. 46.

Fife, I. (2003) Bet against a bubble. *Financial Mail*, 16 May, p. 71.

Finance Week (1998) Demand for stands in Atlantic Beach Estate. *Finance Week*, 30 October, pp. 55–69.

Finance Week (1999) Focus on Cape: Coastal properties. *Finance Week*, 29 October, pp. 47–52.

Financial Mail (2001) Cover story. *Financial Mail*, 7 December, p. 46.

Finansie en Tegniek (1997) Belê nou in kuseiendom. *Finansie en Tegniek*, 7 November, pp. 41–42.

Fine, I.V. and Tuttle, R.E. (1966) *Private Seasonal Housing in Wisconsin*. Madison: State Department of Resource Development.

Fine, I.V. and Werner, E.E. (1960) *Private Cottages in Wisconsin*. Madison: University of Wisconsin, Bureau of Business Research.

Finnveden, B. (1960) Den dubbla bosättningen och sommarmigrationen; Exempel från Hallandskustens fritidsbebyggelse. *Svensk Geografisk Årsbok* 36, 58–84.

Fitchen, J.M. (1991) *Endangered Spaces, Enduring Places: Change, identity, and survival in rural America*. Boulder: Westview Press.

Flognfeldt, T. (1999) Trysilprosjektet. Konsekvens: Og mulighetsanalyse av en foreslått utbygging i Trysilfjellet for strekningen Innbygda-Nybergsund [The Trysil Project: Feasibility study of a proposed private Master Plan of Trysilfjellet, Norway]. Working paper no. 86/1999. Lillehammer: Lillehammer College.

Flognfeldt, T. (2000) Rapid growth in an alpine skiing resort area: A feasibility study for further development in Trysil, Norway. Paper presented at the 29th International Geographical Congress in Seoul, Korea.

Flognfeldt, T. (2002) Second home ownership. A sustainable semi-migration. In C.M. Hall and A.M. Williams (eds) *Tourism and Migration. New Relationships between Production and Consumption* (pp. 187–203). Dordrecht: Kluwer Academic Publishers.

Fountain, J. and Hall, C.M. (2002) The impact of lifestyle migration on rural communities: A case study of Akaroa, New Zealand. In C.M. Hall and A.M. Williams (eds) *Tourism and Migration: New Relationships between Production and Consumption* (pp. 153–168). Dordrecht: Kluwer.

Fraguell, M.J. (1996) *Turismo y territorio*. Valencia: Universidad de Valencia.

Freedman, R. (2000) Grabbing a ray of sunshine. *Realtor Magazine* 33 (3), 50–53.

Fridgen, J.D. (1984) Environmental psychology and tourism. *Annals of Tourism Research* 11 (1), 19–40.

Friedmann, J. (1978) The urban field as human habitat. In L.S. Bourne and J.W. Simmons (eds) *Systems of Cities: Readings on Structure, Growth, and Policy* (pp. 42–52). New York: Oxford University Press.

Friedmann, J. and Miller, J. (1965) The urban field. *Journal of the American Institute of Planners* 31, 312–320.

Fritz, R.G. (1982) Tourism, vacation home development and residential tax burden: A case study of the local finances of 240 Vermont towns. *American Journal of Economics and Sociology* 41, 375–385.

Frontur (2003) *Movimientos Turisticos en Fronteras Avance de Resultados 2002.* Instituto de Estudios Turisticos.

Frost, W. (2000) *Nature-based Tourism in the 1920s and 1930s.* Proceedings of the Council for Australian Universities Tourism and Hospitality Educators Conference, Mt Buller. Melbourne: La Trobe University.

Frost, W. (2003) *Second Homes in Australia: An Exploration of Statistical Sources.* Proceedings of the 2003 Council of Australian Universities Tourism and Hospitality Educators Conference, Coffs Harbour.

Frost, W. and Foster, D. (2002) *Strategies for Effective Tourist Data Collection for Small Regional Areas: A Case Study of the Echuca-Moama Tourism Study.* Refereed proceedings of the 12th Council for Australian Universities Tourism and Hospitality Educators Conference. Fremantle: Promaco.

Gallent, N. (1997) Improvement grants, second homes and planning control in England and Wales: A policy review. *Planning Practice & Research* 12, 401–411.

Gallent, N. and Tewdwr-Jones, M. (2000) *Rural Second Homes in Europe: Examining Housing Supply and Planning Control.* Aldershot: Ashgate.

Gardavsky, V. (1977) Second homes in Czechoslovakia. In J.T. Coppock (ed.) *Second Homes: Curse or Blessing?* (pp. 63–74). Oxford: Pergamon.

Gartner, W.C. (1987) Environmental impacts of recreational home developments. *Annals of Tourism Research* 14: 38–57.

Garvill, J., Malmberg, G. and Westin, K. (2000) *Värdet av att flytta och att stanna: om flyttningsbeslut, platsanknytning och livsvärden.* Rapport 2 från regionalpolitiska utredningen SOU 2000,36. Stockholm: Fritzes.

Gayler, H. (1991) The demise of the Niagara Fruit Belt: Policy planning and development options in the 1990s. In K.B. Beesley (ed.) *Rural and Urban Fringe Studies in Canada: Geographical Monographs No. 21* (pp. 282–313). Toronto: Atkinson College, York University.

Geipel, R. (1989) Territorialität auf dem Mikromaßstab. *Münchener Geographische Hefte* 62, 111–129.

Geipel, R. (1992) Territoriality at the microscale. In S.T. Wong (ed.) *Person, Place and Thing: Interpretive and Empirical Essays in Cultural Geography* (pp. 79–97). Baton Rouge: Department of Geography and Anthropology, Louisiana State University.

Geisler, C.C. and Martinson, O.B. (1976) Local control of land use: Profile of a problem. *Land Economics* 3, 371–381.

Giddens, A. (1990) *The Consequences of Modernity.* Cambridge: Polity Press.

Gill, A. (2000) From growth machine to growth management: The dynamics of resort development in Whistler, British Columbia. *Environment and Planning A* 32, 1083–1103.

Gill, A. and Clark, P. (1992) Second-home development in the resort municipality of Whistler, British Columbia. In P.M. Koroscil (ed.) *British Columbia: Geographical Essays in Honour of A. MacPherson* (pp. 281–294). Burnaby: Department of Geography, Simon Fraser University.

Gillion, M. (1998) Nelson notables. *WINENZ Magazine.* April/May, 8–14.

Girard, T.C. and Gartner, W.C. (1993) Second home, second view: Host community perceptions. *Annals of Tourism Research* 20 (4), 685–700.

Glesbygdsverket (2001) *Planering för åretruntbrunde i kust och skärgård.* Östersund: Glesbygdsverket

Glick Schiller, N. and Fouron, G. (2001) *Georges Woke Up Laughing: Long-distance Nationalism and the Search for Home*. Durham: Duke University Press.

Gmelch, G. (1992) *Double Passage: The Lives of Caribbean Migrants Abroad and Back Home*. Ann Arbor: University of Michigan Press.

Go, F. (1988) Holiday homes in Europe. *Travel & Tourism Analyst* 1, 20–33.

Gober, P. and Zonn, L.E. (1983) Kin and elderly amenity migration. *The Gerontologist* 23 (2), 288–294.

Godbey, G. and Bevins, M.I. (1987) The life cycle of second home ownership: A case study. *Journal of Travel Research* 25 (3), 18–22.

Goelder, C.R., Ritchie, J.R.B. and McIntosh, R.W. (2000) *Tourism: Principles, Practices, Philosophies*. New York: Wiley.

Gordon, C. (1989) *At the Cottage: A Fearless Look at Canada's Summer Obsession*. Toronto: McLelland and Stewart.

Gosar, A. (1989) Second homes in the alpine region of Yugoslavia. *Mountain Research and Development* 9 (2), 165–174.

Goto, J. and Ouchi, M. (1996) The resilience and fragility of Japanese rural communities: Implications for other Asian countries. In H. Sasaki, I. Saito, A. Tabayashi and T. Morimoto (eds) *Geographical Perspectives on Sustainable Rural Systems: Proceedings of the Tsukuba International Conference on the Sustainability of Rural Systems* (pp. 181–187). Toyko: Kaisei Publications.

Grault, J. (1970) Les résidences secondaires. *Tendances* 68, 5–10.

Green, G.P., Marcouiller, D., Deller, S., Erkkila, D. and Sumathi, N.R. (1996) Local dependency, land use attitudes, and economic development: Comparisons between seasonal and permanent residents. *Rural Sociology* 61 (3), 427–445.

Greer, T. and Wall, G. (1979) Recreational hinterlands: A theoretical and empirical analysis. In G. Wall (ed.) *Recreational Land Use in Southern Ontario* (pp. 227–246). Waterloo: Department of Geography, University of Waterloo.

Grey Community Association (1995) *Grey Community Association Minutes of Meetings*. Grey: Grey Community Association.

Groves, D.L. and Timothy, D.J. (2001) Festivals, migration, and long-term residency. *Téoros: Revue de Recherche en Tourisme* 20 (1), 56–62.

Gustafson, P. (2002a) Place, place attachment and mobility: Three sociological studies. *Göteborg Studies in Sociology No 6*. Göteborg: Department of Sociology, Göteborg University.

Gustafson, P. (2002b) Tourism and seasonal retirement migration. *Annals of Tourism Research* 29 (4), 899–918.

Hägerstrand, T. (1984) Escapes from the cage of routines. Observations of human paths, projects and personal scripts. In J. Long and R. Hecock (eds) *Leisure, Tourism and Social Change*. Edinburgh: Centre for Leisure Research.

Hägerstrand, T. (1985) *Time-geography: Focus on the Corporeality of Man, Society, and Environment. The Science and Praxis of Complexity*. Tokyo: The United Nations University.

Hägerstrand, T., Carlestam, G. and Sollbe, B. (1991) *Om tidens vidd och tingens ordning. Texter av Torsten Hägerstrand*. Stockholm: Byggforskningsrådet.

Halfacree, K. (1994) The importance of 'the rural' in the construction of counter-urbanization: Evidence from England in the 1980s. *Sociologia Ruralis* 34, 164–89.

Halfacree, K.H. (1995) Talking about rurality: Social representation of rural as expressed by residents of six English parishes. *Journal of Rural Studies* 11, 1–20.

Hall, C.M. (2000) *Tourism Planning*. Harlow: Prentice Hall.

Hall, C.M. (2004a) Space–time accessibility and the tourist area cycle of evolution: The role of geographies of spatial interaction and mobility in contributing to an improved understanding of tourism. In R. Butler (ed.) *The Tourism Area Life-Cycle* (Vol. 1). Clevedon: Channelview.

Hall, C.M. (2004b) *Tourism*. Harlow: Prentice-Hall.

Hall, C.M. and Jenkins, J.M. (1998) The policy dimension of rural tourism and recreation. In R. Butler, C.M. Hall and J. Jenkins (eds) *Tourism and Recreation in Rural Areas* (pp. 19–42). Chichester: Wiley.

Hall, C.M. and Johnson, G. (1998) Wine and tourism: A new relationship in sustainable rural tourism management? In D. Hall (ed.) *Sustainable Rural Tourism Management*. Auchencruivre: Scottish Agricultural College.

Hall, C.M. and Keen, D. (2001) Second homes, curse or blessing? A New Zealand case study. In *New Directions in Managing Rural Tourism and Leisure: Local Impacts, Global Trends* (CD-ROM). Auchencruivre: Scottish Agricultural College.

Hall, C.M. and Page, S.J. (2002). *The Geography of Tourism and Recreation: Space, Place and Environment* (2nd edn). London: Routledge.

Hall, C.M. and Williams A.M. (2002) *Tourism and Migration: New Relationships Between Production and Consumption*. Dordrecht: Kluwer Academic Publishers.

Halseth, G. (1992) Cottage property ownership: Interpreting spatial patterns in an Eastern Ontario case study. *Ontario Geography* 38, 32–42.

Halseth, G. (1993) Communities within communities: Changing 'residential' areas at Cultus Lake, British Columbia. *Journal of Rural Studies* 9 (2), 175–188.

Halseth, G. (1996) 'Community' and land use planning debate: An example from rural British Columbia. *Environment and Planning A* 28, 1279–1298.

Halseth G. (1998) *Cottage Country in Transition: A Social Geography of Change and Contention in the Rural-Recreational Countryside*. Montreal: McGills-Queen's University Press.

Halseth, G. (1999) Disentangling policy, governance, and local contention over change in Vancouver's rural urban fringe. In O. Furuseth and M. Lapping (eds) *Contested Countryside: The Rural Urban Fringe in North America* (pp. 151–178). Hampshire: Ashgate.

Halseth, G. (forthcoming) Recreation and tourism land uses in New Caledonia. *Western Geographer*.

Halseth, G. and Rosenberg, M.W. (1990) Conversion of recreational residences: A case study of its measurement and management. *Canadian Journal of Regional Science* 13 (1), 99–115.

Halseth, G. and Rosenberg, M.W. (1995) Cottagers in an urban field. *Professional Geographer* 47 (2), 148–159.

Hannerz, U. (1996) *Transnational Connection: Culture, People, Places*. London: Routledge.

Hansen, J. C (1969) Fritidsbebyggelsen i Eidanger [Holiday cottages in Eidanger]. In A. Sømme (ed.) (1969) *Fritid og feriemiljø [Leisure and Holiday Environment]: Ad Novas no. 8*. Oslo: Universitetsforlaget.

Harris, B. (2002) Families rev up for RV travel. *Los Angeles Times*, 14 April, T5.

Harvey, D. (1989) *The Condition of Postmodernity: An Enquiry into the Orgins of Cultural Change*. Oxford: Basil Blackwell.

Harvey, D. (1996) *Justice, Nature and the Geography of Difference*. London: Blackwell.

Heath, E. (1990) *A Pilot Study of Timeshare and Trends in South Africa*. Port Elizabeth: Institute of Planning Research, University of Port Elizabeth.

Heeringa, S. (2001) Slice of heaven. *Grace* 29, 70–75.

Helleiner, F.M. (1983) Loon Lake: The evolution and decline of a cottage community in Northwestern Ontario. *Recreation Research Review* 10, 34–44.
Heltsley, E. (1997) Rocky Point fast becoming bustling resort. *Arizona Daily Star,* 10 February, D1.
Hepburn, S. (2002) Renaissance for Naseby as farming and tourism boost economy. *Otago Daily Times,* 8 March.
Hepburn, S. (2003) Demand for real estate outstrips supply. *Otago Daily Times,* 24 January.
Hermosilla, J. (1992) La residencia secundaria en la perifia occidental del área metropolitana de Valencia. *Cuaderos de geografia* 51, 95–109.
Hobsbawm, E. (1983) Introduction: Inventing traditions. In E. Hobsbawm and T. Ranger (eds) *The Invention of Tradition* (pp. 1–14). Cambridge: Cambridge University Press.
Hodge, G.D. (1970) Cottaging in the Toronto Urban Field: A probe of structure and behaviour. *Research Paper No. 29.* Toronto: University of Toronto, Centre for Urban and Community Studies.
Hoggart, K. and Buller, H. (1994) Property agents as gatekeepers in British house purchases in rural France. *Geoforum* 25, 173–187.
Hoggart, K. and Buller, H. (1995) Geographical differences in British property acquisitions in rural France. *Geographical Journal* 161, 69–78.
Huber, A. (2000) La migracion internacional de tercera edad: El caso de los juibilados europeos en la Costa Blanca (Alicante) y los problemas de plazas en residencias. Paper presented at the II Congreso sobre la inmigración en Espana, Universidad de Comillas, Madrid, 5–7 October.
Hugo, G. (1994) The turnaround in Australia: Some observations from the 1991 census. *Australian Geographer* 25, 1–17.
Hugo, G. and Smailes, P. (1985) Urban-rural migration in Australia: A process view of the turnaround. *Journal of Rural Studies* 1, 11–30.
Hulan, R. (2002) *Northern Experience and the Myths of Canadian Culture.* Montreal: McGill-Queen's University Press.
ICOMOS (2000) 'Heritage at risk'. On WWW at www.international.icomos.org/risk/newze_2000.htm. Accessed 14.03.03.
Ilbery, B. and Bowler, I. (1998) From agricultural productivism to post-productivism. In B. Ilbery (ed.) *The Geography of Rural Change* (pp. 57–84). Harlow: Longman.
Inglis, A. (1999) *Beside the Seaside: Victorian Resorts in the Nineteenth Century.* Carlton: Melbourne University Press.
Instituto Nacional de la Vivienda de Portugal (1991) Localización de segundas residencias y efectos derivados de su concentración. Paper presented at Coloquio Internacional sobre desarrollos de segundas residencias, Palma de Mallorca (pp. 293–305). Madrid: Ministerio de Obras Públicas y Transportes.
Irvine, C. and Cunningham, B. (1990) *Second Homes.* New York: Bantam Books.
Itzigsohn, J., Cabral, C.D., Hernandez Medina, E. and Vazquez, O. (1999) Mapping Dominican transnationalism: Narrow and broad transnational practices. *Ethnic and Racial Studies* 22 (2), 316–339.
Iyer, P. (2000). *The Global Soul: Jet-lag, Shopping Malls and the Search for Home.* London: Bloomsbury.
Jaakson, R. (1986) Second-home domestic tourism. *Annals of Tourism Research* 13, 357–391.
Jackson, P. (1989) *Maps of Meaning.* London: Routledge.
Jamieson, D. (2002) Rates sought from rental of private houses. *Otago Daily Times,* 21 September.

Jansson, B. (1994) *Borta bra men hemma bäst: Svenskars turistresor i Sverige under sommaren*. Umeå: Geografiska institutionen.

Jansson, B. and Müller, D.K. (2003) *Fritidsboende i Kvarken*. Umeå: Kvarkenrådet.

Japan (2001) *Survey Concerning Awareness of Urban Residents and Farmers about the Sybiosis and Migration between Urban and Rural Japan*. Tokyo: Ministry of Agriculture, Forestry, and Fisheries.

Jarlöv, L. (1999) Leisure lots and summer cottages as places for people's own creative work. In D. Crouch (ed.) *Leisure/Tourism Geographies: Practices and Geographical Knowledge* (pp. 231–237). London: Routledge.

Jenkins, J., Hall, C.M. and Troughton, M. (1998) The restructuring of rural economies: Rural tourism and recreation as a government response. In R. Butler, C.M. Hall and J. Jenkins (eds) *Tourism and Recreation in Rural Areas* (pp. 43–68). Chichester: John Wiley.

Jordan, J.W. (1980) The summer people and the natives: Some effects of tourism in a Vermont vacation village. *Annals of Tourism Research* 7 (1), 34–55.

Jordan, T.C. and Kaups, M. (1989) *The American Backwoods Frontier: An Ethnic and Ecological Interpretation*. Baltimore: Johns Hopkins University Press.

Kaltenborn, B.P. (1997a) Nature of place attachment: A study among recreation homeowners in Southern Norway. *Leisure Sciences* 19, 175–189.

Kaltenborn, B.P. (1997b) Recreation homes in natural settings: Factors affecting place attachment. *Norsk Geografisk Tidsskrift* 51, 187–198.

Kaltenborn, B.P. (1998) The alternative home: Motives of recreation home use. *Norsk Geografisk Tidsskrift* 52 (3), 121–134.

Kaltenborn, B. (2002) Bo i naturen: Meningen med hyttelivet [To live in nature: The meaning of cottage life]. *Utmark No. 3, 2002*. On WWW at www.utmark.org.

Kearney, R. (1997) *Post-Nationalist Ireland: Politics, Culture, Philosophy*. London: Routledge.

Keen, D. (2002) The interaction of community and business in rural tourism. Paper presented at Small Firms in the Tourism and Hospitality Sector Conference. Leeds: Leeds Metropolitan University.

Keenan, T. (1999) Knysna Quays: The pearl of the Gardens Route. *Finance Week,* 29 October, pp. 49–52.

Kelly, L. (2000) Rocky Point housing for sale: Development is banking on Americans. *Arizona Republic*, 18 February, D2.

Kennedy, J.R. (1984) *South Elmsley in the Making 1783–1983*. Lombardy: Township of South Elmsley.

Keogh, B. (1982) L'Impact social du tourism: Le cas de Shédiac, Nouveau-Brunswick. *Canadian Geographer* 26 (4), 318–331.

Kerry County Council (2001) *Kerry County Development Plan*. Tralee: Kerry County Council.

King, D. (2000) Value of visitors calculated. *Otago Daily Times,* 7 June.

King, R. and Patterson, G. (1998) Diverse paths: The elderly British in Tuscany. *International Journal of Population Geography* 4 (2), 157–82.

King, R., Warnes, A.M. and Williams, A.M. (2000) *Sunset Lives: British Retirement to the Mediterranean*. London: Berg.

Kinsella, A. (1982) *The Windswept Shore: A History of the Courtown District*. Dublin: Graphic Services.

Kremarik, F. (2002) A little place in the country: A profile of Canadians who own vacation property. *Canadian Social Trends* 65 (Summer), 12–14.

Krueger, R. (1978) Urbanization of the Niagara Fruit Belt. *Canadian Geographer* 22 (3), 174–194.

Krueger, R. (1980) The geographer and rural Southern Ontario. *Ontario Geography* 16, 7–18.

Langdalen, E (1965) Natur og menneskeverk i fjellet [Nature and human work in the mountains]. In A. Sømme (ed.) *Fjellbygd og Feriefjell [Rural Communities and Holiday Mountains]* (pp. 25–53). Oslo: Cappelens forlag.

Langdalen, E. (1980) Second homes in Norway: A controversial planning problem. *Norsk Geografisk Tidsskrift* 34, 139–144.

Langdalen, E. (1992) Fjellbygd og feriefjell, 30 år etter [Rural communities and holiday mountains, after 30 years). In M. Jones and W. Cramer (eds) *Levekår og planlegging [Welfare and Planning]*. Festskrift til Asbjørn Aases 60 år (pp. 11–30). Trondheim: Tapir.

Lash, S. and Urry, J. (1987) *The End of Organized Capitalism*. Cambridge: Polity Press.

Lees, D. (2001) Subdivide and conquer. *Cottage Life*, March, pp. 41–46.

Lehr, J.C., Selwood, H.J. and Goatcher, R. (1984) Wilderness suburbias: Winnipeggers and their vacation homes. *Bulletin Association of North Dakota Geographers* 34, 17–23.

Lehr, J.C., Selwood, J. and Badiuk, E. (1991) Ethnicity, religion, and class as elements in the evolution of Lake Winnipeg resorts. *Canadian Geographer* 35, 46–58.

Lengfelder, J.R. and Timothy, D.J. (2000) Leisure time in the 1990s and beyond: Cherished friend or incessant foe? *Visions in Leisure and Business* 19 (1), 13–26.

Leppänen, J. (2003) Finlands skärgårdsprogram och fritidsboende 2003–2006. Paper presented at Fritidsboende och strandskydd: Seminarium om regional utveckling i Kvarkenområdet, Umeå, Sweden, 25 June. Helsinki: Skärgårdsdelegationen.

Lister, M.R.S (1977) Second home ownership: A case study of Blueskin Riding, Dunedin. Dissertation submitted in partial fulfilment of the requirements for the degree of BA (Hons), Department of Geography, University of Otago.

Ljungdahl, S.G. (1938) Sommar-Stockholm. *Ymer* 58, 218–242.

Local Government New Zealand (2001) *Review of Local Government Act*. Wellington: Local Government New Zealand.

Löfgren, O. (1999) *On Holiday: A History of Vacationing*. Berkeley: University of California Press.

Lundgren, J. (1989) Patterns. In G. Wall (ed.) *Outdoor Recreation in Canada* (pp. 133–161). Toronto: Wiley.

Lundgren, J.O.J. (1974) On access to recreational lands in dynamic metropolitan hinterlands. *Tourist Review* 29, 124–131.

Mabotja, S (2003) A slice of holiday pie still attractive. *Finance Week*, 14 May, p. 40.

MacCannell, D. (1976) *The Tourist: A New Theory of the Leisure Class*. Macmillan. London.

MacCannell, D. (1992) *Empty Meeting Grounds: The Tourist Papers*. London: Routledge.

MacFarlane, D. (1999) *Summer Gone*. Canada: Alfred A. Knopf.

Malmberg, B. and Lindh, T. (2000) *40-talisternas uttåg: En ESO-rapport om 2000-talets demografiska utmaningar*. Stockholm: ESO.

Marcouiller, D.W., Green, G.P, Deller, S.C., Sumathi, N.R and Erikkila, D.C. (1998) *Recreational Homes and Regional Development: A Case Study from the Upper Great Lakes States*. Madison: Cooperative Extension Publications.

Marsh, J. and Wall, G. (1982) Themes in the investigation of the evolution of outdoor recreation. In G. Wall and J. Marsh (eds) *Recreational Land Use: Perspectives on its Evolution in Canada* (pp. 1–11). Ottawa: Carleton University Press.

Marshall, J. and Foster, N. (2002) 'Between belonging': Habitus and the migration experience. *The Canadian Geographer* 46 (1), 63–83.

Marshall, V.W. and Longino, C.F. (1988) Older Canadians in Florida: The social networks of international seasonal migration. *Aging and Society* 10, 229–235.

Massey, D. (1991) A global sense of place. *Marxism Today*, June, pp. 24–29.

Massey, D. (1993). Power geometry and a progressive sense of place. In J. Bird, B. Curtis, T. Putnam, G. Robertson and L. Tickner (eds) *Mapping the Futures: Local Cultures, Global Change*. Routledge: London.

Massey, D. (2000) Travelling thoughts. In P. Gilroy, L. Grossberg and A. McRobbie (eds) *Without Guarantees: In Honour of Stuart Hall* (pp. 225–232). London: Verso.

Massey, D. and Jess, P. (eds) (1995) *A Place in the World? Places, Cultures and Globalization: 4 The Shape of the World. Explorations in Human Geography*. Oxford: Oxford University Press.

Massey, J.C. and Maxwell, S. (1993) Second houses and summer homes. *Old House Journal* 21 (4), 28–34.

Mathieson, A. and Wall, G. (1982) *Tourism: Economic, Physical and Social Impacts*. London: Longman.

McGregor, R. (2002) *Escape: In Search of the Natural Soul of Canada*. Toronto: McClelland and Stewart.

McHugh, K.E. (1990) Seasonal migration as a substitute for, or precursor to, permanent migration. *Research on Aging* 12 (2), 229–245.

McHugh, K.E. (2000) Inside, outside, upside down, backward, forward, round and round: A case for ethnographic studies in migration. *Progress in Human Geography* 24 (1), 71–89.

McHugh, K.E., Hogan, T.D. and Happel, S.K. (1995) Multiple residence and cyclical migration: A life course perspective. *Professional Geographer* 47 (3), 251–267.

McHugh, K.E. and Mings, R. (1996) The circle of migration: Attachment to place in aging. *Annals of the Association of American Geographers* 8, 314–28.

McHugh, P., Raffel, S., Foss, D.C. and Blum, A.F. (1974) *Travel On the Beginning of Social Inquiry* (pp. 137–153). London: Routledge and Keenan Paul.

McMillian, E. (1982) Pauanuia and Whitianga: Contrasts in second home development. Unpublished MA thesis, Department of Geography, University of Canterbury.

McNaughten, P. and Urry J. (1998) *Contested Natures*. London: Sage.

McNicol, B.J. (1997) Views about industrial tourism pressures in Canmore, Alberta. *Western Geography* 7, 47–72.

Miljøverndepartementet [Ministry of Environment] (1981) *Hytter og fritidshus* [*Cabins and Recreational Dwellings*]. NOU 1981, 2. Oslo: Universitetsforlaget.

Ministerio de Fomento (1998) *Statistical Atlas of Housing*. Madrid: Ministerio de Fomento.

Mintel (2002) *Family Holidays: The Irish Market*. London: Mintel International Group.

Miranda Montero, M.J. (1985) *La segunda residencia en la provincia de Valencia*. Valencia: Universidad de Valencia, Facultad de Geografia e Historia.

Mitchell, C.J.A. (1998) Entrepreneurialism, commodification and creative destruction: A model of post-modern community development. *Journal of Rural Studies* 14 (3), 273–286.

Mitchell, D. and Chaplin, G. (1984) *The Elegant Shed: New Zealand Architecture Since 1945*. Auckland: Oxford University Press

Montgomery, J (1991) The future prospects of Twizel becoming a major tourism Centre. Unpublished Postgraduate Diploma of Tourism dissertation, Centre for Tourism, Dunedin.

Morley, D. (2000) *Home Territories: Media, Mobility and Identity*. London: Routledge.

Morley, D. and K. Robins. (1990) No place like heimat: Images of homeland in European culture. *New Formations* 12, 1–23.

Mottiar, Z. and Quinn, B. (2003) Shaping leisure/tourism places: The role of holiday home owners: A case study of Courtown, Co. Wexford, Ireland. *Leisure Studies* 22, 109–128.

Müller, D.K. (1999) *German Second Home Owners in the Swedish Countryside: On the Internationalization of the Leisure Space*. Umeå: Kulturgeografiska institutionen.

Müller, D.K. (2001) Second home tourism and sustainable development in North European peripheries. Paper presented at the TTRA European Chapter Annual Conference, Kiruna, Sweden, April.

Müller, D.K. (2002a) German second home development in Sweden. In C.M. Hall and A.M. Williams (eds) *Tourism and Migration: New Relationships between Production and Consumption* (pp. 169–186). Dordrecht: Kluwer.

Müller, D.K. (2002b) Second home ownership and sustainable development in Northern Sweden. *Tourism and Hospitality Research* 3, 343–355.

Müller, D.K. (2002c) German second homeowners in Sweden: Some remarks on the tourism-migration-nexus. *Revue Européenne des Migrations Internationales* 18, 67–86.

Müller, D.K. (2002d) Reinventing the countryside: German second home owners in southern Sweden. *Current Issues in Tourism* 5, 426–446.

Müller, D.K. (2002e) Second home tourism in the Swedish mountain range. *Conference Proceedings: Ecotourism, Wilderness and Mountains: Issues, Strategies and Regional Development* (pp. 129–141). Dunedin: Department of Tourism.

Müller, D.K. (2004) Tourism, mobility and second homes. In A.A. Lew, C.M. Hall and A.M. William (eds) *A Companion to Tourism*. Oxford: Blackwell.

Müller, D.K. and Hall, C.M. (2003) Second homes and regional population distribution: On administrative practices and failures in Sweden. *Espace, populations, sociétés* 2003 (2), 251–261.

Muller, J. (1999a) Holiday property once again attracts investment. *Finance Week*, 29 October, pp. 47–48.

Muller, J. (1999b) Tomorrow's Clifton and Plet. *Finance Week*, 29 October, p. 52.

Muller, J. (1999c) Ruyteplaats offers exclusive country lifestyle. *Finance Week*, 29 October, p. 48.

Muller, J. (2003) Hartebeesport loses momentum. *Finance Week*, 14 May, p. 38.

Naish, J. (2001) Holiday home ban a threat to Exmoor idyll. *The Times*, 5 September, p. 1.

Nash, C. (2002) Genealogical identities. *Environment and Planning D: Society and Space* 20, 27–52.

National Parks and Nature Conservation Authority (1999) *Wedge and Grey Draft Master Plan*. Perth: Department of Conservation and Land Management.

National Statistics Institute (1991) *Population and Housing Census 1991*. Madrid: National Stastics Institute.

Navalón, M.R. (1995) *El planeamiento urbano y turismo residencial en los municipios litorales alicantinos*. Alicante: Instituto de Cultura Juan Gil-Albert.

Nelson (1994) Architectural assessment: Rotten Row baches, Taylor's mistake, Bank's Peninsula. *Historic Places Trust*, 12 October, H10.

Neville, P. (2002). 'Sea change' on holiday. *New Zealand House and Garden* Autumn/Winter, 124–141.

New Zealand Heritage (2002) New on the register. *New Zealand Heritage*, Spring, 47.

Newig J. (2000) Freizeitwohnen: Mobil und stationär. In *Nationalatlas Bundesrepublik Deutschland: Freizeit und Tourismus* (CD-ROM). Heidelberg: Spektrum.

Niedzviecki, H. (1998) *Concrete Forest: The New Fiction of Urban Canada*. Toronto: Mclelland and Stewart.

Nordin, U. (1993a) Fritidshusbebyggelse för skärgårdsbor? Studier av fritidsboendets betydelse för sysselsättningen i Blidö församling, Norrtälje kommun 1945–1987. *Meddelanden från Kulturgeografiska institutionen vid Stockholms universitet* B86. Stockholm: Kulturgeografiska institutionen.

Nordin, U. (1993b) Second homes. In H. Aldskogius (ed.) *Cultural Life, Recreation and Tourism: National Atlas of Sweden* (pp. 72–79). Stockholm: Royal Swedish Academy of Science.

NZHPT (1995) Proposal for registration. *Historic Areas Trust Board* 27 October. Paper No. BD1995/10/22. New Zealand Historic Places Trust.

Okahashi, H. (1996) New development strategies in Japan's mountain villages: Sustainable or unsustainable. In H. Sasaki, I. Saito, A. Tabayashi and T. Morimoto (eds) *Geographical Perspectives on Sustainable Rural Systems: Proceedings of the Tsukuba International Conference on the Sustainability of Rural Systems* (pp. 285–292). Toyko: Kaisei Publications.

Olwig. K.F. (1993) *Global Culture, Island Identity: Continuity and Change in the Afro-Caribbean Community of Nevis.* London: Routledge.

Olwig, K.F. (1997) Cultural sites: Sustaining a home in a deterritorialized world. In K.F. Olwig and K. Halstrup (eds) *Siting Culture: The Shifting Anthropological Object* (pp. 15–32). London: Routledge.

Olwig, K.F. (2001) New York as a locality in a global family network. In N. Foner (ed.) *Islands in the City: West Indian Migration to New York* (pp. 142–160). Berkeley: University of California Press.

Olwig, K.F. and Halstrup, K. (1997) Introduction. In K.F. Olwig and K. Halstrup (eds) *Siting Culture: The Shifting Anthropological Object* (pp. 1–13). London: Routledge.

O'Reilley, K. (1995) A new trend in European migration: Contemporary British migration to Fuengirola, Costa del Sol. *Geographical Viewpoint* 23, 25–36.

O'Reilley, K. (2001) *The British on the Costa del Sol: Transnational Communities and Local Identities.* Routledge, London.

Osborne, B.S. (1988) The hinterland. In D. Gagan and R. Gagan (eds) *New Directions for the Study of Ontario's Past: Papers of the Bicentennial Conference on the History of Ontario, McMaster University September 5 to 8, 1984* (pp. 267–283). Hamilton: McMaster University.

Otago Daily Times (2002) The valley for value. *Otago Daily Times*, 23 January.

Ouren, T. (ed.) (1965) *Fritid og Feriemiljø. Festskrift i anledning av professor Axel Sømmes 70-årsdag. Ad Novas no. 8.* Oslo: Universitetsforlageto.

Pacione, M. (1979) Second homes on Arran. *Norsk Geografisk Tidsskrift* 33, 33–38.

Pacione, M. (1984) *Rural Geography.* London: Harper and Row.

Pahl, R.E. (1965) Urbs in rure: The metropolitan fringe in Hertfordshire. *Geographical Papers No. 2.* London: London School of Economics and Political Science.

PANZ (1994) *Taylor's Mistake: A Legacy of Civic Dereliction.* On WWW at www.publicaccessnewzealand.org/files/local_issues_roads.htm#anchor218987. Accessed 08.04.01.

Parks Victoria (2001) *Cape Liptrap Coastal Park: Draft Management Plan.* Melbourne: Parks Victoria.

Paterson, V. (1999) Access rights agreed to. *Otago Daily Times*, 6 August.

Paulson, M.C. (1989) Vacation homes: It's a buyer's market. *Changing Times* 43 (6), 37–43.

Pearce, D. (1988) Tourist time-budgets. *Annals of Tourism Research* 1, 106–121.

Phillips, M. (1993) Rural gentrification and the processes of class colonisation. *Journal of Rural Studies* 9, 123–140.

Phillips, M. (2002) The production, symbolization and socialization of gentrification: Impressions from two Berkshire villages. *Transactions of the Institute of British Geographers* 27 (3), 282–308.

Philpott, S.B. (1973) West Indian migration: The Montserrat case. *London School of Economics Monographs in Anthropology 47*. London: Athone Press.

Pierce Colfer, C.J. and Colfer, A.M. (1978) Inside Bushler Bay: Lifeways in counterpoint. *Rural Sociology* 43 (2), 204–220.

Pihl Atmer, A.K. (1998) *Livet som leves där måste smaka vildmark: Sportstugor och friluftsliv 1900–1945*. Stockholm: Stockholmia.

Portes, A. (1999) Conclusion: Towards a new world. The origins and effects of transnational activities. *Ethnic and Racial Studies* 22 (2), 463–477.

Portes, A., Guarnizo, L.E. and Landolt, P. (1999) The study of transnationalism: Pitfalls and promise of an emergent research field. *Ethnic and Racial Studies* 22 (2), 217–237.

Pressley, D. (2002) Govt eyes foreign land ownership. *Business Day*. On WWW at http://www.bday.co.za/bday/content/direct/1,3523,1224767-6078-0,00.html. Accessed 14.11.02.

Priddle, G. and Kreutzwiser, R. (1977) Evaluating cottage environments in Ontario. In J.T. Coppock (ed.) *Second Homes: Curse or Blessing?* (pp. 165–180). Oxford: Pergamon.

Priestley, G. and Mundet, L. (1998) The post-stagnation phase of the resort cycle. *Annals of Tourism Research* 25 (1), 85–111.

Priskin, J. (2001) Nature-based tourism in the Central Coast region of Western Australia. Unpublished discussion paper on the outcomes of the workshop held in Jurien Bay 23 March. Department of Geography, University of Western Australia.

Property24 (2002) New homes in Clarens. *Property24*. On WWW at http://www.property24.co.za/property24/news/FullArticle.asp?id=954&Archive=true. Accessed16.08.02.

Ragatz, R.L. (1969) *The Vacation Home Market: An Unrecognized Factor in Outdoor Recreation and Rural Development*. Ithaca: Cornell University.

Ragatz, R.L. (1970a) Vacation homes in the north eastern United States: Seasonality in population distribution. *Annals of the Association of American Geographers* 60, 447–455.

Ragatz, R.L. (1970b) Vacation housing: A missing component in urban and regional theory. *Land Economics* 46, 118–126.

Ragatz, R.L. (1977) Vacation homes in rural areas: Towards a model for predicting their distribution and occupancy patterns. In J.T. Coppock (ed.) *Second Homes: Curse or Blessing?* (pp. 181–193). Oxford: Pergamon.

Ragatz, R.L. and Gelb, G.M. (1970) The quiet boom in the vacation home market. *California Management Review* 12, 57–64.

Recreation Vehicle Industry Association (2003) *RV Quick Facts*. On WWW at www.rvia.org. Accessed 15.01.03.

Relph, E. (1976) *Place and Placelessness*. London: Pion.

Resort Municipality of Whistler (1995) *1995 Community and Resort Monitoring Program*. Whistler: Planning Department, RMOW.

Rideau Valley Conservation Authority (1992a) *Rideau Valley Conservation Strategy*. Manotick: Rideau Valley Conservation Authority.

Rideau Valley Conservation Authority (1992b) *Rideau Lakes Basin Carrying Capacities and Proposed Shoreland Development Policies*. Manotick: Rideau Valley Conservation Authority (prepared by Michael Michalski Associates and Anthony Usher Planning Consultants).

Robertson, R.W. (1977) Second-home decisions: The Australian context. In J.T. Coppock (ed.) _Second Homes: Curse or Blessing?_ (pp. 119–138). Oxford: Pergamon.

Rodriguez, V. (2001) Tourism as a recruiting post. _Tourism Geographies_ 3 (1), 52–63.

Rodriguez, V., Casado-Diaz, M.A. and Huber, A. (2000) Impactos de la migración internacional de retirados en las costas espanolas. _OFRIM Suplementos 7, Revista Especializada en Inmigracion,_ 117–138.

Rodríguez, V., Fernández-Mayoralas, G. and Rojo, F. (1998) European retirees on the Costa del Sol: A cross-national comparison. _International Journal of Population Geography_ 4, 183–200.

Rogers, A.W. (1977) Second homes in England and Wales: A spatial view. In J.T. Coppock (ed.) _Second Homes: Curse or Blessing?_ (pp. 85–102). Oxford: Pergamon.

Rogerson, C.M. (1998) Restructuring of the post-apartheid space economy. _Regional Studies_ 32, 187–197.

Rogerson, C.M. (2000) Manufacturing change in Gauteng 1989–1999: Re-examining the state of South Africa's economic heartland. _Urban Forum_ 11, 311–340.

Rogerson, C.M. (2002) Tourism: An economic driver for South Africa. In A. Lemon and C.M. Rogerson (eds) _Geography and Economy in South Africa and its Neighbours_ (pp.95–110). Aldershot: Ashgate.

Rogerson, C.M. and Browett, J.G. (1988) _Research in Human Geography: Introductions and Investigations._ Oxford: Blackwell.

Rojek, C. and Urry, J. (eds) (1997) _Touring Cultures. Transformations of Travel and Theory._ London: Routledge.

Rojek, C. (1995) _Decentring Leisure: Rethinking Leisure Theory._ London: Sage Publications.

Rojek, C. (1998) Cybertourism and the phantasmagoria of place. In G. Ringer (ed.) _Destinations: Cultural Landscapes of Tourism._ London: Routledge.

Rose, J. (2002) Quiet city uneasy with wild image. _Arizona Republic,_ 16 March, A1, A6.

Rose, L.S. and Kingma, H.L. (1989) Seasonal migration of retired persons: Estimating its extent and its implications for the State of Florida. _Journal of Economic and Social Measurement_ 15, 91–104.

Roseman, C.C. (1992) Cyclical and polygonal migration in a western context. In P.C. Jobes, W.F. Stinner and J.M. Wardwell (eds) _Community, Society and Migration_ (pp. 33–45). Lanham: University Press of America.

Rosenberg, M.W. and Halseth, G. (1993) _Recreational Home Conversion in Canada._ Ottawa: Canada Mortgage and Housing Corporation.

Rouse, R.C. (1992) Making sense of settlement: Class transformation, cultural struggle, and transnationalism among Mexican migrants in the United States. In N. Glick Schiller, L. Basch and C. Szanton Blanc (eds) _Towards a Transnational Perspective on Migration: Race, Class, Ethnicity, and Nationalism Reconsidered: Annals of the New York Academy of Sciences_ (Vol. 645, pp. 25–52). New York: New York Academy of Sciences.

Royal Lepage (2002) _Royal Lepage Recreational Property Report 2002._ On WWW at www.royallepage.ca.

Russis, M.E. (1998) Second homes: A well-rounded house. _Professional Builder Luxury Homes_ 63 (15), 12–31.

Rykwert, J. (1991) House and home. _Social Research_ 58 (1), 51–62.

Salvå, P. and Socias, M. (1985) Las residencias secundarias y la agricultura a tiemp parcial. _El Campo_ 100, 64–67.

Salvà-Tomàs, P. (2002) Foreign immigration and tourism development in Spain's Balearic Islands. In C.M. Hall and A.M. Williams (eds) _Tourism and Migration: New Relationships between Production and Consumption_ (pp. 119–134). Dordrecht: Kluwer.

Sanders, D. (2000) Holiday towns in the Leeuwin-Naturaliste region: Another Gold Coast? *The Journal of Tourism Studies* 11, 45–55.

Scholte, J.A. (2000) Global civil society. In N. Woods (ed.) *The Political Economy of Globalization* (pp. 173–201). London: Macmillan.

Selwood, J. and May, A. (1992) Holiday squatters in Western Australia: Problems and policies. *Australian Journal of Leisure and Recreation* 2 (2), 19–24.

Selwood, J. and May, A. (2001) Resolving contested notions of tourism sustainability on Western Australia's 'Turquoise Coast': The squatter settlements. *Current Issues in Tourism* 4, 381–391.

Selwood, J. (1981) Patterns and processes of residential subdivision in the Perth metropolitan region, 1829–1969. Unpublished PhD thesis. The University of Western Australia, Department of Geography.

Selwood, J., Curry, G. and Koczberski, G. (1995) Structure and change in a local holiday resort: Peaceful Bay, on the southern coast of Western Australia. *Urban Policy and Research* 13, 149–157.

Selwyn, T. (ed.) (1996) *The Tourist Image: Myths and Myth Making in Tourism.* Chichester: John Wiley and Sons.

Shaw, G. and Williams, A.M. (1994) *Critical Issues in Tourism: A Geographical Perspective.* Oxford: Blackwell.

Shearer, G. (1980) The Maniototo as a recreation resource: A study in second home development. Unpublished BA (Hons). University of Otago, Department of Geography

Shields, R. (1991) *Places on the Margin: Alternative Geographies of Modernity.* London: Routledge.

Shucksmith, D.M. (1983) Second homes. *Town Planning Review* 54, 174–193.

Shukla, S. (2001) Locations for South Asian diasporas. *Annual Review of Anthropology* 30, 551–572.

Smailes, P.J. (2002) From rural dilution to multifunctional countryside: Some pointers to the future from South Australia. *Australian Geographer* 33 (1), 79–95.

Smith, D. (2001) How's it going in Wanaka? *Otago Daily Times*, 18 December.

Smith, D. (2002a) Tourists numbers rise. *Otago Daily Times*, 16 February.

Smith, D. (2002b) Average ratepayer facing hike of 12.3%. *Otago Daily Times*, 24 August.

Smith, M.D. and Krannich, R.S. (2000) 'Culture clash' revisited: Newcomer and longer-term residents' attitudes toward land use, development, and environmental issues in rural communities in the Rocky Mountain West. *Rural Sociology* 65 (3), 396–421.

Smutny, G. (2002) Patterns of growth and change: Depicting the impacts of restructuring in Idaho. *The Professional Geographer* 54 (3), 438–453.

Snyder, R. (1967) *Seasonal Recreation Properties in Minnesota.* St Paul: University of Minnesota, Department of Agricultural Economics.

Somerville, P. (2001) Ratepayers may lose vote. *Otago Daily Times*, 30 June. On WWW at www.odt.co.nz/cgi-bin/getitem?date=30Jun2001&object=HQF48E0 697LS&type=html. Accessed 09.07.01.

Sømme, A. (ed.) (1965) *Fjellbygd og Feriefjell* [*Mountain Communities and Holiday Mountains*]. Oslo: Cappelens forlag, Universitetsforlaget

Spanish Ministry of Development (1998) *Statistical Atlas of Housing.* Madrid: Spanish Ministry of Development.

Spoonley, P. (2000) Reinventing Polynesia: The cultural politics of transnational communities. Working paper (WPTC-2K-14); Transnational Communities Research Programme, Institute of Social and Cultural Anthropology, University of Oxford. On WWW at www.transcomm.ox.ac.uk/working_papers.htm.

SSB (2002) *Statistics Norway.* On WWW at http://www.ssb.no.

Statistics Canada (1973–1992) *Household Facilities and Equipment: Catalogue 64-202.* Ottawa: Minister of Supply and Services.

Statistics Canada (1977–1999) *Survey of Household Spending*. Ottawa: Minister of Supply and Services.

Statistics Canada (1982–1985) *Household Facilities by Income and Other Characteristics: Catalogue 13-567 (occasional)*. Ottawa: Minister of Supply and Services.

Statistics Canada (1987–1991) *Household Facilities by Income and Other Characteristics: Catalogue 13-218 (annual)*. Ottawa: Minister of Supply and Services.

Statistics Canada (1997–2001) *Canadian Travel Survey Microdata User's Guide*. Ottawa: Statistics Canada.

Statistics Finland (2001) *Free-time Residences 2000.* Helsinki: Statistics Finland

Statistics New Zealand (2001) *Census New Zealand.* Wellington: Statistics New Zealand.

Statistics Norway (2001) *Fritidsbygg 2001: Statistical Databases.* On WWW at http://statbank.ssb.no/statistikkbanken.

Stern, L. (1994) Vacation homes. *Newsweek,* 4 July, p. 62.

Stroud, H.B. (1985) Changing rural landscapes: A need for planning and management. *Land Use Policy* 2 (2), 126–134.

Stroud, H.B. (1995) *The Promise of Paradise: Recreational and Retirement Communities in the United States Since 1950.* Baltimore: Johns Hopkins University Press.

Suffron, R.V. (1998) Perceived impacts of outdoor recreation development on benefits of cottage owners at Aylesford Lake: A test of the social exchange theory. *Journal of Applied Recreation Research* 23 (1), 23–41.

Suiter, J. (1999) Cash finds it way into holiday hideaways. *The Irish Times,* 24 June.

Svenson, S. (2002) Cottaging in Canada: A spatial and demographic analysis of domestic activity. Report submitted to the Canadian Tourism Commission and Statistics Canada.

Swarbrooke, J. (1992) The impact of British visitors on rural France. In *Tourism in Europe: The 1992 Conference* (s.32–s.40). Newcastle upon Tyne: Centre for Travel and Tourism.

Swarbrooke, J. (1996) Culture, tourism, and the sustainability of rural areas in Europe. In *Managing Cultural Resources for Tourism, Proceedings of the Tourism and Culture: Towards the 21st Century Conference* (Vol. 2, pp. 447–470). Morpeth: Centre for Travel and Tourism, University of Northumbria.

Tame, A. (1996) *The Matriarch: The Kathy Pettingill Story.* Sydney: Macmillan.

Taylor, L.O. and Smith, V.K. (2000) Environmental amenities as a source of market power. *Land Economics* 76 (4), 550–568.

The Age (2001) Developers spark rush of Venus envy. *The Age,* 31 December.

The Age (2002) Clouds build over the rising popularity of Mornington Peninsula land. *The Age,* 15 September.

Thomas, M. (2002) Task force to tackle labour shortage affordable accommodation the key. *Otago Daily Times,* 20 March.

Thomas-Hope, E. (1992) *Explanation in Caribbean Migration.* London: Macmillan.

Thompson, J.B. (1995) *The Media and Modernity.* Cambridge: Polity Press.

Thompson, M.E. (1990) Forty-and-one years on: An overview of Afro-Caribbean migration to the United Kingdom. In R.W. Palmer (ed.) *In Search of a Better Life: Perspectives on Migration from the Caribbean* (pp. 39–70). New York: Praeger.

Thompson, P. (1985) *The Bach.* Wellington: Crown Printer.

Thompson, W. (2000) Bach owners fight to keep beach paradise. *New Zealand Herald Online,* 23 November. On WWW at www.nzherald.co.nz/storyprint.cfm?story ID=161783. Accessed 30.04.02.

Thrift, N. (1997) The still point. In M. Keith and S. Pile (eds) *Geographies of Resistance.* London: Routledge.

Thrift, N. and Pile, S. (eds) (1995) *Mapping the Subject.* London: Routledge.

Timothy, D.J. (1995) The decline of Finnish ethnic islands in rural Thunder Bay. *Great Lakes Geographer* 2 (2), 45–59.

Timothy, D.J. (2001) *Tourism and Political Boundaries.* London: Routledge.

Timothy, D.J. (2002) Tourism and the growth of urban ethnic islands. In C.M. Hall. and A.M. Williams (eds) *Tourism and Migration: New Relationships Between Production and Consumption* (pp. 135–152). Dordrecht: Kluwer.

Timothy, D.J. (forthcoming) The supply and organization of tourism in North America. In D.A. Fennell (ed.) *Tourism in North America: A Handbook.* Clevedon: Channel View Publications.

Tombaugh, L.W. (1970) Factors influencing vacation home location. *Journal of Leisure Research* 2, 54–63.

Tomlinson, J. (1999) *Globalization and Culture.* Chicago: The University of Chicago Press.

Tonts, M. and Greive, S. (2002) Commodification and creative destruction in the Australian rural landscape: The case of Bridgetown, Western Australia. *Australian Geographical Studies* 40, 58–70.

Topham-Kindley, L. (2000) For a change of pace, try Naseby. *Otago Daily Times,* 22 August.

Torres Alfosea, F. (1995) *Aplicacion de un sistema de informacion geografica al estudio de un modelo de desarrollo local.* Alicante: Instituto de Cultura Juan Gil-Albert.

Tourism Research Council (2000) *New Zealand Domestic Travel Survey 2000.* Wellington: Ministry of Tourism.

Tress, G. (2002) Development of second-home tourism in Denmark. *Scandinavian Journal of Hospitality and Tourism* 2, 109–122.

Troughton, M.J. (1981) The rural-urban fringe: A challenge to resource management. In K.B. Beesley and L.H. Russwurm (eds) *The Rural-Urban Fringe: A Canadian Perspective: Geographical Monographs No. 10* (pp. 218–243). Toronto: Atkinson College, York University.

Truly, D. (2002) International retirement migration and tourism along the Lake Chapala Riviera: Developing a matrix of retirement migration behaviour. *Tourism Geographies* 4 (3), 261–281.

Tuan, Y.-F. (1980) Rootedness versus sense of place. *Landscape* 24 (1), 3–8.

Tuan, Y-F. (1977) *Space and Place: The Perspective of Experience.* Minneapolis: University of Minnesota Press.

Tuan, Y-F. (1998) *Escapism.* London: Johns Hopkins University Press.

Tyler's Cottage Rental Directory (2002) *Tyler's Cottage Rental Directory* (17th edn). Barrie: Tyler Publishing.

United Nations (1998) *The Ageing of the World's Population.* New York: United Nations Division for Social Policy and Development

Umcobase (1996) *Umeå Cottage Database of Sweden, 1991–1996*. Research database created by Statistics Sweden and located at the Department of Social and Economic Geography, Umeå University.

Urry, J. (1990) *The Tourist Gaze: Leisure and Travel in Contemporary Societies*. London: Sage.

Urry, J. (1994) Cultural change and contemporary tourism. *Leisure Studies* 13, 233–238.

Urry, J. (1995) *Consuming Places*. London: Routledge.

Urry, J. (2000) *Sociology Beyond Societies. Mobilities for the Twenty First Century*. London: Routledge.

US Census Bureau (2000) *American Housing Survey for the United States, 1999*. Washington, DC: US Census Bureau.

US Census Bureau (2002) *Housing Vacancies and Homeownership Annual Statistics*. Washington, DC: US Census Bureau.

Velvin, J. (2002) Hyttebasert reiseliv, hvordan øke brukstid og lokale inntekter. *Utmark* 2002, 3. On WWW at www.utmark.org. Accessed 31.10.03.

Vera Rebollo, J.F. (1987) *Turismo y urbanizacion en el litoral alicantino*. Alicante: Instituto de Cultura Juan Gil-Albert.

Vera Rebollo, J.F. (1995) *Programa de revitalización de municipios con turismo residencial: Investigaciones básicas*. Alicante: Diputación de Alicante.

Vertovec, S. (1999) Conceiving and researching transnationalism. *Ethnic and Racial Studies* 22 (2), 447–462.

VPIRG (1977) *A Coastal Retreat*. Melbourne: Victorian Public Interest Research Group.

Visser, G. (2002) Gentrification and South African cities. *Cities* 19 (6), 419–423.

Visser, G. (2003a) *Trekking South Africa: A Survey of Backpacker Tourism*. Bloemfontein: Department of Geography, University of the Free State.

Visser, G. (2003b) Gay men, tourism and urban space: Reflections on Africa's 'gay capital'. *Tourism Geographies* 5 (2), 168–189.

Visser, G. (in press, a) Unvoiced and invisible: On the transparency of white South Africans in post-apartheid geographical discourse. *Acta Academica Supplementum*.

Visser, G. (in press, b) Gentrification: Prospects for South African urban society? *Acta Academica Supplementum* 3.

Visser, G. and Van Huyssteen, K. (1999) Guest houses: The emergence of a new tourist accommodation type in the South African tourism industry. *Tourism and Hospitality Research* 1 (2), 155–175.

Visser, G. and Van Huyssteen. K. (1997) Guest houses: New option for tourists in the Western Cape winelands. *Acta Academica* 29 (2), 106–137.

Waldsmith, L. (1997) Councils view agricultural tourism as untapped mine. *The Detroit News*, 12 October. On WWW at htttp://www.detnews.com/1997/biz/9710/13/10120016.htm.

Walker, G.E. (1987) An invaded countryside: Structures of life on the Toronto fringe. *Geographical Monographs No.17*. Toronto: Atkinson College, York University,

Walker, J.W. St G. (1984) *The West Indians in Canada* (Booklet 6). Ottawa: Canadian Historical Association.

Wall, G. (1979) Recreational land use in Muskoka. In G. Wall (ed.) *Recreational Land Use in Southern Ontario* (pp. 139–154). Waterloo: Department of Geography.

Ward, J.C. (1999) Vacation homes: Design in context. *Custom Builder* 14 (1), 31–49.

Ward, N. (1993) The agricultural treadmill and the rural environment in the post-productivist era. *Sociologica Ruralis* 33, 348–64.

Warnes A.M. (2001) The international dispersal of pensioners from affluent countries. *International Journal of Population Geography* 7 (6), 373–88.

Warnes, A.M. (1992) Migration and the life course. In A.G. Champion and A. Fielding (eds) *Migration Processes and Patterns* (Vol. 1): *Research Progress and Prospects* (pp. 175–187). London: Belhaven.

Warnes, T. (1994) Permanent and seasonal international retirement migration: The prospects for Europe. *Nederlandse Geografische Studies* 173, 69–79.

Washer, R. (1977) Holiday homes on Banks Peninsula: An impact assessment. Unpublished thesis submitted for Masters Degree. University of Canterbury.

Watts, L. (2002) Sand, surf, location. *New Zealand Investor Monthly* December/January 93, 10–16

Webb, C. (2000) Personal interview. Chairman, North Wexford Tourism.

White, P. (1985) On the use of creative literature in migration study. *Area* 17, 277–283.

Whyte, D. (1978) Have second homes gone into hibernation? *New Society* 45, 286–8.

Wickens, E. (2002) The sacred and the profane: A tourist typology. *Annals of Tourism Research* 29 (3), 834–851.

Wild, R. (1978) *Bradstow: A Study of Class, Status and Power in a Small Australian Town* (rev. edn). Sydney: Angus and Robertson Publishers.

Wilkinson, P.F. and Murray, A.L. (1991) Centre and periphery: The impacts of the leisure industry on a small town (Collingwood, Ontario). *Society and Leisure* 14 (1), 235–260.

Williams, A.M. (2001) Tourism on the fabled shore. In R. King, P. de Mas and J.M. Beck (eds) *Geography, Environment and Development in the Mediterranean* (pp. 156–175). Brighton: Sussex Academic Press.

Williams, A.M. (2002) Mobility and culture: Issues for cultural tourism. Paper presented to The Tourist Historic City Conference, Bruges, March.

Williams, A.M. and Hall, C.M. (2000a) Tourism and migration: New relationships between production and consumption. *Tourism Geographies* 2, 5–27.

Williams, A.M. and Hall, C.M. (2000b) Guest editorial: Tourism and migration. *Tourism Geographies* 2 (1), 2–4.

Williams, A.M. and Hall, C.M. (2002) Tourism, migration, circulation and mobility: the contingencies of time and place. In C.M. Hall and A.M. Williams (eds) *Tourism and Migration: New Relationships between Production and Consumption* (pp. 1–52). Dordrecht: Kluwer.

Williams, A.M., King, R. and Warnes, A.M. (1997) A place in the sun: International retirement migration from northern to southern Europe. *European Urban and Regional Studies* 4 (2), 115–134.

Williams, A.M., King, R., Warnes, A.M. and Patterson, G. (2000) Tourism and international retirement migration: New forms of an old relationship in southern Europe. *Tourism Geographies* 2 (1), 28–50.

Williams, D.R. and Kaltenborn, B.P. (1999) Leisure places and modernity: The use and meaning of recreational cottages in Norway and the USA. In D. Crouch (ed.) *Leisure/Tourism Geographies. Practices and Geographical Knowledge* (pp. 214–230). London: Routledge.

WINZ (1997) *Annual Report: Year end June 1997*. Auckland: Wine Institute of New Zealand.

Wolfe, R.I. (1951) Summer cottagers in Ontario. *Economic Geography* 27 (1), 10–32.

Wolfe, R.I. (1952) Wasaga Beach: The divorce from the geographic environment. *Canadian Geographer* 2, 57–65.

Wolfe, R.I. (1962) The summer resorts of Ontario in the nineteenth century. *Ontario History* 54, 149–61.

Wolfe, R.I. (1965) About cottages and cottagers. *Landscape* 15 (1), 6–8.
Wolfe, R.I. (1977) Summer cottages in Ontario: Purpose-built for an inessential purpose. In J.T. Coppock (ed.) *Second Homes: Curse or Blessing?* (pp. 17–34). Oxford: Pergamon.
Woods, R.H. (2001) Important issues for a growing timeshare industry. *Cornell Hotel and Restaurant Administration Quarterly* 42 (1), 71–81.
Wyckoff, W.K. (1990) Landscapes of private power and wealth. In M.P. Conzen (ed.) *The Making of the American Landscape* (pp. 335–354). London: Harper Collins Academic.
Zanon, D. and Frost, W. (2002) Regional tourism trends project. Unpublished draft discussion paper. Melbourne: Parks Victoria and Monash University.

Index